Forgotten Heroes

*A Record of Police Gallantry Awards in the
Lancashire County Palatine*

Forgotten Heroes

A Record of Police Gallantry Awards in the Lancashire County Palatine

Stephen Wilson

Forgotten Heroes

A Record of Police Gallantry Awards in the
Lancashire County Palatine

Stephen Wilson
The moral rights of the author have been asserted

ISBN: 978-1-9164247-0-8

Published by Stephen Wilson in conjunction with WRITERSWORLD, this book is produced entirely in the UK, is available to order from most book shops in the United Kingdom and is globally available via UK-based Internet book retailers.

For information regarding Forgotten Heroes, please contact: enquiries@forgotten-heroes.uk

Cover Design by Jag Lall

Copy edited by Ian Large

WRITERSWORLD
2 Bear Close, Woodstock,
Oxfordshire
OX20 1JX
UK

☎ +44 1993 812500

www.writersworld.co.uk

Foreword

I consider it an honour to be asked to write the foreword to this book entitled *Forgotten Heroes – A Record of Police Gallantry Awards in the Lancashire County Palatine*. This book is the result of extensive research carried out by Stephen Wilson, a retired Lancashire police officer, and covers all national awards for police gallantry since the King's Police Medal was established in 1909.

It is a comprehensive record of extraordinary actions carried out by officers on behalf of the people of the historic Lancashire County Palatine, an area covering most of the modern counties of Lancashire, Greater Manchester and Merseyside and parts of Cumbria, Cheshire and Yorkshire.

Police duties involve danger – whether dealing with explosions and bombings during two world wars; the ever present threats of both criminal and political violence; safeguarding of the public from fire, water and other dangers, or their rescue when danger strikes. All circumstances involving a risk of injury or death and on occasion the awards for their gallantry are posthumous – the officers having made the ultimate sacrifice in protecting their communities.

Many of the incidents described within this book took place a long time ago; this however does not detract from the levels of courage and devotion to duty which were shown. Such actions are a tribute to the Police Service and the individuals involved and deserve to be known about and remembered.

Andy Rhodes, QPM, BA (Hons)

Chief Constable, Lancashire Constabulary

July 2018

Preface

This book is a record of gallantry awards presented to police officers and others in the Lancashire County Palatine. It includes the Palatine areas of Lancashire now within the administrative counties of Cheshire, Cumbria, Greater Manchester, Merseyside and Yorkshire.

The nation began to officially recognise police gallantry in 1909 with the creation of the King's Police Medal. Gallant deeds were acknowledged by other means prior to this. Over the years other gallantry awards were created and awarded to members of the public as well as the police.

Police officers are required to protect life and property, to maintain order, to prevent and detect crime and to prosecute offenders. These form the basis of the actions described and the rationale for the awards given. Police duties will always involve an element of risk of injury or death. Officers go to work daily not knowing what they may face or what may be required of them.

Gallantry awards are not readily given and recognise conscious decisions and actions where risks are involved. Such actions go above and beyond what would normally be expected.

This book covers all sovereigns' national awards for police gallantry since the King's Police Medal was established in 1909, as recorded in the official public record *The London Gazette*. I have attempted to put into historical context the incidents and include further information about what took place and the individuals involved where known.

The first national award was the King's Police Medal awarded to Detective Sergeant James McGuire following an incident in Preston in 1911. His courage was recognised for the arrest of an armed criminal who fired on him and his colleague. Many of the awards since have resulted from incidents involving loss of life.

The police faced unprecedented demands during two world wars. During the First World War many additional responsibilities, including guarding strategic locations such as munitions factories and infrastructure, were introduced. In 1917 Constable James Hardacre lost his life after an explosion whilst bravely fighting fire at an explosives factory near Accrington. Two further major explosions took place at other factories in the North West during the Great War, resulting in awards being given for gallantry.

During the Second World War heavy bombing took place on the industrial and port areas around Manchester and Liverpool but bombs fell widely across the whole of the North West.

The police were in many cases first on the scene of death and destruction and were instrumental in the rescue of many casualties from demolished or burning buildings. Until the formation of the National Fire Service in 1941 firefighting was, in places, the responsibility of the Police Fire Brigades. Many officers were killed as a result of the bombing. Five died after Old Trafford Police Station was hit by a bomb in December 1940.

Away from the major cities Blackpool was the scene of a mid-air collision in 1941 between two R.A.F. aircraft on a training mission. One aircraft crashed on the Central Railway Station causing major damage and fire. Constable Thomas Beeston braved the flames to rescue a small child from the flames. A witness described the incident as follows – '*saw P.C. Beeston pick up the child and carry it to safety, whilst he was doing this another explosion occurred as if a petrol tank had burst. The flaming debris was scattered all about the station entrance, over P.C. Beeston and the child... I witnessed the whole of this P.C.'s courageous conduct and consider it one of the most courageous acts I have witnessed. Whilst working as a Home Guard in London I witnessed many brave acts.*'

The last Queen's Police Medal for Gallantry was posthumously awarded to Detective Inspector James O'Donnell of Blackburn Borough Police who was shot during the Brewery Street siege in 1958. He was attempting to disarm an armed man who had shot and wounded another officer, P.C. Jack Covill, and then shot and killed his wife. O'Donnell was no stranger to danger, being a highly decorated soldier who had served in the Irish Guards during the Second World War, and had been awarded the Military Medal and Bar.

Blackpool was the location in 1971 where the posthumous award of the George Cross (Britain's highest civilian award) was made to Superintendent Gerald Richardson and then Constable Carl Walker who were shot during attempts to arrest an armed gang who raided a jeweller's shop. A third officer Ian Hampson had earlier been shot and wounded.

Superintendent Richardson is the highest ranking officer to have been killed on duty in modern times. Four George Medals and other awards were made to the other officers involved.

Further afield, John Egerton lost his life whilst tackling an intruder at a factory in Farnworth; Raymond Davenport lost his life attempting to arrest car thieves in Liverpool; and Sergeant James Bowden was decorated for his bravery during an incident at Birch Services on the M62 where his colleague Inspector Raymond Codling was shot dead.

The most poignant of these fatal incidents was the loss of three Lancashire officers, Angela Bradley, Gordon Connolly and Colin Morrison, who lost their lives whilst attempting the rescue of a holiday maker from the stormy sea off Blackpool in January 1983. Their colleague Pat Abram was pulled lifeless from the sea and was resuscitated. They are remembered every year by a service of remembrance at the scene of their loss.

Terrorism has also featured in awards given over the years, mainly in connection with the I.R.A. but in recent years Islamist terrorists have come to the fore. In 2003 Constable Stephen Oake was stabbed to death in Manchester whilst protecting his colleagues during the arrest of an Islamist terrorist suspect.

The last gallantry award at the date of publication of this book was the award of the Queen's Gallantry Medal to Constable Claire Louise Murphy of Greater Manchester Police in 2012 for the rescue of a 50-year-old woman who had fallen into the River Irwell in Salford.

This book attempts to retell the stories as to why the awards were made in order they are not forgotten.

Stephen Wilson

July 2018

Acknowledgements

This book could not have been produced without the help and assistance of the staff of the Lancashire Archives, Bow Lane, Preston. Their knowledge and advice has been invaluable.

My thanks also go to the Chief Constable of Lancashire Constabulary for permission to access records and photographs held at Lancashire Archives not normally available to the public.

Wherever possible the ownership of photographs has been acknowledged. Photographs of the Lancashire officers originate from photographs taken by the constabulary when officers were appointed, and others are from other public sources. Similarly, photographs of Salford and Manchester City officers are reproduced with permission of the Greater Manchester Police Museum.

In any document of this nature it will be inevitable that mistakes or omissions will exist, and apologies are made for any errors.

Citations quoted are in the main derived from the *London Gazette* and are quoted with only minor amendments to correct spelling mistakes and are paragraph spaced to improve readability.

Information related to a number of the awards of the King's Police Medal partially originates from J. Peter Farmer's excellent book *Police Gallantry: The King's Police Medal, the King's Police and Fire Services Medal and the Queen's Police Medal for Gallantry 1909-1978*. My thanks go to him for permission to use this information.

Great assistance was provided by Duncan Broady and Katie Henderson of the Greater Manchester Police Museum for their invaluable assistance and access to the archives and photographs held by the museum.

Other great assistance was rendered by Kate McNichol and her staff of Merseyside Police and Will Brown and Paul Carter of the Museum of Policing in Cheshire.

Thanks also go to Anthony Rae for his help, support and assistance with this project and the information provided from his extensive research files.

Contents

A Brief History of the Police in the Lancashire County Palatine 1

The History of National Gallantry Awards 12

The Edward Medal 13

The King's Police Medal 13

Commendation for Brave Conduct 15

The Most Excellent Order of the British Empire 19

The Medal of the Order of the British Empire 19

The British Empire Medal 19

Members of the Order of the British Empire 20

The George Cross 21

The George Medal 22

The Queen's Gallantry Medal 22

The Colonial Police Medal for Gallantry 23

Criteria For Awards 23

Local Awards 24

The William Garnett Cup – Lancashire Constabulary 24

The John Egerton Trophy – Greater Manchester Police 26

The Smith Cup – Burnley Borough Police 27

Other Awards 28

The Award Winners 31

Appendix 1: The Tottenham Outrage 355

Appendix 2: Liverpool City Police Gallantry award winners 1940 – 1941 360

Appendix 3: The William Garnett Cup winners 362

Appendix 4: The John Egerton Trophy winners 366

Bibliography and further reading 369

Index 370

Figures

Figure 1 – Helmet plates of the Lancashire Borough forces amalgamated in 1947 5

Figure 2 – Map showing the boundaries of the Lancashire County Palatine and locations of borough and city police forces existing prior to 1947. 6

Figure 3 – Helmet plates of Lancashire Borough and City Police Forces (1947 to 1967) 7

Figure 4 – Helmet plate of Liverpool and Bootle Constabulary 1967-74 8

Figure 5 – Helmet plate of Manchester and Salford Police 1968-74 8

Figure 6 – Helmet plates of the five police forces covering the Lancashire County Palatine area following reorganisation in 1974 (Cheshire Constabulary, Cumbria Constabulary, Lancashire Constabulary, Greater Manchester Police and Merseyside Police). 9

Figure 7 – Revised boundaries and police force areas after reorganisation in 1974 10

Abbreviations

E.G.   – Edinburgh Gazette

G.M.P.   – Greater Manchester Police

L.A.   – Lancashire Archives

L.G.   – London Gazette

W.O.   – Weekly Order – Lancashire Constabulary

A Brief History of the Police in the Lancashire County Palatine

The Lancashire County Palatine

The ancient county of Lancashire – the County of Lancaster, is situated in the north-west of England. It is bounded to the north with Westmorland and Cumberland, to the east with Yorkshire, south with Cheshire and to the west by the Irish Sea.

The county is approximately 76 miles long and 45 miles wide.

A detached part of the county known as Furness, approximately 25 miles long and 23 miles wide, is separated from the main county area by Morecambe Bay and part of Westmorland.

Lancashire was first termed *'the county of Lancashire'* in the pipe rolls of 1182 (which were the main record of central government transactions) under King Henry II.[1]

The ancient Duchy of Lancaster began in 1265, when Henry III gifted the baronial lands of Simon de Montfort to his son, Edmund. A year later, Henry added the estate of Robert Ferrers, Earl of Derby and then the *'honour, county, town and castle of Lancaster'*, giving Edmund a new title, Earl of Lancaster.

Two years later in 1267, Edmund also received from his father the manor of Newcastle-under-Lyme in Staffordshire, together with lands and estates in both Yorkshire and Lancashire. This substantial inheritance was further added to by Edmund's mother, Eleanor of Provence, who in 1284 bestowed on him the manor of the Savoy in London.

Edmund's inheritance passed to his eldest son Thomas, who was beheaded in 1322. Thereafter, it was conferred on his second son Henry (3rd Earl of Lancaster).

In 1351, Edward III created Henry Grosmont the 3rd Earl of Lancaster as the 1st Duke of Lancaster *'in recognition of astonishing deeds of prowess and feats of arms'* rendered to the crown in France during the Hundred Years War. In the same charter Edward raised Lancaster to a county palatine for Henry's lifetime. This meant that the new duke had sovereign rights in the county in the spheres of justice and administration. The law courts in Lancashire were under the duke's administration and he appointed the sheriff, judges, justices of the peace and other senior officials.

In medieval England palatinate powers were devolved royal powers for use in regions where central government was difficult. The creation of Lancashire as a county palatine may have been intended by Edward III as a protective barrier against the Scots.

Henry, 1st Duke of Lancaster, died in 1361 without a male heir and the palatinate powers reverted back to King Edward III. John O'Gaunt was created 2nd Duke of Lancaster in 1362 and in 1377 the palatinate was recreated for his lifetime. In 1390 this honour was extended to include his heirs. In 1399, Henry Bolinbroke, John O'Gaunt's son was crowned Henry IV. His first act was to stipulate how the Lancaster inheritance was to remain separate from the Crown estate.

The Duke of Lancaster is the hereditary title conferred on the reigning monarch with the palatine forming part of the estate and jurisdiction of The Duchy of Lancaster. The duchy comprises a portfolio of land, property and assets held in trust for the sovereign in their role as the Duke of Lancaster.

---

[1]   http://www.forl.co.uk/online-resources/brief-history-of-lancashire – Retrieved 14/6/2018

In 1974, boundary changes created new metropolitan counties of Greater Manchester and Merseyside and the boundaries with other existing counties were altered. Much of the existing area of the County of Lancashire was lost to these new counties.

In 2013, it was formally announced that the historic counties still exist and are recognised by the government.

This book details incidents where sovereign's gallantry awards were issued to police officers, police and council firemen (before the formation of the National Fire Service in 1941) situated within the Lancashire County Palatine, which appear within the *Gazette*. The *Gazette* (comprising the *London, Belfast and Edinburgh Gazette*) is the official government journal of record. Where civilians and others were involved in the incidents and given awards they are included also.

The birth of policing

Before the police as we know it today, law and order was maintained by a system of constables and watchmen.

Constables were parish employees with their origins dating back to the Danish and Anglo-Saxon invaders, the nearest equivalent being the Saxon *tything-man*. Constables were unpaid and were chosen according to local practices, being appointed to carry out the task as a public duty.

In the later years many wealthier individuals did not want the job due to the time required to carry out the duties and because it was unpaid. They preferred to pay a fine or to hire others to do it for them. In turn the deputies would employ deputies and eventually the office became filled with those who could not find other employment. Thus, the status of constable sank lower in public esteem.

The Statute of Winchester of 1285 provided for watchmen to supplement the duties of the constable. As their title suggests they were employed to watch over towns at night. Originally all townsmen had a responsibility to act as watchmen when called upon. Watchmen guarded the sleeping towns and on their rounds would shout out the hour and remark on the weather. They were provided with sentry-type boxes for their protection in inclement weather.

After about 1689, arising from a number of reasons including population increases, the rapid growth of towns and transport changes, the system became, particularly in urban areas, ineffective and in need of reform. Crime levels grew rapidly in the new industrial towns and across the countryside. Crime statistics first introduced in 1805 showed Lancashire had a considerable crime rate.

Organised policing in the Lancashire County Palatine began with the formation of a police force in Preston. The force was established by the Preston Police Act 1815 (55 Geo. 3, c. xxii), a private Act of Parliament. The Act received Royal Assent on the 1st May 1815. The Act was entitled '*An Act to Light, watch, pave, cleanse and improve the Streets, Highways, and Places within the Borough of Preston, in the County Palatine of Lancaster, and to provide Fire Engines and fireman for the Protection of the Said Borough*'.

Within the Act it empowered the police commissioners (also referred to as the improvement commissioners) to appoint constables, firemen, watchmen and a patrol and to provide watch houses, watch boxes and places for the safe custody of persons apprehended. As part of this they were able to impose rates on property to pay for these improvements.

The police force comprised seven men, with the first superintendent being Thomas Walton.

Lancaster gained its own police in 1824, again by a private Act of Parliament. Both forces predate the formation of the Metropolitan Police in 1829, which was overseen by the Home Secretary, Sir Robert Peel.

The Municipal Corporations Act 1835 reformed local government and set up a system for municipal councils to be elected by ratepayers. Police responsibilities were removed from improvement commissioners. The Act required a watch committee to be set up, formed of councillors and the mayor, who was declared as a Justice of the Peace and to appoint within three weeks sufficient constables to preserve the peace and prevent robberies. The watch committee, formed of councillors, was also given powers to dismiss constables and to frame regulations for them.

The Act applied to the 178 boroughs in England and Wales which had been granted a charter of incorporation by the sovereign. It enabled new charters to be granted under its provisions. Many larger growing industrial towns such as Manchester and Bolton had not yet been granted charters of incorporation and were not obliged to create a police force at this time.

County of Lancaster Constabulary Force (as Lancashire Constabulary was first referred to) was formed in 1839. This followed the County Police Act 1839, which allowed Justices of the Peace to establish police forces in their counties if desired. It was not until 1840 that the fledgling force took to the streets headed by the first Chief Constable, Captain John Woodford. The county force took over policing of towns that did not have its own police force.

Other towns gained their own charters and created their own borough forces, over the years taking policing of their towns from the county force. The Municipal Corporations (New Charters) Act 1877 restricted towns granted charters to have a population in excess of 20,000 before new police forces could be formed. Six Lancashire towns formed their own police forces in 1887.

Twenty-one borough and city forces existed in addition to Lancashire Constabulary in the Lancashire County Palatine.

Accrington Borough Police
Ashton-under-Lyne Borough Police
Bacup Borough Police
Barrow-in-Furness Borough Police
Blackburn Borough Police
Blackpool Borough Police
Bolton Borough Police
Bootle Borough Police
Burnley Borough Police
Clitheroe Borough Police
Lancaster Borough/City Police

Liverpool Constabulary/City Police
Manchester Borough/City Police
Oldham Borough Police
Preston Borough Police
Rochdale Borough Police
Salford Borough/City Police
St Helens Borough Police
Southport Borough Police
Warrington Borough Police
Wigan Borough Police

These forces continued into the 20th Century and although pressure was brought to bear to combine forces this did not take place until after the Second World War.

Police Fire Brigades

In a number of towns and cities, the police also ran the fire brigade with chief constables having responsibility for both functions. Firemen held police ranks, wore police uniform and had collar numbers. In places full-time regular police officers also carried out duties as part-time firemen.

Elsewhere, town councils ran the brigades with full-time staff and firemen who turned out from their regular jobs as required. The Fire Brigades Act 1938 formally designated county boroughs and county district councils as being fire authorities having responsibility for the provision of a fire brigade.

Before the Second World War there were some 1,600 separate fire brigades in operation across the country.

As the Second World War loomed, the Auxiliary Fire Service (A.F.S.) was formed, staffed by unpaid volunteers to supplement fire brigade provision as part of air raid precautions.

All existing fire brigades and the A.F.S. were absorbed into the N.F.S (National Fire Service) in August 1941. This allowed standardisation of equipment and procedures arising from lessons learned from the bombing of the U.K. earlier in the war. After the war, The Fire Services Act 1947 disbanded the N.F.S. giving responsibility back to county and county borough councils, resulting in considerably fewer separate fire brigades which were administered separately from the police.

Ambulance services

Ambulance services were provided by the police and voluntary organisations. Before the advent of the motor vehicle patients were conveyed to hospital by means of hand-wheeled litters and/or horse-drawn and later motor ambulances.

The National Health Service Act 1946 gave county and county borough councils a statutory responsibility to provide emergency ambulance services. The ambulance services were transferred to central government control in 1974, being consolidated under the control of regional or area health authorities.

Other Police Forces in Lancashire

A number of other police forces exist or have existed over the years in Lancashire. These comprised forces outside of the control of the Home Office and have or had limited jurisdiction and powers.

Examples of such forces still in existence are the Mersey Tunnel Police (1936 onwards) and the Port of Liverpool Police (1975 onwards).

Other national forces such as the Ministry of Defence (M.O.D.) Police and the UK Atomic Energy Authority (U.K.A.E.A.) Constabulary (now the Civil Nuclear Constabulary) have operated at various locations in the Lancashire County Palatine over the years.

The British Transport Police (and its predecessor forces) responsible for policing on the railways also operates within the Lancashire County Palatine area.

Other now defunct police forces and their predecessors include:

Liverpool Airport Police	Manchester Airport Police
Liverpool Dock Police	Manchester Park Police
Liverpool Market Police	Manchester Ship Canal Police
Liverpool Parks Police	Ministry of Civil Aviation Constabulary
Liverpool River Police	

Amalgamations

The first amalgamations of police forces in the Lancashire County Palatine took place on 1st April 1947, arising from the Police Act 1946 when five smaller borough and city forces were amalgamated into Lancashire Constabulary. The amalgamated forces were:

Accrington Borough Police
Ashton-under-Lyne Borough Police
Bacup Borough Police
Clitheroe Borough Police
Lancaster City Police

Accrington

Ashton-under-Lyne

Bacup

Clitheroe

Lancaster City

Figure 1— Helmet plates of the Lancashire Borough Forces amalgamated in 1947.

(© David Wilkinson)

Figure 2 – Map showing the boundaries of the Lancashire County Palatine and locations of borough and city police forces existing prior to 1947.

Barrow-in-Furness	Blackburn	Blackpool	Bolton
Bootle	Burnley	Liverpool City	Manchester City
Oldham	Preston	Rochdale	Salford
St. Helens	Southport	Warrington	Wigan

Figure 3 – Helmet plates of Lancashire Borough and City Police Forces (1947 to 1967).

The Police Act 1964 introduced a number of changes including the power for the Home Secretary to force compulsory amalgamation schemes. On 16th May 1966 the Home Secretary, Roy Jenkins, announced that the number of police forces in England and Wales would be reduced from 117 to 49. Where the local authorities would not agree to a voluntary scheme he would make compulsory amalgamations.

Liverpool City Police and Bootle Borough Police were amalgamated and became **Liverpool and Bootle Constabulary** on 1st April 1967.

Manchester City Police and Salford City Police were amalgamated to form **Manchester and Salford Police** on 1st June 1968.

Figure 4 – Helmet plate of Liverpool and Bootle Constabulary 1967-74.

Figure 5 – Helmet plate of Manchester and Salford Police 1968-74.

On 1st April 1969, despite strong opposition, the remaining twelve borough forces were amalgamated into Lancashire Constabulary, comprising:

Barrow-in-Furness Borough Police
Blackburn Borough Police
Blackpool Borough Police
Bolton Borough Police
Burnley Borough Police
Oldham Borough Police

Preston Borough Police
Rochdale County Borough Police
St Helens Borough Police
Southport Borough Police
Warrington Borough Police
Wigan Borough Police

Chief Constable's Message – 29th March 1974

On the 1st April 1974 the Lancashire Constabulary as we have known it since 1969 ceases to exist. Nearly one half of the Constabulary area and almost two-thirds of its personnel will be transferred to the new Cumbria, Cheshire, Greater Manchester and Merseyside forces.

I know many of you are as concerned as I am at the breaking up of the Lancashire Constabulary which has been moulded into a highly efficient Police Force of international prestige following the 1969 amalgamation.

The referendum in November 1972 showed that a thousand or so police officers in the areas designated to become parts of other Forces would have liked to have remained in Lancashire but the number was so large that the wishes of only a few could be met. I very much regret that it should be so, but knowing the calibre of our men and women, I am sure that all our officers who join the new successor Forces will serve their new Chief Constables and Forces with the same devotion and loyalty to duty they have given to the Lancashire Constabulary.

To all police officers, police cadets, civilian staff, traffic wardens, school crossing patrols and members of the Special Constabulary, who will be joining the new Forces, I offer my sincere thanks and to them and their wives and families, my wife and I send our best wishes, good health and happiness for the future.

These amalgamations resulted in Lancashire Constabulary becoming the largest police force outside London, with an establishment of around 7,000 officers.

The enlarged Lancashire Constabulary was, however, to be short lived when on 1st April 1974, as a result of boundary changes arising from the Local Government Act 1972, new metropolitan counties and the Police Forces of Greater Manchester Police and Merseyside Police were created.

Much of the Lancashire Constabulary area and establishment was lost to these new forces as well as to Cumbria Constabulary and Cheshire Police Forces, which resulted in a smaller establishment for Lancashire Constabulary of less than 3,000 officers.

A large rural area incorporating the towns of Barnoldswick and Earby, Bowland Rural District and the parishes of Bracewell, Brogden and Salterforth from the Skipton Rural District were incorporated into the north-easterly part of the Lancashire administrative county. This area had previously been part of the West Riding of Yorkshire. A number of other small boundary adjustments also took place.

The five forces of Cheshire Constabulary, Cumbria Constabulary, Greater Manchester Police, Lancashire Constabulary and Merseyside Police have continued to this day.

In 2005 the Home Office, following a report by Her Majesty's Inspectorate of Constabulary, made proposals to create larger 'strategic police forces' by further amalgamating forces. It was thought that larger forces would be more capable of dealing with areas of "protective services", comprising: counter terrorism and extremism; serious organised and cross border crime; civil contingencies and emergency planning; critical incident management; major crime (homicide); public order; and strategic road policing.

In the North West it was proposed that Cheshire and Merseyside Police and Cumbria and Lancashire Constabularies should merge, with Greater Manchester Police remaining unaffected as they had an establishment in excess of 4,000 officers which was above the criteria proposed to operate effectively.

Lancashire and Cumbria Constabularies voluntarily agreed to merge but the merger was called off after failure to agree on how the combined force would be financed. Lancashire and Cumbria were the only two forces in the country which voluntarily agreed to merge. Nationally the proposals were abandoned in 2006.

Figure 4 – Helmet plates of the five police forces covering the Lancashire County Palatine area following reorganisation in 1974.

(Cheshire Constabulary, Cumbria Constabulary, Lancashire Constabulary, Greater Manchester Police and Merseyside Police).

Figure 5 – Revised boundaries and police force areas after reorganisation in 1974.

Table 1

Timeline & dispositions of amalgamated predecessor forces within current forces.

Police Force	Formed		Amalgamated			1974 reorganisation
	Year	Size	Year	Size	Amalgamated with	
Preston	1815	7	1969	283	Lancashire Constabulary	Lancashire Constabulary 1974 = 2880
Lancaster	1824	7	1947	62	Lancashire Constabulary	
Lancashire County Constabulary	1839	500	1969	4,246	Borough forces (establishment at 1/4/1969 – 7,000)	
Blackburn	1852	12	1969	243	Lancashire Constabulary	
Accrington	1882	32	1947	62	Lancashire Constabulary	
Bacup	1887	26	1947	28	Lancashire Constabulary	
Blackpool	1887	23	1969	356	Lancashire Constabulary	
Burnley	1887	70	1969	186	Lancashire Constabulary	
Clitheroe	1887	9	1947	15	Lancashire Constabulary	
Liverpool	1836	390	1967	2,322	Liverpool & Bootle	Merseyside Police 1974 = 4,345
Southport	1870	7	1969	203	Lancashire Constabulary	
Bootle	1887	47	1967	203	Liverpool & Bootle	
St Helens	1887	65	1969	237	Lancashire Constabulary	
Wigan	1836	7	1969	189	Lancashire Constabulary	Greater Manchester Police 1974 = 6,628
Bolton	1839	12	1969	398	Lancashire Constabulary	
Manchester	1839	347	1968	2,115	Manchester & Salford	
Salford	1844	40	1968	420	Manchester & Salford	
Ashton-under-Lyne	1848	13	1947	63	Lancashire Constabulary	
Oldham	1849	12	1969	272	Lancashire Constabulary	
Rochdale	1857	17	1969	212	Lancashire Constabulary	
Warrington	1847	5	1969	180	Lancashire Constabulary	Cheshire Constabulary
Barrow-in-Furness	1881	48	1969	158	Lancashire Constabulary	Cumbria Constabulary

The History of National Gallantry Awards

Bravery been recognised on the battlefields of war since the introduction of the Victoria Cross and other military decorations, but there was no general equivalent for acts of bravery by the civilian population.

Various organisations such as The Royal Humane Society, The Royal Society for the Protection of Life from Fire and others, such as the Liverpool Shipwreck and Humane Society, issued medals and scrolls commemorating gallant actions but there were no official awards issued by the Crown.

Liverpool Shipwreck and Humane Society General Medal in bronze awarded to Sgt. Wyatt, Liverpool City Police in 1907.

(© Dix Noonan Webb)

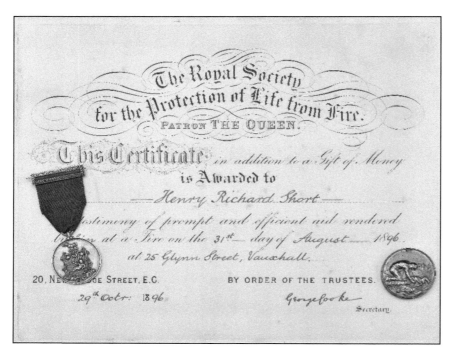

Scroll and medal of the Royal Society for the Protection of Life from Fire.
(© Dix Noonan Webb)

The Carnegie Hero Fund Trust, established in Britain in 1908, also provides awards recognising civilian heroism and aids where necessary people who have been injured or the dependants of persons killed attempting to save another human life in peaceful pursuits.

Two medals were later instituted by Royal Warrant to reward civilians.

The **Albert Medal** was instituted in 1867, for acts of bravery in saving life at sea, and later The **Edward Medal** in 1907, specifically for acts of bravery in saving life in mines, which was later widened to include bravery in factories and workshops.

Only a small number of such awards were made nationally to police officers and as far as can be established no officer from the North West was awarded the Albert Medal and only one person associated with the police, namely Thomas Coppard, a works police sergeant at a

Carnegie Hero Fund Medallion.
(© Dix Noonan Webb)

munitions factory, the National Filling Factory, White Lund, Morecambe, was awarded an Edward Medal following a disastrous fire there in 1917.

Chief Constables, Watch Committees and the Courts gave commendations to officers which were formally recorded on the officer's service records. Chief Constables awarded Merit Badges and Watch Committees awarded monetary rewards recognising officer's actions.

Some forces awarded their own medals for bravery, one such was Manchester City Police who awarded the Watch Committee Medal for Bravery, which was instituted in February 1894, with the last award being made in 1948. Rochdale Borough Police awarded a similar medal for bravery.

The Edward Medal

In 1907, it was suggested by Sir Henry Cunningham of the Home Office, who took a great interest in mining matters, that acts of gallantry occurring underground should be recognised by the award of silver and bronze medals.

Manchester City Watch Committee Medal for Bravery.

Mr Hewlett, a leading colliery owner, offered to subscribe £600 to defray the cost of establishing the medal. It was originally intended that the award

The Edward Medal (Industry). (© Dix Noonan Webb)

should be confined to mines and quarries in the U.K., but further funding was pledged, and the award was extended to the Empire. The scheme was approved by the King who suggested the medal be called the Edward Medal. The medal was instituted on the 13th July 1907 by Royal Warrant.

Further funding was obtained and the scope for the medal was extended to acts arising in factories and workshops and the reverse of the medal was amended to have two separate versions (Mining or Industry) dependant on the industry for which the award was given.

In 1949, the silver medal awards were discontinued, and the bronze medal was awarded only posthumously. In 1971, living recipients of the medal were deemed to have been awarded the George Cross and the medals *might* be exchanged for the George Cross.

The medal is one of the rarest gallantry awards, with only 77 silver and 318 bronze medals being awarded.

Four silver Edward Medals were awarded following the disastrous fire at the National Filling Factory at White Lund, Morecambe in 1917. One of these was to Thomas Coppard a police sergeant with the Factory Police. Coppard was a retired Detective Inspector from Hastings.

The King's Police Medal

The medal was created as a consequence of the 'Tottenham Outrage', which took place in 1909.

During this incident, which began as a wages robbery, one police officer and a ten-year-old boy were shot dead, seven police officers and seventeen civilians were wounded. A full account of this incident is included at the rear of this book.

The country was shocked at this incident, and the Commissioner of Police, Sir Edward Henry, pressed the

1st pattern King's Police Medal (George V issue).
(© Dix Noonan Webb)

King's Police Medal (Edward VI issue) – note FOR GALLANTRY wording on reverse.

(© Dix Noonan Webb)

Home Secretary, Mr H.J. Gladstone to reward the officers involved. In due course, a recommendation was placed before His Majesty, King Edward VII for an award to be created.

This award was to become the King's Police Medal. The first officers awarded the medal were those singled out for their actions during the Tottenham Outrage.

The medal was inaugurated by Royal Warrant on July 7th, 1909 and was named **The King's Police Medal**.

The Proclamation read as follows:

'It is ordered that the medal shall only be awarded to those of our faithful subjects and others who, being members of a recognised Police Force or of a properly organised Fire Brigade within our Dominions or in Territories under our protection or Jurisdiction, have performed acts of exceptional courage and skill, or have exhibited conspicuous devotion to duty, and that such award shall be only on a recommendation to us by our Principal of State for the Home Department.'

The medal is of silver, and to be suspended from the left breast by a riband, one inch and three eights in width, coloured dark blue with a narrow silver stripe on either side.

The front of the medal bears the Sovereign's effigy and reverse of the medal bears a design emblematic of protection from danger. All awards bear the recipient's name on the rim.

The number of medals to be awarded in any one year was not to exceed one hundred and twenty, of which at the most, forty to be awarded for services in the United Kingdom of Great Britain and Ireland, the Channel Islands and the Isle of Man; thirty for services in His Majesty's Dominions beyond the seas, and fifty for services in the Empire of India. In very special circumstances, which, in His Majesty's opinion would justify an exceptional grant, His Majesty could award medals exceeding the above numbers.

Initially recipients were required to have shown:

(a)   Conspicuous gallantry in saving life and property, or in preventing crime or arresting criminals; the risks incurred to be estimated with due regard to the obligations and duties of the officer concerned.

(b)   A specially distinguished record in administrative or detective service.

(c)   Success in organizing Police Forces or Fire Brigades or Departments, or in maintaining their organization under special difficulties.

(d)   Special services in dealing with serious or widespread outbreaks of crime or public disorder, or of fire.

(e)   Valuable political and secret services.

(f)   Special services to Royalty and Heads of States.

(g)   Prolonged service; but only when distinguished by very exceptional ability and merit.

In October 1916, by Royal Warrant, the medal riband was altered to dark blue with a narrow silver stripe on either side and a similar silver stripe in the centre.

On 12th December 1933, by Royal Warrant, The King's Police Medal for Gallantry was ordered to be distinguished from the medal awarded on other grounds as follows:

'The medal when awarded for Gallantry shall bear on the reverse the words "For Gallantry" and shall be suspended by a blue riband with white and red stripes. The medal when awarded on other grounds shall bear on the reverse the words "For Distinguished Service" and shall be suspended by a blue riband with white stripes as at present.'

Thus, the medal from that date came in two different forms, namely the medal for gallantry which bore the legend "FOR GALLANTRY" on the reverse and was accompanied by the blue and silver ribbon bearing the additional red stripes.

The distinguished service medal bore the legend "FOR DISTINGUISHED SERVICE" and was accompanied by the existing blue and silver ribbon without the additional red stripes.

On August 20st, 1940, by Royal Warrant, it was ordained that the medal shall be designated and named **The King's Police and Fire Services Medal**. The medal could be, and was, issued to fire service officers before this, but was now reflected formally in the title of the medal.

In a warrant of 19th May 1954 the current version of the medal, named **The Queen's Police Medal** was introduced; at the same time a separate medal for the Fire Service was created, **The Queen's Fire Service Medal**.

The Queen's Police Medal for gallantry after this time was only awarded posthumously, and from 30th November 1977 no further awards have been made, as the Queen's Gallantry Medal could then be issued posthumously.

The Queen's Police Medal is still issued for distinguished police service.

The largest number of awards made for one incident, for actions at a fire at a munitions works at White Lund, Morecambe in Lancashire in October 1917, was when eight members of Lancashire Fire Brigade were awarded the King's Police Medal. Four Edward Medals in silver and fifteen Medals of the Order of the British Empire were also awarded.

Bars to medal

Further awards of the medal for gallantry were denoted by the issue of a horizontal bar worn on the medal ribbon. There are 5 bars recorded as being issued to recipients of the King's Police Medal. The winners were:

> Constable William George, of Kincardineshire Constabulary in 1912 & 1914.
> Detective Sergeant William Tait Brown of Glasgow City Police in 1918 & 1922.
> Constable John Barton of Dublin City Police in 1917 & 1918.
> Sergeant John Jones of Wigan Police Fire Brigade in 1922 & 1927.
> Constable (later Inspector) James Cole of Metropolitan Police, 1930 & 1944.

The only north-west recipient of a bar to the medal was Sergeant John Jones of the Wigan Police Fire Brigade. Jones had already been awarded a **The Medal of the Order of the British Empire** for gallantry at a fire at the Gathurst Munitions Works, Wigan on 15th May 1916. Prior to 1934 the bar comprised a dated bar and after that date it comprised a laurel leaf patterned bar.

Commendation for Brave Conduct

During the First World War 1914-18, it was acknowledged that there was no suitable award to recognise acts of bravery by civilians that did not merit a specific gallantry medal, and for acts of gallantry during which the person performing the act lost their life (only the Victoria Cross could be awarded posthumously at that time).

The formal introduction of 'Commendations' was the solution approved by King George V. After the end of the war the award fell into disuse.

It was re-introduced in 1939 by King George VI when it was referred to as the **King's Commendation** before being officially titled the **King's Commendation for Brave Conduct**. Awards for bravery in civil defence were gazetted accordingly in the *London Gazette*.

The award can be thought of as the civilian equivalent of the military mention in dispatches.

The King's Commendation originally simply comprised a certificate alone. However, in 1943, a gold-coloured plastic emblem was issued to denote civil commendations.

The small plastic badge was replaced by alternative insignia in the form of a silver metal laurel leaf for civilians and a bronze oak leaf for armed forces personnel (including merchant seamen during time of war). The award continues to be issued in this form.

The award is worn on the coat after any medals awarded or, if no other medals are held, in the position a single medal would be occupy.

In 1952 the honour was renamed the **Queen's Commendation for Brave Conduct**, which was replaced in 1994 by the title **Queen's Commendation for Bravery**.

King's Commendation for Brave Conduct emblem.
(© Dix Noonan Webb)

All such awards are accompanied by a named certificate, which for civilian awards is signed by the Prime Minister.

King's/Queen's Commendation emblems in presentation case.
(Author's collection)

King's/Queen's Commendation emblem.

By the KING'S Order the name of
James Macpherson, M.B.
Medical Practitioner,
Westminster.
was published in the London Gazette on
25 April, 1941.
as commended for brave conduct in
Civil Defence.
I am charged to record His Majesty's
high appreciation of the service rendered.

Winston S. Churchill

Prime Minister and First Lord
of the Treasury

Commendation certificate for brave conduct in Civil Defence – certificate bearing the signature of
Prime Minister Winston S. Churchill. (Author's collection)

By the QUEEN'S Order the name of

Peter Halliwell,

Constable, Blackburn Borough Police Force,

was published in the London Gazette on
14 August, 1959,
as commended for brave conduct.
I am charged to record Her Majesty's
high appreciation of the service rendered.

Prime Minister and First Lord
of the Treasury

Commendation certificate for brave conduct – certificate bearing the signature of
Prime Minister Harold Macmillan. (Author's collection)

The Most Excellent Order of the British Empire

This Order of Knighthood was founded by King George V in 1917 to reward important services to the Empire at home, in India and in the overseas dominions and colonies other than those rendered by the Navy and Army, although it could be awarded for services of a non-combative nature to Navy and Army personnel. For the first time, women of all classes could be admitted to the Order and coincided with parliament's acceptance of women's suffrage.

In addition to the five classes of the Order, a medal was created in order that the services of many persons who could not be admitted to one of the classes of the Order could be recognised. Such persons included significant numbers of largely working class men and women performing civilian roles who had given long and meritorious service in their duties and performed acts of bravery and lifesaving.

On the 27th December 1918 King George introduced a Military Division of the Order with the Division indicated by a central red stripe on the riband.

The Medal of the Order of the British Empire

The Medal of the Order of the British Empire comprised a circular silver medal with a representation of Britannia within the circle and motto of the Order and on the reverse the Royal Cypher and was suspended by a purple riband. The medals were issued un-named and holders were not permitted to use post nominal letters.

A total of 2,015[2] medals were awarded to U.K. and Empire recipients. Around 900 were awarded to foreign nationals, mainly those involved in secret service organisations operating on the Western Front.

Recommendations for the posthumous award of the Medal of the Order of the British Empire were made. However, these were declined using the pretext that the medal was not authorised to be so awarded. Such decisions were made despite the fact that medals were being quietly granted to Belgian and French secret service agents who had been captured and executed by the Germans.

The medal was superseded on the 29th December 1922 by two medals, namely the British Empire Medal and the Empire Gallantry Medal. (See next entry concerning these awards.)

Medal of the Order of the British Empire.

(© Dix Noonan Webb)

The British Empire Medal

The Medal of the Order of the British Empire was discontinued in 1922, being replaced with two separate honours, namely the *Medal of the Order of the British Empire for Meritorious Service* (usually referred to as British Empire Medal, **B.E.M.**) and the *Medal of the Order of the British Empire for Gallantry* (usually referred to as Empire Gallantry Medal, **E.G.M.**) which was replaced by the George Cross in 1940. Existing holders of the Empire Gallantry Medal were invited to exchange their medals for the George Cross.

When instituted in 1922 the medal ribbon comprised a purple ribbon 1 1/16" wide with the Military Division versions indicated by a central red stripe. This was changed in 1937 to a rose-pink ribbon with pearl grey edges and for the Military Division medal an additional central grey stripe.

The British Empire Medal: **(B.E.M.)** which may be awarded posthumously, is granted in recognition of meritorious civil or military service. From June 1942 recipients were entitled to use the post-nominal letters B.E.M.

---

[2]   Revised figure from recent research carried out by Roger Willoughby – see *For God and the Empire – The Medal of the Order of the British Empire 1917-1922.*

However, also starting in 1940, the statutes were amended so that it could again be awarded for acts of gallantry, but now for such acts of bravery, not in the face of the enemy, which were below the level required for the George Medal.

From 14 January 1958, awards of the B.E.M. made for acts of bravery were formally designated the **British Empire Medal for Gallantry** and consisted of the B.E.M. medal with the addition of a silver oak leaf emblem worn on the ribbon.

This was done so that the B.E.M. awarded for gallantry would physically be distinguished from the B.E.M. awarded for other services. The emblem was not retrospective to the earlier awards issued.

British Empire Medal (Civil Division)
George V issue. (© Spink)

Silver oak leaf emblem.
(© Dix Noonan Webb)

Unlike the George Cross and George Medal, the B.E.M. for Gallantry could not be awarded posthumously and was eventually replaced in 1974 with **The Queen's Gallantry Medal**.

Members of the Order of the British Empire

MBE (Civil Division)
Post-1937 ribbon.
(© Dix Noonan Webb)

There are five classes of member of the order, namely:

Grand Cross of the British Empire, **G.B.E.**
Knights & Dames Grand Cross of the British Empire, **K.B.E. & D.B.E.**
Commanders of the British Empire, **C.B.E.**
Officers of the British Empire, **O.B.E.**
Members of the British Empire, **M.B.E.**

A number of the lower appointments to the Order were awarded in recognition of gallantry.

Such appointments were generally to senior police officers who received this appointment rather than the British Empire Medal, which was awarded to lower ranks.

As with the B.E.M., from 14th January 1958 awards made for acts of gallantry consisted of the medal with the addition of a silver oak leaf emblem worn on the ribbon.

This was done so that the medal awarded for gallantry would physically be distinguished from those awarded for other services. The emblem was not retrospective to the earlier awards issued.

The George Cross and George Medal

The George Cross

The George Cross: (G.C.) is the second highest award of the United Kingdom honours system.

It is awarded for gallantry *'not in the face of the enemy'* to members of the British armed forces and to British civilians. It has always been able to be awarded posthumously.

It may be awarded to a person of any military rank in any service and to civilians including police, emergency services and merchant seamen.

During the height of the Blitz, there was a strong desire to reward the many acts of civilian courage.

The existing awards open to civilians were not judged suitable to meet the new situation, therefore it was decided that the George Cross and the George Medal would be instituted to recognise both civilian gallantry in the face of enemy action and brave deeds more generally.

Announcing the new award, the King said:

George Cross.
(© Dix Noonan Webb)

'In order that they should be worthily and promptly recognised, I have decided to create, at once, a new mark of honour for men and women in all walks of civilian life. I propose to give my name to this new distinction, which will consist of the George Cross, which will rank next to the Victoria Cross, and the George Medal for wider distribution.'

The Warrant for the G.C. (along with that of the G.M.), dated 24th September 1940, was published in the *London Gazette* on 31st January 1941 and stated:

'The Cross is intended primarily for civilians and award in our military services is to be confined to actions for which purely military Honours are not normally granted.'

and

'It is ordained that the Cross shall be awarded only for acts of the greatest heroism or of the most conspicuous courage in circumstances of extreme danger, and that the Cross may be awarded posthumously.'

and

'The Cross shall be worn by recipients on the left breast suspended from a ribbon one and a quarter inches in width, of dark blue, that it shall be worn immediately after the Victoria Cross and in front of the Insignia of all British Orders of Chivalry.'

Bars are awarded to the G.C. in recognition of the performance of further acts of bravery meriting the award, although none has yet been awarded. Recipients are entitled to the post-nominal letters G.C.

In common with the Victoria Cross, a distinction peculiar to these two premier awards for bravery, in undress uniform or on occasions when the medal ribbon alone is worn, a miniature replica of the cross is affixed to the centre of the ribbon.

The George Medal

George Medal. (© Dix Noonan Webb)

The George Medal: **(G.M.)** was instituted at the same time as the George Cross and is granted in recognition of *'acts of great bravery'*.

The original Warrant for the George Medal did not permit it to be awarded posthumously.

This was changed in December 1977 to allow posthumous awards, several of which have been subsequently made.

Bars are awarded to the G.M. in recognition of the performance of further acts of bravery meriting the award.

In undress uniform or on occasions when the medal ribbon alone is worn, a silver rosette is worn on the ribbon to indicate each bar.

Recipients are entitled to the post-nominal letters G.M.

The Queen's Gallantry Medal

Queen's Gallantry Medal.
(Author's collection)

The Queen's Gallantry Medal: **(Q.G.M.)** is awarded to both military and civilians for acts of gallantry where the services were not so outstanding as to merit the award of the George Cross or the George Medal. The Q.G.M. is awarded for *'exemplary acts of bravery'*.

It was instituted on 20th June 1974 to replace the Order of the British Empire for Gallantry and the British Empire Medal for Gallantry.

The Q.G.M. ended the situation where the Order of the British Empire for Gallantry was awarded for lesser acts of bravery than the George Medal but took precedence over it in the Order of Wear.

The Q.G.M. has been awarded posthumously since 30th November 1977 and no further awards of either the Queen's Police Medal for Gallantry or the Colonial Police Medal for Gallantry have been gazetted. Holders of the Queen's Gallantry Medal are permitted to use the post nominal letters Q.G.M.

The Colonial Police Medal for Gallantry

The Colonial Police Medal (C.P.M.) is a medal awarded to members of police forces and members of fire brigades in British Overseas Territories and formerly in Crown Colonies and British Dependent Territories.

This award has been made to UK officers serving overseas attached temporarily to the police forces of such territories.

Holders of the Colonial Police Medal are entitled to use the post nominal letters C.P.M.

Between 1938 and 1979 a total of 465 Colonial Police Medals for Gallantry have been awarded.

The medal was instituted by Royal Warrant dated the 10th May 1938. The qualifications for the award are:

Colonial Police Medal for Gallantry.
(© Dix Noonan Webb)

   (i)   Conspicuous gallantry;

   (ii)   Valuable service characterised by resource and devotion to duty, including prolonged service marked by exceptional ability, merit and exemplary conduct.

The medal is thus awarded in two versions, namely for gallantry or distinguished service.

The gallantry award is differentiated from the meritorious service award by a different ribbon bearing red stripes and the wording on the reverse of the medal reads 'COLONIAL POLICE MEDAL FOR GALLANTRY'.

As of 14th June 2012, this medal was renamed the Overseas Territories Police Medal.

Only one Lancashire officer has been awarded this medal.

This was Detective Constable Alan Sewart who was awarded this medal for service with the British Police Unit in Cyprus.

Criteria For Awards

In 1975, following the institution of The Queen's Gallantry Medal, guidance was issued to government departments detailing the criteria for the different awards.

This was further updated in 1977 to allow posthumous awards when the levels of gallantry were set out as follows:

> Of the highest order
> Of an extremely high order
> Of a high order
> Not up to the foregoing standard but entailing risk to life and meriting recognition

The levels of available awards were set out as follows:

> The George Cross
> The George Medal
> The Queen's Gallantry Medal
> The Queen's Commendation

This guidance also detailed how submissions should be made. This guidance was further updated in 1997, which led to the issue of Home Office Circular 67/1997.

This Circular provides advice and guidance to those considering nominations for a gallantry award and laid out factors to be considered when making nominations and included the degree of the risk of death.

George Cross	Over 90%
George Medal	50% to 90%
Queen's Gallantry Medal	20% to 50%
Queen's Commendation	Below 20%

The Circular also laid out other factors for consideration, including a knowledge or awareness of danger, preparedness, persistence, third party protection, saving life, injury and the physical surroundings.

This guidance remains in force to this day.

Local Awards

The William Garnett Cup – Lancashire Constabulary

The William Garnett Cup was donated to Lancashire Constabulary in 1930 and is awarded to the Constabulary officer judged to have performed the most gallant deed of the year. The cup and its purpose is detailed within the Constabulary records as follows:

> *The 'William Garnett' Cup was donated in 1930 by the late Alderman William Garnett in memory of his father and is awarded annually to the Lancashire police officer or officers performing the most gallant deed of the year.*
>
> *Throughout the year many acts of meritorious conduct are performed by members of the Constabulary, some unreported, and yet these acts alone may not meet the high criteria required to qualify the officer for this most prestigious award.*
>
> *Such are the lofty standards required before this award is made that the Chief Constable, after consultation with senior officers, considers each individual act of bravery in the previous 12 months, not only looking for the most meritorious deed, but also ensuring that the act itself merits the presentation of this prestigious award.*
>
> *In this light, it would be fair to say that the 'William Garnett' Cup is 'special' in that it is awarded to officers who have acted in the highest tradition of the Constabulary by performing an extreme act of bravery.*

The presentation of the cup was detailed within the Force General Order of 26th April to 27th May 1930 as follows:

26th April 1930.

The 'William Garnett' Cup presented to the Force by

W. J. Garnett, Esq., J.P.

I am pleased to announce to the Force that Mr. W. J. Garnett, J.P., Quernmore Park, Lancaster, has kindly presented a Trophy in memory of his father, the late Mr. William Garnett, D.L., J.P. for many years a member of the Lancashire County Council and the Standing Joint Committee and, at the time of his death, Chairman of the Lonsdale South Petty Sessional Division, and Deputy Constable of Lancaster Castle. The Trophy will be styled the 'William Garnett Cup' and will be awarded to the member of the Force who, in my opinion, performs the most gallant act of the year. If in any one year no act has been performed of sufficient gallantry to merit the award of the Cup, it will be withheld and in all cases of award or otherwise my decision will be final.

It should also be noted that the award is for exceptional courage and skill and not for devotion to duty or meritorious service.

The member of the Force to whom the Cup is awarded will be allowed to retain possession of it during the remainder of the year of the award, after which it should be returned to this office, he will also receive a memento in the form of a medal suitably inscribed and indicating the year he held the Cup.

The Cup will be inscribed with the name of the holder and the year for which it is held and will be covered by insurance, the annual premium for which will be paid out of the Lancashire Constabulary Reward Account.

W. Trubshaw, Chief Constable

Sergeant John Henry Barber with the William Garnett Cup 1930. Note: Merit Badge to right sleeve and The R.S.P.C.A. Silver Medal. On the table next to the cup is the memento medal.

Since then the cup has been awarded annually, apart from the war years when no awards were made and several years where no suitable events occurred.

The first award was made in 1930 jointly to P.S. 656 John Henry Barber and P.C. 563 Thomas Edward Bradburn.

Both officers were involved on 2nd March 1930 in the attempted rescue of Charles Redvers Henry Walsh, a seaman who fell 120 feet to the bottom of Delph Lane Quarry, Prescot at night.

The officers obtained ropes and were lowered into the pit to assist but the man was found to be dead and they recovered his body.

Both officers were awarded the Merit Badge and granted £5 for brave conduct for their actions that day.

John Henry Barber was born in December 1886 at Dromoyle, Ireland and was appointed to Lancashire Constabulary in May 1914. He had previously served for 12 years with the Irish Guards and the Leinster Regiment.

In 1923, he was awarded the Royal Society for Prevention of Cruelty to Animals (R.S.P.C.A.) Silver Medal for descending a disused pit shaft to rescue a dog from drowning. He was commended by the Chief Constable for his actions and awarded £7 and the merit badge. He was previously commended by the Chief Constable in 1919 for the arrest of a man for dog stealing.

He served at Lonsdale North and Prescot Divisions. On promotion to sergeant on 6th May 1930 he transferred to Rochdale Division. Sergeant Barber served until retirement in 1945. He died in 1957.

Thomas Edward Bradburn was born at York in 1883 and joined Lancashire Constabulary in July 1909.

He had previously served with the Grenadier Guards for three years and was an Army reservist when appointed. He was recalled to the Army on 6th August 1914. He was wounded in France in May 1915, sustaining a gunshot wound to his left shoulder. He was discharged from the Army in June 1918, returning to police duties.

Miniature copy of the William Garnett Cup presented to P.S. 1808 Rae, jointly awarded the trophy for 1989.
(© Anthony Rae)

He was commended in June 1912 and October 1913 and served at Rochdale, Wigan, Leyland, Prescot and Widnes Divisions.

He retired after 25 years and 18 day's service on 31st July 1934 and died in 1955.

The William Garnett Cup continues to be awarded annually by Lancashire Constabulary. A list of the winners of the cup is included at the rear of this book.

A miniature trophy is now presented rather than a memento medal.

The John Egerton Trophy – Greater Manchester Police

On 11th March 1983, Constable John Egerton, aged 20, and Constable David O'Brien were in the yard premises of Dynamic Plastics, Emlyn Street, Farnworth near Bolton searching for an intruder.

Inaugural presentation of the John Egerton Trophy to P.C. Alan Shaw by Chief Constable Sir James Anderton and members of John Egerton's family in 1983. (G.M.P Museum)

P.C. Egerton radioed that he had disturbed an intruder in the yard. Nothing further was heard from him. P.C. Egerton had been repeatedly stabbed. He had caught the intruder, Arthur Edge, siphoning petrol from a car in the factory yard. John Egerton was awarded the Queen's Commendation for Brave Conduct.

Arthur Edge, a former employee at Dynamic Plastics, was jailed for the murder of P.C. Egerton

Students of the Police Training Centre at Bruche, Warrington, presented the John Egerton Trophy to Greater Manchester Police in order it should be awarded to the officer who performs the bravest act of the year.

The first recipient of the trophy was P.C. Alan Shaw (Oldham) who was attacked by a frenzied man with a knife.

The trophy continues to be awarded annually to the member of Greater Manchester Police who performs the bravest act of the year. A list of the recipients of the trophy is included at the rear of this book.

The Smith Cup – Burnley Borough Police

Alfred Victor Smith V.C.

Burnley Borough Police awarded The Smith Cup annually for courageous and gentlemanly acts by its officers.

The Smith Cup was donated to the force on retirement in 1924 by William Henry Smith, Chief Constable of Burnley in memory of his son Alfred Victor Smith V.C.

Alfred Victor Smith was born in Surrey and was educated at Burnley Grammar School and joined Blackpool Borough Police Force on 12th August 1912. Following the outbreak of war in 1914 he joined the East Lancashire Regiment as a 2nd Lieutenant in October 1914.

Alfred Victor Smith died, aged 24 years, on 23rd December 1915 at Gallipoli, whilst serving with 'D' company of the 1/5th Battalion of the East Lancashire Regiment.

The citation for his Victoria Cross published in the *London Gazette* reads as follows:

'For most conspicuous bravery. He was in the act of throwing a grenade when it slipped from his hand and fell into the bottom of the trench, close to several of our officers and men. He immediately shouted out a warning, and himself jumped clear and into safety; but seeing that the officers and men were unable to get into cover and knowing well that the grenade was due to explode, he returned without any hesitation and flung himself down on it. He was killed instantly by the explosion. His magnificent act of self-sacrifice undoubtedly saved many lives.'

PC Tom Harker, winner of the Smith Cup 1971 for the rescue of a man from a burning house on Colne Road, Burnley.

The Victoria Cross and French Croix de Guerre awarded to Lieutenant Alfred Victor Smith are in the collection of the Towneley Hall Museum, Burnley, Lancashire.

The Smith Cup was awarded from 1924 onwards with the recipient being chosen by a committee of officers rather than by the Chief Constable. The last Burnley Borough Police winner was P.C. 84 Ronald Harker in 1968/69.

Ronald Harker was awarded the cup for the arrest of a man on the roof of a warehouse in Burnley when, during a struggle, he and the man narrowly avoided falling off the roof from a height of 30 feet.

On amalgamation with Lancashire Constabulary at the last meeting of the Burnley Branch Board of the Police Federation, it was decided that the cup would be retained at Burnley Police Station to be presented annually if deserved to any police officer of whatever force for the most appropriate deed done within the area.

Other Awards

The Rhodes Marshall Trophy.
(Author's collection)

Trophies

Other borough forces gave similar awards such as **The Kay Taylor Trophy**, awarded by Preston Borough Police, and **The Rhodes Marshall Trophy**, awarded by Blackpool Police for meritorious conduct. The Rhodes Marshall Trophy continues to be awarded to officers in Blackpool Division.

Blackburn Borough Police awarded **The O'Donnell Trophy**, which has recently been brought back into use within Lancashire Constabulary. (See the entry for **Detective Inspector James O'Donnell** later for further information about the circumstances the award commemorates.)

In East Lancashire the **Roland Cree McGowan Cup** is awarded. It was presented by the parents of P.C. Roland Cree McGowan to be awarded annually for bravery. He died in a car accident whilst on duty in Burnley Road, Bacup on 22nd January 1978 whilst responding to an emergency call.

Merit Badges and Commendations

Lancashire Constabulary and many of the borough and city forces issued Merit Badges to officers to recognise significant deeds which fell below the criteria for National Awards.

In many cases officers awarded National Awards would also be issued with Merit Badges. Such badges appear to have generally fallen out of use in most forces by the 1960s but Merseyside Police still have the option of awarding such badges as of 2017.[3]

Merit Badges were worn on the right tunic sleeve and the award of the badge attracted in some forces an enhanced pay rate for the officer.

In addition, commendations by the Chief Constable, Watch Committees, Courts and Chief Constables from other areas were recorded on officer's record sheets and service registers along with the circumstances of the commendation. In certain circumstances, monetary awards were also made.

---

[3]   Merseyside Police Recognition & Reward Policy and Procedure – Retrieved 21/6/2017
https://www.merseyside.police.uk/media/12834/recognition_reward_policy_procedure_2014-02-28.pdf

Lancashire Constabulary Merit Badge.
(first pattern)

Lancashire Constabulary Merit Badge
(later pattern).

Preston Borough
Police Merit Badge.

Merseyside Police
Merit Badge 2017.

Southport Police
Merit Badge.

The Award Winners

At 8.30p.m. on the evening of Saturday, 7th October 1911, Detective Sergeant James McGuire was with Detective Rawcliffe on Church Street, Preston when they saw John Whittle (22 years).

As a result of what was said to them previously they began to follow him. They walked along Church Street, Deepdale Road and onto Castleton Road where Whittle went down a back passageway trying back doors of houses. Whittle then went onto Holmrook Road and onto St. Georges Road North and knocked loudly on a front door of number 275 standing there for several minutes before a man and woman came up the street.

He then walked away and stood around the corner for a few minutes. Seeing the two officers approach he ran away down a back passageway of St. Georges Road with the officers following him. When they were about ten yards away he turned around and fired at them twice with a revolver. Rawcliffe ran around the houses to catch him at the other end and McGuire continued to run after him.

When on Kingfisher Street, Whittle stopped, and McGuire ran forward and shouted, *'If you fire again, I will knock your brains out'*. Whittle hesitated, and McGuire grabbed hold of the hand holding the revolver.

A violent struggle ensued and he and Rawcliffe managed to get Whittle to the floor and take the weapon away. The revolver contained three live rounds and two spent cases. Whittle also had in his possession a jemmy, a skeleton key and 45 ball cartridges.

Alfred Moore a local gunsmith examined the revolver which contained three ball cartridges. He stated a shot from the revolver would kill a person at a range of about 150 yards.

Whittle appeared at Preston Magistrates Court on Monday 9th October 1911 charged with loitering with intent to commit a felony and with attempting to murder Detective Sergeant McGuire and Detective Rawcliffe. Whittle was committed by the Magistrates to Liverpool Assizes for trial. Both officers were commended by the magistrates on their very courageous action. At the Assizes Whittle was convicted and sentenced to seven years penal servitude.

Whittle appealed, and the case was heard at the Court of Criminal Appeal in March 1912. His appeal was dismissed.

FURTHER INFORMATION:

James McGuire was born in Preston in 1869 and joined Preston Borough Police on 21st September 1892. He became a detective in 1904 and was promoted to Detective Sergeant in 1908 and to Inspector in 1913. James McGuire left Preston Borough Police in February 1920 and became the licensee of the Lime Kiln public house on Aqueduct Street, Preston. He died aged 51 years on the 28th May 1921, following a short illness.

James McGuire was involved in one of the earliest recorded police pursuits in Lancashire using a motor vehicle. In September 1905, two men and a woman were circulated as wanted for theft of wages by Bolton Police. McGuire had seen a hansom cab travelling towards Blackpool on his way to work with two well-dressed males and a female passenger on board matching the description. McGuire made enquiries and found that they had stayed overnight at a hotel in Preston. He obtained the use of a motor car and chauffeur and made towards Blackpool to attempt to catch up with the hansom cab. After half an hour the cab was seen at Freckleton Marsh. The chauffeur forced the cab to stop and McGuire arrested William Woods who was one of the wanted persons. The other wanted persons, Charles Roscoe and Maria Lowe, were also present.

After a sharp struggle Woods was placed in the motor car and the cabman was told to follow them back to Preston. Whilst on route the cab turned around and went in the opposite direction.

McGuire and his colleague Detective Moss left Woods at Preston Police Station and then went back in pursuit of the cab and caught up with it prior to reaching Lytham when it was being driven by Charles Roscoe. Roscoe swerved the cab from side to side to prevent the car passing.

The chauffeur however managed to pass and the cab was again forced to stop by the chauffeur who drove the car across its path. Roscoe refused to come down and was pulled down and placed in the car. Maria Lowe also had to be forcibly removed from the cab and placed into the car. The chase generated much excitement in the district.

Inspector Edward Rawcliffe (pictured in 1922)

The wanted persons were returned to Bolton where the two men were sentenced to three months hard labour and the woman discharged. The Preston officers were praised by the Bolton Magistrates.

Edward Rawcliffe was born in Preston in 1875 and joined Preston Borough Police on 19th July 1899. Promotion to Sergeant followed in 1914 and to Uniform Inspector in 1919. He served until 1925 and died in 1957.

Edward Rawcliffe was awarded the Merit Badge and publicly commended by the Mayor of Preston on 11th March 1912 for his actions on 7th October 1911.

L.G. 2/1/1912 Issue 28568 Page 30

3rd November 1911

Henry LINAKER, Constable 301	**Lancashire Constabulary**
Christopher ADAMSON, Constable 1579	**Lancashire Constabulary**

King's Police Medal

For conspicuous gallantry and exceptional coolness, courage and determination displayed in apprehending Albert Wright, alias Harry Webster, a powerful, well-built man known to carry a loaded firearm, and having previously expressed an intention to use it.

He was wanted by the Lincolnshire Police for burglary, and had twice previously escaped, when on the point of arrest during the previous four months.

At 5.45p.m. on 3rd November 1911, Sergeant Linaker and Constable Adamson were in plain clothes, and entered a house at Rishton, where they saw Wright facing them, about eight feet away, with his hand in his jacket pocket.

Linaker told Wright that he was a Police Sergeant, and Wright levelled a revolver at him, and hit him in the left eye with the muzzle, after the revolver misfired. The Sergeant knocked the hand with the revolver to one side, and Adamson seized it, trying to keep the muzzle pointing downwards. A short struggle ensued, and Wright backed away, saying, *'I will kill you both'*.

He fired three shots, one of which grazed the Sergeant's ribs, and one hit the Constable in the thigh, also searing his left hand by the revolver flash. After a long struggle on the stairs, Sergeant Linaker drew his truncheon, hit Wright on the head. Wright was then overpowered and arrested.

The extreme gallantry displayed on this occasion cannot be too highly commended and is a credit to both of these courageous officers.

Lancashire Constabulary award file – PLA/ACC6849   L.G. 31/12/1912 Issue 28677 Page 4

FURTHER INFORMATION:

Incident location – Burton Street, Rishton.

Albert Wright (23) appeared at Manchester Assizes on 20th November 1911 and was sentenced to ten years penal servitude by Mr Justice Avory. The defence was that Wright had no intention of firing the revolver and the jury passed over the more serious charge of attempted murder and convicted him instead of unlawful wounding.

It was stated that in 1905 Wright was sentenced to nine months imprisonment for housebreaking and later six years penal servitude for attempting to shoot a constable at Nottingham in 1906.[4]

Stolen property was found in his possession and arrest warrants had been issued later at Rotherham, Grimsby and the East Riding of Yorkshire for burglary.

Henry Linaker and Christopher Adamson were presented with their medals by King George V at Buckingham Palace on 6th February 1913.

Henry Linaker

Henry Linaker was born at Leyland, Lancashire in 1872. He was appointed to Lancashire Constabulary on 4th November 1892, giving his previous occupation as being an asylum attendant at Prestwich County Asylum.

He served at Manchester, Blackburn, Bolton, Church and Wigan Division on promotion to Sergeant. In 1914 he was promoted to Inspector and returned to Bolton Division where he was promoted to Chief Inspector in 1919. In 1920 he was promoted to Superintendent and took charge of Rossendale Division. In 1928 he moved to Blackburn Lower and Higher Divisions and in 1935 was awarded the King's Silver Jubilee Medal.

He served until January 1937. In 1939 he was appointed to the First Police Reserve, serving until 1940. He died in 1944.

His son William Henry Linaker also joined Lancashire Constabulary and attained the rank of Assistant Chief Constable. He served for 24 years, retiring in 1967.

Christopher Adamson was born at Bolton, Lancashire in 1878. He was appointed to Lancashire Constabulary on 9th August 1901, stating his previous occupation as being a factory operative.

He served at Ormskirk and Church Divisions. Following the arrest of Albert Wright, he was promoted to Merit Class. He was transferred to Manchester

Christopher Adamson

---

4   Wright was one of three men who entered 11 Lewis Street, Nottingham, an empty house, on 21st November 1905 where stolen property had been hidden. After being detained Wright produced a pistol and pointed it at P.C. Willoughby and pulled the trigger twice, but the gun misfired. A violent struggle took place and Willoughby subdued Wright with his truncheon but not before Wright had struck him a severe blow to the head with the gun butt. (*Nottingham Daily Post*, 3/12/1906)

Division on promotion to Sergeant in 1913 and to Ashton-under-Lyne Division in 1918. He was promoted to Inspector in 1919 and transferred to Blackburn Higher Division. In 1927 he was promoted to Chief Inspector.

He served until 1st July 1930 and died in 1950.

8th April 1912

Thomas ROTHERY, Sergeant 1408 **Lancashire Constabulary**

King's Police Medal

At 10.40am on 8th April 1912, a riotous mob of about 1,100 men tried to get into the weaving and engine shed of the Dicconson Lane Mill, Aspull, to stop the engines.

A number of weavers had been on strike since October 1911, and these men supplemented by colliers, demanded that those still working, should be brought out. The manager of the mill requested Sergeant Rothery to save the engines. The Sergeant went towards the engine house, when a half brick hit him on the helmet, and bounced through a window.

Sergeant Rothery with two Constables succeeded in preventing serious damage being done before the arrival of reinforcements of police, when the crowd dispersed.

This is indeed a case of real courage accompanied by coolness in emergency, so very desirable in a Police Officer.

Lancashire Constabulary award file – PLA/ACC6849 E.G. 2/1/1914 Issue 12630 Page 10

FURTHER INFORMATION:

Location of incident – Halliday and Constantine's Mill, Dicconson Lane, Aspull, Wigan.

Two men, Hugh Swinwood, a collier of Westhoughton, and his son William Swinwood appeared at Wigan County Police Court on 9th April 1912 charged with creating a breach of the peace by unlawful obstruction of the police in the execution of their duty and with inciting the crowd to violence.

Sergeant Rothery told the court that there were around 1,000 people outside the mill and they assumed a very threatening attitude. Some of them got hold of him and tried to put him into the fire hole.

Rothery entered the weaving shed and prevented damage occurring after having produced his truncheon and threatening to knock down the first man who entered.

The younger defendant attempted to strike Sergeant Rothery with a large stick but Rothery wrenched it from his grasp. Later, following the arrest of another man, John Pilkington, Hugh Swinwood went to the police station where, after causing a disturbance and being violent, he was arrested. His son later came to the station and was arrested after shouting and demanding his father's release. Sergeant Metcalfe and Constable Ashton gave evidence that the Swinwoods were the ringleaders of the mob. Constable Ashton had taken a half brick off Hugh Swinwood which he was about to throw at Sergeant Rothery at the mill. Both were convicted and fined 40s. and costs.

John Pilkington of Aspull also pleaded guilty to breaking two windows at the mill valued at 10s. and to inciting the mob to violence. He was fined 40s. and 10s. representing the amount of the damage caused. (*Wigan Observer*, 13/4/1912)

Thomas Rothery was born at Maryport, Cumbria in 1864. His previous occupation is recorded as being a labourer resident at Frizzington, Whitehaven.

He was appointed on 29th June 1886 and posted to Wigan Division and transferred to Manchester Division in April 1893. During this time, he was promoted to Merit Class for '*the arrest of a man in the face of opposition*' and was given monetary awards for stopping a runaway horse and cart and, along with another constable, for '*great courage in arresting a man in the face of a hostile crowd*'.

On 10th July 1902 he was promoted to Sergeant and transferred to Bolton Division, and returned to Wigan Division the following year. Following the events of April 1912, he was promoted to Merit Sergeant for '*courage and determination during a disturbance*'.

Thomas Rothery pictured after being awarded the Coronation Medal 1911.

Rothery was one of the six Lancashire officers awarded the 1911 Police Coronation Medal. He served until 1st February 1915 and died in December 1942.

14th May 1912

George BEESLEY, Fireman   **Colne Borough Fire Brigade**

King's Police Medal

Fireman Beesley is one of the permanent drivers of the Fire Brigade and when a call was received at the Fire Station on 14th May 1912, he drove the No. 2 Steamer to the place where the fire had occurred.

On arrival at the scene it was found that flames and smoke were issuing from the windows and doors of the dwelling, and immediately a cry was heard from the crowd – '*I hope they have saved the child!*'

Fireman Beesley, hearing this, at once handed over the hose he was using to another fireman, and after several fruitless attempts, in the face of almost insurmountable difficulties and continually at the risk of his own life, was able to gain access to the bedroom of the dwelling, and bring away the child, although, unfortunately, too late to save its life.

PRO Ref: H045/10999/217900

L.G. 1/1/1913 Issue 28677 Page 5

FURTHER INFORMATION:

Location of incident – 27, Reginald Street, Colne.

The child was the nine-month-old daughter of Herbert Hartley, a warp dresser. The inquest decided there was no evidence as to how the fire started as both parents were at work. The jury returned a verdict of accidental death.

George Beesley was presented with the King's Police Medal at Buckingham Palace at an investiture held on 6th February 1913.

(See later entry for Fireman Hariph Robert Taylor, also presented with the King's Police Medal, relating to an incident in March 1918 in which Beesley was involved.)

On 13ᵗʰ July 1914, Constable Monks was off duty and in plain clothes, when he was told that a man had just shot a solicitor's clerk who was trying to serve a writ on him.

The Constable immediately went to the house and knocked at the front door. He found it locked, and after trying the back door, also found that locked. He saw a man at the kitchen window, told him that he was a police officer, and that he intended to take him to the police station, and charge him with attempted murder. Constable Monks searched the man, who was powerfully built, and took him to the police station.

On returning to the house, the Constable found a five-chambered revolver, and he had already been warned that the man would shoot to kill, even before he reached the house.

PRO Ref: HO 45/10771/275562   L.G. 31/12/1915 Issue 29423 Page 85

FURTHER INFORMATION:

On Monday 13ᵗʰ July 1914, Frank Hinchcliffe, a solicitor's clerk, went to serve a writ on James Hargreaves (44) a retired solicitor at 52, Osbourne Road, South Shore, Blackpool. The writ was from his former housekeeper for alleged assault and breach of contract. After the writ was served and some conversation took place about the weather, Hinchcliffe went down some steps towards the street and heard a bang and realised had been shot. He turned and saw Hargreaves with the revolver in his hand.

Hinchcliffe was pushed onto the street through the garden gate by Hargreaves who then returned to the house. Hinchcliffe was taken to hospital and it was found that he had been shot in the back with the bullet passing into his spinal column, producing partial paralysis. Hinchcliffe was gravely ill and the Justices at the first hearing went to the hospital to take his deposition. Hinchcliffe died from his injuries on 30ᵗʰ November 1914.

Hargreaves was charged with murder and appeared at Manchester Assizes in January 1915. It was admitted that Hargreaves had shot Hinchcliffe after he had served the writ, but the prisoner did not know what he was doing, that insanity ran in his family and that he exhibited characteristic symptoms. Medical evidence was given by Dr Cassidy from the Lancaster County Asylum and Dr Douglas from the Royal Albert Institution, based on interviews and family history, that Hargreaves did not know what he was doing when he shot Hinchcliffe.

Jack Monks as a Sergeant in the uniform of the Lancashire Fusiliers.

In summing up, Mr Justice Sankey told the jury that the prisoner must be found guilty of murder, which meant a death sentence or a verdict of guilty but insane, which meant he would be sent to a criminal lunatic asylum and it was a matter for the jury to decide if he knew he was doing wrong when he shot Hinchcliffe.

After a short absence, the jury returned a verdict of guilty but insane and the prisoner was ordered to be detained during His Majesty's pleasure.

Jack Monks was born in Manchester in 1890 and was appointed to Blackpool Borough Police on 30ᵗʰ October 1911 as Constable 81. He gave his previous occupation as being a paper maker.

He was commended by the Watch Committee and awarded the Merit Badge and one guinea gratuity for his actions on 13th July 1914. Monks had served as a territorial soldier for four years in the 1/5th Lancashire Fusiliers prior to being appointed. On 15th August 1914 at the outbreak of the Great War he left to join his regiment. Jack Monks is reported as having served as a sergeant at Gallipoli where he was severely wounded in August 1915.

The King's Police Medal was presented to him by the King at Buckingham Palace on Saturday 15th January 1916. He later served in the Labour Corps, being discharged with the Silver War Badge awarded in respect of his army service.

On discharge from the Army he was reappointed to Blackpool Borough Police in January 1919. He was commended on eleven further occasions during his service.

He remained with Blackpool Borough Police, being promoted to Sergeant in 1927 and to Inspector in 1937. He retired on 28th August 1942 and died in 1962.

22nd October 1915

Thomas Parnell GIBBONS, Constable 1289   **Lancashire Constabulary**

King's Police Medal

At about 3p.m. on October 22nd, 1915, when off duty, this officer was passing Banks House Farm, Heysham, when he noticed Anthony Hilton and a man servant being attacked by an enraged bull. Hilton was tossed, and the bull commenced to gore him.

The man servant took refuge in a building, whereupon Constable Gibbons ran to Hilton's assistance, managed to draw the bull's attention from Hilton on to himself by prodding it with a fork. The Constable was only just able to make his escape followed by the infuriated animal, which was eventually secured by him with the help of three other men. Hilton was able to get away to safety, and undoubtedly owed his life to the prompt and most courageous conduct of Constable Gibbons.

As an example of rapidity of action, high sense of duty and disregard of danger this act must take a high place among other instances of courage.

It is worthy of note that Constable Gibbons made no report of the occurrence to his superior officer, and it was not until letters from Mr. Hilton and Mr. Baldwin Bent, of Heysham Lodge, Morecambe, were received that anything was known about his act of courage.

Lancashire Constabulary award file – PLA/ACC6849   L.G. 9/2/1917 Issue 29938 Page 1460

FURTHER INFORMATION:

Banks House Farm no longer exists and now forms part of the site of the Heysham Nuclear Power Station.

Thomas Parnell Gibbons was born at Wigan, Lancashire in 1880. He was appointed to Lancashire Constabulary on 21st January 1902, stating his previous occupation as being a labourer in a local pit and residing in Standish. He was commended on a number of occasions and served at Kirkham, Bolton and South Lonsdale Divisions. Following the events of October 1915, he was promoted to Merit Constable and for a brief time was seconded to H.Q. for armed duty, guarding the North Union Railway Bridge in Preston.

In June 1917 he was promoted to Sergeant and transferred to Seaforth Division. In November that year he saved a woman's life by application of first aid.

In May 1924 he was promoted to Inspector and transferred to Garstang Division. He remained there after promotion to Superintendent in 1929. In 1931 he took command of Lonsdale North Division until pensioned on 1st August 1934.

He died in 1971.

20th November 1915

William GREEN, Constable 1898   **Lancashire Constabulary**

King's Police Medal

At about 2.30p.m. on 20th November 1915, four boys were sliding on the ice in a pit at Elliscales, Dalton, when the ice suddenly gave way, and one boy, Peter Phizaclea disappeared under the ice.

The alarm was given, and Constable Green ran three quarters of a mile to the pit, where he found a considerable portion of the ice broken. The pit is about seven feet deep with rocks and refuse at the bottom. He immediately obtained a rope, fastened it round his body and dived twice under the ice in the endeavour to rescue Phizaclea. He was unfortunately unsuccessful and was drawn up out of the pit in an exhausted condition.

This Officer was awarded the Bronze Medal of the Royal Humane Society and Testimonial in Vellum for his praiseworthy and gallant action. Courage of an unusually high order is required for such a very dangerous act. This Officer must have been fully aware of the risks he was taking, which makes what he did the more creditable.

Lancashire Constabulary award file – PLA/ACC6849   L.G. 9/2/1917 Issue 29938 Page 1460

FURTHER INFORMATION:

Location of incident – Shuttleworth's Tarn, Elliscales, Dalton, Lancashire.

At the inquest held at Dalton Police Court it was stated that there were three boys, namely James Corkill, Tom Wilson and Peter Phizaclea who went to the tarn. Whilst on the ice, all three fell through but Phizacklea was unable to get out.

At about 3.30p.m. P.C. Green was on duty in Princes Street, Dalton when he overheard a woman say a boy had drowned and he enquired who had told her and then ran to James Corkill's house. From what he was told he sent a youth to the police station for grappling irons and ran to the tarn, on route getting a man to fetch a rope. Entering the water, he unsuccessfully dived under the ice, attempting to recover the child, having to be dragged out. He later assisted with the recovery of the child, performing artificial respiration in an attempt to revive the child.

The coroner praised P.C. Green's actions. Councillor Shaw, the foreman of the jury, commented, *'I think the constable deserves every praise for the steps he took. We all know what dangerous places these old pits are, with old rails and other things about. The officer went in at great danger to himself to try and save the boy'.*

William Green was born in July 1893 at Tebay, Westmorland.

He was appointed to Lancashire Constabulary on 9th September 1914, giving his previous occupation as being a railway porter residing in Morecambe. His first posting was to the North Lonsdale Division, serving at Dalton. On 10th June 1917 he joined the Army and served with the Royal Garrison Artillery, reaching the rank of Quarter Master Sergeant. He returned to Lancashire Constabulary in February 1919, returning to Dalton.

The following year he was appointed to detective duties at Ulverston and in 1921 he was promoted to Sergeant and transferred to Seaforth Division. He was promoted to Detective Inspector in 1935, serving in the Manchester Division and then to Detective Chief Inspector in 1936, serving at H.Q. In January 1939 he was promoted to Superintendent and transferred to Garstang Division.

During his career he was commended on many occasions and was involved in a number of high-profile cases, one of which was the Dr Buck Ruxton murder case[5] and several other murder cases. For his involvement in the Ruxton case, in addition to being commended by the Lancashire Chief Constable, letters of appreciation were received from the Director of Public Prosecutions and the Lancaster Chief Constable.

He served with Lancashire Constabulary until 1st October 1942 when he left to become the Chief Constable of Burnley Borough Police, where he served until his death on 15th March 1948, aged 54 years. At his funeral service at St. Peters Church, Burnley, twelve chief constables (including two previous Burnley Chief Constables) formed a guard of honour and the funeral cortege was headed by 40 officers.

Peter Walmsley Phizacklea was ten-years old at the time of his death, having been born at Galgate, Lancashire on 29th May 1905. In 1911, he was living at 26 Napier Street, Dalton-in-Furness with his parents and four siblings. His father, Thomas James Phizacklea, was an iron ore miner.

12th December 1915

John CLYNES, Detective Inspector   **Manchester City Police**

King's Police Medal

On 12th December 1915, when Detective Inspector Clynes was arresting a well-known dangerous criminal, who was much younger and stronger than himself, a struggle took place and both men fell down the steps of a moving tramcar onto the road, where the criminal then attacked the Inspector and severely kicked him.

The Inspector nevertheless overcame the man, but on the way to the police station, the man pulled out a life preserver [club] with which he did further injury to the Inspector. As a result of his injuries, Inspector Clynes was under medical treatment for seven weeks.

PRO Ref: H045/10954/306338   L.G. 9/2/1917 Issue 29938 Page 1460

---

[5] Detective Inspector William Green gave evidence at the trial of Dr Buck Ruxton, held at Manchester Winter Assizes before Mr Justice Singleton. His evidence related to statements made by Dr Ruxton of 2 Dalton Square, Lancaster to him, seizure of exhibits and tests he carried out using Dr Ruxton's car to establish travelling times from Lancaster to the scene where the dismembered remains of his wife and maid were found near Moffat in Scotland. Dr Ruxton was convicted of murder and despite an appeal was executed on 12th May 1936 at Strangeways Prison, Manchester.

The case made use of innovative forensic techniques to identify the remains and to establish that the murders took place at 2 Dalton Square, Lancaster. The bath from 2 Dalton Square remains in the possession of Lancashire Constabulary and was used as a horse trough at the Mounted Branch H.Q. at Hutton, Preston.

FURTHER INFORMATION:

Location of incident – Corporation Street and Deansgate, Manchester.

The arrested man was Harry Firth (28) who lived at Bignor Street, Cheetham, Manchester. Firth was a convicted criminal released on licence who had failed to report as required to the police. Firth had been convicted for housebreaking in Leeds and sentenced to three years imprisonment. Clynes had recognised the man after seeing him in custody 7 or 8 years previously.

Firth after release had joined and then deserted from the West Riding Regiment. Firth appeared at the City Police Court on 21st December 1915 charged with failing to report to police and assaulting Inspector Clynes. He was sentenced to six months hard labour for each offence to run consecutively.

Also appearing at court was his wife Edith Firth (22) who was charged with being in possession of valuable jewellery and cash, which she could not give an explanation as to how she obtained them. This arose after officers searched the house at Bignor Street. It was believed that the items were the proceeds of robberies in the Huddersfield area. She was handed over to Huddersfield officers.

Two other persons also appeared at court, namely Firth's brother William Firth (35) and a watchmaker,

Max Kalmanovich, charged with similar offences. During a search of their premises by armed officers further jewellery and a fully loaded revolver and jemmies were recovered. Both prisoners were handed over to Liverpool Police and it was stated that charges against them would be brought there and at Blackburn. (*North-Eastern Daily Gazette*, 14/12/1915)

John Clynes was born at Stockport, Cheshire and joined Manchester City Police on 7th July 1890, aged 22 years. His previous occupation was as a groom. He served until 6th March 1918 when he was pensioned at the rank of Detective Inspector.

15th May 1916	
Ralph AINSCOUGH, Fireman	**Wigan Fire Brigade**
John JONES, Fireman	**Wigan Fire Brigade**
John S. PERCIVAL, Chief Constable and Superintendent	**Wigan Fire Brigade**
Willie RYLANCE, Sergeant	**Wigan Fire Brigade**
Thomas Brett COOKSEY	
Medal of the Order of the British Empire	

Ainscough, Jones, Percival and Rylance

For conspicuous courage and devotion to duty on a fire at an explosives factory.

L.G. 7/7/1920 Issue 31967 Pages 7301, 7308, 7311

Thomas Brett Cooksey

For services in connection with the war.

L.G. 24/8/1917 Issue 30250 Page 8798

FURTHER INFORMATION:

Location of incident – Roburite and Ammonal Explosives Company Ltd, Gathurst, Shevington near Wigan.

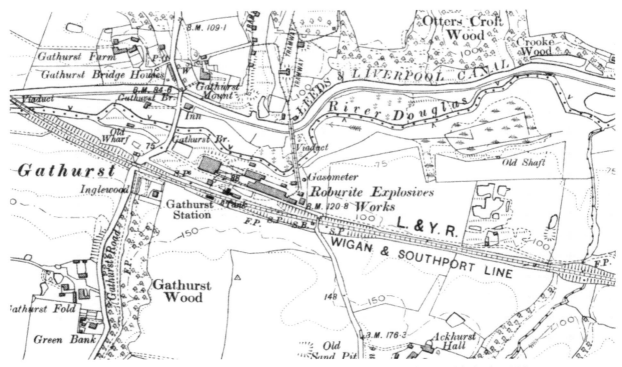

Ordnance Survey Lancashire XCIII.NW, Revised: 1906 to 1907, Published: 1909.

The original recommendation for the Fire Brigade award states:

Fire at the High Explosive Mixing and Filling Sheds of the Robwrite [sic] Explosives Company, near Wigan, 15 May 1916:

The Police Brigade was the only one in attendance at the fire. On arriving at the scene they found No.1 Mixing Shed well alight. It was found impossible to get the motor pump on the works side of the canal and the machine was taken to the other side and set to work a distance of 150 yards from the fire. Jones and Ainscough were within 40 yards of the shed running out a length of hose which had been thrown across the canal to them, when a terrific explosion occurred completely demolishing that shed, killing 6 men (1 soldier and 5 civilians) and wounding 50 others. Jones and Ainscough were covered with debris and Ainscough was slightly injured in the back.

The explosion of this shed set fire to No. 2 Mixing Shed and 'Z' Filling Shed about 75 yards away. In close proximity to these sheds was a shed containing a number of loaded bombs as well as a large quantity of explosives. The work of extinguishing these fires was consequently attended with considerable risk. (TNA ref: HO 45/11016/377171).

The Roburite and Ammonal Explosives Company Ltd works were situated at Gathurst, Shevington near Wigan. Roburite was a flameless explosive which did not give off noxious fumes and was used in the mining industry. In addition, the factory also began to produce T.N.T. explosive for the war effort.

At about 6.15p.m. on 15th May 1916, a fire broke out in one of the mixing machines in which explosive was being made. The operator, William Edward Gore, and foreman, Alfred Evans, used a fire extinguisher but the fire was too fierce and both were forced from the building. Along with other men who had run to the building they connected a hose to a hydrant and water and other fire extinguishers were used to try and put out the fire without success. The fire spread and, fearing an explosion, staff not engaged in fighting the fire were ordered to safety. The Wigan Fire Brigade attended promptly and at around 7p.m. four small explosions took place. Mr Cooksey noted that the smoke prior to the explosions was light brown but changed to black at the moment just prior to the explosions. It was decided the building could not be saved and that everyone should leave the area.

To ensure everybody had left Mr Cooksey ran around the outside of the burning building and on seeing a column of black smoke he shouted to the men who had been fighting the fire, *'Run for God's sake and drop'*. It was at

Members of the Wigan Police aboard the motor fire engine 'LAYLAND' named on 12/8/1909 in honour of Alderman Layland, Chairman of the Watch Committee. The fire engine had a capacity of 450 gallons of water.

that instant the building exploded with Mr Cooksey only just managing to take cover. The six men (including a soldier – Lance Corporal Jonathan Rhodes of the Lancashire Fusiliers) who had been using the hose were caught by the blast and were killed instantly and Mr Alfred Evans the foreman who had been using a fire extinguisher died the following day from his injuries.

The official report states that twenty-three persons were injured including other employees and soldiers guarding the factory. Mrs Annie Liptrot, a farmer, was struck by flying debris outside the factory boundary. Within the site widespread damage was caused to other buildings and windows were broken in Shevington village. The explosion was heard as far away as Manchester 20 miles away and also at Fernilee (near Macclesfield) about 32 miles from the factory.

It was believed the cause of the explosion was due to a stone present in the charcoal used in the production process, which had ignited other material causing the fire. A recommendation was made by the Inspector of Explosives that all ingredients should be sifted to remove any foreign matter.[6]

The Gathurst site commenced operation in 1887 and continued in production and became one of the sites operated by the I.C.I. (Explosives). A further minor explosion took place at the site in 1989. In 1997 I.C.I. sold the explosives business to ORICA, which was previously I.C.I Australia. The site is now closed and is at present earmarked for housing development.

Four members of the Wigan Fire Brigade were presented with their awards on 18th November 1920 by Lord Shuttleworth, the Lord Lieutenant of Lancashire, at Manchester Town Hall. Nine members of the Accrington, Church and Oswaldtwistle Fire Brigades were also decorated for their actions at the Cote Holme Chemical Works, Church, Accrington on 27th April 1917.

(See later entries for further awards to Jones and Rylance.)

John Samuel Percival was born in Gosport, Hampshire around 1871. He was appointed Chief Constable of Wigan Police on 30th March 1914. Forty candidates applied and eight were shortlisted. Mr Percival had 23 years police service, having served with the Royal Irish Constabulary (R.I.C.) and then with Liverpool City Police. He is recorded as holding the rank of Sergeant on the 1901 census

[6]   H.M. Inspector of Explosives Report No. CCXVIII – TNA ref: EF2.

and in 1911 as an Inspector. At the date of his appointment to Wigan Police he held the rank of Chief Inspector.

He served as Wigan Chief Constable and Superintendent of the Fire Brigade until 1920 when he resigned, retiring from Wigan Police on 21st March 1921. He died, aged 58 years, in 1929.

Thomas Brett Cooksey was the Chief Engineer at the Roburite site and commenced work there in 1915. He was the company's North of England expert in the demolition of bridges, chimneys and quarry work.

Cooksey was born in 1868 and a native of Tipton, Staffordshire. He died, aged 55 years, on 15th August 1924 at Manchester Royal Infirmary after being dangerously ill for six weeks, having been in failing health for some time. It was reported that he received his O.B.E. for his devotion to duty during the explosion at Gathurst where he was injured in the side by flying timber. (*Wigan Observer*, 23/8/1924)

T. B. Cooksey's award was gazetted within the first listing of 53 winners of the Medal of the Order of the British Empire.

9th March 1917

John Nelson KENT, Constable 64   **Blackpool Borough Police**

King's Police Medal

On 9th March 1917, at 10.45p.m. Constable Kent went to the rescue of a woman who was in the sea shouting for help.

He waded in for a distance of about 50 yards, and with great difficulty, owing to the darkness and the tide, brought the woman ashore alive, although she died on the way to hospital. The temperature of the water was 38 degrees Fahrenheit, and the air temperature was below freezing.

Constable Kent was conveyed home and was seriously ill for several weeks with cardiac depression, and it was considered at the time that his health may have been permanently impaired.

PRO Ref: H045/10832/326629

L.G. 28/12/1917 Issue 30451 Page 85

FURTHER INFORMATION:

Location of incident – Sea off Blackpool.

The woman who died was Mrs Margaret Edith Miller-Parker (44 years) of 64 Osborne Road, South Shore. Evidence was given that the cause of death was drowning. P.C. Kent told the inquest that he was alerted by Sergeant Paine of the Military Foot Police who told him the woman was in the water. PC Kent told the inquest that he entered the water within two minutes and there was nobody else in the water. The inquest jury returned an open verdict as it was unclear as to how the woman entered the water. The coroner praised P.C. Kent who told the coroner that he could only swim a little.

John Nelson Kent was born at Skipton, Yorkshire in 1877 and was appointed as Constable 64 in the Blackpool Borough Police on 15th September 1899. His previous occupation was as a weaver and previously lived in Nelson. He resigned on pension on 31st December 1917. John Nelson Kent died on 18th

March 1955, aged 78 years.

The King's Police Medal was presented to John Nelson Kent by Lord Shuttleworth, Lord Lieutenant at Preston on Saturday 20th April 1918. Also presented were medals to P.C. Herbert Bradbury and Mrs Hardacre (widow of P.C. James Hardacre) and P.C. Ambrose Jolleys.

A total of 33 medals were presented at the ceremony, including 26 British Empire Orders and three Edward Medals in addition to the four police medals.

John Nelson Kent was also presented an award by the Carnegie Hero Fund.

27th April 1917	
Herbert BRADBURY, Constable 1031	**Lancashire Constabulary**
James HARDACRE, Police Constable 819 (Posthumous)	**Lancashire Constabulary**
King's Police Medal	
Frank BARNES, 2nd Officer	**Accrington Fire Brigade**
John ROBERTS, 3rd Officer	**Accrington Fire Brigade**
Edward Samuel WARE, Superintendent	**Accrington Fire Brigade**
Eli Hudson RILEY, Sergeant	**Church (Lancs) Fire Brigade**
Walter Riley SCHOFIELD, Fireman	**Church (Lancs) Fire Brigade**
Richard Thomas WALKER, Superintendent	**Church (Lancs) Fire Brigade**
John BOOTH, Fireman	**Oswaldtwistle Fire Brigade**
John William DUCKWORTH, Fireman	**Oswaldtwistle Fire Brigade**
Edward SMALLEY, Late Superintendent	**Oswaldtwistle Fire Brigade**
Medal of the Order of the British Empire	

Constables Bradbury and Hardacre

At 4.20a.m. on 27th April 1917, Police Constable Bradbury in company with James Heyes, a workman found that a drying room at the Cote Holme Chemical Works, containing 1000lbs. of picric acid was on fire.

Aware of the danger should the fire reach the acid Bradbury and Heyes attached a hose pipe to the nearest hydrant. They were joined by Hardacre and all three showed the greatest courage in trying to subdue the fire and to prevent an explosion.

As a matter of fact, at 4.41a.m. the worst occurred, and a violent explosion wrecked the works and the Kirk Chemical Works nearby and Bradbury found himself a considerable distance from where he had been playing the hose on the fire, and, although suffering from shock and many superficial injuries to his head, neck and face, he yet returned to search for Hardacre and Heyes without success. Hardacre was killed. Bradbury was off duty, suffering from his injuries and shock until July 11th.

What was passing through the minds of these two extremely brave officers, apparently indifferent to danger, but fully aware of the grave risks to which they were exposing themselves, can only be left to imagination.

Lancashire Constabulary award file – PLA/ACC6849

L.G. 28/12/1917 Issue 30451 Page 84

FURTHER INFORMATION:

Location of incident – Cote Holme Chemical Works, Church, Accrington.

James Hardacre was born at Penwortham near Preston, Lancashire. He was appointed to Lancashire Constabulary on 1st March 1910. On joining he was living at Hoghton, Lancashire and was working as a labourer.

In June 1910, he was posted to Lonsdale North Division and the 1911 census shows him as being a single man residing at Ulverston Police Station.

He married Ann Braithwaite in 1913 at Ulverston and was transferred to Church Division. At the time of his death in 1917 he was 34 years old and had two children, James born in January 1914 and Margaret born in November 1915.

The family lived at Talbot Street, Rishton. His funeral took place at Ulverston Cemetery on 2nd May 1917.

James Hardacre

His widow was paid a pension by Lancashire Constabulary at 1/3rd of her husband's annual pay and an allowance of 1/15th of his annual pay was made for his children until they attained the age of fifteen. His widow Ann died in May 1957.

James Hardacre's son also became a police officer, serving for 30 years, and later worked as a civilian employee with Lancashire Constabulary.

The St. John Ambulance Brigade, at Rishton, produced a postcard with a picture of P.C. Hardacre, and a poem by Kate Leeming, called *A Noble Deed*, about the tragedy. It sold for 2d. with proceeds going to his widow and children.

To the Glorious Memory of Police Constable Hardacre,

Who gave his life in the recent explosion,
on April 27th, 1917,
and was interred at Ulverston Cemetery
on May 2nd.

A NOBLE DEED.

Come, listen to my story, a story great and true,
Which tells us of a policeman, a gallant man in blue,
When near an explosive factory, to his dismay he found
Something which meant destruction to the districts all around.

The connection of the magazines in one place was alight;
Just think of that man's feelings, as he saw the sickening sight!
No thought of self was in his mind, no thought of dread nor fear;
He simply thought of his fellowmen, and the danger lurking near.

Regardless of personal danger, he tried to extinguish the flame;
But, alas! it cost a noble life, yet won a hero's name.
It's a story of amazing love, where self was overthrown;
It reminds us that heroic deeds aren't done at the front alone.

This brave man's name and story, will live for many years;
And though his dear ones mourn for him, there'll be pride amid their tears.
He has shown to us all a Greater Love; for his friends he has given his life;
Now he's wearing a Crown of Glory, safe from all danger and strife.

Herbert Bradbury was born at Bury, Lancashire. He was appointed, aged 23 years, to Lancashire Constabulary on 30th November 1903. At that time, he was living in Bury and his previous occupation was as a labourer. He was posted to Church Division in February 1904 serving at Church, Great Harwood and Oswaldtwistle. In 1907 he was commended by the Chief Constable for vigilance resulting in the conviction of a fowl stealer.

Herbert Bradbury

Arising from the incident at Cote Holme he was promoted to the rank of Merit Class for prompt and courageous conduct.

On 29th July 1921 he was transferred to Bolton Division, serving at Wingates and Farnworth. He was pensioned on 30th November 1929 having served for 26 years. He died in August 1943.

The King's Police Medal was presented by Lord Shuttleworth, Lord Lieutenant at Preston, on Saturday 20th April 1918 to Mrs Hardacre (widow of P.C. James Hardacre) and P.C. Herbert Bradbury. Also presented were medals to P.C. Ambrose Jolleys and P.C. John Nelson Kent.

A total of 33 medals were presented at the ceremony, including 26 British Empire Orders and three Edward Medals in addition to the four police medals.

The Explosion

Cote Holme is the area situated to the west of the Leeds and Liverpool Canal and Bridge Street, Church. This area in 1917 had a number of chemical works, cotton mills, a soap works and industrial buildings, including a canal wharf.

The Cote Holme Chemical Company produced picric acid (a high explosive) and was situated at the northerly end of Bridge Street adjacent to the canal. Following large loss of life and destruction at an incident at another picric acid works at Low Moor, Bradford in August 1916, it was recommended by the government that such works should be dispersed over a wider area.

The site was extended and a new company called the Kirk Chemical Company Limited was formed to manage the extension. This was in effect another complete factory. However, for practical purposes both works operated together. The new site included a considerable number of small magazines separated from the main site. The magazines had brick walls, corrugated iron roofs and wooden doors. The completed picric acid from both sites was stored within the new magazines, which was fortuitous.

The Cote Holme Chemical Company, Kirk Chemical Company and High Explosives Ltd (situated at Lytham) were subsidiary companies of William Blyth and Company producing picric acid.

The night shift at the factory comprised the foreman, Alma Sayers, along with Dennis Barnes and Michael Kennedy. Police

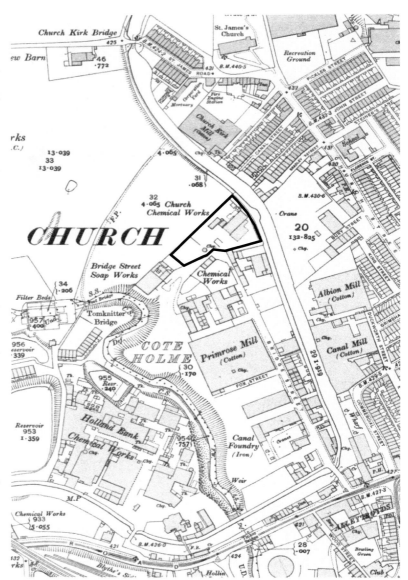

Ordnance Survey Lancashire Sheet LXIII.10 & LXIII.14 1911 Edition (Cote Holme Chemical works highlighted).

Constables Hardacre and Bradburn were the night guards at the works along with John Barnes, the boiler house fireman. Another man present was James Heyes who was the fireman of the neighbouring works of the North Western Chemical Company.

P.C. Bradbury told the official enquiry that he was standing near the entrance gate to the site, talking to James Heyes, when he heard a fizzing noise and both commented that it sounded like a fire. On investigating they found one of the Cote Holme drying rooms on fire. Bradbury instructed John Barnes to raise the alarm and he and Heyes obtained a hose.

P.C. Hardacre came up with the other workers and he set up another hose assisted by Heyes who left, going to P.C. Bradbury to assist him. Eventually a third hose was set up and both the officers and the five workers were all involved in fighting the fire. The fire spread to another of the buildings and after about ten minutes from the discovery of the fire the explosion took place, killing James Hardacre and injuring the others.

Debris from the explosion set fire to other buildings at both sites, which burned without further explosions. The magazines where the finished picric acid was stored were badly damaged, but the picric acid remained unaffected. Most of the buildings on both sites were demolished and large craters were created by the explosion.

It is reported that there was little structural damage outside the works but there was widespread minor damage throughout Church, mainly broken glass with doors and window frames blown in. A number of persons in the town received injuries from broken glass.

The houses on nearby Canal Street and Bradley Street bore the brunt. St. James Church, Church Kirk was damaged and remained closed for some time. These properties are situated on the easterly side of the canal. Opposite the works the canal wharf, associated buildings along with electric and steam derricks were damaged.[7]

The origin of the fire was never established but the Inspector of Explosives criticised the instructions given to the night shift workers in the event of fire and the actions to be taken.

The inquest of Constable Hardacre was held on 30th April 1917. The jury returned a verdict of death arising from the explosion following the fire, which he and others were attempting to put out. The jury added a rider that the works should not be re-erected on the present site and that the praiseworthy conduct of both constables be brought to the attention of the Chief Constable.

A previous fire had taken place at the works in September 1916 and Church Urban District Council complained to the Ministry of Munitions about the safety of the works. In April 1917, a fire took place at a nearby works after which the council expressed their concerns about possible danger to the chemical works. After the explosion, Church U.D.C. wrote to the Ministry of Munitions to protest about the site being returned to use.

On Thursday, 18th November 1920, at Manchester Town Hall, Lord Shuttleworth, the Lord Lieutenant of Lancashire, presented nine members of the Accrington, Church and Oswaldtwistle Fire Brigades awards for their actions during this incident.

The men were awarded **The Medal of the Order of the British Empire** for services in connection with the war. The citations read: *'For conspicuous courage and devotion to duty on the occasion of a fire at a chemical works.'* (*London Gazette*, 7/7/1920, Issue 13612)

Four members of the Wigan Fire Brigade were also decorated that day for their actions at the Roburite explosive works fire at Gathurst on 15th May 1916.

The Medal of the Order of the British Empire awarded to Fireman Walter Riley Schofield is held in the collection of the Howarth Art Gallery, Accrington.

For further information about the firemen awards, see *For God and the Empire: The Medal of the Order of the British Empire 1917-1922* by Roger Willoughby.

SMALLEY, Edward, late Superintendent, Oswaldtwistle Fire Brigade

The original recommendation for the award states: *'On 27 April 1917 the Brigade attended the premises of Blythe & Co. Cote Holme Chemical Works, Church, where an explosion had occurred. The company were manufacturers of trinitrotoluene[8] and trinitrophenol[9] and there was considerable danger of other explosions occurring. In fact several minor explosions did actually occur whilst the Brigade were engaged. The Superintendent states that every member of the Brigade performed his duty unflinchingly, and he cannot mention any one individual for special merit.'*

---

[7]   http://www.mikeclarke.myzen.co.uk/Accrington.html

[8]   T.N.T.

[9]   Picric acid

Edward Smalley
(Author's collection)

A further consideration of this notes: *'Serious explosion of picric acid at the Cote Holme Chemical Works, 27 April 1917: This Brigade were asked to select the names of three men. In reply the Council stated that there were five men all equally entitled to recognition and they asked whether it would be possible to extend the number of medals. They were informed in reply that it would not be possible for the Secretary of State to recommend more than three names, and the Brigade therefore submitted the names of Edward Smalley, John Booth and John W Duckworth, but asked that the medals should not be engraved as it was the intention to have the medals placed in a frame and hung on the walls of the Station.*

In reply to a subsequent letter from the Home Office, asking whether the five men mentioned in their first letter had performed specially distinguished service, the Council stated that the desire for the further medals had been abandoned both by the Council and the members of the Brigade.' (TNA ref: HO 45/11016/377171)

Superintendent Smalley and men of the Oswaldtwistle Fire Brigade pictured outside the Town Hall, Union Road, Oswaldtwistle. The Brigade was based there with stabling for the horses at the rear of the building.
(Courtesy of Lancashire County Council Red Rose Collections)

WARE, Edward Samuel, Superintendent, Accrington Fire Brigade

Two original recommendations for the award survive, the first stating: *'Serious explosion of Picric Acid at Messrs Blyth's Works at Cote Holme Church in April 1917: Superintendent Ware was fully conscious of the explosives being on the site and although the doors of the magazines had been destroyed by the explosion, he fearlessly worked among them and accompanied his firemen so as to effectually prevent the spread of the fire. Large quantities of the explosives were stored on the site but this owing to the efforts of the Brigade were saved.'*

While the second notes:

'Serious explosion of picric acid at the Cote Holme Chemical Works – 27 April 1917: Although there were no further explosion after the arrival of the Brigade, considerable danger was involved as the first explosion had loosened the roofs of the adjoining magazines containing picric acid and there was danger of further explosion from the sparks which were flying about.

The Brigade Authority was asked to select the names of two men, in addition to the Chief Officer. They suggested in reply that in addition to the medal for the Chief Officer a second medal might be awarded to the Brigade collectively. On being informed that it was not possible to carry out this suggestion the names of Second Officer Frank Barnes and Third Officer James Roberts were selected by ballot, but all the men appear to have rendered services of equal merit.' (TNA ref: HO 45/11016/377171)

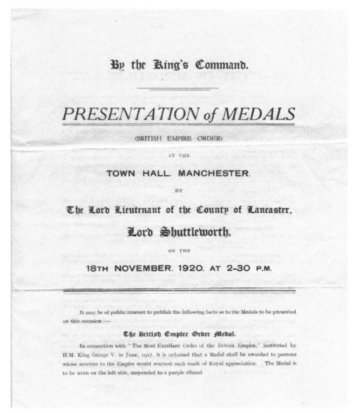

(Author's collection)

WALKER, Richard Thomas, Superintendent, Church (Lancs) Fire Brigade

The original recommendation for the award states: *'On 27 April 1917 at 4.37am an explosion occurred at the Cote Holme Chemical Works where picric acid was being made on a Government contract for military purposes. The Church Fire Brigade received the call at 4.50am and were at the works at 5am and were continuously engaged until 11am and at intervals through the day. Although there was not a further explosion, the first explosion had loosened the roofs of the 17 adjoining magazines containing some tons of picric acid and there was considerable risk of the picric acid being fired by sparks and burning fragments from the fire.'* (TNA ref: HO 45/11016/377171)

William Blyth Chemicals was founded in 1845 and remains in operation. The head office is situated at Bridge Street, Church, Accrington, south of the site of the Cote Holme works nearer to the junction with Blackburn Road. In 1998 it became a wholly owned subsidiary of Synthomer, formerly known as Yule Catto & Co. plc.

The site of the Cote Holme Chemical Works is now occupied by modern industrial units forming part of the Bridge Street Industrial Estate.

Church Fire Brigade. (Courtesy of Lancashire County Council Red Rose Collections)

29th August 1917

Ambrose JOLLEYS, Constable 1597   **Lancashire Constabulary**

King's Police Medal

At 6.45p.m. on August 29th, 1917, Constable Jolleys was informed that a boy had fallen down a disused iron ore mine shaft at Dalton with water at the bottom.

He obtained grappling irons and ran about one and half miles to the pit, procured cart ropes from a farm close by and ignoring the danger of noxious gases, and the rotten state of the shaft, was lowered to the water level about 75 feet down.

After grappling for about an hour, suspended at the end of the rope, half the time in absolute darkness, he found the body, brought it to the surface of the water and attached a rope to it. Eventually both Constable Jolleys and the body were drawn up from the shaft, the Officer being wet through and exhausted.

Very little imagination is required to picture the scene. Constable Jolleys dangling at the end of a rope, which might easily have parted, making strenuous and skilful use of the grapnel for no less than one hour.

Lancashire Constabulary award file – PLA/ACC6849

L.G. 28/12/1917 Issue 30451 Page 85

FURTHER INFORMATION:

Location of incident – Disused pit, Goldmire, near Dalton, Lancashire.

At the inquest held at Dalton Police Station it was stated that Thomas Ross, aged 11 years, and his brother Walter, aged 12, were gathering blackberries near the top of the disused pit shaft. Walter saw his brother climb over the railings and then heard a shout for help followed by a splash. Running across he shouted down and got no reply. Walter then found an adult and showed him the place and then went home. P.C. Jolleys ran to the scene and commenced rescue operations. The mouth of the pit was overgrown with brambles and there was a small hole through which the child had fallen.

It was stated that the pit shaft was fenced but the railings were not very sound. George Coward, manager of the Goldmire Quarry, stated the place was within his district and that nine warning signs had been recently posted warning people not to trespass. He said that it was not a public place where the deceased was drowned.

The coroner recorded a verdict of accidentally drowning and hoped that Thomas's death would be a warning to other children.

The coroner, Mr Shaw, foreman of the jury, and Mr Crellin, another member of the jury, expressed their sympathy to the parents and commented that P.C. Jolleys had acted very bravely. P.C. Jolleys thanked the coroner and jury for their remarks. In closing, the coroner said, *'You deserve every one of them, Constable Jolleys. It was a great pity you could not save the poor little fellow's life; but of course, you did your best'.*

Ambrose Jolleys was also presented with an award by the Carnegie Hero Fund.

Thomas Ross was 11 years old and lived at 8 Church Hill, Dalton. His father, Thomas, was a slinger at the shipyard of Messrs Vickers Ltd, Barrow.

Ambrose Jolleys was born at Ellel, near Lancaster in 1889. He was appointed to Lancashire Constabulary on 6ᵗʰ February 1911, stating his previous occupation as being a joiner residing at Galgate near Lancaster. In addition to the King's Police Medal he was awarded the Merit Badge and a certificate from The Royal Humane Society.

He was promoted to Sergeant in 1927. During his career he served at Lonsdale North, Widnes, Prescot, Lonsdale South and following his promotion Warrington Division. He died, aged 52 years, whilst still serving in July 1941. He is buried at Ellel Parish Churchyard. Jolleys was a married man with three sons.

The King's Police Medal was presented to P.C. Ambrose Jolleys by Lord Shuttleworth, Lord Lieutenant, at Preston on Saturday 20ᵗʰ April 1918. Also presented were medals to P.C. Herbert Bradbury and Mrs Hardacre (widow of P.C. James Hardacre) and P.C. John Nelson Kent.

A total of 33 medals were presented at the ceremony, including 26 British Empire Orders and three Edward Medals in addition to the four police medals.

Goldmire Quarry is a limestone quarry and remains in operation today.

1st October 1917

Fred BROCKLEHURST, Superintendent	Bolton Fire Brigade
William Bramwell HODGSON, Superintendent	Morecambe Fire Brigade
D'Arcy Benson MOFFAT, Superintendent	Barrow (Vickers Armstrong) Fire Brigade
Richard NEWSHAM, Superintendent	Barrow Corporation Fire Brigade
George Albert OAKES, Chief Inspector	Liverpool Fire Brigade
Alonzo SAVAGE, Superintendent	Preston Fire Brigade
Daniel Devine SLOAN, Second Officer	Manchester Fire Brigade
William Andrew WEARING, Inspector	Lancaster Fire Brigade

King's Police Medal

Abraham Clark GRAHAM, Railway Shunter

Thomas KEW, Engine Driver

Thomas TATTERSALL, Works Fireman

Thomas COPPARD, Police Sergeant

Silver Edward Medal

On account of their gallant conduct on the occasion of a fire which occurred at a munitions factory on 1st October 1917.

L.G. 10/5/1918 Issue 30678

Grace CALROW, Driver of factory motor car

John CATON, Boiler Attendant

Alexander CHAMBERLAIN, Shift Engineer

Lily COPE, Nurse

William DISBERRY, Pump Attendant

Richard GARTH, Sergeant, Lancaster Fire Brigade

William HEALD, Feed Pump Attendant

George HUTCHINSON, Boiler Fireman

Jilbert JOHNSON, Works Constable

George NUTT, Boiler Attendant

William SEERY, Works Constable

Maisey J. SHEPHERD, Nurse, Factory Nursing Staff

Charles TAYLOR, Foreman

Richard TAYLOR, Fireman, Factory Fire Brigade

Mary Agnes WILKINSON, Telephonist

Medal of the Order of the British Empire

Abraham Clark Graham, Railway Shunter

When the alarm was given, he was at home, and he at once made his way to the place of danger, from which the employees were fleeing in terror. His occupation was that of a shunter, and he saw a train of wagons in the fire zone filled with shells, some of which were exploding.

Graham sought the engine driver, Thomas Kew, now of Blackburn, and together they determined to draw the wagons and shells out of the fire. Graham coupled up the wagons, whilst shells were bursting, and shrapnel was flying about. He seems to bear a charmed life, for he escaped injury and so did Kew.

By coolness and courage long sustained, the two men got not less than 49 wagons (laden with shells) away out of 57, drawing them out of the raging fire in successive journeys, and thus averted an even more terrible disaster than really occurred. It meant risking their lives over and over again, but they stuck to their self-appointed task with a determination and grit that amazed all who saw what they attempted and accomplished.

Albert Graham, Thomas Coppard and Thomas Kew leaving Buckingham Palace after receiving their Edward Medals on 7th May 1918. (© Lancaster City Museum)

Thomas Kew, Engine Driver

He drove the train of shells through the fire zone but also mended a water tank under great difficulty from which firemen were drawing their water supply. Mr Kew climbed up to the tank to repair the hole and managed to block it up so that the firemen could continue playing their hoses on the fire. Mr Kew was formerly an engine driver with the North-Eastern Railway. He drove ammunition trucks holding 250,000 live shells out of the danger zone.

Thomas Tattersall, Works Fireman

For bravery in firefighting. Tattersall had previously served in the Royal Field Artillery landing in France on 25th December 1915. He was discharged from the Army on 26th April 1917.

Thomas Coppard, Police Sergeant

For his part in rescuing several people from a blazing factory at which he was one of the police guards. Police Sergeant Thomas Coppard was a retired Detective Inspector of the Hastings Police. Coppard was also awarded a framed testimonial and a cheque from The Society for the Protection of Life from Fire in June 1919.

Silver Edward Medal

On account of their gallant conduct on the occasion of a fire which occurred at a munitions factory on 1st October 1917.

Mary Agnes Wilkinson, Telephonist

Rendered invaluable service at a telephone exchange on the occasion of a fire and serious explosion at a munition works close by, proceeding to her post through the danger zone at grave personal risk.

L.G. 8/1/1918 Issue 30464

Grace Calrow, Driver of factory motor car

For courage and devotion to duty at a fire at a filling factory, when she was on duty continuously for forty-eight hours in circumstances of very great danger.

L.G. 7/6/1918 Issue 30738 Page 6894

John Caton, Boiler Attendant

Remained on duty the whole time during a severe fire and explosion at a national filling factory in spite of great danger.

L.G. 7/6/1918 Issue 30738 Page 6895

Alexander Chamberlain, Shift Engineer

Displayed conspicuous courage and devotion to duty on the occasion of a very serious fire and explosion at a munition factory.

Lily Cope, Nurse

Behaved with great courage on the occasion of a severe fire and explosion at a national filling factory, performing her duties quietly and without regard to personal safety.

William Disberry, Pump Attendant

Although 70 years of age, he remained at his fire pumps the whole night on the occasion of a severe explosion and fire at a national filling factory. The position was one of great danger throughout.

Richard Garth, Sergeant, Lancaster Fire Brigade

Behaved with great gallantry on the occasion of a severe fire and explosion at a national filling factory.

William Heald, Feed Pump Attendant

Remained on duty the whole time during a severe fire and explosion at a national filling factory, in spite of great danger.

George Hutchinson, Boiler Fireman

Remained on duty the whole time during a severe fire and explosion at a national filling factory in spite of great danger.

Jilbert Johnson, Works Constable

Behaved with coolness and resource on the occasion of a severe fire and explosion at a national filling factory.

George Nutt, Boiler Attendant

Remained on duty the whole time during a severe fire and explosion at a national filling factory, in spite of great danger.

William Seery, Works Constable

Displayed courage and resource on the occasion of a severe fire and explosion at a national filling factory. He was thrown down and injured by an explosion.

Maisey J. Shepherd, Nurse, Factory Nursing Staff

Behaved with great courage on the occasion of a severe fire and explosion at a national filling factory, performing her duties quietly and without regard to personal safety.

Charles Taylor, Foreman

Displayed great coolness and courage in carrying out vitally important repairs on the occasion of a fire at a national filling factory whilst a large number of shells were exploding in the immediate neighbourhood.

Richard Taylor, Fireman, Factory Fire Brigade

Displayed great courage and resource on the occasion of a severe explosion at a national filling factory.

Medal of the Order of the British Empire

L.G. 7/7/1918 Issue 30738

FURTHER INFORMATION:

On 1st October 1917, a disastrous fire occurred at the Number 13 National Filling Factory, at White Lund, Morecambe. White Lund was one of 218 factories which were directly administered by the Ministry of Munitions as National Factories. Construction at White Lund began in November 1915 on a 400-acre site.

The site needed to be so large because explosive safety was a key issue and the site used parallel production facilities in separate small, wooden huts to reduce the risk. The N.F.F. filled a range of shells with Amatol, a mixture of TNT and ammonium nitrate, but they also produced gas shells. As of September 1917, there was a workforce of 4,621 employees with 64.4% of the employees being female.

The fire started at around 10.30p.m. on the upper floor of Building 6c, which contained large amounts of TNT. The lower floor contained 12-inch shells, partly filled. These exploded after about 20 minutes. The largest explosion of ammunition occurred four and a half hours after the initial fire. The largest of the blasts was heard at around 3a.m. as far away as Burnley, more than 40 miles away from the factory. A total of 20 fire brigades from across Lancashire were summoned to help tackle the inferno, including squads from Preston, Bolton, Blackpool and Kendal.

Red hot shrapnel was fired across the area, with residents reporting chunks landing in Quernmore and Scotforth, more than seven miles away, while windows were smashed by falling metal as far away as Lancaster. Fortunately, the workforce was at supper at the time, and no loss of life occurred except amongst those engaged in fighting the fires. There were on the premises at the time a large number of shells wholly or partially filled, and about 300 tons of high explosives.

The works fire brigade made a heroic attempt to extinguish the fire at the outset, but they were unsuccessful, and it spread rapidly in a short time. Three violent explosions shook the place, killing or injuring firemen and civilians helping them. A total of ten men died at the time or from their injuries after the incident.

Violent explosions continued at frequent intervals for the next 36 hours, for as the shells became heated they detonated, throwing masses of burning debris on neighbouring buildings and spreading the fires.

It was impossible to save the factory, but there was valuable property nearby, including sheds where a million shells were stored. The work of isolating and subduing the fire was extremely dangerous, and the measure of success attained was largely due to the courage, resource, and self-sacrifice of many persons who took part, including members of various fire brigades who came from all parts of the county to assist in fighting the fires.

After the explosion, the White Lund factory was not brought back into production, but disaster struck again on two further occasions. The first was in April 1918 when two men died when an explosion took place whilst they were salvaging shells. On January 14th, 1920, when there was another explosion as staff defused bombs and emptied shells, nine people were killed.

L-R: King's Police Medal, Jubilee Medal 1935, Coronation Medal 1937, Liverpool Police Silver Medal for 25 Years' Good Service – George Albert Oakes, Liverpool Fire Brigade (Author's collection)

The medals of Thomas Coppard, Charles Taylor and Mary Agnes Wilkinson are displayed in the Lancaster City Museum.

The medals awarded to George Albert Oakes from the Liverpool Fire Brigade are also displayed.

The site of the factory is now the White Lund Industrial Estate where a small number of the original buildings remain. In October 2017, to mark the centenary of the disaster, a black granite memorial plaque paying tribute to those killed or injured was unveiled.

20th March 1918

Hariph Robert TAYLOR, Fireman   **Colne Fire Brigade**

King's Police Medal

On March 20th, 1918, the Fire Brigade was called to a fire in a dwelling house. Three persons were rescued, and then it was discovered that a fourth had remained behind. Fireman Taylor at once rushed back into the house, which was by this time filled with smoke and flames and searched the bedrooms. After some time, he found the body of an unconscious woman, and with great difficulty dragged her to the window, and handed her over to another fireman, who brought her down a ladder. Fireman Taylor then collapsed and had to be helped to the ground.

PRO Ref: H045/11066/354481   L.G. 2/1/1919 Issue 13376 Page 59

FURTHER INFORMATION:

Location of incident – 9/11 Skipton Road, Colne, Lancashire.

The fire took place at a grocer's shop tenanted by Mr J.W. Crossley who was away on active war service. The business was being carried on in his absence by his wife and her sister Gertrude Alderson. The fire was discovered by a neighbour, Mr Lanham, 22 Skipton Road, who was awakened at 2.30a.m. by the sound of breaking glass, he then alerted the fire brigade.

In the meantime, Mr Fred Rook, 24 Skipton Road, was awakened and, on going outside, saw Mrs Crossley standing at the bedroom window with two children aged six years and eight months respectively in her arms. A ladder was obtained, and Mr Rook ascended, taking the children, the elder child being unconscious.

Second Officer Preston then arrived and with the assistance of Rook brought Mrs Crossley down the ladder and on reaching the ground she collapsed but recovered and said her sister remained inside. Fireman Taylor ascended the ladder and entered the building and found her unconscious at the top of the stairs. Taylor dragged her to the window where Fireman Beesley carried the woman to the ground. Meanwhile, Taylor collapsed and was assisted to the ground. He was then taken home to receive medical attention.

Miss Alderson was taken to a neighbour's house and was unconscious for half an hour. The fire originated in the shop, which was completely gutted. Furniture in the upstairs room was also destroyed.

Fireman Taylor was presented with the King's Police Medal at a ceremony at Liverpool by Lord Shuttleworth the Lord Lieutenant on Thursday 22nd May 1919. On Wednesday 24th September 1919 Fireman Taylor was presented with a testimonial and cheque for £10 from the Carnegie Hero Fund at a council meeting by the Mayor, Alderman E. Carr.

The Mayor said that during his term of office he had the privilege of presenting many medals for military service and one thing that had struck him was the modesty of the recipients. Brave men were generally modest. Medals had been won in the war and had been well won, but the medal Fireman Taylor had won in peace was equally well deserved. In the hum and noise of battle men were excited, and for the love of their country they performed great acts but what Fireman Taylor had done facing fire in cold blood was an equally meritorious act.

Hariph Robert Taylor was born in 1880 at Padiham, his occupation was as a house painter. He is shown as being a Special Constable in 1939. He died, aged 75 years, in 1955.

NOTE:

Fireman George Beesley was also the holder of the King's Police Medal awarded for a rescue in May 1912. (See earlier entry.)

29th December 1918

Nicholas CORK, Constable 1600   **Lancashire Constabulary**

King's Police Medal

At 9.30 p.m. on 29th December 1918, Constable Cork was told that there had been a subsidence of ground

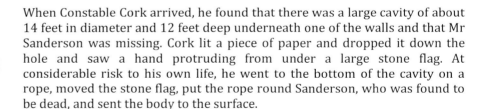

underneath No. 8, Commercial Street, Rishton, which is partly shop and partly residence and occupied by a Mr Sanderson and his family.

When Constable Cork arrived, he found that there was a large cavity of about 14 feet in diameter and 12 feet deep underneath one of the walls and that Mr Sanderson was missing. Cork lit a piece of paper and dropped it down the hole and saw a hand protruding from under a large stone flag. At considerable risk to his own life, he went to the bottom of the cavity on a rope, moved the stone flag, put the rope round Sanderson, who was found to be dead, and sent the body to the surface.

During all this time Constable Cork displayed the utmost coolness and contempt for the grave danger of being buried under the very probable further collapse of the premises and is deserving of the highest commendation and reward.

Lancashire Constabulary award file – PLA/ACC6849   L.G. 30/12/1919 Issue 31712 Page 8

FURTHER INFORMATION:

Mr Robert Duckworth Sanderson was aged 65 years. It is described that Mr Sanderson had sustained a head injury and his left shoulder was broken. The cause of the subsidence was attributed to the presence of a brook which ran under or near to the building. The collapse was to the shop part of the premises. (*Lancashire Evening Post*, 30/12/1918)

Nicholas Cork was born at Nelson, Lancashire in 1878 and was appointed to Lancashire Constabulary, aged 23 years, on 21st April 1902.

His previous occupation was as a factory operative residing in Nelson. He served in Wigan, Church and Rochdale Divisions. He was promoted to Merit Class after the incident in Rishton and then to Sergeant in 1919. He was transferred to Rochdale Division, serving at Shaw.

Nicholas Cork served until 1st October 1929 before retirement with 27 years, 163 days service. He served briefly in the First Police Reserve in 1932 and died, aged 57 years, in 1936.

Race Riots – Liverpool 1919

There had been a black community in Liverpool for centuries, largely by reason of the shipping trade. The Great War brought many more people from all corners of the British Empire either to fight or to fill gaps in the labour force left by recruitment and conscription. These new arrivals were British subjects and there was no work permit system.

At the end of the War, following demobilisation of the armed forces unemployment was widespread. Black ex-servicemen were cast adrift and found homes in communities like Liverpool's South End. At the same time, white ex-soldiers and sailors demanded civilian employment that had been promised them in 'a land fit for heroes'.

It appears that in the neighbourhood of Pitt Street, Liverpool in the evening of Wednesday, 4th June 1919 a man was stabbed by a negro resulting a feeling of resentment on the part of the white inhabitants.

At about 9.30 p.m. on Thursday 5th June 1919 evening a number of Swedes and Danes were leaving a public house in the neighbourhood of Great George's Square, when one of them was attacked by several negroes and badly stabbed. The Constable on duty intervened, whereupon he was assaulted using razors and knives.

Assistance was summoned, and the Police arrived in force from Argyle Street Station. The offenders left the scene going to Upper Pitt Street. When the Police followed, revolver shots were fired at them resulting in P.C. Brown being wounded in the mouth. The bullet passed through the back of his neck and wounded Sergeant Getty.

By this time a considerable crowd had gathered, and the Police were also present in force.

A negro who was suspected of having fired a revolver started running down Pitt Street and was chased by a mob with several policemen also following. The man made in a straight line for the Queen's Dock where he was seized by one of the Policemen who intended to take him to the police station.

The officer was pushed aside by the mob and the negro was either thrown or jumped into the dock and he drowned. His body was later recovered from the dock by the Police.

This man was Charles Wooten[10] a 24-year-old ships fireman from Bermuda residing at 18 Upper Pitt Street, Liverpool.

In total four officers were injured during this incident including P.C. Brown and Sergeant Getty.

The other injured officers were Constable Fox and Constable Parkinson. Constable Parkinson is stated to have been badly slashed with a razor about his face and neck.

At Liverpool Police Court, thirteen coloured men were charged with attempting to murder police officers, and with riotous assembling. Only evidence of arrest was offered, and the prisoners were remanded.

Unrest continued for several days with crowds - at times several thousand strong, attacking black-occupied homes and hostels. Buildings were vandalised, emptied of their furniture and even set alight.

---

10   Race Riots in Liverpool 1919 – http://www.blackpresence.co.uk/race-riots-in-liverpool-1919/ – Retrieved 10/6/2017

On 5th June 1919, during the race riots in Liverpool, Constable Fox, on hearing shouting coming from the direction of Great George Square, ran to the place, and found a gang of coloured men armed with knives and open razors, attacking two old men. Constable Fox drew his baton and rushed to their assistance.

The gang then turned and set upon the Constable, beating and kicking him savagely, and stabbing and slashing him with knives and razors.

Constable Fox was rendered unconscious and taken to hospital with a fractured wrist, and severe head injuries, necessitating a stay in hospital of nearly two months.

L.G. 1/1/1921 Issue 32178 Page 8

On 5th June 1919, during the race riots in Liverpool, Constable Brown saw a black man pull out a revolver from his pocket.

He went up to the man, and struck him on the arm with his baton, but the man passed the revolver to his other hand, and fired at point blank range at the Constable, the bullet entering his neck, rendering him unconscious. The Constable was in hospital for nearly three months.

L.G. 1/1/1921 Issue 32178 Page 8

Just after 2.30p.m. on 2nd July 1920, in the yard of the Atherton Gas Works, a man called Matthews descended a dry well which was about 30 feet deep and 6 feet in diameter, in order to empty accumulated water from gas mains by means of a tap. The dry well is built round the inlet and outlet pipes of the gas holder, both of which are about 16 inches in diameter and run from top to bottom of the well. They consequently greatly impeded any work of rescue.

There was also about 3 feet 6 inches of water which had accumulated at the bottom of the well. While he was doing this, he was overcome by the fumes of coal gas. Two other men, named Marsh and Whitlam went to the assistance of Matthews, but were themselves knocked out by the gas and subsequently died.

Sergeant Brown, although warned of the danger involved, volunteered to go down, and put on a respirator and gas mask, no real protection as he must have known quite well, and was lowered down on a rope. At the bottom of the well he saw Marsh suspended by his left foot from a pipe with his head under water. Brown could not release Marsh, but tied a rope to his leg, and then, becoming partly unconscious, was drawn up to the surface.

There is no doubt that Sergeant Brown showed courage of a very high order by going down to the bottom of the well, hardly protected at all from coal gas, and doing his best to rescue the three men. A fine act which is very much to his credit.

Lancashire Constabulary award file – PLA/ACC6849   L.G. 1/1/1921 Issue 32178 Page 8

FURTHER INFORMATION:

Location of incident – Atherton District Council Gas Works, Water Street, Atherton.

The men who died that day were Samuel Marsh, Inside Foreman; William Whitlam, Outside Foreman of Drains; and David Mathews, labourer. The bodies were later recovered by the Lancashire and Cheshire Mines Rescue Service when it was apparent that in addition to the effects of gas they had been submerged in the water. (*The Manchester Guardian*, 3/7/1920)

Thomas James Brown was born at Matlock, Derbyshire in 1876.

He was appointed to Lancashire Constabulary, aged 22 years, on 15th January 1900, stating his previous occupation as a railway porter, residing at Halton near Lancaster. He served at Manchester, Bury, Warrington and Bolton Divisions. In 1915 he was promoted to Sergeant and to Inspector in 1921.

He was commended on a number of occasions and was awarded the Merit Badge and £10 for his actions in July 1920. He served until 30th June 1927 and died in August 1958.

28th October 1920

John JONES, Sergeant   **Wigan Borough Police Fire Brigade**

King's Police Medal

On 28th October 1920, Sergeant Jones and the Wigan Police Fire Brigade arrived at Water Heyes Cotton Mill, Greenough Street, Wigan and found the engine house well ablaze and there was dense smoke.

Sergeant Jones was told there was a man in the building and he entered the engine house, groped his way through the smoke and found the steel ladder leading to the middle platform.

The ladder was hot, and flames were rushing up by the side of it. He reached the top of the ladder and then proceeded along the gangway. The heat was almost unbearable, and Sergeant Jones could not stand up. Guided by the sounds of moans, he groped his way forward and found Mr Alfred Little on the floor.

Sergeant Jones got hold of him by the shoulders and tried to drag him out, but he was stuck fast. He tried for a considerable time to release him and the smoke and heat worsened all the time. He ultimately succeeded in releasing him and dragged him to the top of the ladder but was unable to carry him. By this time Jones was exhausted and had to rest and shouted for help.

That part of the engine house was now a mass of flames. Engineer Ainsworth[11] came to his assistance and Jones carried Little on his shoulders down the ladder and out of the building. Jones then collapsed. Little was badly burned about the head, face, neck and arms and died the following day.

FURTHER INFORMATION:

Alfred Little was aged 52 years and was employed as a general labourer at the mill. He lived at 7 Soho Street, Pemberton, Wigan. A verdict of accidental death was recorded at the inquest held on 1st November 1920, with his cause of death being recorded as due to burning caused by fire.

The coroner at the inquest commended Sergeant Jones, stating he had performed an act of great bravery and gallantry and congratulated the Fire Brigade on having so efficient and gallant officer.

The mill owners were so impressed by Sergeant Jones' bravery they presented him with an inscribed silver cigarette case containing a £5 note, and the Wigan Watch Committee made him a special grant of £10 10s. to mark their appreciation. In addition, he was awarded the Watch Committee Merit Badge.

Jones' heroism was recognised by the Carnegie Hero Fund and his name is inscribed in the Roll of Honour.

(See previous and later entries for John Jones.)

PRO Ref: H045/11562/402261

L.G. 30/12/1921 Issue 32563 Page 10717

John (known as Jack) Jones was born in Wigan on 6th November 1884 and started work, aged 13 years, with a Wigan veterinary surgeon. He later joined Wigan Fire Brigade in 1906 as the driver of the horse-drawn fire engines.

Jones was promoted to the rank of Sergeant in February 1920 and to the rank of Inspector in 1928 and became responsible for the administration of the Fire Brigade under the direction of the Chief Constable, Mr T. Pey. On the reorganisation of fire services on the lead up to WW2 he was responsible for the organisation of the Auxiliary Fire Service (A.F.S.) in the area.

When the National Fire Service (N.F.S.) was formed in 1941 he was seconded by the Wigan Borough Police Fire Brigade and was appointed as the Divisional Commander for 'F' Division, comprising Wigan, Golborne, Westhoughton, Blackrod, Horwich and Skelmersdale. In April 1942 Jones retired at his own request to continue in service on a part-time basis.

During his career he was awarded the King's Police Medal and Bar as well as the Medal of the Order of the British Empire. He was also the winner of the Joseph Watson Memorial Medal and Bar and the winner of the Medal of the Society for Protection of Life from Fire. (*Wigan Observer and District Advertiser*, 4/4/1942)

---

[11] This appears to have been Ralph Ainsworth, one of the other recipients of the Medal of the Order of The British Empire, awarded for actions at the Roburite Explosive Site at Gathurst in 1916. (See previous entry.)

I.R.A. Operations in Britain 1919-1923

Between 1919 and 1923 Ireland was engulfed in violence as the I.R.A. (Irish Republican Army) fought a guerrilla campaign against the British State and later against fellow Irish men and women in pursuit of an Irish Republic.

The Royal Irish Constabulary (R.I.C.) could not recruit sufficient officers in Ireland to deal with the violence due to the threats and intimidation of Irish recruits. Rather than sending in the Army, the British Government boosted the R.I.C. establishment by the recruitment of thousands of mainly ex-military veterans from England as constables who were nicknamed the 'Black and Tans'. Their nickname arose from the colours of the improvised uniforms they wore, which comprised a mixture of British Army khaki and dark coloured R.I.C. uniforms.

In addition, a temporary force, the Auxiliary Division Royal Irish Constabulary (A.D.R.I.C.) was formed, which was a heavily armed and motorised paramilitary force comprised of ex-British military and naval officers. They dressed in distinctive uniform and were organised in military-style companies. These units appear to have been the brainchild of Winston Churchill.

In support of their colleagues in Ireland, emigrants and their descendants resident in Britain undertook gun running and the smuggling of weapons to Ireland. They later began a campaign of violence in retaliation for British State activities in Ireland where farms and houses were burnt in response to the rebellion, allegedly by the 'Black and Tans' and the 'Auxiliaries'.

It has been estimated that there were approximately 1,000 Irish volunteers in Britain with several hundred taking part in operations. Lancashire had large Irish communities concentrated in Liverpool and Manchester and bore the brunt of attacks launched.

In total, 239 attacks were recorded in mainland Britain with 103 of these taking place in Lancashire. The majority of these attacks being against farms and crops as well as communications, infrastructure and warehouses. (See entry for Constable Bowden, shot in Salford on 2nd January 1921 following an attack at a warehouse.)

A number of other attacks took place on mills and factories and houses of R.I.C. men and their relatives.

On 19th February 1921, the I.R.A. mounted attacks against ten farms in the Manchester area, where fires were set by igniting straw and hay soaked with paraffin. A further farm was attacked and when the farmer went to investigate a disturbance he was fired on but was not hit. Two further attacks took place on the 21st and 22nd at Bury and Woodley where buildings were destroyed by fire. On 22nd March a constable on patrol in Manchester was fired on after he disturbed three men outside Manchester United's football ground. Fortunately, he was not hit.

On 9th March 1921, farms were attacked in the Liverpool area. One incident at Roby resulted in the shooting and subsequent arrest of an I.R.A. volunteer. This incident led to a revenge attack on the 23rd May where shots were exchanged between the I.R.A. and the Police. (See entries for Inspector Lewis and Constable Jones relating to both of these incidents)

On the 2nd April 1921, co-ordinated attacks took place at commercial premises in Manchester City Centre, resulting in the wounding of Constable Boucher. This led to the later raid on the Irish Club on Erskine Street, Hulme, where shots were exchanged resulting in the death of I.R.A. man Sean Morgan and the wounding of several other persons. (See entry for Tongue, Bailey, Bolas and Boucher.)

In total, four deaths resulted from the campaign, including Inspector Robert Johnson who died when thirty armed men attacked a van taking a wanted I.R.A. officer from court to prison in Glasgow. Another police officer was seriously wounded in this incident. A number of other persons were injured during the campaign.

The campaign ended on 11th July 1921 when a truce was implemented between the Irish Republican Government and the British Government, which came into effect at 12 noon that day.

In January 1921, Constable Bowden saw several suspicious persons loitering near a large railway grain warehouse.

He kept them under observation for some time, and when they separated, he followed two of them for some distance into Salford, where he decided to stop and question them. A struggle ensued, and the Constable seized one of the men.

The other man pulled out a revolver and fired at the Constable, wounding him in the chest and hand. As a result of the loss of blood he had to let go of his prisoner who was then able to escape.

From the information which Constable Bowden provided, five arrests were made, but he spent several months in hospital as a result of the wounds.

PRO Ref: H045/11562/402261

L.G. 30/12/1921 Issue 32563 Page 10717

FURTHER INFORMATION:

Location of incident – Oldfield Road, Salford.

On 2nd January 1921, Police Constable Henry Bowden was patrolling some warehouses on Ordsall Lane, Salford when he came across ten men near a large grain warehouse, owned by the Lancashire & Yorkshire Railway Company.

The men supplied him with their names and addresses, but Constable Bowden still insisted that they accompany him to the police station. When they reached Oldfield Road one of the men suddenly produced a revolver and fired at the policeman. Fortunately for him the bullet passed through his wrist and entered his shoulder. The men ran off.

A fire was later discovered in Miller Street, Shudehill. Police later arrested four men in connection with the shooting: Patrick Flynn (22), Jeremiah Roddy (20), Daniel O'Connell (25) and Charles Forsythe (32). Forsythe was the landlord of a boarding house at 3 Poole Street, Salford, where the other men were lodgers.

They and another man, Patrick Waldron, were later charged under the Defence of the Realm Act. On 22nd February, Flynn was sentenced to ten years penal servitude for attempted murder.

He was released in 1922 as part of an amnesty for political prisoners following the signing of the Anglo-Irish Treaty in December 1921.

Henry (Harry) Bowden was born in Heaton Norris in 1883 and was appointed to Salford Police in February 1908. Following his wounding in January 1921 he was unable to perform police duty for a period of 116 days. Harry Bowden also carried out duties as an auxiliary fireman. He died in 1938, aged 55 years.

At about 7.45p.m. on 9th March 1921, a party of Sinn Feiners attempted to fire a stack-yard at Roby Farm, near Liverpool.

One of their number called Patrick Lowe was wounded by a gun fired by the occupier Mr John Rimmer.

Inspector Lewis arrived very soon after, and saw that Lowe had a revolver, fully loaded, in his hand and was threatening to use it. Mr Lewis by a most daring ruse arrested and secured Lowe without any further shots being fired.

When Lowe was secured another revolver, fully loaded, was found on him. Inspector Lewis was in charge of a Police Section close to Liverpool, in which Sinn Feiners had for some time been very active, and he had carried out his extremely dangerous and exacting duties with singular ability and courage, at all times showing a fine example to his men.

This is a very worthy case of the award of the King's Police Medal for Gallantry [sic].

Lancashire Constabulary award file – PLA/ACC6849   L.G. 30/12/1921 Issue 32563 Page 10717

FURTHER INFORMATION:

This incident was one of a number attributed to Sinn Fein members which took place at farms around the Merseyside area where stacks and barns were set on fire. It was also found that in some places telephone wires were cut to hinder communications. Such fires were in retaliation for farms being burned in Ireland by 'Black and Tan' R.I.C. men. An order was received by the Liverpool City I.R.A. Company in February 1921 ordering the attacks.

Thirteen fires occurred at Ormskirk, Little Crosby, Childwall and on the Wirral peninsula. Other fires took place in the boundaries of Liverpool at Woolton, Gateacre, Wavertree, Garston and West Derby. In total, thirteen fires took place with damage estimated to total £20,000. Police had previously advised farmers to be alert and to guard their premises.

Mr John Rimmer, a prominent local member of the local rural district council, was in his stack yard at Roby Farm on armed guard when he saw the figures of two men approaching from the direction of the tram terminus. Once they entered his stack yard, Mr Rimmer challenged them, warning that he would fire and told them to put up their hands. They refused and continued making towards a barn. Mr Rimmer fired at them twice, aiming for their legs. One man fell, and the other ran away. The injured man was Patrick Lowe who was found armed with two revolvers and combustible materials.

Elsewhere, five other men were arrested. Two men were detained by a former Special Constable and his son after a group of eight men had been seen earlier alighting from a train at Hall Road and were seen entering a wood. Two farm fires later broke out nearby and the former Constable and his son tackled two men after they ran past. The two men had earlier thrown their guns away. Another was arrested on the shore at Seaforth after being challenged by police officers.

Sadly, the night did not pass without loss of life when Edward Jones, Constable 350 'H' of Liverpool Fire Brigade, a fireman who had attended a fire at Childwall, was killed.

Whilst travelling up a steep incline the motor stopped. Whilst being reversed to attempt to restart the engine it ran backwards and overturned after running up an embankment, trapping fireman Edward Jones, the driver, underneath the engines ladders. He was taken to hospital but died on the way. Medical evidence showed he died of a fractured skull.

Patrick Lowe was convicted at Liverpool Assizes on 11th April 1921 of attempted arson, conspiracy and possession of firearms. He received a sentence of ten years penal servitude.

The other detained men received sentences of between five and ten years. As they were led away the prisoners shouted, *'Up the rebels'*.

All were released in 1922 as part of an amnesty for political prisoners following the signing of the Anglo-Irish Treaty in December 1921.

Roby Farm was situated to the south of Broad Green Road at Roby. It no longer exists with the area now occupied by the M62 motorway.

Richard Lewis was born in Skelmersdale, Lancashire, in 1873. He joined Lancashire Constabulary, aged 21 years, on 7th July 1894 as Constable 764. He served at Lonsdale South, Bury, Prescot and Widnes Divisions.

He gained promotion through the ranks and retired as a Superintendent on 1st January 1934, having served for 39 years and 178 days. He died on the 12th August 1934, aged 61 years.

(See later award of King's Police Medal to P.C. 1910 Jones, also relating to a later incident at this property.)

2nd April 1921

Samuel TONGUE, Superintendent	**Manchester City Police**
Richard BAILEY, Constable	**Manchester City Police**
Michael BOLAS, Detective Constable	**Manchester City Police**
William Edwin BOUCHER, Constable	**Manchester City Police**

King's Police Medal

During the Fenian firebombing outrages in Manchester, Constable Boucher entered a large city warehouse on 2nd April 1921, which some suspected I.R.A. persons had been seen to enter.

He was immediately shot and wounded. The men ran out of the building, and Constable Boucher, despite his wounds followed them, and called for help.

Later that day Superintendent Tongue with other officers went to a club in the City known to be frequented by the suspected men. On arrival Detective Constable Bolas, and Constable Bailey arrested two suspects, but were attacked on the landing by two more armed men. Shots were exchanged, and Constable Bailey's jaw was broken.

Constable Bolas shot and wounded both assailants. Reinforcements were rushed to the club, and several arrests were made. A search of the premises revealed a large store of arms, ammunition, and high explosives.

PRO Ref: H045/11562/402261   L.G. 30/12/1921 Issue 32563 Page 10717

FURTHER INFORMATION:

On Saturday 2nd April 1921, P.C. Boucher was called to Bridgewater House, 60 Whitworth Street, Manchester, a large warehouse, as a result of information given to him by a woman. The woman, a cleaner, had managed to slip out of the building after a number of men entered. On entering the building, he met one man and asked who the other men were. He was told they had come to repair the lift.

Going down to the basement, Boucher saw three men and was shot and hit in the chest. On pursuing them he was shot again in the left arm by a man Boucher later identified as Patrick O'Donoughue. Constable Boucher was later also able to identify two of the other men in the warehouse.

P.C. Boucher pursued them, blowing his whistle, but collapsed on Whitworth Street. He was taken to hospital by tram. Medical evidence indicated the bullet had passed through his chest just under the heart, penetrating his lung before exiting leaving a wide exit wound. The other shot had fractured his left forearm.

Attempts had also been made to set fire to a number of other warehouses and premises in Manchester between 6 and 7a.m. that day and some of the men who carried out these incidents were armed. These premises included a café on Piccadilly where five employees were held at gunpoint whilst oil was poured before being ignited. In three hotels terrorists had booked overnight rooms and piled up furniture, dousing it in paraffin before setting it on fire. Damage fortunately was not significant.

As a result of these incidents, officers from Manchester City Police headed by Sergeant Crowther entered the Irish Club on Erskine Street, Hulme in force at 10.30p.m. that day.

Constable Bailey and Detective Bolas stated that after they had entered the building Sean Morgan had confronted them with a revolver in each hand and had fired, wounding Bailey in the jaw. Bolas shot Morgan dead and also wounded another man, Sean Wickham.

A third man pulled out a revolver which Sergeant Crowther managed to knock away, but he was unable to prevent the man's escape. Fighting broke out in the club and reinforcements (including Lancashire Constabulary officers) responded and were called to assist. It is estimated that over a hundred officers were involved in fighting in the club with a crowd of over 5,000 people gathered outside. The police arrested a number of men at the Irish Club and also picked up others over the weekend, including Patrick O'Donoghue.

Also wounded at the club, in addition to Constable Bailey, was Constable Skidmore who received a scalp wound. Another officer, Detective Constable Valentine, escaped injury when he was struck by a bullet which entered his clothing and was deflected by his watch, passing out through his clothing on his left side.

Eleven men were arrested at the club. Shaun Wickham was taken to the Infirmary.

The club was searched, and 20 revolvers and ammunition were found along with grenades, a uniform and Irish National flag, bottles and jars containing petrol, and four boxes of gelignite. A prisoner later showed the location of hidden areas in the club containing further weapons, including rifles.

The death of Sean Morgan was registered on 14th April 1921 after an inquest, the cause of death being officially given as *'Bullet wound to the head due to being shot by a police officer whilst the said John Morgan* [sic] *was resisting the said police officer in the legal exercise of his duty. Justifiable homicide'*. A memorial to Sean Morgan was unveiled in Moston Cemetery on the ninth anniversary of his death in 1930.[12]

On the 15th July 1921, nineteen men were convicted of treason felony at Manchester Assizes and received sentences ranging from three to fifteen years imprisonment. There was uproar in the court when the sentences were announced, and the judge ordered that the public gallery be cleared.

At the conclusion of the trial the judge addressed the Attorney General and asked that his appreciation of

---

[12] *Irish Republican Operations in Manchester 1920-1922*
https://radicalmanchester.wordpress.com/2009/10/17/irish-republican-operations-in-manchester-1920-1922/ – Retrieved 8/6/2017

the conduct and courage of the whole of the Manchester Police Force be conveyed to the Chief Constable and whole force.

Patrick O'Donoghue and Sean Wickham were convicted and sentenced to fifteen years imprisonment. They were released in 1922 along with the other prisoners as part of an amnesty for political prisoners following the signing of the Anglo-Irish Treaty in December 1921.

The Chief Constable submitted recommendations for the award of the King's Police Medal to four officers, with promotions for Boucher, Bolas and Bailey, along with monetary awards.

In addition, Sergeant Crowther, Detective Constable Oakden and Constable Longworth were recommended for promotions and the award of the Watch Committee Medal for Bravery.

Further consideration was to be given to the actions of other officers and further awards.

Samuel James Tongue was born at Stalybridge, Cheshire, and was appointed, aged 22 years, to Manchester City Police on 30th October 1890. He served until 14th September 1924 when he was pensioned at the rank of Superintendent. He died in 1955.

Richard Bailey was awarded the King's Commendation for Brave Conduct in 1940 – see later entry for further information.

Michael Bolas was born at Boyle, Roscommon, Ireland and was appointed to Manchester City Police on 14th September 1904, aged 23 years. He was pensioned as a Sergeant in March 1926. After being pensioned he worked as a private inquiry agent. He died in Manchester in 1945.

D.S. Michael Bolas – 1922. (© Lancashire Police Museum)

William Edwin Boucher was born at Birmingham and was appointed to Manchester City Police on 25th August 1920, aged 28 years. His previous occupation was as a railway porter and he had served with the Royal Field Artillery from 30th January 1915 to 30th May 1919 as a gunner. He was a territorial soldier prior to the outbreak of the war. Boucher was discharged from the RFA on 30th May 1919 as being unfit due to sickness and was awarded the Silver War Badge (see below).

He served with Manchester City Police until 1st May 1934 when he was pensioned at the rank of Constable as being medically unfit. He died ,aged 48 years, in 1940.

The **Silver War Badge** was issued to UK and Empire service personnel who had been discharged due to wounds or sickness from military service in the Great War. Each badge was made from silver and individually numbered.

The purpose of the badge was to recognise service and to indicate that the wearer was no longer fit for military duties. This was to prevent harassment from individuals who saw apparently able-bodied men not in uniform and presented white feathers as a suggestion of cowardice.

Badges were also issued to male workers employed in vital war industries who were exempted from military service to indicate their status.

This is an award for exceptionally gallant conduct on the part of Constable Jones, when attacked by a body of armed Sinn Feiners who, after setting fire to farm buildings, attempted to murder Mr Rimmer, the occupier, in revenge for his action on a previous occasion on March 9th, when Patrick Lowe was wounded by a gun fired by Mr Rimmer.

As a consequence of threats police protection was afforded to Mr Rimmer and his farm premises. At 11p.m. on 23rd May 1921, P.C. Jones was on armed duty near Roby Farm, and observed a fire in the stack yard behind the house. He hurried to warn Mr Rimmer and on arriving at the front door was fired at by two men from behind a wall, Jones fired back, and the two men bolted. He was again shot at by a third man and fired two shots in return, after which all Sinn Feiners present decamped.

Previous to the arrival of Jones attempts had been made to induce Mr Rimmer to open the door without success, shots were fired through windows etc. and it is evident that an attempt was about to be made to enter the house by force, when Jones came on the scene, and by most exceptionally gallant conduct caused the entire murderous gang to retreat.

The whole affair represents coolness and courage of a very high order and is an inspiration to all. Mr Rimmer would undoubtedly have been murdered, had it not been for the intervention by Jones.

Lancashire Constabulary award file – PLA/ACC6849   L.G. 30/12/1921 Issue 32563 Page 10717

FURTHER INFORMATION:

The farm was attacked by 14 masked and armed men in response to boasts made by John Rimmer. The I.R.A. were unimpressed: *'To have ignored it would have been to admit fear, and the moral effect on other citizens in encouraging them to emulate this boasting fellow, might have had disastrous results for us.'*[13]

The men divided into two groups – five men setting light to the outhouses and sheds whilst the remainder went to the farmhouse. Failing to gain entry they fired shots through the windows before the arrival of P.C. Jones and the ensuing firefight.

In addition to the stack yard, two barns were also destroyed at Roby Farm, which was situated on the southerly side of Broad Green Road, Roby. The farm no longer exists, with the site now occupied by the M62 motorway. Damage was estimated to be £2,000. In addition, nearby haystacks owned by Messrs Bibby and Sons of Liverpool were set alight at Court Hey.

Thomas Jones was born at Kersall, Manchester on 3rd December 1889.

He was appointed, aged 24 years, to Lancashire Constabulary on 14th September 1914, stating his previous occupation as being a farm labourer. He was posted to Blackburn Higher Division before being transferred for duty at the explosives factory at Litherland in 1917 and was lent to Flintshire Constabulary for similar duty at Queensferry.

He later served with the Army from April 1918, returning to Lancashire Constabulary in December 1918. He served until 1st November 1948, retiring as an Inspector after 34 years' service. He served at Kirkham and Prescot and on

13   Edward Brady, *The I.R.A. in Britain 1919-1923*

promotion to Sergeant at Widnes and Seaforth, then to Blackburn Lower Division as an Inspector in 1935. For his actions in 1921 he was awarded the Merit Badge and the sum of £10. He died on 25th January 1967.

(See previous award of King's Police Medal to Inspector Lewis relating to earlier incident at these farm premises.)

8th March 1922

William HANDLEY, Constable   **Liverpool City Police**

King's Police Medal

On the evening of 8th March 1922, Constable Handley went to 64, Tyneville Road, Fazackerley, as a result of a complaint from the woman occupier that an armed Russian named Blazhko was watching her house, and intended to see her daughter, whom he had apparently married and then left some three years previously.

The Constable found Blazhko, and while questioning him, he suddenly pulled out a pistol and fired at the Constable's face. Blazhko ran off but turned and fired again at Constable Handley.

The Constable had almost caught up with him, when Blazhko turned the gun on himself and fired. Despite the first aid rendered by Constable Handley, he died as a result of the self-inflicted wound.

PRO Ref: H045/15646/88771   L.G. 1/1/1923 Issue 32782 Page 12

FURTHER INFORMATION:

This incident involved a Russian Canadian named Fred Blazhko[14] who had married Bertha Coghlan in 1918. He arrived in Britain on a troop ship at Liverpool as a member of the Canadian Forces during the Great War. A small tin box was thrown from the ship and was picked up by Bertha Coghlan who, on opening the box, found it to contain Blazhko's name. She corresponded with him for sixteen months and in October 1918 they married before he returned to France.

At the inquest, Bertha stated she only married him as he threatened to take his life if she didn't. At the end of the war she refused to return to Canada with him. He returned to Canada alone but returned to try to persuade her unsuccessfully to return with him.

On 8th March 1922, Blazhko was seen outside Tyneville Road and both Mrs Coghlan and P.C. Handley tried to induce the man to go away. When asked if he was armed and to turn out his pockets he produced a revolver and fired point blank at P.C. Handley, missing him.

He then ran off, pursued by P.C. Handley. As they ran he turned around and fired a second shot, which again missed. The bullet went through a bedroom window, but nobody was hurt.

As P.C. Handley gained on him, Blazhko put the revolver in his mouth and fired, dying almost immediately.

At the inquest, it was revealed that Blazhko had also been corresponding with another girl who had written to him for several years after a note was dropped by him from a troop ship in dock. On 6th March, she received a note from Blazhko asking her to meet him, when he asked her to marry him and return to Canada, to which she refused.

His apartments were searched, and several other letters were found addressed to other females. A verdict of suicide whilst of unsound mind was recorded by the Coroner.

---

14   Canadian military records and the UK register of deaths show his name as being Theodosy Blazhko. Blazhko was born in Kiev, Russia, and enlisted in the Canadian Forces on 22nd January 1917 at Toronto. He served with the 124th Battalion of the Canadian Expeditionary Force in France, being demobilised on 25th August 1919.

At about 5.20a.m. Sergeant Tate, who was in bed, was told that there was a fire at the School House, Rishton, occupied by Mr. and Mrs. Knowlson and their four children. He went at once to the house and there found that Mr. Knowlson and three of the children were safe, but that Mrs. Knowlson and one child were still in the burning building.

Several attempts at rescue had already been made by a Police Constable and a civilian, both of whom had been overcome by the smoke and heat. Sergeant Tate tied a scarf over his mouth and entered the house by a ladder, crawled through a room and passage to the room where the mother and child were supposed to be.

They were not there, but Tate heard a moan from another room which he entered. The room was full of smoke and fire; but he found both Mrs. Knowlson and the child unconscious. He first carried the child to the window and turned him over to a Constable, returned for the mother, and dragged her to the window and got her down to safety. Both regained consciousness by artificial respiration, but the child died the next day. All spectators are unanimous in describing the house as a mass of fire and that to them it appeared an impossibility for anyone to enter the building and come out alive. A silver medal was presented to Sergeant Tate by The Society for the Protection of Life from Fire.

This is a fine example of the greatest courage and determination on the part of Sergeant Tate. Others had failed before his arrival; but this fact does not appear to have deterred him in the slightest.

Lancashire Constabulary award file – PLA/ACC6849

L.G. 29/12/1922 Issue 32782 Page 12

FURTHER INFORMATION:

Location of incident – School House, St Peter and Paul's School, Harwood Road, Rishton, Blackburn.

Mr Knowlson, the school headmaster, and the three eldest children jumped from the first-floor window during which Mr Knowlson broke his ankle. Previous rescue attempts had been made by Mr Tom Robinson, a neighbour, who obtained a ladder entering the bedroom but was overcome by smoke and had to be taken from the building.

P.C. Barnes, who arrived prior to Sergeant Tate, also entered the building by ladder, making his way to the middle bedroom but failed to find the mother and child. It was reported that Mrs Knowlson and her child were found by Sergeant Tate underneath the bed in the room they slept in.

Ordnance Survey – LXIII.9 (Blackburn; Rishton)
Published 1911.

The child who perished was two-year-old Howard Robert Ivan Knowlson, who died as a result of shock and carbon monoxide poisoning. At the inquest, the Superintendent of the Rishton Fire Brigade said in his opinion the cause of the fire was a cinder falling from the boiler fire onto a rug.

On 13th June 1923, at Blackburn County Police Court, Thomas Tate was presented with a framed testimonial from the Carnegie Hero Trust in recognition of his actions that day. He was also awarded ten guineas and the Silver Medal of The Society for Protection of Life from Fire.

The school occupied a site on the easterly side of Harwood Road between High Street and Brook Street. The site is now occupied by a small supermarket.

Thomas Tate was born at Bolton, Lancashire, in 1884. He was appointed to Lancashire Constabulary on 4th March 1909, stating his previous occupation as being a factory operative. His police service record indicates that he had previous Army service for eight years with the Loyal North Lancashire Regiment.

Private 6486 Thomas Tate served with the Loyal North Lancashire Regiment and with the 17th Mounted Infantry in South Africa. It is recorded that he was transferred to the 2nd Battalion L.N.L.R. Tate was awarded the Queen's South Africa medal for his service.

He served at Rochdale, Warrington, Wigan, Church, Blackburn Higher, Manchester, Lonsdale North and Wigan Divisions. He was pensioned on 1st May 1934, retiring as a Sergeant. In 1939 he was working as a County Court Bailiff. He died in 1950.

25th April 1922

James BENSTEAD, Constable   **Liverpool City Police**

King's Police Medal

On the night of 25th April 1922, Constable Benstead heard screams coming from the direction of a landing stage on the banks of the River Mersey, and shouts that a woman was in the water.

When he arrived at the place, he took off his overcoat and helmet, and jumped into the water, and after swimming out about 20 yards, found a 17-year-old girl, who struggled, grabbed him round the neck, and kicked him.

He was able to free himself and then turning the girl round, held onto her waist with one hand, he managed to grasp a lifebuoy which had been thrown to him.

The Constable brought the girl to the bank and applied artificial respiration until her natural breathing was restored. The water was nearly 30 feet deep, and it was a dark and stormy night, with a strong flood tide flowing.

PRO Ref: H045/15646/88771   L.G. 1/1/1923 Issue 32782 Page 12

On the afternoon of 30th August 1922, three men raided a post office in Manchester and succeeded in escaping with cash and stamps worth nearly 800 pounds.

Constable Corlett was on traffic duty nearby, and on being informed of the robbery, chased the two men, who took refuge among some empty lorries on the canal wharf. The Constable who knew that the men were armed, jumped over a wall and approached the men, who pointed their weapons at him.

He drew his truncheon, and attempted to get within striking distance, when one of the men fired, the bullet hit his arm, and entered his body. Constable Corlett fell to the ground badly wounded, and both men escaped, but were captured in another part of the country some weeks later.

PRO Ref: H045/15646/88771   L.G. 29/12/1922 Issue 32782 Page 12

FURTHER INFORMATION:

Location of incident – Sub Post Office, 182 Great Ancoats Street, Manchester.

The three robbers were convicted at Manchester Crown Court on 26th November 1922. They were Horace Eldridge (24), an engineer; James Harker (35), a cook; and Harry Carlton (24), a seaman. All were convicted of robbery and Eldridge and Harker were convicted of shooting to do grievous bodily harm and guilty of possessing firearms with intent to endanger life.

Eldridge and Harker entered the post office whilst Carlton kept watch outside. Harker and Eldridge were later arrested in Worcester and Carlton at Southend-on-Sea.

The defendants also admitted a previous post office raid in Goswell Road, London on 14th August 1922, where the postmistress was tied up and £248 was stolen. Eldridge had no previous convictions. However, Harker had nine previous convictions and was believed to be a deserter from the armed forces. Carlton, whilst serving in the military, had been sentenced to five years hard labour, which was suspended in September 1918. All three had been in receipt of relief from the Poor Law Guardians in London prior to the Goswell Road raid. Eldridge had fired the shot wounding Constable Corlett.

Eldridge was sentenced to ten years penal servitude and Harker, although he had not fired the shot, was adjudged equally guilty, having a poor record, and was also sentenced to ten years penal servitude. Carlton's part in the incident was not as reprehensible and he was sentenced to seven years penal servitude.

Following the sentencing, the judge called P.C. Corlett forward and complimented him on his courageous conduct and stated he wished to make a public appreciation of the officer's conduct.

Robert Alfred Corlett was born at Douglas in the Isle of Man. He was appointed to Manchester City Police, aged 21 years, in August 1920. His previous occupation is recorded as having been a labourer. He had also previously served for just over four years with the Cheshire and South Lancashire Regiments. He served with Manchester City Police until 20th October 1942 when was pensioned. He died in 1973.

At about midnight on 14th December 1922, Mr. and Mrs. Cullen and their three children were all asleep at 15 Ashton Road, Denton, when Mr. Cullen was aroused by finding their room full of smoke.

He and his wife went downstairs and found the living room on fire. Mr. Cullen tried to put the fire out, his wife returned upstairs to bring the three children down. She took one child out of bed but was unable to get any further than the top of the landing when she was overcome by smoke.

Constable Hudson and a civilian called Daniel Connell heard the cry of fire. Hudson ran and gave the alarm at a fire box[15], and Mr. Connell got a ladder to the window and tried to enter the bedroom; but was unable to do so on account of the dense smoke. Hudson hearing that three children were up in the bedrooms, entered through the window, and brought out all three children one after the other and handed them through the window.

He went back again and brought Mrs. Cullen from the landing and handed her out. Hudson then collapsed on the window sill, was assisted down the ladder and taken to a house next door, where he became totally unconscious for the space of about an hour.

Mrs. Cullen and the three children when rescued were quite unable to help themselves. Had it not been for the high courage and persistence of Hudson, they would certainly have lost their lives.

This is a fine example of daring and a credit to the whole Force.

Lancashire Constabulary award file – PLA/ACC6849   L.G. 30/12/1924 Issue 33007 Page 6

FURTHER INFORMATION:

Location of incident – Confectioner's shop, 15 Ashton Road, Denton, Manchester.

It was reported that the fire originated in a recess in the shop where Christmas goods were stored. Considerable damage was caused to both stock and furniture in the property. Constable Hudson was awarded the Merit badge and £5 in recognition of his actions.

Stephen Hudson was born at Church, near Accrington, Lancashire, in 1900. He was appointed to Lancashire Constabulary on 10th October 1921, stating his previous occupation as being a wood sawyer residing at Accrington. He served at Ashton-under-Lyne, Lonsdale South and Garstang Divisions. He was promoted to Sergeant in October 1934. During his career he was commended on two occasions and awarded Merit Badges. He also received a letter of appreciation from the Northumberland Chief Constable for the arrest of three men for larceny.

He served until 30th August 1953 and died in 1971.

---

[15] Before the advent of public telephones, telephone boxes were placed allowing members of the public to contact the Police and Fire Brigade.

At 4.30p.m. on 4th March 1924, Constable Thomas was on patrol in Great Clowes Street, Broughton, when he saw two horses drawing a coach galloping at full speed towards him.

He immediately ran into the roadway, and grabbed one of the horses by the head, but failed to stop it.

He then jumped onto the step of a passing motor car, and after overtaking the runaways, he jumped off, and as the horses passed him again, he seized a rein and succeeded in dragging the horses head downwards, causing both horses to swerve onto the footway, where they slipped and fell, with Constable Thomas just avoiding being crushed.

PRO Ref: H045/12639

L.G. 30/12/1924 Issue 33007 Page 6

FURTHER INFORMATION:

Albert Thomas was born in Salford on 24th September 1896 and joined Salford Police on 20th September 1920. His previous occupation was as a labourer. Albert Thomas served during the Great War from 1914 to 1919 in the Royal Warwickshire Regiment. He was promoted to Sergeant in 1933 and was pensioned in 1945 on account of ill health.

(The King's Police Medal awarded to Albert Thomas is held within the collection of the Manchester Police Museum.)

At about 10.30p.m. on 25th April 1925, Police Constable Barrett observed that Bank Cottage, Walshaw, near Bury, was on fire, and that the occupier James Connaughton was by the window of the front bedroom with his head and arms hanging outside.

Barrett got a ladder, and went up, and after breaking a window asked Connaughton to try and get out, but the latter collapsed and became unconscious. The windows were mullion, the glass being only 2 feet 6 ins. by 12 ins., consequently Barrett went down to get a hammer with which to break the mullion.

At this moment, the Bury Fire Brigade arrived, and Barrett and a fireman broke the mullion. Fireman Heap followed by Sergeant Peter, went up and entered through the opening made, but Heap was overcome by smoke and heat. Peter assisted the fireman through the window and down to the ground, and immediately ran up the ladder again. After tying a handkerchief over his mouth and nose, Peter entered the bedroom, dragged Connaughton to the window and handed him over to Constable Barrett and a fireman. He then got out and came down the ladder, when he himself became unconscious, and remained so for about half an hour. Connaughton was taken to the Bury Infirmary in an ambulance but died on the way from burns and shock.

This is a fine example of determination and bravery. A fireman had already been driven out of the bedroom by smoke and heat, but Sergeant Peter was not put off in any way and took every conceivable risk in the endeavour to save Connaughton. A fine act and most worthy of the award given.

This case was reported to The Society for the Protection of Life from Fire with the result that Sergeant Peter was awarded the Society's Bronze Medal.

Lancashire Constabulary award file – PLA/ACC6849   L.G. 29/12/1925 Issue 33119 Page 8

FURTHER INFORMATION:

Bank Cottage was attached to High Bank Farm, situated on Walshaw Lane, Walshaw, Bury, and was occupied by Mr Connaughton, a gardener.

The inquest was held at Bury on 28th April 1925. Mrs Connaughton expressed the opinion that the fire was likely caused by a spent match when Mr Connaughton took out a candle from a drawer and the match fell into a drawer below containing paper.

Medical evidence attributed the death of James Connaughton (51 years) as due to shock and asphyxiation due to burning and smoke producing cardiac failure. The coroner and jury complimented Police Sergeant Peter, Constable Barrett and Fireman John Heap.

In May 2017, a fire took place at a barn at the farm, which required six fire engines to extinguish. No animals or persons were injured arising from the fire, which was suspected to be arson after hay was set on fire, suspected to be by children. Damage was caused to the barn and ninety tons of hay was destroyed.

William Parker Peter was born at Sabden, Lancashire, in 1881. Prior to appointment he had served with the Coldstream Guards and the Royal Garrison Artillery for 3 years and 3 weeks.

He was appointed to Lancashire Constabulary on 8th May 1903, stating his previous occupation as being a textile machine fitter. As a Constable he was commended on three occasions and was promoted to Merit Class P.C. for rescuing a man from the River Calder. He was promoted to Sergeant in 1924. Peter was awarded the Merit Badge and £10 for his actions in April 1925. He served until 26th May 1929, serving at Wigan, Blackburn, Lonsdale, Garstang and Bury Divisions. He joined the First Police Reserve, serving in 1940 and 1941, and died in 1961 whilst residing in Preesall.

3rd February 1926	
Cyril MACLACHLAN, Constable 31	**Manchester City Police**
George Rigby SOUTHERN, Constable 103	**Manchester City Police**
King's Police Medal	

At 11.45a.m. on 3rd February 1926 the two Constables were on duty in plain clothes, when they saw a man, who they recognised as being wanted for shop breaking in Manchester and Salford. The officers approached the man and asked his name. He admitted that there was a warrant out for his arrest and was taken into custody. After a few minutes the prisoner turned around suddenly and ducked under P.C. MacLachlan's left arm and made off.

The officers gave chase. When the prisoner had gone about 15 yards he stopped, turned around, pulled something out of his right-hand pocket, and fired two shots, one of which passed through P.C. MacLachlan's hat. He continued to run, with the officers in close pursuit. After proceeding about 18 yards the prisoner again turned and fired two more shots at P.C. Southern who was then about 10 or 12 yards away from him. He again made off, and after proceeding about 30 yards he threw the firearm away. At length, with the help of a civilian, the officers secured the prisoner after a violent struggle.

PRO Ref: H045/19447

L.G. 31/12/1926 Issue 33235 Page 7

FURTHER INFORMATION:

Location of incident – Altrincham Street, Manchester.

The man arrested on suspicion of shop breaking and larceny was Joseph Sagar (27) of Herbert Street, Manchester. He was sentenced to ten years penal servitude at the Assizes. Mr George Walker, a civilian who assisted with the capture, was presented with a framed testimonial from the Watch Committee.

Cyril MacLachlan was born at Ipswich, Suffolk and was appointed to Manchester City Police on 28th June 1922. His previous occupation was as a fitter. He had also served in the Royal Air Force for 354 days. He was pensioned as medically unfit, having reached the rank of Sergeant on 1st January 1938.

George Rigby Southern was born in Victoria, British Columbia, Canada and was appointed to Manchester City Police on 7th January 1920, aged 27 years. His occupation was as a farm labourer. He had also served in the 1st Battalion of the Welsh Guards for three years and 182 days. He enlisted in the Welsh Guards on 13th June 1916 and joined the 1st Battalion in France on 22nd February 1917.

Whilst in France he was kicked by a mule which resulted in his jaw being broken, requiring treatment back in the UK. He returned to France in 1918 and was transferred to the Army Reserve and finally fully discharged from the Army on 31st March 1920. He was pensioned as a Sergeant on 6th January 1950. He died on 13th December 1957.

31st March 1926

Thomas Herbert WARDLE, Sergeant 1071   **Lancashire Constabulary**

William JAMES, Constable 5   **Lancashire Constabulary**

King's Police Medal

In the early hours of March 31st, 1926, a fire broke out in the kitchen of No. 16 Sutherland Street, Colne. Seven people were asleep in the house at the time, namely Mr. Hartley, occupier aged 80, Mrs. Hartley, their invalid daughter Mary Ann, George Parkin (son-in-law of occupier), Mrs. Parkin and their son and daughter.

At about 5.20a.m. Parkin was aroused by smoke in the back bedroom, where he and his wife slept. Parkin got up at once, ran out of the house to the Police Station to report the fire.

He met Wardle and James near the Station, and afterwards returned to the burning house. Police Sergeant Wardle immediately informed the Fire Station and then ran to the house with James. The kitchen of the house appeared to be a roaring furnace, the door immediately at the bottom of the staircase, was already on fire and the staircase in great danger of catching light.

In spite of this Wardle and James ran up the staircase, and met Parkin carrying his daughter down. James went into the back bedroom and brought Mrs. Parkin and her son down through the flames at the bottom of the stairs. Sergeant Wardle met Mrs. Hartley coming out of the front bed-room and brought her down stairs.

He was then told that Mary Ann Hartley, an invalid, unable to move was in the front bedroom on the ground floor. He went into the room which was full of smoke and rescued the woman. The Sergeant was then told that Mr. Hartley was still upstairs in the front bedroom. In spite of the increasing flames he went up again and found Mr. Hartley in a great state of terror, so much so that he refused to leave the room, but by this time a ladder had been obtained, and Sergeant Wardle persuaded the old man to go down the ladder.

By this time, the woodwork at the bottom of the stairs was fully alight. Sergeant Wardle then came out of the house. A large crowd of the people of Colne had collected and loudly cheered both Police Officers.

Thus, the extremely gallant conduct of Wardle and James had saved the lives of no less than five people and had added one more page to the fine record of the Lancashire County Police, at all times prepared to risk their lives in the protection of the people under their charge.

Lancashire Constabulary award file – PLA/ACC6849

L.G. 31/12/1926 Issue 33235 Page 7

FURTHER INFORMATION:

Thomas Herbert Wardle was born at Ulverston, Cumbria, in 1883. He was appointed to Lancashire Constabulary on 8th November 1904, stating his previous occupation as being an iron worker. He served at Garstang, Wigan, Kirkham, Ormskirk and Blackburn Higher Divisions.

He served until 10th November 1930, retiring as a Police Sergeant. After his retirement he served for a number of periods in the First Police Reserve and died in March 1958 whilst residing at Blackpool.

William James was born at Heaton Norris, Stockport, in 1881. He was appointed to Lancashire Constabulary on 8th October 1907, stating his previous occupation as being a pattern maker and resident at Hulme, Manchester. He served at Ashton-under-Lyne and Blackburn Higher Divisions.

Thomas Herbert Wardle

William James

He served until 1st November 1933, retiring as a Sergeant and later joined the First Police Reserve. He died in 1960 and lived at Colne.

The General Strike 1926

'Not a minute on the day, not a penny off the pay' – Miners' slogan

The General Strike took place over a period of nine days between Monday 3rd May and Wednesday 12th May 1926. The strike was as a result of long standing problems in the coal mining industry arising from the combined effects of the Great War and the economic problems afterwards. During the war and up to 1921 the mines were under the control of the government. The miners' union favoured continued state control.

To avoid industrial conflict the government set up a Royal Commission headed by Lord Sankey. The Sankey Commission recommended the coal industry remain under government control. Despite a previous promise, Prime Minister Lloyd George decided to give control back to the mine owners.

On 31st March 1921, control was formally handed back to the mine owners who locked out miners who would not work for lower pay rates and also attempted to suspend national agreements. The government issued regulations under the 1920 Emergency Powers Act and recalled troops from Ireland and abroad to quell the miners and their supporters. The government feared the other two members of the 'Triple Alliance', the National Union of Railwaymen and the National Transport Workers Federation would support the miners.

On 15th April 1921, a day which was to become known as 'Black Friday', expected support from the other unions did not materialise and the miners were forced to fight on their own. Eventually the miners were forced to accept pay cuts and return to work.

Red Friday, 31st July 1925

On 30th June 1925, the coal owners decided they would abolish the national minimum wage agreement of 1924 and cut wages by 10%. This was in response to reduced coal exports due to increased production on the Continent and the return to the Gold Standard, which made U.K. exports more expensive. The miners rejected the proposals.

The T.U.C. (Trades Union Congress) made it clear to Prime Minister Stanley Baldwin that they would support the miners. The government was ill-prepared to deal with a major dispute at this time, especially as it was thought that public sympathy was with the miners. To avoid a dispute the government agreed to provide a subsidy for nine months to the mining industry and to set up another Royal Commission on Coal (headed by Sir Herbert Samuel) that was announced on Friday 31st July 1925, which became known as 'Red Friday'.

The subsidy was estimated to cost £10 million but in fact cost £23 million, although it had bought the Government nine months of peace.

August to May 1926

Both sides regarded Red Friday as simply postponing the inevitable. The government began to make preparations. It strengthened its counter strike organisation, the Supply and Transport Committee, and began stockpiling essential supplies. On a local level they set up voluntary networks for the transport and distribution of supplies with the help of bodies such as the Organisation for the Maintenance of Supplies (O.M.S.) and the Economic League. In Liverpool it is estimated that approximately 20,000 volunteers were available.

In February 1926, the Home Secretary reported to the Cabinet that preparations were complete with the country divided into ten divisions each with its own Civil and Road Commissioners, Coal, Finance and Food Officers. Within the divisions were 150 Road Officers and 150 Haulage Committees as well as extensive local arrangements.

The T.U.C. and the unions in contrast made virtually no effective plans for mounting a general strike. The T.U.C. General Council was keenly aware of the need for planning but the individual unions were reluctant to relinquish control of events to the General Council until the eve of the dispute. It was later revealed that the General Council only began to plan for a strike on 27th April 1926.

It appears both sides pinned their hopes that the Royal Commission might somehow achieve a compromise between the miners and the coal owners.

The Royal Commission on the Coal Industry, known as the Samuel Commission, rejected the idea of nationalising the coal industry and focussed on ways the industry could be reorganised. Both sides opposed areas of the recommendations of the Commission.

The government subsidy to the coal industry expired on 30th April and the mine owners wage reduction notices began to take effect, informing miners that those who would not accept the pay cuts need not turn up for work – in effect they were locked out. By lunchtime, 40,000 miners had been locked out. The mine owners issued proposals for wage reductions and a longer working day for a period of three years. A period of negotiation began between the two sides, but the issues proved to be intractable.

On Saturday 1st May, the General Council called for a strike to begin at midnight on Monday 3rd May. In the last days, orders were sent out by the government to the Civil Commissioners and the military. Warships were docked in Liverpool and other ports and Army and Naval leave was cancelled. Army units and Naval ratings were dispatched to a number of locations.

Negotiations continued but in the early hours of 3rd May the government broke off negotiations with T.U.C. representatives, citing the refusal of the *Daily Mail* printers to publish a government notice, which was regarded as evidence that a strike had already begun.

The Nine Days

Word that negotiations had broken down was broadcast by the B.B.C. at 1.10a.m. on Monday 3rd May and when the country awoke it was to a curious lull. The government announced a state of emergency, which triggered the strike arrangements. A national appeal was launched in the morning for volunteers.

> *MESSAGE FROM*
> *THE PRIME MINISTER*
>
> *Constitutional Government is being attacked. Let all good citizens whose livelihood and labour have thus been put in peril bear with fortitude and patience the hardships with which they have been so suddenly confronted. Stand behind the Government, who are doing their part, confident that you will cooperate in the measures they have undertaken to preserve the liberties and privileges of the people of these islands. The laws of England are the people's birthright. The laws are in your keeping. You have made Parliament their guardian. The General Strike is a challenge to Parliament and is the road to anarchy and ruin.*
>
> Stanley Baldwin,
> *British Gazette, 6th May 1926*

On Tuesday 4th May, in towns and cities across the country, people awoke to silence with virtually no public transport operating, no building work or normal rush hour taking place. The response to the T.U.C. instructions startled everyone, not least the T.U.C. In total it is estimated that 1.5 to 1.75 million workers came out on strike supporting 1 million miners.

The non-striking workers were forced to find their way to work without public transport. Roads and pavements were choked with pedestrians and all types of vehicles jostling each other to reach their destinations.

In towns and cities throughout the country thousands of volunteers queued to enrol. In Manchester alone 12,000 enrolled. The Police Reserve was recalled to duty across the country and thousands of special constables were enrolled.

Miners outside the Miners' Hall, Tyldesley, May 1926. (Public domain)

The T.U.C. called upon the print workers to strike. The government had anticipated the loss of the national press and had made plans to publish a government news sheet called *The British Gazette* and had commandeered the offices and presses of *The Morning Post*. The only newspaper which continued to be published was *The Times*. Winston Churchill, then Chancellor of the Exchequer, had made plans to commandeer the B.B.C. but this was resisted by the Director John Reith who ensured that its independence was guaranteed.

As the strike progressed one focus of the strikers' attentions was to disrupt movements of people and goods. The government volunteers began to operate trains and other transport. This led to a number of incidents where buses were stopped or stoned.

The inexperience of the volunteers led to a number of railway incidents and crashes. Their inexperience in the use of railway engines and rolling stock led to costly damage being caused.

Sabotage and damage was caused in a number of locations, the most potentially serious of which took place on 10th May near Cramlington in Northumberland when striking miners removed a section of rail to prevent trains from running. This resulted in a passenger train being derailed. This train was the *'Flying Scotsman'* service operating between Edinburgh and London on the East Coast Main Line and not the now famous preserved steam engine of that name. There were 270 people on board the train. Fortunately, only one person was injured. Eight miners were convicted of displacing a rail with intent to overthrow a train and endanger the safety of passengers, although many other strikers were involved. They received sentences of between 4 to 8 years imprisonment.

Serious unrest took places in Glasgow and Edinburgh and a number of other towns and cities, but the North West remained generally calm.

In Preston crowds of strikers gathered around bus depots and other places where volunteer or blackleg labour was likely to be employed. Preston Borough Police at this time did not own any motor vehicles and was dependent entirely on cars owned and driven by Special Constables to rush them around between places where trouble could start.

Things passed off without major incident until Saturday 8th May when a baton charge was required to disperse a large crowd of hostile strikers who had assembled under the Covered Market next to the Police Station at Earl Street. Stones had been thrown through the Police Station windows and it was feared an all-out attack would be made to release a man from custody. Assistance was requested from the County Force. The strikers mistakenly thought that a man who had been taken by taxi to the police station with an escort was a striker who had been arrested. He had in fact been arrested for an offence of larceny.[16]

Press reports state the crowd numbered 4,000 and that the disturbance lasted over an hour. It is stated that four baton charges took place and six persons were arrested including a woman. A number of officers were hit by bricks and stones and a number of other persons were injured.[17]

In Preston the docks remained closed until Saturday 8th May where there had been considerable interference with the unloading of foodstuffs and petrol. Volunteers were organised, and with police protection the docks reopened. Liverpool Docks also quickly began functioning. In Manchester, however, the docks remained closed until almost the end of the strike.

As the strike progressed it became apparent to the T.U.C. that the government would not or could not accede to the demands for them to prevent further wage losses in the coal industry. The T.U.C. did not wish to escalate the strike as it risked further inconveniencing the public and risked losing their support.

Sir Herbert Samuel was in Italy when the strike began and telegraphed the Prime Minister, offering his assistance as a negotiator, which was rejected. Nevertheless, he returned on 6th May and contacted various parties involved including the T.U.C. Negotiating Committee. His suggestion was that a National Mines Board could be set up with an independent chairman. The board would set up a wage agreement and would fix minimum wage levels.

Bronze medal awarded by the L.M.S. Railway Company to staff who continued to work and volunteers who filled roles left by striking workers. (Author's collection)

The General Council met with the miners' leaders on 11th May, indicating their view was that the proposal was a fair basis for negotiating a settlement. The miners refused to accept these proposals as they believed it would result in a reduction in wage rates. Despite this, the General Council arranged for a meeting to take place with the Prime Minister at noon on 12th May to end the strike.

Workers gradually returned to work. However, the coal mining dispute, the cause of the General Strike, continued until November 1926 when the miners were forced back to work on the employers' terms.

At Pemberton Colliery, Wigan, on Monday 13th October 1926, coal was being mined for the first time after the strike had been called, by 400 miners who had returned to work. A crowd of around 2,000 assembled, awaiting the day shift to come to the surface. Part of the crowd became threatening and the Wigan Chief Constable, Mr Pey, ordered the crowd to disperse without effect and he ordered a baton charge. Many of the crowd were knocked down and injured in the rush and stones were thrown. This was the only incident in Wigan where the police had to use force. This incident became known as the 'Battle of Enfield Street'.

---

[16] *'The Special'* Official Publication of the Preston Borough Special Constabulary – Tom Lightfoot

[17] *Londonderry Sentinel* – Tuesday 11 May 1926 (and others)

6th May 1926

William COOPER, Sergeant 1213   **Lancashire Constabulary**

British Empire Medal (Civil Division)

On May 6th, 1926, Police Sergeant Cooper was riding pillion on a motor bicycle ridden by Constable Davidson and was escorting a charabanc laden with women from Laburnum Mill, Atherton.

In Wigan Road, Atherton, they were met by a hostile crowd of about 1,000. Cooper saw three men who he did not know throw a baulk of timber about 12 feet long by 8 inches square in front of the wheels of the charabanc.

He jumped off the bicycle and on to two of the men, one man got away, but Cooper fell to the ground with the other man. He got to his feet again, still holding on to his man, whereupon the crowd became very hostile.

He dragged the man to a gateway, bricks were flung at him and one man in the crowd struck him several violent blows on the right arm with a long piece of wood. Cooper used his truncheon as well as he was able until his right arm became useless. He then took the prisoner with him into a house, which was opened for him and remained there. Subsequently Superintendent Whitehead arrived with Police assistance and Cooper and his man were taken to the Police Station.

The courage and determination displayed by Sergeant Cooper in holding a prisoner in the presence of a very hostile crowd and in spite of serious injuries to himself, is deserving of the highest praise.

Lancashire Constabulary award file – PLA/ACC6849

L.G. 31/5/1927 Issue 33280 Page 3619

FURTHER INFORMATION:

Sergeant Cooper was assisted that day by twelve-year-old Kathleen Winifred Baggott of Wigan Road, Atherton, who brought Cooper into her house and barred the door.

She said. *'I was alone in the house when I saw a policeman struggling with a man. Some of the other men were hitting the policeman with pieces of wood with nails in. I could see his arm was hurt and I felt so sorry for him, so I opened the door, helped him into the house and locked the door again. The men threw stones and one came through the window and a piece of glass cut my face.'* (*Illustrated Police News*, Thursday 27/5/1926)

On 21st May 1926, she was further presented with a century-old walnut writing desk and a purse containing a Jubilee half sovereign at Atherton Police Station. Mr C.S. Smith, a Special Constable of Lee, London, who desired to recognise her bravery, presented the gifts.

She later received £2 and a letter of thanks from the Lancashire Chief Constable and was presented with an inscribed gold wrist watch by Superintendent Whitehead at Leigh Police Station on 25th May 1926.

Superintendent Whitehead said that had it not been for the little girl, Sergeant Cooper would have been very seriously assaulted. Sergeant Cooper said it was entirely owing to the girl's presence of mind that he was able to attend the ceremony. (*Lincolnshire Echo*, 26/5/1926)

Sergeant Cooper was presented with his medal on 11th October 1927 at Preston Quarter Sessions by Major General Sir Llewelyn Atcherchley.

William Cooper was born at Gateacre, Liverpool, in 1879 and was appointed to Lancashire Constabulary on 24th September 1900. He gained promotion to Sergeant in 1912 and served until retirement in October 1929. William Cooper served at Manchester, Ormskirk, Lonsdale South, Lower Blackburn and Warrington Divisions. He died in 1958.

8th May 1926

George WOODWORTH, Sergeant 1230   **Lancashire Constabulary**

British Empire Medal (Civil Division)

At about 3.15p.m. on May 8th, 1926, Sergeant Woodworth heard that a number of men were congregating at the end of Hennel Lane, Walton-le-Dale.

He immediately went there on his bicycle and found that about 200 men, all strikers from Preston, were present and someone in the crowd called out *'We are going to stop the Ribble'*.[18] Woodworth advised the men in quiet tones to disperse and not to do anything illegal, at the same time having seen the temper of the men sent for assistance.

Just at this juncture a Ribble Bus came along, someone in the crowd shouted, *'Come on boys let it have it,'* and Woodworth saw a man called Clague and others throw stones at the bus, breaking two windows and doing other damage. He immediately arrested Clague but was knocked down and kicked and Clague was released. Woodworth got up again, pursued Clague through the crowd and re-arrested him.

A man called Nicholas was seen to strike the Sergeant on the helmet with an iron bar and to kick him, but Woodworth eventually got Clague to the Police Station. In the meantime, Inspector Blenkinsop and two Constables cleared the crowd with their truncheons, arrested Nicholas and took him to the Police Station.

The prompt, firm and extremely courageous bearing of Sergeant Woodworth undoubtedly prevented what might have been a very ugly situation. Subsequently the Bench, very rightly, complimented him on his very fine performance.

Lancashire Constabulary award file – PLA/ACC6849   L.G. 31/5/1927 Issue 33280 Page 3619

FURTHER INFORMATION:

Two men, namely Norman Gilling Clague (19 years) and Thomas John Nicholas, were charged under the Emergency Powers Act[19] with attempting to impede transport. Nicholas was also charged with obstructing and assaulting P.S. Woodworth and damaging his helmet. Both were convicted, with Clague being fined £5 and ordered to pay witness expenses. Nicholas was found guilty of assaulting the Sergeant and was sentenced to one month's imprisonment.

The Bench complimented Sergeant Woodworth on his personal actions, which the Chairman said probably prevented much more serious consequences.

George Woodworth was born at Clitheroe, Lancashire and was appointed to Lancashire Constabulary on 19th February 1907. He gained promotion to Sergeant in 1921 and Inspector in 1927.

George Woodworth served at Lonsdale North, Manchester, Ashton-under-Lyne, Widnes, Blackburn Lower, Lonsdale North and Bury Divisions.

---

[18] Ribble was one of the local bus companies in Preston. Ribble Motor Services began in 1919 and became one of the largest bus operators in the North West. It remained in existence until 1988 when it became part of Stagecoach Group.

[19] The Emergency Powers Act 1920 made it an offence to interfere with the supply and distribution of food, water, fuel or light or with the means of locomotion to deprive the community or any substantial portion of the community with the essentials of life. Offenders could be imprisoned for three months, a fine of £100 or both together with forfeiture of goods or money in respect of the offence has been committed.

Sergeant Woodworth was commended and awarded £1 for stopping a runaway cart in Eccles in 1916. He was awarded The Royal Humane Society Certificate and raised to Merit Class Constable in 1916 for the attempted rescue of a drowning man. In 1921, he was awarded the Merit Badge for diving into a canal and recovering a child's body. For his actions on 8th May 1926 he was awarded the Merit Badge and £3 by the Chief Constable.

He was presented with his medal on 11th October 1927 at Preston Quarter Sessions by Major General Sir Llewelyn Atcherchley.

He served until retirement as an Inspector in February 1938 and died in 1964.

10th May 1926

Thomas EGERTON, Inspector   **Lancashire Constabulary**

British Empire Medal (Civil Division)

On May 10th, 1926, during the General Strike, Inspector Egerton was engaged with other policeman in escorting workmen from the Locomotive Works of the L.M.S. Railway at Horwich, to their homes, when they were molested by a crowd of approximately 3,000.

The Inspector signalled to an approaching bus to stop, but, owing to the crowd making a rush, the driver was unable to stop properly and drove off with two of the workmen clinging to the outside of the bus, these men were mauled by the crowd and had to receive medical attention. After the bus had driven away Mr. Egerton found himself and one workman cut off from the remainder of the Police. In spite of attacks by the crowd he got the workman away to his home.

Later on, Mr. Egerton met other workmen being escorted to their homes by Police followed by a large hostile crowd. In view of the size and temper of the crowd, he decided to take the workmen to the Police Station but was forced to make a baton charge with seven other members of the Force before the crowd would disperse.

This is a fine example of bold and determined leadership in highly dangerous circumstances, and certainly prevented serious injury to work people.

Lancashire Constabulary award file – PLA/ACC6849   L.G. 31/5/1927 Issue 33280 Page 3619

FURTHER INFORMATION:

The non-striking workers were a handful of locomotive works clerks. A witness described the strikers as

being a seething mob of 3,000 to 4,000 outside the Police Station with there being a frightening atmosphere. Bricks were thrown at the Police Station windows. Suddenly the doors opened, and the officers 'trotted' down the steps and ran towards the crowd, batons drawn. The crowd dispersed with some sustaining injuries in their attempts to get away. A number were arrested and charged with riotous behaviour.[20] It is reported that only eight officers were involved in repelling the crowd with only three being regular officers. He was presented with his medal on 11th October 1927 at Preston Quarter Sessions by Major General Sir Llewelyn Atcherchley.

The locomotive works was the major employer in Horwich. It had been opened in 1886 as the works for the Lancashire and Yorkshire Railway and was taken over in 1923 by the L.M.S. (London, Midland & Scottish) Railway and remained

---

[20]   Radio Lancashire audio interview 1983. (Lancashire Record Office – RLANCS 1983-6329)

in operation through to 1983. After that the foundry continued in operation up to 2004. The site is now a business park with parts of the site earmarked for conservation and for housing development.

Thomas Egerton was born in Widnes, Cheshire and was aged 28 years when appointed to Lancashire Constabulary as Constable 1509 on 15th August 1898.

His previous occupation was as a forgeman with the L. & N.W. (London and North Western) Railway at Crewe. He gained promotion to Sergeant in 1911 and to Inspector in 1918. He served at Wigan, Seaforth and Bolton Divisions. He retired on 1st August 1928 and died in June 1932.

24th July 1926

Willie RYLANCE, Inspector	**Wigan Borough Police Fire Brigade**
King's Police Medal	
John JONES, Sergeant	**Wigan Borough Police Fire Brigade**
King's Police Medal (Bar)	

John Jones
(*Wigan Examiner*, 18/3/1933)

At 3.28p.m. on the 24th July 1926, the Fire Brigade received a message that an explosion had occurred at a butcher's shop causing a fire.

On arrival it was found there was a leak in the ammonia gas engine in the cellar and a man called John Gore was trapped in the refrigerating room due to the fumes which had become hot and pungent. Sergeant Jones put on a smoke helmet and went into the cellar to cut off the gas supply.

Unfortunately, he was overcome by fumes and returned to ground level. Inspector Rylance then put on the helmet and managed to shut off the gas, but he too was obliged to leave the cellar.

John Gore still trapped in the refrigerating room was knocking as a signal that he was alright. After a time the knocking stopped.

Inspector Rylance then made a second attempt, opened the door of the refrigerator room before returning to the surface with the unconscious Gore. As the Inspector reached the surface he collapsed and soon recovered and was taken home in the Police Ambulance.

PRO Ref: H045/19447   L.G. 31/12/1926 Issue 33235 Page 7

FURTHER INFORMATION:

Location of incident – Ben Turner Ltd, Woodcock Street, Wigan.

It also stated that Police Constable Ainscough also assisted in the rescue and that all three firemen as well as John Gore were badly gassed during the incident.

Ben Turner Ltd had a number of butcher's shops in the Wigan area.

(See previous entries for Ainscough, Rylance and Jones.)

Willie Rylance was born in 1878 at Castleton, Rochdale. In 1939 he was living at 9 Daventry Avenue, Bispham, with his wife. His occupation was recorded as being a retired Fire Brigade Inspector. He died, aged 69 years, in May 1948.

Willie Rylance

On 13th October 1926, a man entered a bank in Liverpool, pointed a revolver at the clerk, and demanded money. On being refused, he shot the clerk, and grabbed a bag of silver, and ran out, pursued by the manager. Constable Clarke was nearby, and saw the man running down the street waving the revolver around. The man turned, and fired a shot at the Constable, which missed.

However, after a short distance, the man stopped, and carefully aimed at Constable Clarke, who did not falter and continued to run straight for the man, but the shot hit him in the shoulder and the man escaped.

PRO Ref: H045/19452   L.G. 2.1.1928 Issue 33343 Page 7

Thomas Burnett Smithwick

L.G. 1/6/1928 Issue 33390 Page 3862

FURTHER INFORMATION:

Location of incident – District Bank, Great Homer Street and other streets in Liverpool.

At Liverpool Assizes on 3rd February 1927, William McAllister (19), a labourer, was sentenced to ten years penal servitude in connection with the bank raid.

On entering the bank at 11.25a.m. on 13th October 1926, McAllister levelled a large revolver at Walter Cecil Tooby (22), the cashier, and instructed him to put his hands up. Tooby threw a file at the gunman and shouted for the manager. McAllister then fired point blank at Tooby, who was hit in the chest. McAllister grabbed the money and ran out of the bank pursued by the manager, Mr Calkeld, shouting, '*Stop thief*'. A Market Constable named Moore joined in the pursuit. While running across North Haymarket, McAllister fired three shots. John Stevenson (34), a civilian who had attempted to stop him, was hit in the head. He then turned and shot at the crowd, wounding a man called Vipond in the chest. The third shot hit the market roof.

The chase continued onto Juvenal Street where Constable Clark and a market constable named Smithwick joined in. He fired at Clarke, missing and splintering a window of a shop. Clarke continued and was within a few yards of him when he turned and fired, hitting Clarke in the chest. McAllister ran onto Grosvenor and Blodwen Street. Police Constable Kerr saw the man running towards him with the revolver in his hand. Five yards from the Constable he stopped and aimed at the officer, pulling the trigger, but had used up all his ammunition. McAllister was then detained and taken to the Bridewell.

Constable Clarke lost the use of his left arm whilst John Stevenson, a labourer, was believed likely to die due to the wound to his head. He recovered but was left with severe paralysis. The other wounded persons were Walter Cecil Tooby (22), bank clerk, and Robert Vipond (57), a gardener. Mr Justice Greer stated that the crime of robbery under arms was punishable by the cat,[21] but in passing a sentence of ten years he would omit that punishment. The judge said that John Stevenson had performed an act of great

---

[21] The *Cat o' Nine tails* was a nine-tailed whip used to inflict severe physical punishment used in the U.K. Army, Royal Navy and as a judicial punishment in the U.K. Such punishment was removed from the Statute Book in 1948 for most offences although it was retained for serious assaults on prison staff until 1967.

courage in assisting the police and had suffered enormously in consequence of that act. Under the statutory powers he awarded him £50. *'The reward, I am afraid,'* the judge added, *'is no sort of compensation for what he has suffered.'* (*The Manchester Guardian*, 15/10/1926)

It is not known whether Constable Clarke's injury was permanent. It is stated that at the time of the incident he had been a police officer for about five years and had served for over two years with the Manchester Regiment during the Great War. He had been married two weeks previously and had recently been awarded a certificate for gallantry in stopping a runaway horse.

He was presented with the King's Police Medal by his Majesty the King at an Investiture held at Buckingham Palace on 14th February 1928.

William Burnett Smithwick was presented with the British Empire Medal on 2nd August 1928 by the Lord Mayor of Liverpool, Miss Margaret Beavan. The Chief Constable of Liverpool, Mr L.D.L. Everett,[22] said Smithwick's courageous act resulted in the capture of a dangerous criminal. *'We police,'* he added, *'are merely paid citizens in uniform who are looking after the interests of the community, and I appeal to citizens to help the police whenever their assistance is needed.'*

William Burnett Smithwick was born in October 1888, at Kirkdale, Liverpool. He joined Liverpool City Police around 1908 and married in December 1914. He joined the Army and served with the 17th Battalion of the King's Liverpool Regiment, entering France on 8th November 1915. He was discharged from the 3rd Battalion King's Liverpool Regiment on 12th September 1917 due to wounds received. He was awarded the Silver War Badge.

He returned to Liverpool City Police and joined the National Union of Police and Prison Officers (N.U.P.P.O.), becoming one of the union officials. He gave evidence to the Desborough Committee into police pay and conditions on 25th April 1919. He took part in the Police Strike of 1919 and was one of the 954 Liverpool officers who were sacked.

He later gained employment as a Market Constable where he remained, reaching the rank of Chief Inspector. He died aged, 58 years, on 19th January 1947.

10th December 1926

Frank LEECH Constable 34   **Salford Borough Police**

King's Police Medal

During the evening of 10th December 1926, two workmen were buried by the sudden collapse of a narrow trench, twelve feet deep, and were in immediate danger of suffocation.

The bottom of the trench was soft sand, and the slightest movement caused them to sink deeper. Constable Leech, despite the danger of being sucked down, or buried by further falls, immediately jumped into the trench, and began to dig the men out.

With the help of others, he finally rescued both men after some seven hours work.

PRO Ref: H045/19452   L.G. 2/1/1928 Issue 33343 Page 7

---

[22] **Lionel Decimus Longcroft Everett** – Chief Constable, Preston Borough Police, 1913-1917, then First Assistant Head Constable and later Chief Constable, Liverpool City Police, 1925-1931.

FURTHER INFORMATION:

During the day workmen had been excavating in the garden of Malvern House, a large private residence facing Bury Old Road, Cheetham Hill, Manchester. The property is described as having its rear garden abutting Catherine Road, which places the property as being between Middleton Road and Park Road.

A trench, approximately 30 to 40 feet long and 16 or more feet deep, had been dug to locate a sewer.

Part of the trench gave way at about 4.45p.m., burying two workmen, namely David Inglis (19) of Baguley Street, Cheetham Hill and Ernest Johnson (23), a plumber of Bellowe Street, Ardwick. The ground in which they were buried was found to comprise quicksand.

Inglis was completely buried with only the top of his head visible and was kept alive by clearing earth away from his nose and mouth. Johnson was less deeply buried but to release him would have precipitated another fall which would engulf Inglis. To safely rescue the trapped men, it was first necessary to secure the men and to shore up the excavation. The rescuers worked by light provided by acetylene flares.

It was not until 11.45p.m. that it was safe to extricate Johnson. Inglis by now had been raised until all of his body was clear to the knees, but it took a further hour until he could be released.

Reporting to the Watch Committee on 20th December 1926, Major C.V. Godfrey, the Chief Constable of Salford, described the *'outstanding bravery'* of Police Constable Leech, Sergeant Blakeley and Police Constables Kehoe and Howarth, describing the bravery as follows: *'Without waiting for the trench to be made safe, Police Constable Leech climbed down and started digging. He was assisted by Sergeant Blakeley and the other officers, and it is due to their prompt action that the men were not suffocated. The lives of the officers were in jeopardy all the time they were working in the trench.'*

The Watch Committee awarded each of the officers £5 and recommended Constable Leech for the grant of the King's Police Medal. Major Godfrey, saying of the officer, *'He was the first on the scene and he worked continuously in the trench before any precautions whatever had been taken, and he ran the greatest risk.'*

He was presented with the King's Police Medal by his Majesty the King at an Investiture held at Buckingham Palace on 14th February 1928.

Frank Leech was awarded the King's Commendation for Brave Conduct for his actions on the 22/23rd December 1940. (See later entry for further information.)

1st June 1927

William Henry SMITH, Constable 299 'A'   **Liverpool City Police**

King's Police Medal

Late at night on 1st June 1927, Constable Smith was at George's Landing Stage, when he saw a man called McDonald in the water. He threw him a lifebuoy, but the man disappeared.

The Constable jumped into the water fully dressed, and caught hold of McDonald, and put him in the lifebuoy. A rope was thrown from a ferry, and Constable Smith took hold of it, and swam with McDonald towards the ferry. As he was being pulled on board by a passenger, the passenger slipped, and both ended up back in the water.

Constable Smith then secured both of them in lifebuoys and swam around until the other two were rescued before he was taken on board.

PRO Ref: H045/19452   L.G. 2/1/1928 Issue 33343 Page 7

FURTHER INFORMATION:

The rescued man was Henry McDonald, aged 29 years. McDonald fell from the landing stage near to the bows of the Wallasey cross ferry steamer the S.S. *Francis Storey*. Constable Smith entered the water fully dressed and reached the man and swam with him between the boat and the landing stage. The lifeboat was lowered from the *Francis Storey* but meanwhile Constable Smith was becoming exhausted.

A stageman, George Jackson, was lowered, head first with passengers holding his feet over the side of the boat from which position he supported Constable Smith who was dragged onto the ferry boat by passengers whilst Jackson held onto McDonald. A passenger, Mr H.E. Weston (40), attempted to climb down the mooring ropes but slipped and fell into the water and also got into difficulty but managed to grasp hold of McDonald, meaning Jackson was supporting both men.

The life boat from the ferry then arrived and both were dragged into the boat and all three were later taken to hospital for treatment.

William Henry Smith was presented with the King's Police Medal by his Majesty the King at an Investiture held at Buckingham Palace on 14th February 1928.

The Great Storm of October 1927

The North West was battered with 80mph winds, which continued unabated for close to six hours on 28th October 1927. It caused the waters of Morecambe Bay to sweep away sea defences, resulting in Fleetwood and the surrounding area being flooded.

The flooding prevented any vehicles entering the town for two days. Telephone lines were brought down, and the electricity works was flooded, plunging the town into darkness. Electricity was not restored for several days.

Roofs were torn off and the gable ends of several houses collapsed. Lord Street was flooded, and the tram track was strewn with dead livestock and hundreds of pit props, which had been washed from a timber yard half a mile away. Some streets were flooded to a depth of 10 to 15 feet.

The three Fleetwood lighthouses had no power and resorted to using oil lamps, making navigating the channel hazardous.

Five caravan occupants were reported dead. These were two women and three children who lived in the Peel Road area of Fleetwood. Another death occurred when a man attempting to reach his wife in the flooded area died of heart failure. Around nine persons were treated at hospital for injuries arising from the storm.

The storm rendered around 400 people homeless and damage to property amounted to several thousand pounds.

At Blackpool a double deck tram car was blown over. Fortunately, there were no passengers on board and the driver and conductor escaped injury. In Preston, the gable ends of two properties were blown down and there was extensive flooding around the Broadgate and the Dock areas of the town.

Aftermath of the 1927 floods – Lord Street, Fleetwood. (Author's collection)

At Lancaster, the Luneside Sanatorium[23] was flooded when the River Lune burst its banks. Forty-eight patients were at the hospital. Three lives were lost when water flooded huts in the grounds of the hospital where patients were sleeping. Patients in the main building were rescued by boat after being carried upstairs by members of the nursing staff.

At Lytham, a tide of 25 feet was produced and the sea defence broke, allowing water to flood in, inundating a number of houses and washing the ballast from the rail tracks at Lytham. Similar flooding took place in the area of the Ormerod Home, causing extensive damage with a number of workmen being marooned.

Further afield in the North West, at Spring Vale Dye Works near Rawtenstall, a 50-year-old night watchman was killed when a derelict wall was blown down onto him and at Morecambe Football Club a director was killed when a corrugated iron fence at the club's ground fell on him.

---

[23] The Luneside Sanatorium was a council operated isolation hospital situated at Marsh Point at the westerly end of New Quay Road, Lancaster, adjacent to the River Lune. The site of the sanatorium is now occupied by a builder's merchants. The sanatorium was replaced in 1934 by a new Lancaster and District Isolation Hospital, situated on Slyne Road, which became known as Beaumont Hospital. It closed in 1990.

At Blackburn, the chimney stack of a house at Bolton Road fell, injuring two boys who were sleeping in the back bedroom. Also, at the Blackburn Electricity Works at Whitebirk, four cooling towers over 100 feet tall and weighing hundreds of tons were torn from their foundations and destroyed. At Tanpits Road, Church, Accrington, a 120-feet high stone chimney owned by the Antley Manufacturing Company was blown down.

At Morecambe, a 60-feet section of the West End Pier was carried away, as was a 100 yard long section of Sandylands Promenade.

At Barrow-in-Furness, four children escaped without injury when a chimney was blown down, crashing into the bedroom where they were asleep. At Park Road, Blackpool, a 72-year-old woman escaped injury when the chimney collapsed and debris fell onto her bed.

In Dale Street, Manchester, a man walking along the Rochdale Canal was blown into the water and was rescued by police. In Great Ancoats Street, a house collapsed, fortunately resulting in only minor injuries being caused. In Hulme, a man was knocked down in the street by a falling chimney pot, sustaining only minor injuries.

Sailings were disrupted from Liverpool with wind speeds of 92mph being recorded there.

Much destruction and loss of life took place nationally due to the storm. The most serious loss of life took place off the west coast of Ireland where many fishermen were lost.

28th October 1927

John BRITCH, Constable 790   **Lancashire Constabulary**

Thomas SUMNER, Constable 862   **Lancashire Constabulary**

British Empire Medal (Civil Division)

At 11.55p.m. on October 28th, 1927 news was received at St. Annes Police Station from three workmen that at 11.30p.m. on the same day they were in a cabin on the foreshore, situated between North Promenade and Ormerod Homes, St. Annes, accompanied by four other men, when the tide suddenly swamped the cabin, owing to a fierce wind which was blowing at the time.

The three men had succeeded in reaching the road, 150 yards away, after wading in 5 ft. of water. They stated that four men, named J. Peach, F. Jackson, A. Boardman and W. Jackson were still in the cabin, and if help could not be given at once they would all be drowned.

The two Constables with Inspector Rosbotham and Police Sergeant Ormerod went out to the place, taking ropes with them. They found the roadway flooded to a depth of five feet, and on the sandhills the depth rose to between nine and twenty feet. Ropes were attached to Britch and Sumner, who in the face of the fierce gale struggled out to the position where the cabin should have been, but it was discovered that it had been washed away and was floating about.

A flicker of light was then observed, and at about 1.30a.m. the four men were reached, having taken refuge on the gib of a large crane which was partially under water, Britch and Sumner remained with the four men until the tide receded at about 2.30a.m. to enable all to wade ashore to safety.

This gallant and prolonged effort on the part of Britch and Sumner is all the more meritorious, since neither of them is a good swimmer, the weather conditions were exceedingly bad, a full gale in progress and a dark night.

Lancashire Constabulary award file – PLA/ACC6849   L.G. 1/6/1928 Issue 33390 Page 3861 & 3862

FURTHER INFORMATION:

The three men who escaped the cabin and made their way to the Police Station were W. Saunders, W. Reynolds and Alfred Lees (or Rees). The workmen were employed working on a sewerage scheme at St. Annes.

The Ormerod Convalescent Home for Children and Orphanage was situated on Todmorden Road, St. Annes and was established in 1890. The home was funded by the two daughters of Abraham Ormerod, a wealthy cotton manufacturer from Todmorden. The home had 110 beds and provided convalescent care for poor children from Lancashire and Yorkshire. The home closed in 1971 and was demolished in 1984. The site is now occupied by modern housing.

FURTHER INFORMATION:

John Britch

John Britch was born at St. Helens in 1900 and was appointed to Lancashire Constabulary on 29th July 1925. His previous occupation was a collier. He served at Kirkham Division until he was transferred on promotion to Sergeant to Bury Division on 19th February 1937.

He retired on completion of his service on 20th September 1955 and died aged 78 years in 1978.

Thomas Sumner was born at Westhoughton and was appointed to Lancashire Constabulary on 6th November 1924. His previous occupation was as a drawer in a colliery.

Thomas Sumner

He served at Fylde Division until 1938 when on promotion to Sergeant he transferred to Manchester Division. In 1949 he transferred to Lonsdale Division.

During his career, he was awarded the Merit Badge for the events of October 28th 1927 and was commended by Magistrates for the arrest of two housebreakers in 1938. He retired on 29th July 1951 and died in 1981.

Both officers were presented with the British Empire Medal by Major-General Sir Llewellyn William Atcherley, C.M.G, C.V.O., His Majesties Inspector of Constabulary, at a ceremony held at Lancaster Castle on Thursday 9th August 1928.

28th/29th October 1927	
Thomas JOHNSON, Constable 1649	**Lancashire Constabulary**
George BROTHWOOD, Constable 12	**Lancashire Constabulary**
King's Police Medal	

These two officers were selected by the Chief Constable as having rendered services of outstanding merit during severe floods at Fleetwood. The floods broke out after a gale on the evening of October 28th 1927 and covered an area of about three and a half miles to a depth of between two and nine feet and affecting about 1,200 houses.

Constable Johnson, who was on night duty on the 28th October, after warning the occupants of a house which had been seriously damaged, patrolled the area at great risk to himself.

On being informed that the tide was flowing towards the town, he waded waist deep into the road and warned the inhabitants in a lane near the docks. He then waded into other streets and although very exhausted continued to warn the inhabitants of their danger. After a short rest, cold and wet through, he continued to patrol the flooded area until was compelled to stop on account of floating wreckage. He waded out again later on and managed to drive some cattle to a place of safety.

After changing his sodden clothes, he proceeded to distribute food by boat to the marooned residents. This he continued to do until the evening of the following day. During most of the time he was in great danger from floating baulks of timber and other heavy objects and displayed great gallantry and fortitude and exceptionally high sense of duty.

Constable Brothwood on the morning of October 29th, was instructed by his Superintendent to obtain a boat and try and rescue a number of caravan dwellers who were in grave danger. Accompanied by two other men, he rowed through a tangled mass of dangerous wreckage and rescued a woman and a little girl from a van which was nearly submerged and under very difficult circumstances rescued a man, woman and two children from another van.

Turning these people over to another boat, he went back to the caravan and after breaking through fences and wire saved another four people from a partly submerged vehicle. At another place, Brothwood waded through water five feet deep, broke open the front door of a house and carried out a woman who was seriously ill.

He then broke open the door of another house and carried an old woman and her daughter on his back to the boat. Brothwood remained on duty until late at night carrying food and drink to flooded houses and bringing people to safety.

He displayed great gallantry, fortitude and exceptional courage and together with Johnson deserved the greatest credit for splendid work done under very difficult weather conditions.

Lancashire Constabulary award file – PLA/ACC6849   L.G. 2.1.1928 Issue 33343 Page 7

FURTHER INFORMATION:

Thomas Johnson was born at Morecambe, Lancashire, in 1883.

He was appointed to Lancashire Constabulary on 4th January 1912, stating his previous occupation as being a labourer resident in Morecambe. He served at Wigan, Kirkham, Ashton-under-Lyne and Church Divisions. For his actions in 1927 he received the Merit Badge and £10.

Thomas Johnson

He served until 14th January 1937 and died in 1943.

George Brothwood

George Brothwood was born at The Nabb, St Georges, Wellington, Shropshire.

He was appointed to Lancashire Constabulary on 20th September 1912, stating his previous occupation as being a store keeper residing at St. Georges, Wellington, Shropshire. He served at Garstang, Blackburn and Kirkham Divisions.

During the Great War Brothwood was allowed to enlist in the Army. He served as Lance Corporal P2437 in the Military Police in France from 15th December 1915 to 11th November 1918. He was reappointed to Lancashire Constabulary in 1919.

For his actions in 1927 he received the Merit Badge and £10. He was promoted to Sergeant in 1928 and transferred to Manchester Division. He served until 1st October 1937 and died in 1963 whilst residing in Davyhulme.

Thomas Johnson and George Brothwood were presented with the King's Police Medal by his Majesty the King at Buckingham Palace on 14th February 1928.

25th January 1928

William Guthrie MATTINSON, Detective Sergeant   **Liverpool City Police**

King's Police Medal

Detective Sergeant Mattinson was one of the Liverpool detectives assigned to trace and arrest a man called Kennedy, wanted for the murder of Constable Gutteridge in Essex on 27th September 1927.

Late on the evening of 25th January 1928, Sergeant Mattinson and other police officers were keeping observation on a house frequented by Kennedy.

The Sergeant saw a man nearby and followed him. The man was walking quickly, and his coat collar was turned up, but as the Sergeant drew alongside, he recognised him as Kennedy, and spoke to him. Kennedy turned, with an automatic pistol in his hand, and growled, 'Stand back Bill, or I'll shoot you'.

He pushed the gun into the Sergeant's side, and a distinct click was heard, but the gun did not fire. The Sergeant then grabbed the muzzle of the weapon, and ripped it out of Kennedy's hand, and then the Sergeant turned the gun on Kennedy, stuck it in his back, and took him into custody.

PRO Ref: H045/13418   L.G. 1/3/1928 Issue 33472 Page 1445

FURTHER INFORMATION:

At around 6a.m. on 27th September 1927, the body of P.C. George William Gutteridge of Essex County Constabulary was found on the side of a road near Howe Green, between Romford and Ongar in Essex. P.C. Gutteridge had been shot four times.

A huge manhunt was started for the killer or killers and from the outset his murder was connected with the theft of a Morris Cowley car, registration number TW 6120, belonging to Dr Edward Lovell from Billericay on the same night. The vehicle was subsequently found abandoned in Stockwell, London.

A search of the vehicle revealed an empty cartridge case on the floor. There was also blood on the running board of the car. The search for the persons responsible for the crime extended over the whole country and even abroad, but it was not until January 1928 that evidence came to light that implicated Frederick Guy Browne, a well-known London criminal with a garage business in Clapham.

The Metropolitan Police kept watch and Browne was arrested as he returned to his premises in Clapham. When arrested, Browne was found in possession of several loaded firearms including a .45 Webley pistol, the same calibre as that used to kill P.C. Gutteridge. A further suspect was William Kennedy who was well known to the Liverpool Police. Following the arrest of Kennedy in Liverpool by Sergeant Mattinson, he was brought back to London where he admitted being present at the time of the murder but implicating Browne as being the killer.

Forensic evidence linked the cartridge case found in the Morris to having been fired by the Webley revolver recovered from Browne when he was arrested.

Both defendants appeared before the Central Criminal Court and were convicted and subsequently hanged. Kennedy admitted his part in the killing, but Browne went to the gallows protesting his innocence, his defence being he had obtained the gun from Kennedy after the murder had taken place.

A memorial to P.C. Gutteridge stands close to the spot where the murder took place.[24]

William Guthrie Mattinson was born in September 1891 at Lancaster, Lancashire. During the Great War he attested on 2nd December 1915 under the Derby Scheme, being called up for service on 2nd September 1918 and served with the Coldstream Guards in the U.K. At the time he was enlisted he was a single man, living with his mother at Luxmore Road, Liverpool.

He was demobilised on 3rd February 1919 and returned to Liverpool City Police. He retired in 1937 having served for 26 years and died, aged 78 years, in 1969.

9th May 1928

Edward RICHARDS, Constable 1848   **Lancashire Constabulary**

Joseph ENTWISLE, Second Officer   **Farnworth Urban District Fire Brigade**

King's Police Medal

At about 1.30a.m. on May 9th 1928, Richards was told that the Golden Lion Hotel, Farnworth, a three-storey building was on fire. He went there at once and found that the first two floors were in flames and the fire brigade there.

Among others present were Supt. A. Entwisle, Second Officer J. Entwisle and Fireman W. Whittaker. The Licensee Mr Kay, Mrs Kay and their daughter, had escaped by jumping out, but there were still three persons in the building, Mr Kay's mother, his son Walter and a maidservant named Jane Seddon, all of whom were on the top floor.

Richards assisted in placing the fire brigade's ladder up to the top floor left hand window at the front of the hotel and in company with Second Officer Entwisle went up the ladder but owing to the fierce flames from the window on the second floor burning the ladder, both men had to come down.

Another ladder was erected at the rear of the hotel. Richards went up with the Second Officer, broke the window of a top storey room with his truncheon and entered the room with the Second Officer. The place was very hot and full of smoke, but they made a search and found nobody there.

The Second Officer became very faint and Richards helped him down the ladder. Soon after this Richards saw Fireman W. Whittaker climb a ladder to a window at the front of the hotel. He followed him, both entered a bedroom and found Jane Seddon and lowered her to the ground. They also found Walter Kay and got him out and lowered him down the ladder. Richards then came down himself and then heard Second Officer Entwisle call out for assistance from the back upper storey room.

He went up, discovered Entwisle in a state of collapse from heat and smoke, helped him to the window and the fresh air. The Second Officer then told Richards that Mrs. Kay was behind the bed in the room. Richards dragged her to the window and both he and Entwisle lowered her down the ladder.

---

24   George William Gutteridge – Essex Police Roll of Honour – Retrieved 11/6/2017
     http://www2.essex.police.uk/memorial/roll-of-honour.php?rollOfHonourId=35

Richards then saw Second Officer Entwisle enter the ground floor where the fire had been somewhat subdued, followed him in, and watched him climb the staircase of the second floor. Almost immediately the Second Officer reached the top, the floor gave way and he fell through a hole till he was only held up by his armpits. Richards ran to him, got his shoulders under the Second Officer's feet and supported him until help arrived.

Unfortunately, it was not possible to effect any saving of life since all the persons extricated were dead.

As an example of cool courage, determination and devotion to duty, the work of Constable Richards must take a high place in any list of brave deeds.

It must be remembered that this Officer, after considerable exposure to fire and smoke, assisted completely helpless people down a ladder from the top floor of a three-storey building, no easy task even for fully trained fire officers.

Lancashire Constabulary award file – PLA/ACC6849   L.G. 1/3/1928 Issue 33472 Page 1445

FURTHER INFORMATION:

The fatalities from the Golden Lion were Mrs Sarah Ann Kay, aged 86 years; Walter Kay, aged 18 years; and Jane Seddon, aged 21 years. The licensee, Walter Kay (55), his wife Margaret and daughter Netta (16) escaped the building with Netta sustaining a broken arm after jumping from a third-floor window.

The Golden Lion Hotel, 18, Gladstone Road, Farnworth ceased to be a public house and the premises are now occupied by an automotive paint retailer.

Edward Richards was born at Wigan, Lancashire, in 1891.

He was appointed to Lancashire Constabulary on 28th September 1914, stating his previous occupation as being a collier and residing in Wigan. Richards saw military service with the Army during the Great War.

He served at Rossendale, Ashton-under-Lyne, Bolton, Bury and Manchester Divisions. He was promoted to Sergeant in 1931.

He served until 8th October 1940 and died in 1965.

Second Officer **Joseph Dack Entwisle** of the Farnworth Urban District Fire Brigade was also awarded the King's Police Medal for his actions that day. His father, Superintendent Alfred Entwisle, was also present at the fire.

The Entwisle family was involved with the Farnworth Fire Brigade for four generations, with the first chief being Thomas Entwisle in 1867, James Entwisle in 1886, Alfred in 1906 and Joseph Dack Entwisle from 1937 to 1940.

Joseph Dack Entwisle left to become Chief Officer at Barnoldswick in 1940. In 1941, on the formation of the National Fire Service, he became a Column Officer in Cheshire.

National Fire Service cap badge.

The National Fire Service (N.F.S.) was formed as a result of lessons learned in the Blitz period of 1940/41, which highlighted the need for a unified approach nationally. Previously there were a large number of brigades with each local area having its own Fire Authority with its own methods and equipment.

When formed, the N.F.S. amalgamated all brigades and included the Auxiliary Fire Service. At its height, the N.F.S. had 350,000 members. The unified structure allowed movement of resources nationally, which would not have been possible under the old system.

On 29th November 1941, he died after being electrocuted whilst attending a house fire at Crewe. It is stated that his steel helmet was contacted by a live wire at the incident.

16th June 1929

William James WOOFF, Constable 1504　　　　　　　　**Lancashire Constabulary**

King's Police Medal

At about 1p.m. on June 16th 1929, Wooff was told that a woman had been noticed in a position of great danger on one of the walls which hold the River Ribble on its course.

The estuary of the Ribble is highly treacherous and dangerous, consisting of a series of channels of varying depths, at the bottom of which is soft mud and sand. Wooff set off at once and on arrival noticed a woman, afterwards identified as Elsie Heywood, at the edge of the water about a mile from the shore.

He immediately made his way towards her, hurried across the treacherous sands and after going about 400 yards sank up to his knees but persevered through channels and very heavy going till he eventually reached the mud bank on which the woman was standing.

When she saw him close to, she jumped into the water of a channel about 40 feet wide and was in grave danger of being washed away by the ebb tide. Wooff, though he was unable to swim and handicapped by heavy clothing and nearly exhausted by his previous efforts, plunged in the mud and water up to his armpits and secured the woman who made a violent struggle which took both her and Wooff under water.

In spite of this Wooff managed to hold on and dragged the frenzied creature to a mud bank where he, being completely exhausted, collapsed. By this time Inspector Dewhurst and Constable Fox arrived and all three subsequently conveyed the woman to Lytham Police Station.

The energy and complete disregard for the danger involved in crossing the treacherous estuary and securing the unfortunate creature at great risk to his own life must form an inspiration to the whole Force and was very worthy of the award granted.

Lancashire Constabulary award file – PLA/ACC6849　　　　　　　L.G. 31/12/1929 Issue 33566 Page 12

FURTHER INFORMATION:

(See later entry for P.C. Fox, also involved in this incident.)

On the morning of 16th June, the police were informed that a housekeeper was missing from St. Annes and a search was instituted. Shortly after 1p.m. a telephone message was received by the police from the Preston Corporation navigation barge, which was anchored in the River Ribble, stating a woman had been seen on one of the walls which form the river channel.

Mr Charles Molloy who was in charge of the barge saw the woman through his binoculars whilst checking for debris in the river. Becoming concerned, he and Major Miller, who was nearby in his motor yacht *Repose* went across towards the woman who ran off shrieking. As they could not reach her they returned to the barge and contacted the police.

P.C. Wooff, wearing heavy motorcycle clothing, went to her despite being impeded by the deep clinging mud and slime. He saw the woman in the water of a deep channel and, though he could not swim, he entered the water and seized the woman who gripped him by the throat. Both went under the water and Wooff was kicked, bitten and struck many times. Wooff overpowered the woman and dragged her to higher ground.

Inspector Dewhurst and Constable Fox joined Wooff and the woman made a furious attack, trying to escape into the water. Between them they carried the woman back to shore and conveyed her to Lytham Police Station where the woman collapsed and was very ill. All of the officers were absolutely exhausted.

After the woman had received medical treatment she was taken before a magistrate and was certified as insane and was taken to the Kirkham Institution.

Mr Molloy afterwards said, *'The first constable is a very brave man. I watched him through my glasses and saw him absolutely fight to reach the woman, and then fight to save her. I cannot speak too highly of that man for he did a splendid piece of work. All the policemen had a terrible struggle to reach the woman and they had a more terrible struggle with her. They deserve the very highest praise.'* (LEP, 17/6/1929)

William James Wooff was born at Hulme, Warrington. He was appointed to Lancashire Constabulary on 21st February 1923. He had previously served with the King's Liverpool Regiment as a Lance Corporal and as a Sergeant with the Seaforth Highlanders, serving from 2nd August 1918 to 29th January 1923.

He rose through the ranks, attaining the rank of Chief Superintendent in command at Bolton, Wigan and Leigh. He died whilst still serving on 19th March 1957.

During his career, he was commended and complimented a number of times and had been awarded the Merit Badge.

(See image of P.C. Braithwaite and P.C. Wooff at Buckingham Palace on 4th March 1930 receiving the King's Police Medal later within this section.)

16th June 1929

Albert Edward FOX, Constable 1131   **Lancashire Constabulary**

British Empire Medal (Civil Division)

At about 1.15p.m. on June 16th 1929, Fox was on point duty at the White Church, Ansdell, when he saw the Police motor cycle combination with Inspector Dewhurst and Constable Wooff race towards the Promenade and stop there.

Fox followed at once and was informed by the Inspector that a woman had been seen running along the edge of the channel in the estuary of the Ribble.

He set off over the sands and very treacherous mud and struggled on until he got within about 8 yards of the water's edge, he saw a woman lying on the mud bank, and Wooff wading towards her, a few seconds later he reached them both, and subsequently he, Inspector Dewhurst and Wooff removed the woman through the sand and mud to the hard ground on the Promenade. The poor creature who was afterwards found to be insane, added greatly to their difficulty by struggling violently. On this occasion, Constable Wooff was awarded that coveted decoration The King's Police and Fire Services Medal for gallantry [sic].

The action taken by Fox was exceedingly gallant, the estuary of the Ribble is known to be most dangerous and to abound in quicksand, but this did not deter him in the least and he thoroughly deserved the award which was granted.

Lancashire Constabulary award file – PLA/ACC6849

L.G. 31/12/1929 Issue 33566 Page 12

FURTHER INFORMATION:

(See previous entry for P.C. Wooff, also involved and additional information about the incident.)

Albert Edward Fox was born at Alston, Lancashire and was appointed to Lancashire Constabulary on 7th March 1912. He served at Blackburn, Rochdale, Prescot and Kirkham Divisions. Following the incident in June 1929 he was awarded the Merit Badge and awarded £5.

Albert Edward Fox retired in March 1937. In June 1937, he was appointed to the First Police Reserve briefly and again in 1938.

He died in November 1951.

20th August 1929

Thomas BRAITHWAITE, Constable 122   **Lancashire Constabulary**

King's Police Medal

At about 10.20p.m. on August 20th 1929 Constable Braithwaite was told that five boys whose ages ranged from eight to eleven years, from Sykeside, Haslingden, had been missing from their homes since about 1p.m. the same day and that they were believed to be in some old drifts in Pike Law Quarry, Haslingden, the boys having been heard to state their intention of exploring the workings.

During the afternoon and evening the boys' parents had searched the workings but without success. Braithwaite immediately went to the quarry, searched one drift thoroughly without finding the children; he was told that the other two drifts had already been searched but in company with John Paton and Joseph Holden, civilians, decided to look again.

After going through one drift for about 200 yards they came to a place where there had been an extensive fall from the roof, leaving a hole of about 2 feet in diameter through which Braithwaite and his companions crawled.

They went on along a low passage dripping with moisture and in a very foul atmosphere for a distance of over half a mile, calling out and flashing a torch when they discovered the boys huddled together on a heap of shale. The children were all brought out to safety at about 12.45a.m. on August 21st and turned over to their parents.

It was a very dark wet night and it is difficult to give sufficient praise to Braithwaite, evidently the leader of the rescue party for his perseverance and high courage in forcing a way through the hole along a dangerous low passage in foul air and in great peril from falling stones.

The five children undoubtedly owed their lives to Braithwaite and his brave companions.

Lancashire Constabulary award file – PLA/ACC6849   L.G. 31/12/1929 Issue 33566 Page 12

FURTHER INFORMATION:

The five children were Vincent Butler (11) and his brother Terence (8), Charles Fulshaw (11), Walter Metcalf (9) and another boy. George Schofield. They went to explore the 'caves' at the disused quarry at Pike Law. The holes or tunnels had long been a play place for generations of boys in the area.

The boys entered the tunnels at about 1.30p.m., equipped with some candles and matches. George Schofield went only a short distance into the tunnels before turning around and making his way out without difficulty.

Charles Fulshaw did not return for his tea at 7p.m. and feeling uneasy Mrs Fulshaw went to search for him and met Mr Brown, also searching for his son. Another younger boy, who the group had refused to take with them, told the parents where the children had gone to. A search was begun at the quarry by men who knew the tunnels and other places without success. At 10p.m. the police were informed.

Constable Braithwaite and his two companions, John Paton and Joseph Holden, entered the tunnel and found the collapse with the small hole through which Braithwaite crawled. Hearing a boy's voice, he continued and after about 12 minutes he found the boys and brought them out.

P.C. Braithwaite (left) and P.C. Wooff at Buckingham Palace on 4th March 1930 to receive the King's Police Medal – note Merit Badges to right sleeves.

The boys had crawled through the hole but as Fulshaw passed through behind the others a fall of earth partially blocked the hole and a stone fell on his foot, severely injuring him. On the far side of the hole the foul air in the tunnel put the candles out and they could not be relit. In the darkness they could not find their way out and after walking for some time due to the foul air they fell asleep.

It was only later that one of the boys awoke and saw the light from the constable's lamp and by shouting they guided him to where they were. Due to the foul air it was stated it was unlikely the children would have survived until the morning. (*The Rossendale Free Press*, 24/8/1929)

Thomas Braithwaite was born at Cleator Moor, Cumberland, in 1899.

He was appointed to Lancashire Constabulary on 1st February 1922, stating his previous occupation as being an iron ore miner, resident at Cleator Moor. Thomas Braithwaite had also served with the Loyal North Lancashire Regiment during the Great War.

In addition to the King's Police Medal and Lancashire Constabulary Merit Badge, he was also awarded a Certificate of Honour by The Order of St. John of Jerusalem in 1929.

He served until 18th November 1947, having reached the rank of Sergeant. Thomas Braithwaite died on 23rd November 1960 and was living at Feniscowles near Blackburn.

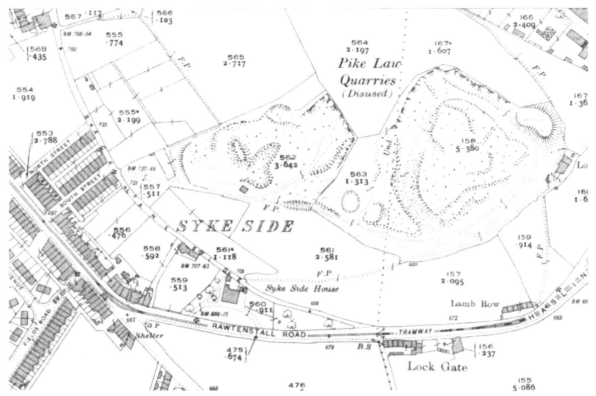

Ordnance Survey - Lancashire LXXI.16 (Haslingden; Rawtenstall) – Published 1929.

16th July 1931

William Alexander MARR, Constable   **Oldham Borough Police**

King's Police Medal

Shortly after midnight on 16th July 1931, P.C. Marr, on plain clothes duty, was checking property in Waterloo Street, Oldham. On looking over the backyard gate of a grocer's shop, the officer noticed that the rear window was partly open.

Almost immediately he also heard a noise coming from inside the shop. As he climbed quietly through the open window, P.C. Marr armed himself with an iron case-opener he found lying beneath the window sill. He made his way through to the small back room into the shop itself, and there, by the light of his torch, saw a man backing away from him in the direction of the shop door.

The man had a soft felt hat pulled down low over his forehead and the lower half of his face was concealed by a handkerchief mask. And in one hand the intruder was pointing a revolver straight at P.C. Marr. When he was asked what he was doing in the shop the man said, *'Stand where you are'*. But the officer moved towards him and, as he was later to say in court, *'As soon as I moved he fired the revolver. I saw the flash and heard the explosion. I did not feel the bullet.'*

The constable immediately threw the case-opener he had picked up a few seconds earlier and hit the man on the chest, at the same time rushing forward and wresting the revolver from the man's right hand. Almost in the same instant he was struck a violent blow on the head with an iron bar the man was holding in his other hand. P.C. Marr briefly lost consciousness, but before his assailant could escape he closed with him again. The man swung the iron bar once more. This time he missed the officer and, instead, smashed the shop's side window.

Then he began raining vicious blows on the policeman's arms. More blows to his head again momentarily stunned the officer, his attacker broke loose and made his escape. P.C. Marr gave chase along Hardy Street and Brompton Street and at the junction of Bismarck Street succeeded in catching the fugitive.

Reaction to this was a further attempt by the shop-breaker to escape. P.C. Marr responded by taking from his pocket the revolver he had earlier wrested from the man and hitting him over the head with it. The man then said he would go quietly with the officer, but as the pair turned out of Bismarck Street into Park Road, enroute for Glodwick Road and the nearest fire alarm box, the man broke away. After a chase of about 20 yards P.C. Marr again caught the man, but immediately was stabbed eight times in his left arm by a spring clasp-knife the man took from a haversack he was carrying.

The officer's cries for help were answered by an Oldham Corporation night watchman, Mr. Harry Kipling, of Manchester Street, who had been on duty in Hardy Street. Mr. Kipling had a crippled arm, but he and the police officer succeeded in getting the arrested man to the top of Glodwick Road, even though P.C. Marr was by now bleeding copiously from his head and arm wounds.

At Glodwick the arrested man made yet another bid to escape, but once more he was caught before he had got very far. And this time more help was readily to hand. Three men attracted by the noise of the running battle, sat on the arrested man until police help arrived.

By this time both P.C. Marr and his prisoner were unconscious, the officer suffering from severe head and arm injuries and loss of blood and the prisoner from facial and head wounds and a broken hand. Other police officers found the revolver which had been fired at P.C. Marr. All but one of its chambers were still loaded. The revolver had originally been manufactured to fire blank cartridges but had been made into a lethal weapon by the re-boring of the barrel and the chambers

On November 20th 1931 at Manchester Assizes the shop-breaker having pleaded guilty to wounding with intent to do grievous bodily harm, and guilty to shop-breaking was sentenced to four years penal servitude. The Judge called P.C. Marr into the witness box and publicly commended him for the service he had done to Public Justice.

P.C. Marr in addition to the award of the King's Police Medal was awarded the Oldham Watch Committee's Merit Badge.

FURTHER INFORMATION:

The shop-breaker disturbed by P.C. Marr was John Dakin, aged 24 years. Dakin was a chemist's assistant of 15, Brook Lane, Oldham.

William Alexander Marr was a native of Oldham and joined Oldham Borough Police in 1928. He was attached to the CID for most of his service. He retired from the police service in October 1958, having attained the rank of Inspector. He died suddenly, aged 67 years, in 1973.

Edith Marr, his widow, presented his medals to the head of Oldham Police in 1974. Presenting the medals, she said, *'It was his last wish that the medal should be returned to the force on his death'.*

His medals, the revolver and the knife used in the attack are displayed at the Greater Manchester Police Museum at Newton Street, Manchester.

L.G. 30/12/1932 Issue 33898 Page 14

24th May 1932

Herbert HAYES, Constable 180	**Lancashire Constabulary**

King's Police Medal

Eric Watt BONAR, Flight-Sergeant **Chief Pilot**	**R.A.F. Reserve** **Northern Air Transport Ltd.**

British Empire Medal (Civil Division) for Gallantry (exchanged for George Cross)

At 2.35p.m. on May 24th, 1932, Constable Hayes was on motor patrol duty near Barton Airport, near Manchester, when he saw an R.A.F. two-seater aeroplane crash and burst into flames in a field about 400 yards from the airport hangar.

He immediately made his way to the crashed aircraft from which flames were rising to a height of about 30 feet. A Flight Sergeant named J. Treadwell, was strapped in the rear cockpit and surrounded by flames with his clothes on fire.

Hayes fully realised the danger of an explosion of the petrol tank, got onto the blazing aircraft and commenced to unfasten the straps securing Treadwell, preparatory to lifting him from the cockpit.

The Deputy Manager of the Airport, Mr. E. Bonar, then arrived with an asbestos blanket, together with several members of the general staff of the airport who played on Bonnar and Hayes with Snowfire chemical extinguishers and so helped them to get Treadwell out of the aircraft. There was another man in the front cockpit but owing to his position and the extreme heat all round him it was impossible to do anything for him. Hayes was burnt on the right side of his face and the back of his right hand and his uniform clothing was ruined by fire.

Both Bonar and Hayes were awarded the Bronze Medal of The Society for the Protection of Life from Fire. Sergeant Treadwell unfortunately did not survive his injuries and died on June 10th 1932.

This supreme act of courage and rapid decision entirely deserved the award of the King's Police Medal for Gallantry which was subsequently made to Hayes.

Lancashire Constabulary award file – PLA/ACC6849   L.G. 30/12/1932 Issue 33898 Page 14

Awarded 'William Garnett' Cup.

Eric Watt Bonar

'For an act of conspicuous courage in rescuing the pilot of a burning aeroplane of the Royal Air Force at Barton in May last. Under the protection of an asbestos blanket he unfastened the straps binding the pilot, released him from his parachute harness, and with assistance dragged him from the burning wreckage. He gave first aid to the airman, who was then conveyed to hospital but died about a fortnight later.'

L.G. 5/8/1932 Issue 33852 Page 5055

FURTHER INFORMATION:

The aircraft involved in the crash was an R.A.F. Armstrong Whitworth Siskin DC. This was a two-seat biplane training aircraft. It had taken off from No. 5 F.T.S. (Flying Training School), R.A.F. Sealand, near to Queensferry in Flintshire. The two occupants, instructor Flight Sergeant 341550 Jack Treadwell (29) and his pupil, Leading Aircraftsman 560860 William Patrick Lane (22) both lost their lives. Treadwell was an experienced pilot and had been flying for about 7½ years, four of which was as an R.A.F. Instructor.

R.A.F. Sealand was operational from 1916 to 2006 when the last R.A.F. units moved out. Part of the site is now used as a civilian MoD site and other parts of the site are planned for redevelopment.

Single seat Armstrong-Whitworth Siskin IIIa in R.A.F. service. (Public domain)

Herbert Hayes was born at Preston, Lancashire, in 1901. He was appointed to Lancashire Constabulary on 17th October 1921, stating his previous occupation to have been an engineer and was residing in Preston. For his actions on 24th May 1932 he was awarded the Merit Badge.

He served in a number of divisions and was promoted to Sergeant in 1937. He retired from Seaforth Division on 1st February 1955 and died on 15th September 1961 and at that time was residing in Ormskirk.

At the inquest on Leading Aircraftsman Lane, Police Constable Hayes stated that he was at the airport and saw the plane approach from the west.

The plane appeared to descend, rise in the air, and crash. *'I drove my motorcycle over the aerodrome, climbed the boundary fence, and saw flames rushing up from the plane. I ran to get the airmen out and was burned on the face. The airport fire engine then arrived, and I helped Mr. Bonnar to get Treadwell out.'*

The jury returned a verdict of accidental death and commended both Constable Hayes and Mr Bonar for their bravery.

Eric Watt 'Jock' Bonar, the Chief Instructor of the flying school of Northern Airlines at Barton Airport, was awarded the Empire Gallantry Medal for his actions that day. Following the introduction of the George Cross 8 years later, Bonar's medal was exchanged for the George Cross.

Bonar was born on 22nd September 1899 in Edinburgh, Scotland. He joined the

2/7th Cameronians (Scottish Rifles) in the British Army underage in February 1915. Prior to being posted to Gallipoli his true age was discovered and he was discharged, returning to his apprenticeship as a motor engineer.

After completing his apprenticeship, he joined the Royal Navy, serving with the Motor Boat Reserve and with the Dover Patrol and was later involved with mine clearance operations in the North Sea. On discharge in 1919 he went into business in Glasgow but in 1922 he joined the R.A.F. as a fitter and was later trained as a Pilot, then as an Instructor, being stationed at R.A.F. Sealand from 1926 to 1929.

He left the R.A.F., taking up civilian flying from 1929 to 1936, working as a pleasure flight pilot at Blackpool and as a stunt pilot with a flying circus. He also lived in the U.S.A. for two years and was involved in air racing. Bonar remained as a R.A.F. reserve pilot. In 1937, he became a Test Pilot with Rolls Royce, being involved with the development of the Merlin engine used in the Spitfire, and Chief Test Pilot with D. Napier & Sons, manufacturers of the Sabre aero engines used in the Typhoon and Tempest aircraft. After the war he became a freelance charter pilot and set up his own aviation business at Croydon before giving up flying in 1951.

He died on 26th February 1991, at Richmond, Surrey.

Bonar's recollections were recorded by the Imperial War Museum in 1980. He recalled the incident at Barton Airport and the crash. Bonar had maintained his contacts with R.A.F. Sealand, being invited to mess functions and knew many of the staff there. Barton Airport was regularly used in training for cross country flying instruction and training aircraft from Sealand regularly landed there.

Sgt. Jack Treadwell was nearing the end of his R.A.F. service and had been offered a job as a Flying Instructor by Bonar at Barton Airport. Bonar described the Siskin as flying over at a low altitude and commencing a slow roll before stalling and crashing to the ground. He described the rescue with P.C. Hayes.[25]

8th May 1933

Walter HESKETH, Constable   **Manchester City Police**

King's Police Medal for Gallantry

On a very dark night Constable Hesketh was cycling home from duty when he heard screams coming from the direction of the canal. He went there and saw a man struggling in the water.

The Constable threw off his helmet and tunic, and jumped in, and managed to get hold of the man, and keep him afloat, until the arrival of two other Constables, who threw a rope to him, which he tied round the man. The Constables then started to pull the man up the bank, but half way up the rope broke, and he fell back on top of Constable Hesketh.

After a struggle, Constable Hesketh managed to control the man, who was again tied to the rope, and then both were pulled about 50 yards along the canal to the lock gates where they were easily pulled out and taken to hospital.

PRO Ref: H045/19479   L.G. 29/12/1933 Issue 34010 Page 15

---

[25] IWM Sound collection 4687 – Recorded 2/9/1980.

FURTHER INFORMATION:

Incident location – Rochdale Canal between Minshull Street and Chorlton Street, Manchester.

Hearing shouts from a man and woman about a man being in the canal, P.C. Hesketh discarded his helmet and entered the canal, seizing the man and clung to the bank with one hand and with the other the struggling man.

Those who had raised the alert immediately ran for a rope kept at the lock keeper's lodge and attempted to drag them out, but the rope broke. Constable Riley by now had arrived and, instead of trying to drag them out, towed them to a lock near Chorlton Street, where he was able to help them out.

The rescued man was Robert Heaton of Russell Street who revived quickly. (*The Manchester Guardian*, 9/5/1933)

Walter Hesketh was born in Manchester and was appointed to Manchester City Police on 2nd February 1927, aged 20 years. His previous occupation was as a telephone operator. He was pensioned on 15th September 1953.

27th October 1933	
Arnold YATES, Constable	**Manchester City Police**
King's Police Medal for Gallantry	

At about 4.20p.m. on 27th October 1933, a man named Neszukaitis was seen to mount the parapet of a wall alongside the River Irwell in Manchester and jump into the River.

Constable Yates, climbed over the parapet, and descended some steps to the water, and then plunged in. He swam after the man and succeeded in getting hold of him. The Constable then pulled the man back towards the shore, aiming for Victoria Bridge some 50 yards away.

Another Constable had obtained some rope, and fastened one end to the parapet, lowering the other to the water, where Constable Yates tried to tie it round Neszukaitis, but he lost his grip on the man who slipped under the water. With much difficulty, the Constable grabbed the man again, and got the rope round him, and he was hauled up to safety. During all this time, the man had been unconscious, and unable to give any assistance to Constable Yates.

PRO Ref: H045 /19479

L.G. 29/12/1933 Issue 34010 Page 15

FURTHER INFORMATION:

The location of this incident was at the same place where Constable Jewes lost his life in June 1933. The rescued man was Jonas Neszukaitis, a Russian Jew.

Both Neszukaitis and P.C. Yates were taken to the Roby Street accident ward. P.C. Yates was sent home after treatment and Neszukaitis was later sent to the Crumpsall Institution in a critical condition. When interviewed later, P.C. Yates said, '*It's merely part of a policeman's job. Any of the fellows would have gone in*'. (*Lancashire Daily Post*, 28/10/1933)

Arnold Yates was born in Sale, Cheshire and joined Manchester City Police on 2nd December 1931, aged 20 years. His previous occupation was as a clerk telegraphist. He rose through the ranks, retiring on pension as a Chief Superintendent on 31st March 1962 and died in 1990.

The officer assisting was Constable Bennett who was awarded the Watch Committee's Medal for Bravery.

6th March 1934

Arthur James SKELLERN, Constable   **Liverpool City Police**

King's Police Medal for Gallantry

At 9.40p.m. on 6th March 1934, Constable Skellern was at the Ferry Goods Stage, Liverpool, when he saw an unconscious woman floating about 15 ft. out from the stage in the river.

He took off his greatcoat and dived into the icy water to support her. Sidney Sherlock a van boy aged 19 years also jumped into the water and assisted the Constable.

Together they supported the woman and drifted down to the landing stage, where a small boat was put out from the ferry, and the woman and the boy were taken on board. Constable Skellern swam to the stage and was pulled out of the water. All three were taken to hospital.

There was a strong flood tide running at the time, and it was dark, and all three were in danger of being swept under the pontoons supporting the landing stage.

Constable Skellern and Sidney Sherlock were both awarded a Silver Medal by The Liverpool Shipwreck and Humane Society.

PRO Ref: H045/19488   L.G. 1/1/1935 Issue 34119 Page 17

FURTHER INFORMATION:

Arthur James Skellern was born in Congleton, Cheshire, in 1899. His previous occupation was as a warehouseman and soldier. During the Great War he served with the Royal Welsh Fusiliers from 16th March 1917 to 19th September 1919, reaching the rank of Lance Corporal. During his police career he was commended on three occasions by the Watch Committee.

He was pensioned on 27th February 1954, having reached the maximum age limit for police service and died, aged 66 years, in 1965.

10th September 1934

Edward HALLIDAY, Constable 382   **Lancashire Constabulary**

Richard ROBINSON, Constable 1950   **Lancashire Constabulary**

King's Police Medal for Gallantry

At 2.30p.m. on 10th September 1934, a *'smash and grab'* raid took place on a pawnbroker's shop in Liverpool by three men who escaped in a fast car subsequently found to have been stolen.

At 4.20p.m. information was received at Hurst Brook[26] Police Station that the wanted car had passed

---

[26] Situated just outside Ashton-under-Lyne.

through a town about three miles away at 4.10p.m. Halliday and Robinson immediately set off in an 8 H.P. M.G. Midget 2 seater.

By intelligently anticipating the route likely to be taken they were able to find out from a Cheshire policeman that the car which they were after had passed along the Sheffield road about five minutes before travelling at a very high speed and it was known that the car was a Chrysler.

The car was sighted afterwards and after a series of attempts to wreck the Police car, which was very much smaller and lighter than the Chrysler, during which an attempt was made to injure Robinson with a pick shaft. Halliday was at last able to get ahead of the other car, where after he took a serious risk by pulling up and applying his brakes. The Chrysler swerved, and after striking a wall on the nearside was thrown across to the offside of the road. Three men jumped out, climbed over a wall and ran across the moors.

Halliday and Robinson gave chase, and soon overtook two of the men, one of whom, still armed with the pick shaft, raised it in a threatening manner, while the other put his hand in his pocket as though grasping a firearm. In spite of threats that they would be killed if they advanced any further, Halliday and Robinson did not hesitate in the least, and secured both the criminals. In the meantime, the third man had gone on some way and Robinson went after him, after having been warned by one of the prisoners that the man was armed.

MG Midget type L roadsters at Lancaster Castle c.1934.

Halliday took the two men back to the road where some men of the Cheshire Constabulary and some civilians had arrived. Halliday and a Cheshire Detective Officer then went off in the Police car to intercept the third criminal, after proceeding about five miles, they got out and went over the moors for about a mile, when they saw Robinson still in pursuit. Halliday taking off part of his uniform, gave chase and eventually caught the third and last man, and all the criminals were taken to Dukinfield Police Station. The actual arrest took place on the moors near Woodhead in Cheshire.

Two of the prisoners were wanted for other crimes, and were described as desperate and dangerous criminals, the third was a convict on licence, and all three might be expected to resist arrest with extreme violence.

Halliday and Robinson were fully alive to the fact that they were risking their lives during the repeated attempts to pass the wanted car at speeds of about 60 miles per hour, and all through the chase and capture, showed courage and determination of the highest order.

At the conclusion of the trial of the criminals, Mr. Justice Lawrence said these words to the Jury, *'I think that the County of Lancashire should be proud to have two such officers, who showed such courage and determination in effecting the arrest of such desperate criminals and I am going to communicate with the Chief Constable.'*

Lancashire Constabulary award file – PLA/ACC6849   L.G. 1/1/1935 Issue 34119 Page 17

FURTHER INFORMATION:

The shop raided was the pawnbroker's shop of Messrs. E. Pryor and Son, 110 London Road, Liverpool. These premises are still in use today as a pawnbrokers and jewellers business, now operated by Christopher Brown Jewellers.

On 29th October 1934, sentences were imposed by Mr Justice Lawrence at Liverpool Assizes on the three offenders.

For attempting to break and enter a jeweller's shop in London Road, Liverpool and for stealing two cars, Alexander Howard Jackson (28), a mechanic of London, was sentenced to five years penal servitude; Edwin Melville Jackson (44), of San Francisco, was sentenced to three years penal servitude; and Frederick William Thomas Bungay (22), motor driver from London, was sentenced to twelve months imprisonment.

At the trial it was revealed that Alexander Jackson, whose real name was Stanley George Brown, was from Crouch End, London and had served three years penal servitude for a smash and grab raid and when arrested for that offence he had attacked a police officer with a razor.

Edwin Melville Jackson was from San Francisco and had served three years imprisonment for a train robbery.

Bungay was also from Crouch End where his wildness and love for motor cars led to him being a ringleader of a gang of hooligans despite being the youngest member of the gang.

Jointly awarded 'William Garnett' Cup.

Edward Halliday was born at Blackburn, Lancashire, in September 1903. He was appointed to Lancashire Constabulary on 8th June 1925, stating his previous occupation as being a weaver.

He reached the rank of Sergeant and in 1939 was living in Widnes. In 1947 he was serving with the Army Control Office in Germany. He died, aged 73 years, in 1976.

Edward Halliday

Richard Robinson

Richard Robinson was born at Aspull near Wigan, Lancashire, in August 1908. He was appointed to Lancashire Constabulary on 29th June 1929. His previous occupation is shown as being a clerk. In addition to the King's Police Medal he was awarded the Merit Badge and £10 for his actions on 10th September 1934.

During his career he was complimented and commended on a number of occasions. In 1948 he was promoted to Detective Sergeant, Detective Inspector in 1960 and Uniform Chief Inspector in 1956.

He served until 7th August 1963, retiring as Chief Inspector 2 i/c at Rochdale Division. He died in October 1986.

8th August 1935

Walter GITTINGS, Constable   **Liverpool City Police**

King's Police Medal for Gallantry

At 1.25a.m. on 8th August 1935, Constable Gittings saw a man walk out of a shop doorway and walk quickly down steps leading to the canal.

He quickly checked the shop which appeared alright, and then followed the man down the steps. At the canal, the officer could find no trace of the man. He flashed his lamp up and down, and then onto the water, where he saw a man's face underwater, near the bridge. He immediately took off his jacket and helmet, and went into the canal, which at this place is about seven feet deep, with thick mud at the bottom.

The constable swam about for some time, making several dives to try and find the man, without success. He was getting exhausted, and after a short rest continued the search underwater, until he had to give up. He had become totally exhausted and had to be assisted from the water by other officers called to the scene.

The man's body was later recovered.

PRO Ref: H045/19490   L.G. 1/1/1936 Issue 34238 Page 17

FURTHER INFORMATION:

Location of incident – Leeds and Liverpool Canal, Liverpool.

The man who drowned in the canal was Patrick Donnelly (aged 58 years), a dock labourer of Blenheim Street, Liverpool.

At the inquest held on 9th August 1935 it was revealed that P.C. Gittings was rescued from the canal by John Regan a general labourer. Mr Donnelly's body was brought out of the canal by Alfred Roach, Arlington Street, Liverpool, who dived in at the spot indicated by P.C. Gittings.

The Coroner, returning a verdict of death by drowning with insufficient evidence to show how Donnelly got into the water, expressed warm appreciation of the repeated efforts of Police Constable Gittings to rescue the man.

Walter Gittings was born in 1913 and served for 30 years with Liverpool City Police. He retired as a Chief Inspector in 1964 and died, aged 89 years, in 2002.

16th November 1935

John TIERNAN, Police Constable   **Liverpool City Police**

King's Police Medal for Gallantry

Shortly after 11p.m. on Saturday 16th November 1935, Constable Tiernan was at the South East Gate of the Salthouse Dock, when he saw a woman with her husband and another man walking along the road.

Suddenly the woman ducked underneath the guard chains and threw herself into the dock. The two men went to the edge of the quay, and Constable Tiernan ran to the spot where the woman was thrashing

about in the water. He threw her a lifebelt, which she failed to get hold of, and then he took off his greatcoat and helmet, and dived 15 ft. down into the water, which is 17 ft. deep. He grabbed the woman who was struggling violently, and at one point she pulled him under the water.

Two lifebelts were thrown into the water by one of the men, one of which hit the Constable, causing him severe distress. He then put the woman into one belt, and she was pulled up the side of the dock by the others. However, the rope broke, and she fell back on top of the Constable, nearly drowning him.

After two further attempts she was eventually pulled clear, and Constable Tiernan was assisted from the water by other officers who had by this time arrived.

PRO Ref: H045/19490   L.G. 1/1/1936 Issue 34238 Page 17

FURTHER INFORMATION:

The rescued woman was Sarah McCoy, aged 27 years, of Upper Mann Street, Liverpool, who was detained at hospital.

Constable Harrington also entered the water to assist and was rescued from the water by dock gateman John Rivers, who took to the water in a small boat. Both officers were taken to hospital but were not detained.

John Tiernan was born in 1889 and served with Liverpool City Police, retiring after 30 years' service in 1949. He died, aged 83 years, in 1972.

23rd December 1935

William Anderson CROMPTON, Constable 98   **Salford City Police**

King's Police Medal for Gallantry

At 2.15p.m. on 23rd December 1935, a densely foggy night with patches of ice on the roads, Constable Crompton was on duty in Great Cheetham Street, when he heard the sound of a galloping horse approaching.

The Constable could not see anything until the runaway horse and lorry suddenly loomed at him from out of the fog. The Constable leapt at the passing lorry and scrambled on board.

He took up the reins and tried to halt the animal which was careering down an incline. As it did so it collided with a cart carrying carboys of hydrochloric acid, smashing three of them and showering both the Constables and the horse with acid. Despite his efforts, the Constable could not hold the animal, but managed to steer it past several other vehicles before it came to a stop. Both the Constable and the horse were treated for acid burns.

PRO Ref: H045/19498

L.G. 29/1/1937 Issue 34365 Page 704

FURTHER INFORMATION:

An award of £5 was made by the Salford Watch Committee to Constable Crompton for his bravery in exposing himself to danger and preventing what might have been a serious accident.

William Anderson Crompton was born in Manchester in December 1903 and joined Salford Police on 22nd June 1925. His previous occupation was as a clerk. He had also served in the Grenadier Guards from 4th March 1922 to 3rd March 1925. He was later commended by the Chief Constable in 1939 and 1945 for efficiency and alertness for arrests. He died in 1985.

5th January 1936

James Trott BELL, Constable 1975   **Lancashire Constabulary**

King's Police Medal for Gallantry

At 1a.m. on January 5th, 1936, Constable Bell was patrolling Castle Road, Colne, on his bicycle. This is a lonely road which leads to St. Andrew's Golf Club.

As he approached a house called White Gables, Bell heard a dog barking, got off his bicycle and went on foot towards the house. Here he met two men whom he recognised as Francis Henry Mount, aged 27 years, and Tom Parker, aged 32 years, both men with a very bad criminal record. Bell immediately went up to the two men and asked them what they were doing there. They replied that they were going for a walk in the country.

Bell then told them that he would take them into custody on a charge of loitering with intent to commit a felony, and, on searching Parker he found a flashlamp and a cobbler's knife in his pockets. Whilst Bell was searching Parker he was struck a violent blow by Mount, where upon he released his hold on Parker and closed with Mount.

In the struggle, they fell on a wall at the side of the road with Mount underneath, and Mount then shouted to Parker, *'Hit him with a brick'*, and immediately afterwards Bell, who had lost his helmet in the struggle, felt a heavy blow on the top of his head with something very hard.

Subsequently he received several more blows by an object which he later found to be a stone 4lbs. in weight. He became semi-conscious, and whilst he was lying in the road he felt a severe blow on the face and heard the words *'take that'*. The two men afterwards pulled Bell over the wall into a field and left him there.

Lancashire Constabulary award file – PLA/ACC6849   L.G. 29/1/1937 Issue 34365 Page 703

Awarded 'William Garnett' Cup.

FURTHER INFORMATION:

Giving evidence at the hearing at Colne Police Court on 16th January 1936, P.C. Bell stated that he was on bicycle patrol near White Gables on Castle Road, Colne, when he heard a dog barking furiously at Brown Hill Cottages and went to investigate. This was where he encountered Mount and Parker and the assault took place and he was pulled over the wall into a field. Once he came around he managed to stagger to Lob Common Farm where Mr Alfred Pollard, the farmer, assisted him. Both Mount and Parker were committed by the court to the Lancaster Assizes.

On 20th January 1936, at Lancaster Assizes, Francis Henry Mount (27) of Kensington Street, Nelson and Tom Parker (32) were sentenced by Mr Justice Swift to three years penal servitude for wounding Constable Bell with intent to do him grievous bodily harm. Mr Justice Swift said to the Constable, *'According to everything I have heard you are a brave man determined to do your duty'*.

On 24th May 1937, P.C. Bell was awarded the William Garnett Cup at Lancaster Castle by Lord Cozens-Hardy, Chairman of the County Standing Joint Committee.

Brown Hill Cottages (Row) still exist. However, Lob Common Farm is now the site of Park High School, surrounded by modern housing on the southerly side of Castle Road.

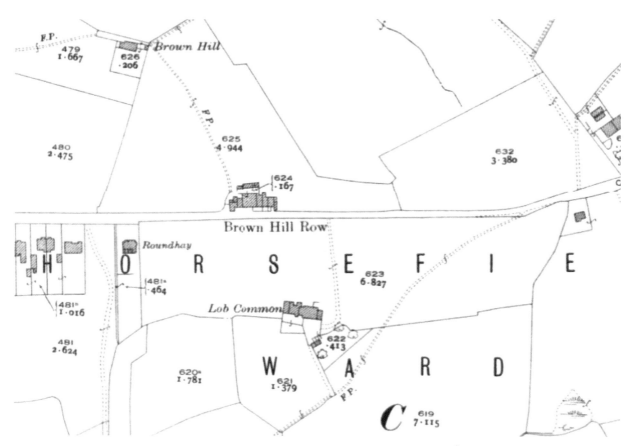

Ordnance Survey - Lancashire XLIX.13 (Colne; Foulridge; Trawden) Published 1932.

James Trott Bell was born at North Bedburn, Durham, in March 1909. He was appointed to Lancashire Constabulary on 13th July 1931, stating his previous occupation as being a labourer. At the time of the incident he was stationed at Trawden. He served until 14th July 1961, retiring as a Sergeant and died, aged 84 years, in 1993.

At about 10.40a.m. on 2nd February 1937, a fire was discovered in the engine room at the Golborne Colliery,[27] and two of the company's employees – Herbert Smith, a blacksmith and Thomas Rigby, a colliery browman, were instructed by the surface engineer to go up to the top platform of the head gear to clamp the two steel wire winding cables as a precaution against the cage falling to the bottom of the shaft in the event of the cable being damaged by fire.

The two men were engaged in this task, when the worst happened, and one of the cables snapped. One of the broken ends, thrashing about the platform, wound itself round Rigby's body, lacerating the flesh of his buttocks, tearing open his stomach and severing his right foot, Smith was uninjured, but was overcome by shock and came down, leaving Rigby up on the platform, from which the guard rails had been torn away.

Constable Dobson, who was on duty in Golborne Village, first heard of the fire at 10.45a.m. and immediately went to the Colliery on his bicycle. When he arrived, he saw about 50 workmen standing round looking up at the head gear, but no one appeared to have made any effort to go up.

Dobson was told that a man was lying severely injured on the top platform, which was at a height of 85 feet from the ground, the last 50 feet of which had to be ascended by a perpendicular 'cat ladder' covered with grease and oil.

Without any hesitation, and indifferent to the clamour around him, Dobson climbed up, and at very great personal risk to himself, got on to the platform, now covered with blood, grease and oil with nothing to get hold of, since all the guard rails had been torn away.

He found Rigby in terrible pain, and did what he could for him, by removing a bit of wood from under him, tying his legs together with a triangular bandage, removing his false teeth and comforting the unfortunate man as much as possible under the circumstances.

All this was done on a very slippery platform at a height of 85 feet from the ground, with nothing to guard against a false step or slip of any sort. There was also a danger that the second wire might break in the same manner as the first, but Dobson completely ignored this danger. He remained with Rigby until the arrival of the Wigan Fire Brigade, when the terribly injured man was lowered to the ground by means of 'Davey' Life Line apparatus. Rigby was taken to the Wigan Infirmary, but died as a result of his injuries.

The above description speaks for itself, nobody else dared to go up, Dobson was fully warned of the extreme danger of doing so, but, upholding the very highest traditions of the Police Service, in the sight of the crowd of excited men, he insisted on carrying out what he considered to be his duty in spite of all the dangers and difficulties.

The prestige of the Lancashire Constabulary must surely never have been higher than on this occasion, and Dobson entirely merited the award which was subsequently made to him.

Lancashire Constabulary award file – PLA/ACC6849   L.G. 1/1/1938 Issue 34469 Page 19

Awarded 'William Garnett' Cup.

---

[27] Golborne Colliery remained in operation until 1989. On 18th March 1979, an underground explosion occurred. The blast was caused after a broken ventilation shaft led to a build-up of methane gas, which ignited after an electrical circuit test. Three men were killed instantly, seven more who were rescued died in hospital. Only one man survived the accident. An inquest held in October 1979 returned verdicts of death by misadventure on the victims.

The site is now occupied by Golborne Enterprise Park, an industrial estate.

FURTHER INFORMATION:

Thomas Rigby, a married man, was aged 48 years and lived at Church Street, Golborne. His colleague named elsewhere as Robert Smith was aged 40 years and also lived at Church Street, Golborne. Rigby was treated by Dr Freda Shaw of Golborne.

At the time of the incident 250 colliers were underground but were safely withdrawn through an emergency shaft.

Involved in the rescue was Inspector John Jones of Wigan Fire Brigade, holder of the King's Police Medal and Bar and Medal of the Order of the British Empire. (See other entries for Jones.)

Stanley Dobson was born at Manchester in January 1912. He was appointed to Lancashire Constabulary on 17th December 1934, stating his previous occupation as being a grocer's assistant.

During his career he served at Wigan, Leyland, Seaforth, Kirkham and Garstang Divisions. He served with the Home Office Motor Patrol Scheme[28] from 1937 onwards and was commended on three occasions. He left the police on 1st September 1946 and died on 15th April 1979.

14th August 1937

Robert Arthur SEBBORN, Constable　　　　　　　　　　**Liverpool City Police**

King's Police Medal for Gallantry

On Saturday afternoon, 14th August 1937, Constable Sebborn was on traffic duty at Bull Bridge, junction with Longmoor Lane, when he was informed that a small boy was lying on the main railway track about 100 yards away. He went to the railway embankment and saw the boy, whose neck and wrists were in contact with the live electric rail, through which over 600 volts were passing.

There was a crowd of some 50 people there, but no one had offered to help. The Constable went down onto the railway and took off his tunic and damp rubber traffic coat, which he folded and laid on the ground. He then stood on them, and grasping the boy by the clothing, pulled him clear. Although artificial respiration was immediately applied, the boy was dead on arrival at hospital.

PRO Ref: H045/19507　　　　　　　　　L.G. 1/1/1938 Issue 34469 Page 19

28　The Home Office Experimental Motor Scheme (funded by the government) was set up in seven areas of England (namely Lancashire, Cheshire, Manchester, Liverpool, Salford, Essex and the Metropolitan Police District) in 1938. Its purpose was to augment the personnel available for uniformed police patrols and to advise rather than prosecute motorists and other road users. Its aim was to encourage a higher standard of road use on behalf of all road users, including cyclists and pedestrians. The underlying purpose was to reduce the large number of road deaths and injuries arising from rapidly increasing vehicle numbers.

The patrols earned the name 'courtesy cops'. In Lancashire it was planned to have an additional 1,100 officers and 452 vehicles. In the event, 300 men were added, operating 92 additional vehicles and 50 lightweight motorcycles. An additional 12 men were employed on clerical duties and 19 officers were allocated to the Motor Patrol Training School. In Lancashire the scheme produced a reduction of 44% in the numbers of casualties in the first year. The scheme, however, was terminated by the outbreak of World War 2. (L.A. PLA 18/15)

Location of incident – Orrell Park Station, Liverpool.

The child was Stanley Watson (6 years) of Weightman Grove, Walton. Constable Sebborn was presented with the King's Police Medal at Buckingham Palace on February 15th, 1938.

Robert Arthur Sebborn was born in 1903 at West Derby. He served with Liverpool City Police for 32 years, retiring in 1963. He died in 1977, aged 74 years, at Heidelberg, Victoria, Australia.

27th April 1938

Edwin William Alfred ASHMAN, Constable 327   **Salford City Police**

King's Police Medal for Gallantry

On 27th April 1938, Constable Ashman was on annual leave when he saw a man throw himself from the Palatine Bridge, into the river below.

This particular section of river is very dangerous with high vertical walls, and where a police officer had drowned a few years before. Constable Ashman climbed over the bridge and dropped 25 feet into the water. He then swam to the man and succeeded in lifting him onto a mudbank, which was exposed due to low tide. Ropes were lowered to him, and the man was hauled to safety.

PRO Ref: H045/19519

L.G. 30/12/1938 Issue 34585 Page 21

FURTHER INFORMATION:

The man rescued was Joseph Dearden (56) of Moreton Street, Strangeways, Manchester.

The previous drowning incident would appear to refer to the death of P.C. Thomas Williamson Jewes of Manchester City Police, who drowned in the River Irwell on 16th June 1933.

It is believed that a local ex-boxer, William Burke, staged the rescue of a kitten from a ledge near the Victoria Bridge to then to take a collection from the crowd. After stranding the kitten, Burke went down a rope, caught the kitten and attempted to climb back up, but dropped the kitten. Burke tried again and fell into the river.

P.C. Jewes heard shouting and entered the river. Both men disappeared under the water and were later discovered drowned. The kitten was later rescued alive. The route of the funeral procession was lined by an estimated 20,000 people.

Edwin William Alfred Ashman was born in Salford in February 1912. He joined Salford Police on 23rd January 1933. His previous occupation was as a book keeper. He resigned on 4th March 1946 and died in 1969.

At about 9.20p.m. on the 6th August 1938, a fire broke out at the NORI Brickworks, Altham, Accrington. The portion of the brickworks involved was the kiln together with the adjoining drying shed, which consisted of a large one storey building of brick and wood, the whole of which was covered with wood and felt roof.

The fire had been in progress for about an hour, and the whole building was alight, particularly the roof, which was burning furiously, when it was discovered that Fireman F. Walsh was trapped inside, and in grave danger of being burnt to death.

A civilian named Hewitt made an attempt to rescue the man, but whilst trying to locate him, was injured about the ribs and back by a falling beam, which necessitated his removal to hospital, where he was detained. Inspector Wild who had been on duty at the scene of the fire, heard someone in the drying shed shouting for help. At the greatest peril to himself he entered the fiercely burning building and forced his way towards where he thought the shouts came from.

He had gone about 20 yards and was almost overcome with the flames and intense heat when he saw Walsh lying on the floor near the wall. Mr. Wild managed to get to him, and with the greatest difficulty half carried and half dragged him to safety. Walsh was taken to hospital suffering from shock and burns, and the Inspector sustained burns to his neck and left hand. His cap and tunic were scorched, his trousers were badly burned and ruined, after receiving first-aid treatment Mr. Wild resumed duty.

There is no doubt that the Inspector's promptitude and great courage saved the life of Walsh, and Mr. Wild's magnificent bravery on this occasion has reflected the greatest credit on himself and on the Police Service generally. In addition to the award to the King's Police Medal for Gallantry Inspector Wild also received the Silver Medal of the Society for the Protection of Life from Fire, and thoroughly deserved both of these distinctions.

Lancashire Constabulary award file – PLA/ACC6849   L.G. 30/12/1938 Issue 34585 Page 21

Awarded 'William Garnett' Cup.

FURTHER INFORMATION:

Richard Hewitt and Fireman Fred Walsh of the Accrington Fire Brigade were the injured persons.

Harry Wild was born in 1895 at Manchester. He was appointed as Constable 771 in the Lancashire Constabulary on 2nd June 1921. His previous occupation was as a transformer erector. Harry served for 4 years 210 days with the East Lancashire Regiment during the Great War. He was promoted to Sergeant on 1st February 1935 and to Inspector on 1st October 1937 and served at Seaforth, H.Q., Warrington, Bury, Leyland and Church.

During his career he was awarded the Merit Badge on two occasions and was commended on four occasions

Harry Wild retired on pension after 25 years police service on 2nd June 1946. He died in October 1971.

2nd October 1938

James McMAHON, Constable 1503   **Lancashire Constabulary**

King's Police Medal for Gallantry

At about 4.20p.m. on 2nd October 1938, two men named Boulton and Westhead, boarded a raft on Turner's Flash, Lower Ince and commenced to fish. Turner's Flash is a large expanse of water of about 70 acres, caused by mining subsidence, it has large patches of surface weeds, and the bottom is covered by slimy mud. The depth in most parts is as much as 17 feet.

After the two men had been fishing for some time, a gale suddenly sprang up, accompanied by heavy rain. The men lost their oars and were blown on to a bank of mud and reeds in the centre of the Flash about a quarter of a mile from the shore. At 7.45p.m. hearing that Boulton and Westhead had gone on the Flash and had not returned, a man called Birchmore and several others went to the spot and efforts were made to rescue the two men in the raft but were unsuccessful.

At 9.40p.m. Constable McMahon was informed of the occurrence and went immediately to the scene, where he found a number of men showing lights to the men on the raft, who could not be seen. McMahon obtained several lengths of rope from a nearby colliery and joined them together. He took of his helmet, tunic and boots, hitched one end of the rope round his waist and entered the water. Birchmore who held the rope and paid it out as McMahon walked and swam out, had to wade in some way to allow the rope to reach the raft. McMahon managed to get to the raft, and found both men exhausted and very cold, particularly Westhead.

The rope was tied round Westhead, McMahon told Boulton to hold on with both hands, and shouted to Birchmore to haul in on the rope, he then proceeded to swim alongside both men and helped them to reach shallow water where Birchmore was standing. Birchmore then waded with his rope to the firm ground on the side of the Flash, and, assisted by onlookers, hauled all three men to safety.

The gale and driving rain, the darkness, the treacherous nature of the bottom, the surface weeds, added to the cold, all combined to increase the danger and difficulty of the extremely gallant deed performed by McMahon who, of all those assembled at the spot, alone saw at once what was required, obtained a rope and went out himself into the darkness to rescue the two men.

In addition to the award of the King's Police Medal for Gallantry, so thoroughly earned, McMahon was awarded the Silver Medal of the Liverpool Branch of the Royal Life Saving Society and the Bronze Medal of the Royal Humane Society, for his extremely gallant and determined act, so happily crowned with success.

Lancashire Constabulary award file – PLA/ACC6849 L.G. 2/1/1940 Issue 34765 Page 19

FURTHER INFORMATION:

James McMahon was presented with his medal by the King on 6th February 1940 at Buckingham Palace.

James McMahon was born in June 1913 at Bury, Lancashire. He was appointed to Lancashire Constabulary on 28th March 1935, stating his previous occupation as being a leather cutter.

McMahon was awarded the Merit Badge, the Bronze Medal and Certificate of The Royal Humane Society and the Silver Medal of The Royal Life Saving Society. He had been stationed at Fulwood and Penwortham between 1935 and 1939. He served until 5th June 1960, retiring as a Police Constable. He died, aged 64 years, in 1978.

16th March 1939

Jack JEAVONS, Constable 2190   **Lancashire Constabulary**

King's Police Medal for Gallantry

At about 11.10p.m. on 16th March 1939, Special Constable Battersby was engaged on patrol duty in the neighbourhood of Barton Bridge, Barton, when he slipped off a platform and fell from a height of 12 feet into the Manchester Ship Canal.

Police Constable Jeavons was on Barton Swing Bridge, when he heard a splash, and, on looking into the Canal, saw Battersby struggling in the water. Jeavons immediately took off his helmet, great coat and tunic and dived off the bridge into the Canal, which was about 15 feet below.

He swam to Battersby, caught hold of him and proceeded to tow him across the Canal. A life buoy was thrown to him, which he secured and attached to Battersby, and then swam with him under Barton Bridge. Jeavons was able to get hold of a wire rope about 3 feet to 3 feet 6 inches above the surface of the water, and whilst holding on to Battersby with his legs, drew himself together with the exhausted man until he reached a low pontoon onto which he and Battersby were both helped by other Policemen who had by this time arrived on the scene.

The Manchester Ship Canal at Barton Bridge is 80 feet wide and 27 feet deep, both banks are vertical and concreted, there is also no form of artificial light anywhere near the place of the rescue and wire ropes stretch across the Canal. It was a cold dark night, and Urmston sewage enters the Canal every night at this point at 11p.m.

Jeavons was well aware of the very great risk he was taking from the wires and the dangers just mentioned, but he did not hesitate for a second. There was a man in the water in distress, so with a total disregard for his own life he plunged in, kept his head in the most admirable manner, and undoubtedly saved the life of Battersby.

This extremely gallant act, which so thoroughly deserved the award of the Police Medal, was also recognised by The Royal Humane Society by the presentation of a Testimonial on Vellum.

Lancashire Constabulary award file – PLA/ACC6849   L.G. 2/1/1940 Issue 34765 Page 19

Awarded 'William Garnett' Cup.

FURTHER INFORMATION:

Jack Jeavons was presented with his medal by the King on 6th February 1940 at Buckingham Palace.

Jack Jeavons was born at Rotherham, Yorkshire in April 1911. He was appointed to Lancashire Constabulary on 1st July 1937, his previous occupation being a miner. Jeavons was an Army reservist and, in 1939, he re-joined his old Regiment, reaching the rank of Captain having served with the Coldstream Guards and East Lancashire Regiment.

He returned to Lancashire Constabulary in January 1946. In 1949 he was awarded the R.S.P.C.A. Bronze Medal and highly commended by the Chief Constable for the rescue of a trapped dog. He served until 2nd April 1966, retiring as a Police Constable and died, aged 75 years, in 1986.

25th March 1939

Thomas Smith HARRISON, Police Constable 251 'A'   **Liverpool City Police**

King's Police Medal for Gallantry

On the afternoon of 25th March 1939, Constable Harrison was near St. George's landing stage when he saw a man jump into the river. The Constable ran to the spot, took off his helmet and overcoat, and jumped in.

Swimming against a strong ebb tide, he caught the man, who struggled violently. It was apparent the man was attempting suicide, and the Constable had difficulty restraining him. He pulled the man to a safety chain under the landing stage, where they remained until a small boat was lowered from a passing ferry.

They were in the water for about 15 minutes, and in continual danger of being washed under the pontoons. They were both pulled to safety and taken to hospital, where they recovered.

PRO Ref: H045/19528

L.G. 2/1/1940 Issue 34765 Page 19

FURTHER INFORMATION:

Thomas Smith Harrison was born in September 1903 and joined Liverpool City Police in 1928.

31st March 1939

Francis Edward DODD, Constable 80 'A'   **Liverpool City Police**

King's Police Medal for Gallantry

In the early hours of 31st March 1939, Constable Dodd saw a suspicious looking parcel lying in a recess of a display window of a shop, which was protected by an iron grille, preventing the parcel from being easily removed. The Constable called the night watchman, and he opened the grille from inside the premises. The Constable then picked up the parcel and threw it into the centre of the deserted roadway. It did not explode, so the Constable then put it into a bucket of water. It was later found to contain gelignite and was primed to explode.

That was the third incident involving explosives that night, but the only one which did not cause damage.

PRO Ref: H045/19528   L.G. 2/1/1940 Issue 34765 Page 19

FURTHER INFORMATION:

Two bombs had previously exploded in Bold Street, Liverpool, one of which had been found by Chief Superintendent Hubert Moore of Liverpool CID, who managed to throw the device into the centre of the road before it exploded.

Constable Francis Dodd of 'A' Division noticed a brown paper parcel between the window and the grille of the Owen Owen store in Clayton Square. He summoned the night watchman and had the grille raised.

Opening the parcel, he found it contained a cigarette packet, from which a wire ran to a stick of gelignite. Throwing the bomb into the roadway he got a bucket of water and plunged the bomb into this. It was then removed for examination.

(Also, see later separate award relating to P.C. Edward Crann for other actions relating to the I.R.A. S-Plan campaign.)

Francis Edward DODD was born in 1914 at Liverpool and joined Liverpool City Police in April 1934. His previous occupation was as a telephone operator. He was commended on 24 occasions and was awarded the Merit Badge and £2 in connection with the incident of 31st March 1939. He received multiple merit awards during his career. He was pensioned after 32 years' service in July 1967, having attained the rank of Inspector.

He died, aged 82 years old, in December 1982.

The I.R.A. campaign (S-plan / Sabotage plan) 1939/1940

On 12th January 1939, the Army Council sent an ultimatum to the British Foreign Secretary, Lord Halifax. The communiqué duly informed the British Government of 'The Government of the Irish Republic' intention to go to 'war' and demanded the withdrawal of all British military forces based in Ireland.

Having had no reply from the British Government, the I.R.A. declared war on 15th January 1939. The campaign was designed not to cause casualties, rather to disrupt the infrastructure and power networks in mainland Britain.

The first bomb exploded under an electricity pylon at Alnwick, Northumberland, causing damage but no loss of power. At Crosby, Liverpool, at 5.48a.m. a loud explosion was heard but it was not until the following day the source was found to have been a bomb under an electricity pylon, which despite damage remained upright.

At 6a.m. three bombs exploded in London outside Willesden, Harlesden and Southwark, targeting electricity control rooms and cabling.

Three bombs also exploded in Manchester City Centre at 6a.m. On Newton Street, at the junction with Hilton Street, a bomb placed in an electricity manhole exploded, killing Albert Ross, aged 27 years, a fish porter passing on his way to work.

A Corporation bus passing at the time had all its windows blown out and the driver and sole passenger received minor injuries. Windows in the area were blown out and a heavy iron manhole was blown over the roof of a five-storey building, falling into a warehouse on Lever Street. For five hours, a great flame of burning gas came from the crater.

The other two bombs also exploded in manholes, fortunately without injury. Unexploded bombs were found in Birmingham and at Clarence Dock, Liverpool.

The following day another attempt was made to blow up a pylon at Barton-upon-Irwell and other bombs exploded or were discovered across the country. This resulted in all power stations, gas works, telephone exchanges and radio transmitters being guarded by the police. All ports serving Ireland were closely monitored.

Manchester and Liverpool Police in the following days arrested a number of persons in connection with the explosions. Nationally, 46 persons were arrested, and 33 people were later convicted.

Following the arrests, the I.R.A. redoubled its efforts, sending more volunteers to the mainland and on 4th February bombs exploded in left luggage offices in the London Underground, seriously injuring two people. An unsuccessful attempt was made to blow up an electricity cable bridge in West London.

On the same day an unsuccessful attempt was made to blow up an outer wall of Walton Jail in Liverpool to release I.R.A. prisoners held there.

On 5th February, there were fires in four department stores resulting from delayed action incendiaries and on 9th February two bombs exploded at Kings Cross Railway station in London. Further attacks continued, including those in Liverpool involving that prevented by P.C. Dodd.

In Liverpool on 5th April, bombs exploded at the railway station and council buildings with telephone kiosks being targeted, one being blown up. On 26th April, five bombs exploded in commercial premises in Liverpool.

On 3rd May, 3,000 people were affected by tear gas bomb attacks at two cinemas, again in Liverpool. The cinemas were the Trocadero in Camden Street and the Paramount in London Road. Fifteen people were treated at hospital with a number of emergency services workers, including police officers, being overcome by the gas on entering the Paramount. Two persons were detained in hospital.

A woman was seen to leave her seat shortly before the explosion. Other incendiary devices exploded in cinemas in Birmingham. The following day similar devices exploded in London cinemas.

Attaché case bomb recovered from bus.
(© Greater Manchester Police Museum)

On the same day a smouldering attaché case was found by a cleaner on the upper deck of a Manchester Corporation bus, which had returned to the depot. The explosive device in the case had failed to explode.

On the previous evening a minor explosion took place at a lodging house at Higher Temple Street, Chorlton-on-Medlock, when three men were seen to run away. When the house was searched, similar materials were found to those within the case.

Three men were arrested and later appeared in July 1939 at Manchester Assizes, charged with terrorist offences.

One man was acquitted, and the others were convicted and sentenced to prison sentences of 20 years each.

On 12th May, five bombs exploded in Manchester City Centre. The first two explosions were at an unoccupied shop on London Road and at a cycle dealer at Peter Street, the third at a jeweller's shop and a shoe shop in Market Street. The devices had been dropped through letter boxes.

A fifth device was found at a car showroom at 129 Deansgate. Water was poured onto the device by Detective Sergeants Lennox and Machent to render it inactive, but it burst into flames and exploded whilst the officers ran for cover. Glass was blown out, but the officers' actions were thought to have averted more serious damage.

On 19th May 1939, seven incendiary devices were planted in resort hotels by men booking in with false names and leaving before the devices ignited. Fires were started at the Carlton Hotel, Blackpool; Victoria Hotel, Southport; The Grand Hotel, Morecambe and at other hotels at Harrogate, Eastbourne, Margate and Southend. All ignited at about the same time and there were many similarities. No great damage was done, although at Morecambe a small explosion took place before the fire.

On 30th May, a tear gas bomb was released at the Tatler News Theatre (a cinema) at Church Street, Liverpool, resulting in 25 persons being taken to hospital. These included a police constable, members of staff, a six-year-old boy and a 74-year-old woman. As well as treatment for gas, two women received burns to their hands and legs. A woman matching the description from the previous tear gas incident was seen leaving the cinema before the device activated.

Damage to motor showroom, 129 Deansgate, Manchester 12/5/1939.
(© Greater Manchester Police Museum)

Attacks continued and included letter bombs, which exploded in sorting offices on 10th June 1939. Three explosions took place at the sorting office at Newton Street, Manchester, injuring five men who were burned. In London twenty pillar boxes were set on fire.

On 27th July, a swing bridge over the Leeds and Liverpool Canal at Green Lane, Maghull, was seriously damaged by an explosion resulting in the canal being blocked. In Liverpool, gelignite was pushed through the letter box of Mount Pleasant Post Office, which exploded resulting in severe damage. Nearby another device exploded and the resulting fire was extinguished by a police officer.

The campaign culminated in the deaths of seven members of the public and seventy injured in Coventry City Centre following an explosion on 25th August 1939. The device was left in the parcel carrier of a bicycle left in the city centre.

In the North West, bombs were detonated in Blackpool on 26th August outside the Town Hall, causing damage and another at Woolworths near to the Blackpool Tower, which detonated without causing much damage; another failed to explode. A further device containing 12 sticks of gelignite was found outside Blackpool Police Station and rendered harmless by a passer-by who saw the device smouldering and stamped it out.

The last explosion took place in March 1940. In total during the campaign there were 300 explosions, 10 deaths and 96 people were injured.

22nd June 1939

George DODD, Constable 119 'B' **Liverpool City Police**

King's Police Medal for Gallantry

At 4.50a.m. on 22nd June 1939, Constable Dodd heard screams coming from a house in Burnley Street, Liverpool. He ran there and saw smoke coming from the first-floor window. Two women, each with a child in her arms, and a young girl were leaning out of the window screaming for help.

The Constable burst open the door and ran up the burning staircase and into the bedroom, which was full of smoke. Although the women were very distressed, he got them all to jump out of the window into blankets held by neighbours below. They all landed safely, and unhurt. The Constable by this time was badly affected by smoke and was unable to jump from the window, but he managed to roll off the window sill and missing the blanket, hit the ground, knocking him unconscious.

He was revived by the Fire Brigade and then removed to hospital.

PRO Ref: H045/19528

L.G. 2/1/1940 Issue 34765 Page 19

FURTHER INFORMATION:

George Dodd was born in 1897 and was pensioned in 1944 after having served for 24 years. He was awarded a special pension for non-accidental disablement after having contracted tuberculosis aggravated by smoke inhalation arising during the rescue and by conditions experienced during the air raids of 1940/1941. He died in July 1945.

Constables G. Dodd, F. E. Dodd and T.S. Harrison

Constable George Dodd, P.C. Francis Edward Dodd and P.C. Thomas Smith Harrison were received and congratulated on the forthcoming award of the King's Police Medal by the Lord Mayor of Liverpool, Sir Sidney Jones, at Liverpool Town Hall on Friday 5th January 1940.

The Lord Mayor commented to Constable George Dodd, *'You have the knowledge that you definitely saved a family of five who were in danger of being swallowed up by flames in their home. You rescued them at the risk of your own life, and at the end you fell out of the window and very nearly caused yourself great injury. But you thought of nothing but your duty.'* Constable George Dodd was also presented with the Gold Medal and Certificate of Thanks by The Liverpool Shipwreck and Humane Society.

The Lord Mayor commented to Constable Francis Edward Dodd, *'Your act in picking up the bomb and putting it in a bucket of water saved a great deal of damage and perhaps many lives.'*

The Lord Mayor said it was a privilege to meet the three policemen and to express the gratitude of the police force and the citizens of Liverpool. He said, *'Human nature in Europe and other places at the present time seems to have descended to the depths, but there are redeeming features in the fact that you three have maintained the pride and reputation of constables, Englishmen, and all who care for the civilisation of the world.'*

The Lord Mayor turned to the Chief Constable of Liverpool (Mr A.K. Wilson) to congratulate him, and Mr Wilson's reply was, *'I am proud of them'.*

The three officers attended Buckingham Palace on 6th February 1940 and were presented with the King's Police Medal by the King. Interviewed afterwards, the three Liverpool policemen spoke of the charm of the King when he decorated them with the medal.

'His Majesty shook hands with each of us after he had pinned the medal to the tunic and said I warmly congratulate you on your pluck,' said Police Constable Harrison.

The Police, Fire and Civil Defence in the Second World War 1939 – 1945

Police

On the lead up to war it was accepted that in the event of war the duties the police would be required to carry out would increase enormously and their numbers would have to be greatly increased.

In the event of war, military reservists would be recalled to their units as had occurred during the Boer War and First World War, depleting the numbers of serving regular officers. Around 25% of police strength was below 25 years of age and would be subject to mobilization in the event of war.

To offset the likely reductions after the declaration of war and to boost police numbers, recruitment of three reserve forces began before the war. These reserves were the **First Police Reserve**, composed of pensioned officers who returned to the service, **Second Reserve**, comprising part-time, unpaid Special Constables and the **Third Reserve**, which was the **Police War Reserve**, comprising a full-time force who were signed up for service during the war only.

In addition, the **Women's Auxiliary Police Corps** (W.A.P.C.) was set up, recruiting women into clerical and administrative duties as well as to be drivers.

Young boys had also been recruited as civilian clerks pre-war to act as messengers and carry out other administrative work. These boys and others were recruited to form the **Police Auxiliary Messenger Service** (P.A.M.S.), delivering messages either on foot or on a bicycle in the event the telephone network was damaged or disrupted.

Regular police officers were designated from June 1940 as being in a 'reserved occupation'. From this date police posts were frozen and officers were required to continue to serve unless there were exceptional circumstances. No retirements or resignations were permitted. As the threat of invasion receded and air raids decreased it was decided to reduce the civil defence services and younger officers became de-reserved and many volunteered for military service.

All police were trained in first aid, firefighting, rescue and anti-gas work. Selected officers were trained in incident control and bomb reconnaissance.

Police stations were strengthened to make them more bomb resistant, either by structural improvements or by the use of sandbags. In many areas reserve stations were set up and equipped in the event of the main stations being put out of action.

By 1945, around 63,000 personnel were in service, which was not far below the pre-war establishment but was largely made up of auxiliaries rather than regular officers. At its peak in 1941, there were 194,000 police personnel in service.

At the end of the war the majority of War Reserve officers returned to their civilian occupations although a number continued to serve for some years afterwards. The W.A.P.C. members either joined the regular forces or took up other employment.

The Police Auxiliary Messenger Service was disbanded and many who met the requirements joined as regular officers. Boy clerks continued to be recruited and employed for a number of years afterwards by certain forces and became officially recognised as the Police Cadet Corps, which was a valuable source of recruitment to the regular force.

The majority of First Police Reservists retired or took up other employment, leaving just the Special Constabulary as the reserve force which remains to this day.

Stretford police officers undergoing gas training in 1937.
The officers wear anti-gas suits and service respirators.

Fire

Fire brigades were before the war run by local authorities and were organised in many places by Chief Constables as part of the police with firemen holding police ranks. The government in 1938, as war loomed, urged local authorities to set up emergency fire brigade organisations including Auxiliary Fire Services (A.F.S.) to supplement the existing brigades.

The National Fire Service (N.F.S.) was formed on 18th August 1941 from the existing fire brigades and the A.F.S. This arose as a result of lessons learned in the Blitz, which highlighted the need for a unified approach nationally. Previously there were over 1,000 separate brigades with each local area having its own Fire Authority and its own methods and equipment. The formation of the N.F.S. entailed a vast reorganisation with all firemen losing their rank with a board then selecting officers according to ability.

The unified structure allowed standardisation of equipment and movement of resources nationally, which would not have been possible under the old system.

At its height, the N.F.S. had 350,000 members. The N.F.S. existed until 1948 when control of the Fire Service reverted back to the control of the local authorities.

Civil Defence

The Civil Defence services were originally formed under the generic title A.R.P. (Air Raid Precautions) in 1937. These included air raid wardens, light and heavy rescue units, gas decontamination units, firewatchers, stretcher parties, ambulance drivers/attendants, first aid and messenger services. At its peak in 1941, the Civil Defence Services comprised over a million members.

The police worked closely with the other Civil Defence organisations during the war and outside of London were usually in charge of incidents. In many places Chief Constables were in operational charge of Civil Defence services.

The police were often the first at the scenes of incidents and took charge organising and summoning the other services. Being the first at the scene, they took an active part in rescue and firefighting operations. During the war, over 100 North West Police and Police Fire Officers were presented gallantry awards for their actions. Fifty-one police officers died during or as a result of enemy air raids in the Palatine of Lancashire.[29]

Enemy Air Activity in the North West – 1940/1941

The North West was subjected to heavy air raids during the Second World War. The main areas attacked were Liverpool and Manchester, but bombs fell in many other places in the North West.

Liverpool was Britain's main transatlantic port during the Second World War. During the war, the city was also a major naval and ship repair base and the headquarters of the Admiralty Western Approaches Command Centre, where Atlantic convoys and their escorts were co-ordinated.

Manchester and Salford also had docks and was a major manufacturing location. Trafford Park was the world's largest industrial estate, measuring three miles from west to east. The Metropolitan Vickers factory manufactured aircraft, whilst the Ford Motor Company manufactured aero engines along with numerous other factories producing items for the war effort. Many other major manufacturing facilities were situated in the area encompassed by Manchester, Salford, Stretford and surrounding areas

Lancashire

The first bombs fell in Lancashire on 20th June 1940 in Altham and Clayton-le-Moors in East Lancashire when four H.E. (high explosive) bombs (one of which failed to explode) and many incendiary bombs were dropped. This resulted in one house being demolished and fires caused to other properties. Nancy Ramsbottom (64) and her daughter Beatrice (21) died at 43 Fielding Terrace, Altham.

---

[29] Lancashire Constabulary (13), Manchester (5), Salford (3), Liverpool (21) (including Parks, Fire Brigade and Fire Salvage), Bootle (7), St Helens (1 – whilst deployed in Liverpool)
http://www.policerollofhonour.org.uk

On 31st August 1940, a single bomb hit Ainsworth Street, Blackburn in the middle of the town, where the last trams and buses were being drawn up. The driver of one tram died from shock, and the conductor died almost three weeks later from his injuries.

On 12th September 1940, seven people were killed and fourteen injured at Seed Street, Blackpool, when 5 H.E. and 1 incendiary bomb fell. Seed Street was near to the Central Railway Station, which appears to have been the target. The Central Railway Station was the scene of another incident later in the war. (See entry for Constable Thomas Beeston who was commended for brave conduct there on 27th August 1941.)

On 1st October 1940, William Fox (72) was killed and nine other people injured when a bomb fell at 202 Church Road, St Annes.

Luftwaffe Junkers Ju-88. (© IWM - MH 6115)

Bombs struck Crown Street, in Darwen, on Monday 21st October 1940. Three bombs fell behind a house, killing six people immediately and demolishing houses in Crown Street and Holme Street. Five hundred people were evacuated from Red Earth Road due to an unexploded bomb.

On the same day, the Leyland Motors complex was attacked. Three people were killed, and many workers were injured when bombs struck the works.

On 27th October 1940, another raid was carried out; it is believed the intended target again was the Leyland Motors site. Before the siren could be sounded bombs fell on Ward Street and Princess Street, Lostock Hall, causing the deaths of 25 civilians with a further 21 injured. Tragically, eight of the victims were from one family.[30]

Leyland Motors was again attacked on 30th October, when two H.E. bombs hit the site, both of which failed to explode and were later safely defused. Little damage was caused and no injuries resulted.

---

[30] LRO – UDWD/68/5 Report – Ward Street bombing. A memorial stone and plaque is placed on Ward Street remembering the dead.

In Chatburn, near Clitheroe, three people died (one later) and five were taken to hospital after two bombs were dropped on 30th October 1940. Two of the dead were local residents and the third, Lawrence Westwood (26) was driving a petrol tanker as part of a convoy passing through Chatburn. His vehicle took the full blast of one of the bombs and was blown off the road, resulting in his death from bomb splinters.

Liverpool & Manchester

Manchester's first bombs fell on 8th August 1940 when a few H.E. bombs and incendiaries fell along with a bundle of leaflets entitled 'A LAST APPEAL TO REASON' by Adolf Hitler. The bundle failed to open and fell upon the head of a police officer guarding the Civil Defence Report and Control Centre in Salford. (It is not known if he was injured!)

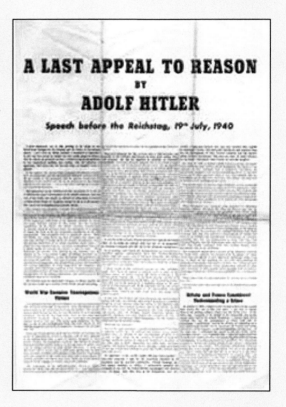

The first bombs fell in the Merseyside area on 9th August 1940 when bombs fell on Prenton, Birkenhead followed by the first bombs on Liverpool itself on the night of 17/18th August.

Further raids followed but these were just a foretaste of what was to come.

The first major raid on Merseyside took place on night of 28/29th November when 324 German aircraft attacked, dropping around 30,000 incendiaries and 356 tons of high explosive bombs, including thirty parachute mines. Severe damage was caused in Bootle with an area of one square mile devastated. The raid resulted in 200 deaths and 2,000 people being made homeless.

The Christmas Blitz 1940

From 20th to 23rd December 1940, Merseyside was again heavily attacked on consecutive nights. The docks were the main target, but the surrounding streets of terraced houses, which housed the dock workers and their families, were also devastated.

The Luftwaffe's attention then switched to Manchester, with the heaviest raids on Manchester taking place on consecutive nights on 22/23rd and 23/24th December. The Free Trade Hall, Smithfield Market and St. Anne's Church were destroyed. Deansgate and Oxford Road were blocked with debris and unexploded bombs. Hope Hospital in Salford was hit, and six members of staff were killed.

Despite the target being Manchester, damage was also caused to dockside warehouses in Wallasey, which were badly damaged with many fires being caused.

On 23rd December, a large bomb struck the Lancashire Constabulary Divisional Police Station at East Union Street, Old Trafford, demolishing the building, resulting in the death of five officers. Lancashire's Chief Constable, Archibald Frederick Hordern,[31] was in the building at the time and escaped with minor injuries. The station was an important communications link and its destruction destroyed telephone communications between the civil defence services. This was countered by the use of car, bicycle and foot messengers. The Trafford Park industrial area was badly damaged by fires. Many of Manchester's firemen and civil defence workers were deployed to Liverpool which had been hit on 20th December and had not returned from there. Fires still burning in Liverpool also helped illuminate the bombers' path to Manchester.

In Manchester, 376 people had died, hundreds were injured. 30,000 houses were damaged with 5,049 people made homeless. Salford was badly affected with 197 dead, 177 seriously injured and 648 slightly injured. Eight thousand houses had been damaged with 5,000 made homeless.

At Stretford, 106 civilians had died, 87 were seriously injured and 184 slightly injured. Twelve thousand houses had been damaged, and 2,000 people made homeless.

Firemen directing hoses on burning buildings in the City of Manchester.
(Believed to be warehouse premises on Portland Street, Manchester – December 1940.)
(© IWM - HU049833)

---

[31] Sir Archibald Frederick Hordern was born on 15th June 1889. He was educated at Cheltenham College and at Royal Military College, Sandhurst. He gained the rank of Captain in the service of the South Staffordshire Regiment. In the First World War he gained the rank of Captain in the Royal Flying Corps and Royal Air Force and was awarded the Air Force Cross.

He was Chief Constable of the East Riding, Yorkshire, between 1926 and 1934;; Chief Constable of Cheshire between 1934 and 1935; and Chief Constable of Lancashire between 1935 and 1950. He was invested as a Commander, Order of the British Empire (C.B.E.) in 1942 and was knighted in 1946 and held the King's Police Medal. He died on 17th April 1950, aged 60. Hordern's medals were sold at Gorringe's Auctions on 21st March 2017.

The May and June 1941 attacks

Commencing on 1st May 1941, Merseyside was attacked for eight consecutive nights. The worst attack took place on the night of 3/4th May when 298 aircraft attacked, dropping 360 tons of H.E. bombs and 50,000 incendiaries. In Liverpool, more than 1,400 people were killed and more than 1,000 people injured.

In Liverpool, Bootle and adjoining areas of Litherland and Crosby, nearly 90,000 houses were destroyed or damaged, representing about 40% of the houses in those areas. In Bootle, about 80% of the houses there were damaged or destroyed. In Merseyside, many thousands of residents had to be evacuated due to the damage caused to their homes.

On 3rd/4th May, the vessel S.S. *Malakand* was berthed in Huskisson Dock, Liverpool, carrying 1,000 tons of bombs destined for the Middle East. The vessel caught fire after fire spread from the burning dockside buildings. Despite several hours of struggle by the crew and firefighters, the ship blew up at about 3a.m., devastated a wide area and four persons were killed.

Mill Road Infirmary was hit by a large bomb resulting in heavy loss of life after three large hospital buildings were destroyed and the remainder of the building and surrounding houses were damaged. Many persons were trapped, and fire broke out in the ambulances and vehicles parked in the courtyard. At Mill Road Infirmary, 17 members of staff, 15 ambulance drivers and 30 patients were killed. Seventy persons were seriously injured and 380 patients had to be evacuated to other hospitals.

During the May week bombing, 11 police officers were killed and 51 injured. Many other civil defence workers and rescue workers were killed and injured.

Manchester was subjected to a heavy attack on the night of 1/2nd June 1941. This was the heaviest raid after those of Christmas 1940 and lasted for 90 minutes. Central Manchester took severe damage and more than 50 people were killed. The Manchester Assize Court at Strangeways and many other buildings were destroyed. At the Bootle Street Police Station, the upper floors were damaged and two Civil Defence Messengers were killed.

In Salford, 14 probationer nurses were killed when Salford Royal Hospital, Chapel Street, Salford was hit by a bomb. In total, 44 persons were killed in Salford and many buildings were damaged.

Intermittent raids occurred across the North West after this date, but nothing matched the intensity of the two periods of heavy bombing in 1940 and 1941.

31st August 1940

Harold Alexander WRIGHT, Sergeant 23 'H'   **Liverpool Fire Brigade**

George Medal

A large building was struck by high explosive and incendiary bombs, structural damage was caused, and a very serious fire resulted. The enemy returned, dropped high explosive bombs all-round the scene of the fire and sprayed the building with machine gun bullets while the Fire Brigade was working to subdue the flames.

Sergeant Wright was given the direction of a party of the Brigade working on the roof of the building. In spite of the intense heat, danger from exploding bombs and from machine gun fire, his party, encouraged by his example and resource, remained on the roof. They were successful in limiting the fire, which at one time appeared likely to involve the whole of the large building, to a section of the top floor.

The Sergeant carried out his duties in charge of a squad of men in a manner which showed his complete disregard of personal danger.

He and his men were operating on the flat roof of the building, and the example and leadership shown by him were an inspiration.

HO 250 Civil Awards case: 224

L.G. 21/1/1941 Issue 35053 Page 483

FURTHER INFORMATION:

Location of incident – Custom House, Canning Place, Liverpool.

I beg to report that at 21.30 hours, Saturday, 31st August 1940 I was on duty at Canning Place, in charge of the police engaged in vicinity of the Custom House which had been set on fire by enemy action. I was patrolling the Custom House, the dome and roof of which were burning furiously when my attention was drawn to the activities of Sergeant 23 'H' Wright. The Sergeant was carrying out his duties in charge of a squad of men in a manner which showed his complete disregard for any personal danger or his own safety.

The Sergeant and his men were operating on the flat roof of the building, and there is no doubt that the example and leadership shown by him were an inspiration to his men to stick to their work. In fact, while so engaged on the roof, they were constantly in grave danger of attack by returning enemy aircraft, who were attracted to the scene by the huge beacon of fire from the dome of the building which could be seen for miles. On one occasion, the building was sprayed by machine gun fire from enemy aircraft.

In my opinion, the action of the Sergeant was worthy of the highest praise.

(Signed) E. Kebby. Inspector

NEW CUSTOM HOUSE, LIVERPOOL.

FURTHER INFORMATION:

Building work began at the Custom House on 12th August 1828 and it took eleven years before the opening in 1839.

Sergeant Wright and his party were able to limit the fire to a section of the top floor, but the huge dome was burnt to a skeleton and eventually collapsed.

During further air raids the building was again hit and partly destroyed although the structure remained. After the war had ended, the council refused to repair the building despite protests and it was subsequently demolished in 1948. The site is now occupied by the Liverpool One shopping centre.

Harold Alexander Wright was born in December 1896 at Liverpool, Lancashire. He joined Liverpool Police Fire Brigade on 6th August 1920, having worked previously as a fitter and then as a sapper with the Royal Engineers from 20th October 1914 to 28th March 1919.

He was promoted to Sergeant in July 1939. On 28/29th November 1940, Wright was injured when he fell into a bomb crater in Greenheys Road, injuring his wrist. He was transferred to the National Fire Service in 1941 as a Senior Company Officer and was retired as medically unfit in October 1945. He died in September 1963.

September 1940 onwards

Leslie Gordon WHYMAN, Sergeant 3   **Bootle Police Force**

British Empire Medal (Civil Division)

Sergeant Whyman's duties as Liaison Officer between the Police and the Bomb Disposal Section have necessitated him searching for unexploded time bombs over a large area in the dark during the height of enemy attacks.

In addition to this highly dangerous work the Sergeant made arrangements for the immediate evacuation of large numbers of people and it is due to his promptness and courage that many lives have been saved.

Sergeant Whyman has shown courage and devotion to duty and his conduct has been an example to all.

HO 250 Civil Awards case: 1781 L.G. 4/11/1941 Issue 35336 Page 6424

FURTHER INFORMATION:

Leslie Gordon Whyman was born at Strood, Kent in 1904. At the time of the award he was 37 years old and had served with Bootle Police for 11 years. He died, aged 63 years, in 1967.

18th September 1940

Thomas Ellis WILSON Constable 1441   **Lancashire Constabulary**

British Empire Medal (Civil Division)

At about 8p.m. on September 18th 1940, eleven high explosive bombs fell at Thornton near Liverpool, one of which exploded at the entrance to a public shelter at the junction of Green Lane and Park View.

A Ribble Bus had pulled up at the roadside close to the shelter and passengers were about to enter it when the bomb exploded killing nine persons and badly injuring a number of others. Wilson, who was on duty nearby, immediately took charge of the incident.

He sent a Special Constable and a Warden to different telephones to inform the Report Centre, attended to all the injured assisted by local First Aid men. He covered the dead, examined all the wrecked houses and checked up on the residents, took precautions to divert traffic from a reported unexploded bomb, which was situated right among the dead and injured.

Wilson took no notice of the danger, and in spite of heavy A.A. fire, falling bombs etc. carried on with the utmost coolness, which had a splendid effect on the local people who arrived to help, whom he organised in such a manner that a great deal of the rescue work etc. was carried out before the several Services arrived.

The above facts speak for themselves, the completely fearless and very gallant conduct of Wilson deservedly won for him the honour which has been awarded.

Lancashire Constabulary award file – PLA/ACC6849

HO 250 Civil Awards case: 546

L.G. 4/3/1941 Issue 35095 Page 1347

FURTHER INFORMATION:

Thomas Ellis Wilson was born in 1897 at Cowan Bridge, Lancashire and was appointed as Constable 1441 on 18th August 1919. At this time, he stated his previous occupation as being a farm labourer. Wilson was awarded the Merit Badge on two occasions and had received a monetary award on 23rd November 1938.

He served at Bury and Seaforth Divisions and was promoted to Sergeant on 1st January 1946. He retired on 1st September 1948 and died in June 1982.

18th/19th September 1940

Edward NICHOLS, Superintendent	**Liverpool Police Force**
John Joseph MEEHAN, Prison Officer	**H.M. Prison, Walton, Liverpool**
The George Medal	
Frederick Albert BOWYER, Chief Officer	**H.M. Prison, Walton, Liverpool**
British Empire Medal (Civil Division)	

When H.M. Prison, Walton, Liverpool, was struck by a high explosive bomb a wing consisting of a basement with four tiers of cells above was severely damaged. A number of prisoners were trapped.

Gas and water were escaping, and the electric light system was put out of order. At the request of the Governor of the prison Superintendent Nichols, with a party of men, arrived to render assistance.

After an examination of the damaged building had been made and a number of prisoners from the damaged upper cells had been removed to safety, a man's voice could be heard coming from somewhere under the rubble which had fallen behind the door of a cell in the basement.

Officer Meehan, Chief Officer Bowyer and others of the prison staff worked hard amid recurrent falls of masonry to release the imprisoned man. The panels of the cell door were broken open, but it was found that owing to the continual falling of debris it was impossible to continue operations at this spot.

It was decided that the only method of rescue was to break through the wall between this cell and the adjoining one, and Superintendent Nichols took charge of this operation. The two prison officers made a hole in the wall and the Superintendent, removing debris with his hands, discovered the trapped man's head. He was conscious and proved to be a prisoner.

With portions of broken steel girders and fiat stones Superintendent Nichols constructed a platform over the prisoner's head and prevented further falls of masonry. The Prison Officer and the Superintendent continued with picks, bars and sledge hammers to enlarge the hole and after a period of 3½ hours the trapped man was released, exhausted but apparently not seriously injured.

This rescue was effected in the worst imaginable conditions, in darkness, apart from the light of pocket lamps, with the danger of the roof and wall of the prison wing collapsing, in a gas polluted atmosphere, amid flooding from fractured water mains, and with enemy aircraft overhead.

Superintendent Nichols was untiring in his efforts, displaying resource and initiative in the way he directed operations. Prison Officer Meehan and Chief Officer Bowyer worked hard and with a disregard for their own safety.

HO 250 Civil Awards case: 319   L.G. 28/1/1941 Issue 35055 Page 531

FURTHER INFORMATION:

Location of incident – 'K' Cell Wing, Walton Prison, Liverpool.

Edward Nichols was a native of Eastham, Cheshire and joined the Liverpool City Police as a recruit in 1911. He was promoted to Sergeant after 8 years' service and Inspector in 1924. 1931 saw further advancement to Chief Inspector and Superintendent 'E' Division in 1937.

In 1942, Superintendent Nichols was promoted to Chief Superintendent and placed in command of the Traffic Division. Four years later, in 1946, he became 2nd Assistant Chief Constable and in 1948 he replaced Sir Charles Martin as 1st Assistant Chief Constable upon Sir Charles being appointed Chief Constable.

In the King's Birthday Honours of 1949, Mr Nichols was awarded the O.B.E. (Civil Division) for Meritorious Service. He died suddenly in June 1952, whilst still serving. He is buried at Anfield Cemetery. Eight Sergeants of the City Police carried his coffin.[32]

(O.B.E. Award – L.G. 3/6/1949 Issue 38628 Page 2806)

26th September 1940

Alfred William HUMBLE, Sergeant 45 'H'   **Liverpool Fire Brigade**

British Empire Medal (Civil Division)

A serious fire, due to enemy action, broke out at some storehouses in Liverpool. In spite of the fact however, that continuous dust explosions were taking place and that the fire appeared to have a hold of the building impossible to subdue, Sergeant Humble courageously handled the position and by prodigious efforts prevented the fire from travelling across a gantry, thereby saving the adjoining building.

There was an ever-present danger of explosion from time bombs and had it not been for the gallant action of Sergeant Humble and his initiative and leadership the fire might well have been far more serious than was eventually the case.

HO 250 Civil Awards case: 318   L.G. 14/1/1941 Issue 35043 Page 335

---

[32] Liverpool City Police http://liverpoolcitypolice.co.uk/edward-nichols/4567444503 – Retrieved 10/9/2017

FURTHER INFORMATION:

Location of incident – East Coburg Dock, Liverpool.

At 10.30p.m. on Thursday 26th September 1940, a serious fire, due to enemy action, broke out at the Granaries, East Coburg Dock, Liverpool. The superstructure of the Coburg Granary was found well alight and was ultimately burned out. The fire was spreading along the bridge which contains the conveyor system connecting with the Brunswick Granary. A naval detachment from a neighbouring depot formed a *'charge party'* and stood by, ready to destroy the bridge if it was found impossible to prevent the fire involving the adjoining warehouse.

After an unsuccessful attempt to attack this fire from a spiral stairway at a height of 50 ft., Sergeant 45 'H' Alfred William Humble of the Liverpool Fire Brigade was driven back by the intense heat and under the direction of Chief Inspector Williams attacked the fire, with his party, from the ground, with the result that the fire round the bridge was extinguished and the Brunswick Granary saved.

Sergeant Humble was untiring in his efforts and displayed courage and commendable qualities of leadership in tackling this work.

At the time several railway trucks loaded with copra standing in the adjoining Dock Avenue were burning fiercely. A time bomb exploded, throwing burning debris in the air. A dust explosion occurred in the basement of the Coburg Granary, resulting in floor collapse killing one man and injuring four others, and a series of minor explosions occurred as water from the hoses struck the burning gantry. None of these dangers deterred the Sergeant from his task of getting the fire under control.

FURTHER INFORMATION:

Alfred William Humble was born in March 1904, at Whitby, Yorkshire. He joined Liverpool Police Fire Brigade on 6th October 1930, giving his previous occupation as being a marine engineer.

On 28th March 1940 he was awarded 10s. by the Watch Committee for courageous action by descending a 60 ft. cutting to render first aid to a man who had fallen down an embankment. In May 1937, he was promoted to Sergeant 6th Class. In November 1940, he was granted a temporary rank allowance to Acting Inspector and on 25th May 1941 he was promoted to 2nd class Sergeant.

In 1941 he was transferred to the National Fire Service. He died, aged 74 years, in 1978.

2nd October 1940

Henry Thomas LISTON, Constable 72   **Salford Police Force**

Joseph Dickinson MORRISON, Constable 263   **Salford Police Force**

Herbert Emsley CLARKSON Constable (Fireman) 13   **Salford City Fire Brigade**

King's Commendation for Brave Conduct in Civil Defence

Copy of letter dated 28/10/1940 from Chief Constable, Salford:

Shortly before midnight on the 2nd instant a high explosive bomb dropped in a working-class district near this Town Hall.

Seven houses were completely demolished and others badly damaged. Constables Liston and Morrison were in a party of police officers sent to the scene, and shortly after their arrival they were informed that a woman was trapped under debris.

They crawled through the debris and found her lying under a small table, which was supporting the main weight of the house. Her legs were trapped, and the officers were at first unable to move her, but after the arrival of a doctor, who gave her an injection to ease the pain, the officers and Fireman Clarkson managed to lever up part of the wreckage and drag her free.

She did not die, as appeared certain but is still in hospital and is unable to give any details of the occurrence. This rescue took place on a particularly dark night and danger was increased by the presence of coal gas.

HO 250 Civil Awards case: 222   L.G. 24/1/1941 Issue 35053 Page 487

FURTHER INFORMATION:

Location of incident – 8 Marsden Street, Salford.

Henry Thomas Liston was born at Birkenhead on 29th December 1916 and joined Salford Police on 12th April 1937. His previous occupation was as a clerk. On 16th March 1939 he was commended by the Chief Constable for the arrest of the occupants of a stolen car. He joined the Intelligence Corps from 3rd September 1942 to 9th September 1945, reaching the rank of Company Sergeant Major. He left Salford Police on 1st March 1946.

Henry Thomas Liston

Joseph Dickinson Morrison was born at Coatbridge, Scotland in 1916 and joined Salford Police on 12th September 1938. His previous occupation was as a tubeworks machinist. Morrison was released for military service in the Royal Marines from 13th January 1943 to 18th April 1946.

Joseph Dickinson Morrison

Herbert Emsley Clarkson was born in Bishop Auckland and joined Salford Police in 1935, his previous occupation is recorded as having been a sailor. He died in June 1978.

Herbert Emsley Clarkson

2nd October 1940

Thomas Harold Reuben FISHER, Police Constable 250   **Salford Police Force**

King's Commendation for Brave Conduct in Civil Defence

Report from the Chief Constable of Salford:

At 11.55p.m. on the 2nd October 1940, Constable Fisher, who is in the Mobile Section of the Force, was on duty near the entrance to this Headquarters when he heard the sound of a bomb falling.

He immediately took cover but after the explosion of the bomb, which had obviously fallen nearby, he promptly returned to the street.

The bomb had dropped alongside the Town Hall, about 30 yards from the Police entrance, and had badly damaged a section of the Town Hall. A shop and a house opposite had been practically demolished, and the debris completely blocked the street.

On investigation, which was rendered particularly difficult owing to the intense darkness, Fisher found that a man and a woman were partly buried beneath the debris of the collapsed shop. He helped extricate the man, and they together were able to free the woman and carry her into this Headquarters for first aid treatment.

I consider that Fisher's action was especially commendable insofar that he searched the debris immediately and alone, regardless of the danger of falling masonry and the risk of further bombs, whereas he could well have waited for the arrival of the Rescue Squad.

HO 250 Civil Awards case: 271

L.G. 28/1/1941 Issue 35058 Page 612

FURTHER INFORMATION:

Incident Location – East Market Street, Salford.

Thomas Harold Reuben Fisher was born in Manchester in 1898 and joined Salford Police on 24th November 1919. His previous occupation was as a grocer's assistant. He had also served during the Great War with the Lancashire Fusiliers from 1915 to 1919. He had previously been commended in 1937 for the arrest of car thieves and the recovery of stolen vehicles.

He retired on pension on 31st December 1948 and died in 1998.

26th October 1940

Thomas Morton SKELTON, Inspector   **Liverpool City Police**

Walter EVANS, A.R.P. Warden   **Liverpool**

Richard ROXBURGH, Sapper 1904638   **Royal Engineers**

British Empire Medal (Civil Division)

A H.E. bomb demolished three houses, causing a number of casualties. Fire added to the difficulties. Inspector Skelton was lowered by a rope into a hole and with the aid of a stirrup pump was able to check the fire and effect some relief to trapped persons by cooling them with water. He had to retire eventually owing to smoke and heat. The trapped people were on the first floor, their escape being due to the fact that the ceiling had not fallen flat on the floor.

Meanwhile Warden Evans and a soldier found another entrance through which they were able to crawl and communicate with the trapped persons. Fire again hindered operations and the stirrup pump had to be brought into play.

A child was first extricated, then the father, whose foot was caught by an iron fender. It was necessary to prop, and clear away debris and the rescuers had to pass over his body to reach the fender.

Eventually, after about two hours, he was dragged away. The mother was trapped face downwards on a wooden bed and mattress with her baby beneath her. After one of the legs of the bed had been sawn through it was possible to drag her away. The baby, however, was dead.

L.G. 11/2/1941 Issue 35074 Page 879

Sapper 1904638 Richard Roxburgh

For gallant conduct in carrying out hazardous work in a very brave manner.

L.G. 7/3/1941 Issue 35099 Page 1428

HO 250 Civil Awards case: 120

FURTHER INFORMATION:

Location of incident – 304a & 308a Netherfield Road, North, Liverpool.

The rescued persons were John Sutton (29), Josephine Sutton (27) and Joyce Sutton (3). Their five-week-old baby was deceased. In total, 13 persons were killed at the location.

Walter Evans was aged 38 years at the time of the incident and was a voluntary A.R.P. Warden. His occupation was as a shopkeeper.

Richard Roxburgh was a Corporal attached to the 3rd Battalion of the Royal Engineers, stationed at Chatham Barracks. He lived at 10 Nicholson Street, Liverpool and was on home leave visiting his wife.

Thomas Morton Skelton was born in 1898 in Liverpool, where he was educated at the Liverpool Nautical College and Liverpool University, where he studied Jurisprudence.

He joined Liverpool Police on 29th October 1920, where he served as Constable 337 'E', stationed at

Inspector G. M. Skelton, of the Liverpool Police Force, being presented with the Belgian Croix de Guerre at the Belgian Independence Day parade at Chelsea Barracks. When a Belgian ammunition ship was set on fire by incendiaries, Inspector Skelton saved the ship from destruction by dumping the cargo in the water. He already holds the British Empire Medal and bar.

Westminster Road, Bridewell. In 1929, he was awarded the Bronze Medal and received a vote of thanks from The Liverpool Shipwreck and Humane Society for stopping a runaway horse in Sandon Dock.

In 1931, he was promoted to Sergeant, then in 1934 promoted to Divisional Inspector.

In 1941, he was to receive three awards for bravery; in February he was awarded the order of the British Empire (Civil Division) in recognition of his very courageous conduct in effecting the rescue of a number of persons buried under the debris of homes destroyed during enemy attack; in May he was awarded the Belgian Croix de Guerre for removing high explosives from a Belgian ship which had been set on fire by incendiary bombs dropped by enemy aircraft; then in October he received the Bar to the British Empire Medal for conspicuous act of heroism in the rescue of men from a ship berthed in Gladstone Dock, which had been severely damaged by a parachute mine; again in the same month he was awarded the Silver General Medal and vote of thanks from The Liverpool Shipwreck and Humane Society for stopping a runaway horse and wagon in No. 2 Alexandra Dock.

In December of that year he also received the Liverpool Shipwreck and Humane Society Silver and Bronze Medal with Certificate of Efficient Performance of Duty in effecting the rescue of a man who had fallen off a ship into Canada Dock. He then was also commended four times by the Liverpool Watch Committee and three times by H.M. Customs.

He was appointed Chief Constable of Hyde Borough Police, Manchester, aged 45 years, on 1st April 1943. During his two years as Chief Constable he received the Silver Meritorious Service Medal and framed Certificate from the R.S.P.C.A. (this is the highest decoration that the Society can bestow) for his devoted service to animal welfare in effecting the rescue of a number of cattle from a ship, which was severely damaged by enemy fire whilst he was an Inspector with Liverpool Police.

During this time, he also received from King George VI the honour of being a serving Brother of the Order of St. John of Jerusalem.

In January 1945, he was seconded to the Allied Control Commission, Germany, to help reorganise the German Police, as members of the police had been asked to volunteer at the outbreak of WWII to act as a Task Force known as Einsatzgruppen with the special charge of executing Jews and other targeted groups; quite a number of these men had managed to slip back into the German Police after the war. Part of the Allied Control Commission, his assignment was to bring these men to trial. In all, one thousand men were arrested but only three hundred and seventy where charged with any offence.

In 1950, he took up a position as Commissioner of Police[33] in Kingston, Jamaica, where he was to remain for several years, returning to the UK in January 1957. On his return, he took a six-month break but could not settle and took a job with Lever Brothers as a Security Consultant. In February 1962, he was admitted to Bootle General Hospital where he passed away. He was 59 years old, leaving a wife and daughter.[34]

29th November 1940

Thomas Arthur DAVIES, War Reserve Constable 656 'R'   **Liverpool City Police**

George Medal

During an air raid a H.E. bomb was dropped on a large building which was demolished. A number of people were trapped in a public shelter in the basement. Fierce fires broke out and made rescue work extremely hazardous.

Police War Reserve Davies was on duty at the time and immediately ran to the wrecked building.

With other police officers, he was successful in clearing a passage to some of the trapped people and in order to prevent further falls of debris he crawled into the aperture he had made and supported the wreckage with his body. Smoke and fumes poured out of the hole. Bricks and earth were continually falling.

The Constable refused to give up and he remained in this dangerous position for over an hour, until rendered unconscious.

He was instrumental in rescuing many people.

HO 250 Civil Awards case: 545   L.G. 18/2/1941 Issue 35081 Page 1059

---

33 The Jamaica Constabulary Force do not record Skelton in their list of previous Commissioners. Jamaica Constabulary Force – Retrieved 01/08/2018 from https://www.jcf.gov.jm/about-us/history/past-commissioners

34 Liverpool City Police – Retrieved 31/5/2017 from http://liverpoolcitypolice.co.uk/thomas-skelton-mbe/4573064205

FURTHER INFORMATION:

Location of incident – Junior Instructional Centre, Durning Road, Edgehill, Liverpool.

The Ernest Brown Junior Instructional Centre on Durning Road in Edge Hill was chosen as the site for an air raid shelter during World War 2. Its basement, and in particular its boiler room with its reinforced ceiling, offered protection to the public from the enemy bombs falling nearby.

At around 1.55a.m. on 29th November, the school took a direct hit from a parachute mine. The building collapsed, sending debris straight onto those sheltering in the basement; many people were buried alive. The boiler burst, streaming out hot water, and burst gas pipes became alight. Anyone not killed outright now faced these horrific dangers. Up above, the building was ablaze, and rescue workers struggled to help free the survivors.

During the next two days the rescue effort went on, as first the survivors, and then the bodies of the dead were brought to the surface. It became clear that retrieving all the bodies was hopeless, and the call was made to cover the area in lime and seal it over.

Police figures gave the total number of dead as 166. However, it is widely believed the figure was much bigger at around 180. Of the survivors, only 30 people escaped unharmed. Many spoke of having to walk over dead bodies to escape. Many of the dead remained unidentified and were buried together in a grave at Anfield Cemetery. Winston Churchill described the bombing as, *'The single worst civilian incident of the war'*.

Thomas Arthur Davies was 31 years of age at the time of the incident and had been a War Reserve Constable for five months. His civil occupation was as a dairy roundsman.

Later incident:

Thomas Arthur Davies was awarded a certificate and £15 by the Carnegie Hero Fund for attempting to stop a runaway horse on 4th May 1945, during which he was seriously injured. (*Liverpool Evening Express*, 15/08/1945)

30th November 1940

Harold Reginald NEWGASS, Temporary Lieutenant   **R.N.V.R.**

George Cross

John James ATKINSON, Police Constable 108 'H'   **Liverpool Fire Brigade**

Harry Charles FISK, Police Constable 279 'H'   **Liverpool Fire Brigade**

King's Commendation for Brave Conduct in Civil Defence

FURTHER INFORMATION:

Location of incident – Garston, Liverpool

Report of Chief Officer Owen:

On Saturday, the 30th November 1940 I was informed that an unexploded land mine had come to rest in a large gasometer at Garston Gas Works, and Sub-Lieut. Clode, R.N.V.R., attached to the R.M.S. Department, requested the services of a fire engine to remove a large quantity of water from the gasometer, in an effort to effect the removal of the mine.

A fire pump and crew in charge of Inspector Blades were sent to the scene, and the dangerous task of removing the water was commenced. In view of the hazardous nature of the task – it is dangerous to operate a fire pump within 200 yards of an unexploded mine – I decided to withdraw all except one man, and from among the volunteers I selected Constables 279 'H' Fisk and 108 'H' Atkinson to take charge of the pump.

Pumping was commenced at 14.30 hours on Saturday, 30.11.40 and the two constables relieved each other in 12 hour shifts until at 17.30 hours on Sunday, 1.12.40 the requisite amount of water (approximately 1¼ million gallons) was removed. It was then found necessary to use a standard Gwynne Pump to feed the Thirlmere Air Compressor for the purpose of removing the residue gas from the holder.

This operation continued under the supervision of the above mentioned constables until 18.00 hours Tuesday 3.12.40 when the Naval Officers were then in a position to commence their dangerous work. When it is realised that the pump was operating for this lengthy period within 120 feet of the mine and the safe distance is 200 yards the high courage and devotion to duty of Constables 279 'H' Fisk and 108 'H' Atkinson merits signal recognition.

HO 250 Civil Awards case: 558 L.G. 4/3/1941 Issue 35095 Page 1347

FURTHER INFORMATION:

In the very early hours of November 29th 1940, a parachute mine landed on the Garston Gas Works. It was not known whether the mine or bomb in the 4,000,000 cubic feet holder tank was magnetic, acoustic, delayed action or just a plain 'dud'. Fearing it might detonate at any time, the authorities evacuated 6,000 people living in the vicinity to escape what would have been an almost unimaginable explosion.

At 7.30a.m., fitters, electricians, plumbers and others were at work disconnecting electrically driven blowers from other plants, rigging them into position on the holder tank and preparing the fire pump to draw water out. These high-risk tasks were carried out by willing volunteers. As the exact location of the mine was unknown, risks had to be taken. First, the fans were started up and nothing happened, then the motor pump, and still no explosion. The men who had assembled the gear were withdrawn. The Liverpool Fire Brigade arrived and put a pump to work, the water was taken down 5' 6" to uncover part of the 'dumping', a brick-faced island inside the holder. This achieved, the air inside the holder tank was no longer considered explosive and means of access were considered.

Fans and pumps were stopped and the job was handed over to Lieutenant Newgass of the bomb disposal unit. Then aged 41, Newgass was a veteran of the Great War and hailed from London.

Donning oxygen apparatus, which only lasted thirty minutes apiece, Lieutenant Newgass entered the holder tank. He lashed the parachute ring of the mine to the top of the pillar against which it was leaning and passed a lashing round the nose. Unfortunately, the fuse was facing the pillar so a special hoisting lug was affixed and the mine was carefully turned round with a 'tommy bar'. This was a great physical effort for one man working under immense pressure and wearing oxygen apparatus for the first time.

For two days Newgass battled to defuse the mine. On 30th November, the fuse, the magnetic primer and the clocks were all removed. Newgass was then able to report that although the detonator was still in, the mine could be considered safe.

Garston employees then entered the holder and uncoupled the lashing. The mine, which in size and appearance resembled a tug boat funnel, was pulled over on its side, dragged across the 'dumping' to a position under the hole on the crown and lifted out by block and tackle. It was then placed on the back of a lorry and driven away.

It is certain that had the mine been detonated, the whole of Garston Works, along with much neighbouring property, would have been completely destroyed in the blast. Lieutenant Newgass was awarded the George Cross, the highest civil decoration available. Local newsagent and tobacconist, Miss Connie Elliot of St. Mary's Road, started a public collection for the mine disposal squad, resulting in generous gifts being presented on behalf of the grateful people of Garston.

The way in which the ordinary man responded to this dangerous incident by selflessly placing themselves at grave risk in order to keep many more thousands of people safe, was hailed as a great example of the 'Blitz Spirit'.[35]

The award of the George Cross was gazetted in the *London Gazette* on 4th March 1941. His medals are displayed in the Lord Ashcroft Gallery, Imperial War Museum, London.

Harry Charles Fisk was 33 years old at the date of the incident. He had served with the Fire Brigade for 10 years at the time of the incident. He resigned in March 1941.

John James Atkinson was born in Hayton, Cumberland, in June 1891. He was appointed to Liverpool Fire Brigade on 19th April 1920. His previous occupation is recorded as being a mechanic and soldier. His record shows he served with the Royal Army Service Corps in Motor Transport between 7th June 1917 and 10th October 1919. Atkinson was transferred to the National Fire Service in 1941.

21st December 1940

Robert PRITCHARD, Member, A.R.P. Rescue Party	**Bootle**
David Charles FORSHAW, Sergeant	**Bootle Police Force**
Thomas Joseph McCARTHY, Constable 27	**Bootle Police Force**
Victor James SCOTT, Constable 101	**Bootle Police Force**

George Medal

A heavy calibre H.E. bomb completely demolished some houses and partially destroyed others. Part of the debris was immediately removed, and a hole made in it towards a window, below ground floor level, in front of the cellar.

Sergeant Forshaw squeezed through and helped the imprisoned persons out. Whilst inside, the wreckage gradually subsided and, shortly after he got out, the debris burst into flames and crashed into the cellar.

The Sergeant, who sustained burns and other injuries, showed courage of an extremely high order. The whole structure of one house had collapsed in a tangled mass of timber and rubble.

Showing considerable daring P.C.s. Scott and McCarthy were able to extricate a mother and daughter. Pritchard made a working space, carefully shifting the bricks. Scott located a child lying face downwards partly protected by a piece of timber.

In a very confined space, with no head room and in a cramped position, Scott cleared the boy's head and shoulders.

Pritchard got half inside the inner clearance and, assisted by McCarthy, they continued to remove the debris covering the victim. After a considerable time, they were able to release the child who was then passed out unharmed.

McCarthy, Scott and Pritchard displayed great courage and daring, knowing that tons of loose debris above were likely to fall at any moment

HO 250 Civil Awards case: 1043   L.G. 18/3/1941 Issue 35111 Page 1641

---

[35] http://www.liverpoolblitz70.co.uk/2011/02/06/the-story-of-harold-newgass – Retrieved 23/5/2018

Merseyside Civil Defence Heroes

More heroes of Merseyside's Civil Defence against enemy air raids. Left to right: Robert Pritchard, rescue squad, Turner-avenue, Orrell, Bootle (George Medal); P.C. T. J. McCarthy, Bootle Police Force (George Medal); Chief Constable of Bootle (Mr. T. Bell); Sergeant D. C. Forshaw, Bootle Police Force (George Medal); the Mayor of Bootle (Alderman J. S. Kelly), congratulating the medallists. Inset: P.C. Victor J. Scott, Bootle Police Force, in hospital (George Medal).

Liverpool Evening Express, 22/3/ 1941

FURTHER INFORMATION:

Location of incident – Pembroke Road, Bootle.

Robert Pritchard was aged 46 years at the time of the incident and had been a member of the Rescue Squad for 12 months. His civilian occupation was as a painter's labourer.

Thomas Joseph McCarthy later received the King's Commendation for Bravery. L.G. 10/10/1941 (See later entry.)

Victor James Scott was later presented in 1941 with the Certificate of the Liverpool Shipwreck and Humane Society for stopping a runaway horse and cart on Irlam Road.

Pembroke Road, Bootle – note fire hoses and smoke. (© Sefton Library Services)

September to December 1940

Albert MOIR, Inspector   **Bootle Police Force**

British Empire Medal (Civil Division)

Inspector Moir has, throughout the period of enemy air attacks, shown courage and devotion to duty.

On one occasion H.E. bombs demolished houses and people were trapped in the cellars. Under the direction of the Inspector a police party set to work to remove wreckage.

The victims were then extricated from the debris which was by this time on fire.

It was largely due to Inspector Moir's efforts that many lives were saved.

HO 250 Civil Awards case: 1854

L.G. 2/1/1942 Issue 35400 Page 58

FURTHER INFORMATION:

Albert Moir was aged 46 years at the time of the incidents. He had served with Bootle Police for 22 years. He died, aged 70 years, in 1968.

James Clark PICKERING, Senior A.R.P. Warden — **Bootle**

Alexander ROSS, Chief Inspector — **Bootle Police Force**

George Medal

Edward PENNINGTON, Special Constable 87 — **Bootle Special Constabulary**

King's Commendation for Brave Conduct in Civil Defence

Four dwelling houses were demolished by bombs and people were trapped under the wreckage. Senior Warden Pickering squeezed through a small hole in the debris and he found the casualties alive but buried. He had very little room to move and further debris was liable to fall and block the aperture completely.

Chief Inspector Ross broke through the fallen woodwork and reached Pickering by crawling under the bottom portion of a doorway. The two women were then in a small triangular space under part of the collapsed roof. A woman and a man were buried up to the shoulders and both were injured about the head.

It was exceedingly dangerous to attempt to release them, as the broken woodwork which was pinning them down was also supporting the angle roof. By passing out the debris bit by bit the two men at last succeeded in freeing the woman who was dragged clear.

Two other persons were discovered completely buried and sufficient weight of debris was removed to make them more comfortable. After Ross and Pickering had been working for nearly an hour the roof was temporarily shored up and the remaining three persons released.

The Chief Inspector and the Senior Warden displayed outstanding courage and performed splendid work in effecting the rescue of the four casualties.

HO 250 Civil Awards case 1699 — L.G. 16/9/1941 Issue 35277 Page 5399

Special Constable Edward Pennington

Soon after the C.I. and Warden Pickering were inside I instructed two Special Constables to try and get to the C.I. from the front and give him all possible assistance. Spec. Con 87 Pennington remained near the entrance where the C.I. was working during the whole of the time the rescue work was proceeding, and to my knowledge he was of great assistance there.

He passed out quantities of debris and bricks and helped the C.I. when the elderly lady who had been trapped, was dragged out. While Spec. Con. Pennington was engaged in this work he was exposed to personal danger if any more of the building has collapsed.

L.G. 16/9/1941 Issue 35277 Page 5402

FURTHER INFORMATION:

Location of incident – Hawthorne Road, Bootle, Lancashire.

James Clark Pickering was aged 33 years at the time of the incident and had been a member of the Warden's Service for four years. His civilian occupation was as a Corporation Rent Collector.

Alexander Ross was aged 47 years at the time of the incident. He had served with Bootle Police for 21 years.

Edward Pennington was aged 41 and had been a Special Constable for two years.

Bomb damage – Hawthorne Road, Bootle. Note the spire of Christ Church, Oxford Road, Bootle in background.
(© Sefton Library Services)

22nd December 1940

Charles BIGLAND, Constable (Fireman) 36　　　　　　　**Salford Fire Brigade**

British Empire Medal (Civil Division)

During an air raid Constable Bigland was one of a detachment sent to a gas works, where an incendiary bomb had penetrated the top of a gasometer, causing a tongue of flame which was acting as a beacon to enemy aircraft.

A hose was placed into position at the side of the gasometer which was then between sixty and seventy feet in height. Bigland immediately climbed up a steel ladder to the top, lay flat on his stomach and remained in that position until he had succeeded in subduing the flame with a powerful jet. Employees of the gas works then sealed the hole with a steel plate and clay.

Bigland's fearless action set a magnificent example to others working with him.

HO 250 Civil Awards case: 633

L.G. 18/3/1941 Issue 35111 Page 1642

FURTHER INFORMATION:

Location of incident – Salford Corporation Gas Works.

Charles Bigland joined Salford Police in 1935. He was commended by the Watch Committee for *'exceptional courage'* in stopping a runaway pony on The Crescent, Salford on 30th September 1939. He was appointed as Acting Sergeant on 31st March 1941. On 24th October 1943, he joined the Royal Air Force. He died in 1982.

22nd December 1940

James CLEGG, Constable 2215   **Lancashire Constabulary**

George Medal

Harry MARTIN, Scaffolder   **Lancashire**

British Empire Medal (Civil Division)

During the first night of the two day's raid on Manchester, between 9p.m. and 10p.m. December 22nd, 1940, a high explosive bomb fell in Shrewsbury Street, Old Trafford, partially demolishing four houses and damaging a large number of others. Constables Clegg and Drysdale went to the scene.

Clegg was informed that an old man was trapped in No. 51 which was partly wrecked with the remains of the upper story on fire.

He made his way through the scullery and wrecked kitchen to what had been the hall, and, by the light of the flames, he saw a man's head sticking out of the debris of plaster and timber, which was all that remained of the staircase.

Assisted by a civilian called Martin, Clegg tore the timber away and succeeded in freeing the trapped man, a Mr. Waterworth, aged 77 years, who was unconscious and injured about the head and chest.

They managed with great difficulty to get the old man out and he was taken to hospital. Clegg returned again to the burning house and was told that another man was inside.

He re-entered the ruins searched the back rooms, pulled away some debris and cleared his way to the cellar, but was unable to find anyone.

By this time, the heat and intensity of the fire had so increased that he was obliged to leave the house. Shortly after this the A.F.S. and rescue parties arrived, and Clegg assisted them to subdue the fire. The body of the man was recovered a fortnight later from under a heap of rubble which was once the front door of the house.

Clegg had previously assisted at many incidents including an electric works fire in Clifton Street, high explosive bombs in Carriage Street and Duke Street, and subsequently assisted in the recovery of bodies of his fellow police officers from the wrecked Divisional Headquarters at Old Trafford.[36]

---

[36] Five police officers were killed or died from their injuries arising from the large bomb which hit the Police Station at East Union Street, Old Trafford on 23rd December 1941, causing the building to collapse. The officers who died were Chief Inspector William A. Chippendale, P.C. Herbert Berry, P.C. John Harrison Burns, P.C. Ian Douglas Steen and Special Constable Henry Edward Heaton. At the time the bomb fell Lancashire's Chief Constable, Archibald Frederick Hordern, was in the Police Station and escaped with minor injuries only. It is believed that Constable Burns was the Chief Constable's driver.

The sustained efforts made by Clegg during the entire night of December 22nd in rescuing and helping the injured, and particularly his most gallant work in a very unsafe and burning house, where he effected the rescue of Mr. Waterworth and made a most courageous effort to save another man were an example to the whole Force, and Clegg thoroughly earned the high honour conferred upon him.

Mr. (Harry) Martin received the honour of the British Empire Medal for Gallantry.

Lancashire Constabulary award file – PLA/ACC6849

HO 250 Civil Awards case: 870   L.G. 13/5/1941 Issue 35162 Page 2780

FURTHER INFORMATION:

Location of incident – 51 Shrewsbury Street, Old Trafford, Manchester.

51 Shrewsbury Street was a lodging house with five persons in the house at the time of the incident. William Henry Waterworth, aged 77 years, a retired butcher was one of the lodgers and appears to have survived the incident having been rescued. He died, aged 80 years, in 1944.

Three other persons survived the explosion. The person found dead in the rubble two weeks later was George Skinner, aged 29 years, also a lodger at the house.

James Clegg was born at Rochdale, Lancashire, in July 1915. He attended Rochdale Secondary School. His father, Mr J.T. Clegg, was the licensee of the Brown Cow Hotel, Milkstone Road, Rochdale. The family left Rochdale in 1929.

He was appointed to Lancashire Constabulary on 31st July 1937. His previous occupation was as a dairyman and he was living at Widnes. He was posted to Farnworth and later posted to Lonsdale South Division in 1938 and 1939 for summer duties. He returned to Farnworth in September 1939 before being posted to Manchester Division on 18th November 1939.

He was allowed to join the Royal Air Force on 8th September 1941 as a pilot/observer. After flight training he joined 101 Squadron based at RAF Ludford Magna, Lincolnshire, as a Flight Sergeant on 23rd December 1943. 101 Squadron operated Avro Lancasters. His first operational sortie was to Berlin on 2nd January 1944. During January and February 1944, he carried out seven sorties, flying to Berlin, Stettin, Leipzig, Stuttgart, Schweinfurt and Augsburg.

On one of the missions his aircraft was hit by friendly fire from another Lancaster, resulting in one of the engines and the mid upper turret being put out of action. On his mission to Augsburg on 25th February 1944, his aircraft was hit by flak, causing damage to the front turret. On 5th February 1944 he was commissioned to Pilot Officer 171637. (L.G. 14/3/1944 Issue 36422 Page 1218)

His final mission with his crew was on 15th March 1944 to Stuttgart. His Lancaster I ME 558 SR-Q was shot down by a German night fighter close to the German border in Alsace, France. Clegg and the other seven members of the crew were killed.

Pilot Officer James Clegg G.M. took off from RAF Ludford Magna at 1900 hours. His aircraft was an ABC equipped plane; ABC was electronic counter measure to jam German radar and carried an additional 8th crew member, namely a German-speaking operator to transmit spoof messages and

(© Isabelle Perrot and Guillaume van der Wende – France)

confuse enemy radio transmissions.

Seven of the crew were found in the wreckage of the aircraft and are buried in a collective grave at Mussig Cemetery, France. The eighth member of the crew, Flight Sergeant John Frederick Ennis, was found dead several days later near Wittisheim, having bailed out from the aircraft. He is buried at the Choloy War Cemetery, Meurthe-et-Moselle, France.

In 1972, a hub and a propeller blade from the aircraft were uncovered and was later placed in front of the grave as a memorial to the seven airmen at the cemetery. It was inaugurated on 17th March 1974.

The collective grave of seven members of the crew of Avro Lancaster ME 558 at Mussig Cemetery, France along with one of the propeller blades and hub recovered from the aircraft crash site.

(© Isabelle Perrot and Guillaume van der Wende – France)

James Clegg was 29 years old and left a wife, Gladys, and a daughter, Patricia Ann.

The inscription of his headstone at Mussig Cemetery reads as follows:

'BEAUTIFUL MEMORIES, SILENTLY TREASURED, HUSBAND, SON AND DADDY.'

A pension of £30 per annum was paid by Lancashire Constabulary to his widow and an allowance of £10 per annum to his daughter up to 1956.

Harry Martin was aged 37 years at the time of the incident and was employed as a scaffolder and attached to the Wright Street, Old Trafford, Demolition Squad. He lived at 49 Barrett Street, Old Trafford, Manchester.

During the whole period between the sounding of the 'alert' at about 6.30p.m. on December 22nd 1940, in the Manchester area, until some 40 to 45 hours afterwards.

Some hours later than the end of the second consecutive night raid, Inspector Holliday was ceaselessly employed in superintending and personally assisting in the highly dangerous work of rescuing and relieving unfortunate people who were trapped or buried under the debris of falling buildings.

Shortly after 6.30p.m. 22nd December, having observed the coolness and great courage displayed by the Police Officers mentioned above, who were then working in two's or three's Mr. Holliday welded them all into one team, placed himself at the head of it, and, utterly ignoring the very great and continuous danger from bombs, fires, falling buildings etc., took them in his car from one incident to another, wherever the danger was greatest or the need for help most urgent.

Mr. Holliday and his team kept up the ceaseless struggle during the whole time, indifferent to the danger and great fatigue which such unaccustomed and prolonged exertions caused.

So many incidents were dealt with, and the work was so shared by all that it was found impossible to commend any one officer above his fellows.

The fine leadership and contempt for danger which was displayed by Mr. Holliday were a source of inspiration to the whole team, and an example to the Police which is impossible to overestimate, his conduct was a credit to the whole Force, and he is a thoroughly worthy recipient of the high honour which was bestowed on him.

Lancashire Constabulary award file – PLA/ACC6849

HO 250 Civil Awards case: 866   L.G. 22/4/1941 Issue 35143 Page 2339

Other members of Holliday's team comprised Cuthbert Dickenson Morrison, Police Sergeant; John Thomas Brewer, Police Constable; John Vincent James Denney, Police Constable; John Robert Leach, Police Constable; and Edward Gerard McClorry, Police Constable. All were awarded the British Empire Medal (Civil Division). – See next entry.

FURTHER INFORMATION:

Thomas Edward Holliday was born at Whinfell near Kendal, Westmorland on 23rd March 1888. He joined Lancashire Constabulary on 17th June 1913 as Constable 298. He was promoted to Sergeant on 10th June 1929 and Inspector on 1st January 1934.

He served at Bury, Blackburn, Ashton-under-Lyne, Rochdale, Garstang and Manchester Divisions. He was pensioned on 1st January 1944 after serving for 30 years, 198 days. He died, aged 81 years, on 22nd November 1969 whilst resident in New South Wales, Australia.

22nd December 1940

Cuthbert Dickenson MORRISON, Sergeant 41	**Lancashire Constabulary**
John Thomas BREWER, Constable 977	**Lancashire Constabulary**
Edward Gerard McCLORRY, Constable 2366	**Lancashire Constabulary**
John Robert LEACH, Constable 863	**Lancashire Constabulary**
John Vincent James DENNEY, Constable 572	**Lancashire Constabulary**

British Empire Medal (Civil Division)

Cuthbert Dickenson Morrison

John Thomas Brewer

Edward Gerard McClorry

John Robert Leach

John Vincent J. Denney

During the whole of the time from the sounding of the 'alert' about 1830 hours on December 22nd 1940, until long after the second raid some 30 hours afterwards, the above named police officers, under the direction of Inspector Holliday, who himself received the award of the George Medal, worked unceasingly and untiringly with spades, picks and their bare hands to relieve or rescue suffering people buried or trapped by the crumbling buildings which failed to withstand the shattering explosions of parachute mines or high explosive bombs.

Indifferent to danger from fires, collapsing property and falling bombs, ignoring the bruises and discomforts arising from so much work of a type to which they were not accustomed, all these men stuck to their work for a period of some 40 to 45 hours, moving from incident to incident by car so as to lose no time in their efforts to minimise the effects from mines and bombs which were so freely strewn around the district.

During the daytime, they were employed dealing with unexploded bombs. So many incidents were dealt with by the whole team, others by two or three of its members, and the work was so shared by the men, that it was impossible to differentiate between them.

Among the outstanding incidents which these officers dealt with were:

a) The rescue of trapped persons from wrecked houses in King's Road, where people were pinned by a wash house roof, which had been reinforced with concrete which had given way.

b) Extinguishing, without the aid of the Fire Brigade, a large fire in a garage, which had gained such a hold that flames and smoke were pouring from the broken windows, no water was available and very little sand.

c) An incident in Milton Road, where two people were killed, and others pinned down in the wreckage. They were freed and the homeless found shelter.

d) Raising and holding for half an hour, a piece of masonry weighing about half a ton which had fallen upon a man in Milwain Road.

e) Forcing an entry into partially demolished cellar under wrecked houses in Urmston Lane, to rescue trapped people.

f) Releasing an injured Warden, who was pinned by the concrete top of a surface shelter which had given way in Victoria Park School Yard

Lancashire Constabulary award file – PLA/ACC6849

HO 250 Civil Awards case: 866   L.G. 22/4/1941 Issue 35143 Page 2339

FURTHER INFORMATION:

Cuthbert Dickenson Morrison was born at Seaton, Cumberland and was appointed to Lancashire Constabulary as P.C. 41 on 26th September 1921. Morrison had previously served during the Great War in the Royal Field Artillery and the Royal Engineers, landing in France on 28th July 1915. He gained promotion to Sergeant in 1936 and Inspector in 1942. He served at Leyland, Kirkham and Manchester Divisions. He died whilst still serving in April 1943.

John Thomas Brewer was born at Quernmore, near Lancaster, in December 1905. He was appointed to Lancashire Constabulary on 1st March 1926. Brewer was a World Champion (Cumberland and Westmorland style) wrestler and had four brothers serving in the police.

He served at Bury and Manchester Divisions. He was promoted to Sergeant in November 1942 and retired on 6th June 1954. He died in 1988.

Edward Gerard McClorry was born at Morecambe, Lancashire and was appointed to Lancashire Constabulary on 6th November 1937. His previous occupation was as a chemist with Standfast Ltd, Lancaster (a fabric manufacturer – still in operation).

During his police career, he served at Manchester and Lonsdale South Divisions. In June 1941, he was awarded the Merit Badge for brave conduct in the recovery of the body of a child who had drowned in a pond. He was awarded the Royal Humane Society Testimonial on Parchment for the same incident.

On 6th October 1941, he was allowed to enlist in the Royal Air Force and in July 1944 was awarded the Distinguished Flying Cross (D.F.C.) for *'successful operations against the enemy when he displayed high skill, fortitude and devotion to duty'*.

At the time of the award he is shown as holding the rank of Flying Officer 139380 with 77 Squadron. 77 Squadron, which was based at Elvington, Yorkshire from Oct 1942 to May 1944, operated Halifax four engine bombers, playing a prominent part of Bomber Command's strategic bombing campaign over Germany.

His two brothers were also serving in the armed forces, one in the Royal Navy and the other also in the R.A.F.

In June 1946, he re-joined Lancashire Constabulary and served until February 1947 when he resigned. He died, aged 72 years, in 1986.

John Robert Leach was born at Churchtown, Garstang, Lancashire in August 1918. He was appointed to Lancashire Constabulary on 4th October 1937 and served until 30th June 1968, retiring as a Chief Inspector. He joined the Army on 20th August 1942. John Robert Leach was also awarded the King's Police Medal for Gallantry in 1950. (See later entry.) He died, aged 85 years, in 2003.

John Vincent James Denney was born in Preston, Lancashire, in 1915 and was appointed to Lancashire Constabulary on 26th February 1938. His previous occupation was as a shipping clerk. He had previous service as a Territorial Soldier with the 88th Field Artillery. He served at Manchester Division for the whole of his career. On the 6th October 1941, he was allowed to enlist in the Royal Air Force, serving as Flight Lieutenant 134534. He resigned from Lancashire Constabulary on 27th May 1946 and died, aged 56 years, in 1972.

22nd December 1940

Norman Blundell GEE, Constable 412   **Lancashire Constabulary**

British Empire Medal (Civil Division)

At about 1915 hours on Sunday December 22nd, 1940, a large high explosive bomb fell and made a crater about 40 feet across and 20 feet deep opposite Nos. 94, 96 and 98 Gilda Brook Road, Eccles. These three houses were demolished, others were damaged, and fractured the water main, electricity cable, main sewer and gas main, the last of which had caught fire.

Constables Gee and Green ran immediately to the spot, assisted by a warden they rescued three women who had been partially buried by debris. Gee then assisted in the rescue work of 40 people who were buried under one of the houses which was used as a first aid post. While the above work was going on, it was realised that the burning gas main which was from 5' to 6' down the crater was throwing flames from 12 to 15 feet long and was acting as a guide to enemy aircraft as bombs and shrapnel were falling all around and machine gunning was taken place.

Inspector Dean called for volunteers to attempt to put the gas main out. Gee and Constable Parr volunteered, and as Parr was a gas fitter before joining the Force, he was lowered head first into the crater; but was unable to reach the main and force the earth into it. He also found that gas was escaping from another unignited fracture of the gas main, and, as he was in danger of being overcome by fumes, he was pulled up into safety. Gee was taller and not so heavy as Parr, was then lowered head first into the crater, being held up by the ankles by Parr and a civilian, after several unsuccessful attempts, he eventually choked the flow of gas by the use of a spade and put the flames out.

Considerable difficulty was experienced in holding Gee up, due to the crumbling state of the edge of the crater, and he was not only in great danger from enemy action, the flames and unignited gas, but also from the fact that there was 12 feet of water and sewer matter at the bottom of the crater.

After having extinguished the flames and recovered from the effects of the gas, Gee returned to assist with the rescue work at the demolished houses, from which the following persons were released:

9 uninjured from No. 94 (First Aid Post)
5 uninjured from No. 98
22 injured from No. 94
13 dead from No. 94
5 dead from No. 96

In spite of his exertions Gee remained on duty till noon on Monday December 23rd, dealing with other incidents. His conduct throughout was a credit to the Force and deserving of the highest praise and award.

Lancashire Constabulary award file – PLA/ACC6849

HO 250 Civil Awards case: 867

L.G. 22/4/1941 Issue 35143 Page 2339

FURTHER INFORMATION:

Norman Blundell Gee was born at Ince, near Wigan, in 1909 and was appointed as Constable 412 in the Lancashire Constabulary on 31st May 1934. During his career he served at Rochdale, Manchester, Bury and Headquarters Divisions.

He served until September 1959 when he retired after 25 years police service. He died, aged 79 years, in 1988.

22/23rd December 1940

Ian Douglas STEEN, Constable 2482   **Lancashire Constabulary**

King's Commendation for Brave Conduct in Civil Defence (Posthumous award)

Undeterred by dangers and difficulties, the late Constable Steen worked untiringly and unceasingly for nine hours, until he was trapped in the wreck of the Divisional Headquarters at Old Trafford about 3am on the morning of the 23rd December, and sustained injuries from which he later succumbed.

Constable Steen was employed on motorcyclists duties and from the very beginning of that intensive raid, he passed from the scene of one disaster to another; crawling on his stomach into a flame enveloped room and extinguished the fire with water pushed in by other helpers who were unable to face the intense heat; searching crumbling ruins for occupants; removing a pregnant woman and children and wounded persons to places of safety; breaking into a large burning mica works and assisting to subdue the flames; removing chickens from a coop adjoining a burning building; struggling on his motorcycle through debris, round craters and over broken glass, conveying vital information to the Police Station – which could not be sent by telephone as the system had broken down – ignoring bombs, shrapnel , fires and falls until he was forced to abandon the machine due to punctured tyres.

Refusing to admit defeat, Constable Steen continued on foot his fight against the effects of enemy action. The is no doubt that this Constable spared no efforts in his determination to assist the public and other services during a most terrifying period, when fires were raging, and bombs and mines were being rained on the district.

Throughout that time, he set an excellent example and was an inspiration to his fellow officers until misfortune overtook him, and he received injuries from which he died three days later. Constable Steen was posthumously commended by His Majesty the King.

Lancashire Constabulary award file – PLA/ACC6849

HO 250 Civil Awards case: 868   L.G. 22/4/1941 Issue 35143 Page 2343

FURTHER INFORMATION:

John Edwin Summers (see next entry), who was trapped in the rubble of Old Trafford Police Station with Steen paid tribute in his statement regarding the incident as follows: *'Looking back over the happenings of the night, I have many times thought what magnificent courage late P.C. Steen showed. He dashed about the night giving help and performing his duty without any regard for his own safety and I have many times been filled with regret that he lost his life after his fine example of bravery and service.'*

Ian Douglas Steen was born in April 1917 at Liverpool.

He was appointed to Lancashire Constabulary on 2nd July 1938 and had previously served with the South Lancashire Regiment (Prince of Wales Volunteers) for five years and 85 days. He is reported as being with the Regiment at the time of the Quetta earthquake in British India (Now Pakistan), which took place in the early hours of 31st May 1935. It is estimated that between 30,000 and 60,000 people were killed in the area. Quetta was a major garrison base and troops were used in the rescue and subsequent operations in the area.

Steen served at Manchester and then Leyland Division as a motorcyclist on the Home Office Motor Patrol Scheme.[37] He returned to Manchester Division on 25th February 1940.

He was injured on 23rd December 1940 and died from his injuries, aged 23 years, on 26th December at Winwick Emergency Hospital.

22/23rd December 1940

John Edwin SUMMERS

Police Auxiliary Messenger   **Lancashire Constabulary**

King's Commendation for Brave Conduct in Civil Defence

Showing exception courage, resource and coolness for a youth of 18 years and only two month's service, Summers played his part wholeheartedly from the time the sirens sounded the 'Alert' about 6.35p.m. on the 22nd December 1940 until he was pinned beneath the ruins of the shattered Divisional Police Headquarters in East Union Street, Old Trafford, when a direct hit by a large bomb caused the building to collapse just after Summers entered to deliver a message at about 3a.m. the following morning.

During the ensuing period which rescuers were struggling to extricate the trapped occupants of the Police station Summers' spirit never faltered although both his arms and legs were trapped in the debris and he was suffering from head injuries and was temporarily blinded.

Only some fifteen days afterwards he was fit to leave hospital with the sight gradually returning in one eye, but still blind in the other. When the telephone system was put out of action in the early stages of the raid, it became necessary for the Police to use to the full their other sources of communication and the boy Summers responded eagerly to every request made to him, regardless of the damage from falling bombs, shrapnel, fires and damaged buildings.

Alone, or accompanying P.C. Steen (who has since died of injuries received in the raid) Summers conveyed particulars from incident after incident to the Police Station. Not content with this, Summers assisted the

---

[37] See entry for Stanley Dobson for an explanation of the scheme.

Police to search damaged property, tended wounded people and removed distressed persons to the safety of a shelter. This youth of 18 rendered an outstanding service to the community – unfortunately at a heavy cost to himself.

Summers subsequently received a Commendation from His Majesty the King.

Lancashire Constabulary award file – PLA/ACC6849

HO 250 Civil Awards case: 869   L.G. 22/4/1941 Issue 35143 Page 2343

FURTHER INFORMATION:

Summers had been a member of the Police Auxiliary Messenger Service since November 1940. He was an apprentice electrical fitter by trade. He was born in May 1922 in Stockport and died, aged 80 years, in 2003.

The **Police Auxiliary Messenger Service (P.A.M.S.)** was set up to provide a backup message service when telephone systems were rendered inoperable due to air raids. Most messengers were below the age of 18 and possessed their own bicycle.

They wore uniform which were usually army surplus items which had been dyed black and wore caps, berets or steel helmets. Most worked full time although in some areas some authorities recruited part-time volunteers who worked only after a raid. Most messengers received basic training in first aid and the use of stirrup pumps and were required to know the locations of civil defence and police posts.

The P.A.M.S. was effectively disbanded after July 1945.

P.A.M.S. lapel badge

> **22nd/23rd December 1940**
>
> **Archibald Idwal JONES, Police Constable 334**   **Salford Police Force**
>
> **British Empire Medal (Civil Division)**

This constable has shown exceptional keenness and zeal during enemy air raids. His work has been an outstanding example of courage and initiative.

He has been responsible for extinguishing many incendiary bombs and incipient fires and showed great courage and entire disregard of personal danger when assisting at rescue a number of casualties trapped in a demolished house.

HO 250 Civil Awards case: 626

L.G. 11/3/1941 Issue 35104 Page 1505

FURTHER INFORMATION:

Archibald Idwal Jones was born at Treorchy, Glamorgan, on 2nd December 1907 and was appointed to Salford Police on 31st December 1938. His previous occupation was as a miner. He was previously commended by the Chief Constable for the arrest of motor car thieves and the recovery of a stolen vehicle on 12th February 1939. He died in 2004.

During the enemy air attacks on Manchester Sergeant Whyte has been conspicuous for his gallant behaviour.

On one occasion, he helped to operate jets inside a warehouse until it became necessary, owing to the intense heat, to withdraw all personnel from the building. Whyte then climbed with his jets to the roof of an adjacent building and from there tackled the fire.

HO 250 Civil Awards case: 1067   L.G. 27/5/1941 Issue 35174 Page 3069

FURTHER INFORMATION:

Location of incident – Major Street, Manchester.

Andrew Whyte was aged 35 years at the time of the incident and had served with Manchester Fire Brigade for 11½ years.

During enemy air attacks on Manchester, Inspector Smith was in charge of a major appliance at many fires. He planned his attack systematically and, despite the injuries he sustained, continued with his work and directed operations so thoroughly that he obtained the maximum effort from personnel and appliances.

Throughout, Inspector Smith showed courage and devotion to duty.

HO 250 Civil Awards case: 1068   L.G. 27/5/1941 Issue 35174 Page 3068

FURTHER INFORMATION:

William Smith was aged 33 years at the time of the incident and had served with Manchester Fire Brigade for 11 years.

When the City of Salford suffered heavy and sustained attack from enemy aircraft, Superintendent Lawrence showed outstanding zeal, efficiency and devotion to duty.

He was indefatigable in his efforts to cope with the various incidents and at no time did the situation get out of hand. By his personal example of grit, coolness and cheerfulness, he did much to minimise the effects of the raid.

He organised voluntary fire parties and successfully effected the evacuation of members of the public from areas affected by unexploded time bombs and serious fires.

Superintendent Lawrence performed his duties in particularly difficult circumstances and was at all times an inspiring leader.

HO 250 Civil Awards case: 623

L.G. 14/3/1941 Issue 35104 Page 1503

FURTHER INFORMATION:

Sydney Lawrence was born at Eccles on 18th January 1905 and joined Salford Police on 1st February 1926. His previous occupation was as a clerk. He was promoted to Sergeant in 1934, Inspector in 1937, Superintendent in 1938 and Chief Superintendent in 1943. He was subsequently appointed Chief Constable of Reading Borough Police in May 1945.

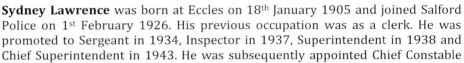

22nd December 1940

Henry Harper DOWNWARD, Police Constable 131   **Manchester City Police**

British Empire Medal (Civil Division)

During heavy air raids on Manchester, P.C. Downward has shown courage and tenacity in dealing with incendiary bombs.

With little regard for his own safety he has dealt very efficiently with a number of fires. His conduct, general bearing and devotion to duty have been an inspiration to other members of the Police Force.

HO 250 Civil Awards case: 619

L.G. 11/3/1941 Issue 35104 Page 1505

FURTHER INFORMATION:

Henry Harper Downward was born in June 1915 and joined Manchester City Police on 11th May 1938, aged 22 years. His previous occupation was as a painter and decorator. On 25th August 1942, he left to join the military forces. He re-joined Manchester City Police on 25th September 1945 and remained as a Constable until he resigned voluntarily on 9th April 1951. He died in 1972.

22nd/23rd December 1940

Francis George MARKIN, Inspector   **Salford Police Force**

British Empire Medal (Civil Division)

Houses were wrecked by high explosive bombs and persons trapped under the wreckage. Inspector Markin attended and organised rescue operations.

Throughout, enemy aircraft dropped incendiary and high explosive bombs. Though the work of rescue was hampered by the danger of the property collapsing, it continued until all persons were extricated. The Inspector helped to recover the dead and injured and took charge of a Police Rescue Party engaged in fighting a nearby fire.

His courage and complete disregard of danger was most encouraging to all.

HO 250 Civil Awards case no: 624

L.G. 21/3/1941 Issue 35111 Page 1643

FURTHER INFORMATION:

Location of incident(s) – Wilson Street and other locations in Pendleton.

Francis George Markin was born in 1900 in Smallburgh, Norfolk and joined Salford Police on 14th May 1923. His previous occupation was as a musician. Markin had served from 1915 to 1922 in the Hussars. He was promoted to Sergeant in 1933, Inspector in 1937, Chief Inspector in 1941 and Superintendent in September 1943.

Markin left Salford and was appointed Chief Constable of Peterborough Police in 1943. He died in 1995.

22nd December 1940

Francis John TAYLOR, Police Constable 112   **Salford Police Force**

British Empire Medal (Civil Division)

Copy of police report dated 8/1/1941:

During a raid, a large explosive bomb fell about forty yards from Constable Taylor, blowing him to the ground and completely demolishing five houses.

Although feeling the effects of the blast, he removed people from the debris and carried them into his own Anderson shelter nearby. He then helped to recover bodies from the wrecked houses. Later, he searched for an unexploded bomb, and, having found it, evacuated people in the district to rest centres.

He returned to give valuable assistance at a works fire. At another demolished house, he excavated some six feet of debris and located a child.

During the whole of the raid Constable Taylor showed indefatigable energy and coolness.

HO 250 Civil Awards case: 628

L.G. 11/3/1941 Issue 35104 Page 1506

FURTHER INFORMATION:

Francis John Taylor was born at Dobcross, near Oldham, on 20th December 1908 and joined Salford Police on 12th January 1931. His previous occupation was as a railway worker. He was commended by the Chief Constable in January 1939 for the arrest of two shop breakers. He died in 1983.

Copy of police report:

Throughout the raids on both nights Inspector Proctor, by his untiring efforts, set an inspiring example to all the men with whom he came in contact.

With many of the men from Divisional Headquarters he entered shops and lock-up premises into which incendiary bombs had fallen and took an active part in dealing with the bombs and resultant fires. He and his party of men were instrumental in saving buildings from total destruction by fire as the fire services were already overtaxed.

Inspector Proctor visited many of the larger incidents in the Division, and in addition to taking charge he joined with the men in the many and varied tasks that were encountered. He showed throughout both nights an utter disregard of personal safety, and whenever a new incident was reported he at once proceeded there with a party of men, in spite of the fact that the bombing was incessant.

He was present at the Regent Road Police Station when it was shattered by a bomb during the early part of the raid on the 23rd December. Although badly shaken himself his only concern was for the safety of the men present and for summoning immediate aid to the injured, two of whom had received fatal wounds. Following this occurrence, he took charge of a party of men and continued to attend other incidents.

Inspector Proctor was on duty almost continuously from the commencement of the first raid until the termination of the second and following these two nights of intensive efforts he remained at work until the situation had considerably eased.

HO 250 Civil Awards case: 625

L.G. 14/4/41 Issue 35104 Page 1507

FURTHER INFORMATION:

Robert Proctor was born at Alston, Lancashire, on 24th December 1892 and joined Salford Police on 7th April 1919. His previous occupation was as an asylum attendant. He had also served in the Grenadier Guards from 1915 to 1919. Robert Proctor was promoted to Sergeant in 1931 and to Inspector in 1934.

The two officers who died arising from the bombing of Regent Road Police Station were:

Inspector John William SALTHOUSE, aged 43 years. He died at Salford Royal Hospital on 24th December 1940. He was the husband of Florence, residing at 25 Wentworth Avenue, Pendleton.

Police War Reserve Constable Franklyn Baden WILKINSON, aged 40 years. He died on 23rd December 1940, also at Salford Royal Hospital. He lived at 16a The Crescent, Salford.

22ⁿᵈ/23ʳᵈ December 1940

Frank LEECH, Police Constable **Salford Police Force**

King's Commendation for Brave Conduct in Civil Defence

Copy of Police Report dated 8/1/1941:

On receipt of the Air Raid warning, Constable Leech turned out for duty and dealt with incendiary bombs which threatened property on the Cromwell Road district. When in Lissadel Street, incendiary bombs fall on Messrs. Reddaway's Mill and fires were started in the works.

Accompanied by another officer and a Warden, Leech climbed through a broken window and attacked the fire with sand and stirrup pump equipment which the men carried with them. They were successful in checking the fire until assistance arrived and prevented extensive damage.

Houses in Westminster Street were wrecked by high explosive bombs and Leech attended and assisted in rescue and evacuation work. Whilst so engaged incendiaries fall on Ward and Goldstone's Works, one falling on the roof and starting a fire, Leech ran to the Works, obtained admittance and found a ladder which enabled him to get onto the roof. He carried a bag of sand with him and succeeded in extinguishing the fire, he performed this work unaided as the firm's night watchers were engaged elsewhere. His action undoubtedly prevented serious damage to the Works which are engaged on important Government production.

Shortly afterwards a high explosive bomb completely demolished property in Strawberry Hill and a number of persons were buried under the wreckage. Leech and others went to this incident and assisted in the work of rescue and the evacuation of persons from nearby dangerous property.

He remained at this incident through the following day and continued through the further raids at night. He worked untiringly through the whole period regardless of danger.

HO 250 Civil Awards case: 627

L.G. 11/3/1941 Issue 35104 Page 1506

FURTHER INFORMATION:

Frank Leech was born at Bolton on 13ᵗʰ February 1903 and joined Salford Police on 1ˢᵗ September 1924. Between 1926 and 1945 he was commended on six occasions. He was promoted to Sergeant in March 1941. He died, aged 92 years, in 1996.

Frank Leech was awarded the King's Police Medal for his actions on 10ᵗʰ December 1926. (See earlier entry.)

22ⁿᵈ December 1940

Thomas ALKER, Police Sergeant 244 **Manchester City Police**

British Empire Medal (Civil Division)

During a heavy air raid, some works premises were set on fire.

Sergeant Alker organised a party of men, and, while A.F.S. units fought the flames, he arranged for the removal of a large number of motor tyres from the burning building.

At the same incident, a fire was discovered near to an ammunition store, and Sergeant Alker, showing a total disregard of danger to himself, went on the roof of a tool shed and extinguished the flames, thereby saving the ammunition.

HO 250 Civil Awards case: 616   L.G. 21/3/1941 Issue 35111 Page 1642

FURTHER INFORMATION:

Location of incident – Crossley Motors Ltd, Gorton Lane, Gorton, Manchester.

Thomas Alker was appointed to Manchester City Police, aged 20 years, on 9th September 1925. His previous occupation was as a miner. He served until 11th September 1955, when he was pensioned at the rank of Sergeant.

22nd December 1940

William GEORGE, Police Constable 117	**Manchester City Police**
British Empire Medal (Civil Division)	
William GREGORY, Police Constable 148	**Manchester City Police**
Arthur DAVENPORT, M.M., Police Constable 178	**Manchester City Police**
King's Commendation for Brave Conduct in Civil Defence	

During an enemy air raid P.C. George went to several places where unexploded time bombs had fallen. He displayed a calm devotion to duty, making thorough investigations and arranging for the evacuation of persons within the danger areas.

At one such incident the bomb exploded, and the Constable was blown against a wall by the blast. Despite the shock, he refused to go off duty and gave valuable help at other incidents.

HO 250 Civil Awards case: 620

L.G. 21/3/1941 Issue 35111 Pages 1642 & 1643

FURTHER INFORMATION:

Chief Constable's report

On the night of the 22nd December 1940, Police Constable William Gregory was engaged as a Bomb Investigation Officer. Together with a senior Constable who has been recommended for the award of the George Medal, P.C. Gregory caused some difficult evacuations on account of unexploded bombs and unexploded land mines.

Inspector's report

Police Constable 'C' 117 was then still suffering from shock after being blown up by a delayed action bomb in Delamere Street, Higher Openshaw. At 3.15a.m. in company with 'C' Inspector Batty I went to assist in the evacuation of people from the Clayton area. I found that P.C. Davenport had located an unexploded land mine which had fallen into the dwelling house, 12 Rushen Street, Clayton.

He had broken into the house and investigated the type of mine and assured himself that the occupants had not been injured. He then organised parties to go round and evacuate all residents within 400 yards.

Meanwhile P.C. 117 had located an unexploded land mine in Ashton New Road, near Park Street, Clayton.

Working in co-operation with P.C. 178 he quickly evacuated people from the vicinity. All the residents in that district were within a very short period evacuated and temporarily housed in various rest centres.

The prompt action and disregard of danger by these two men averted a serious catastrophe had these mines exploded.

William George was born at Monmouth and joined Manchester City Police on 18th February 1925, aged 26 years. His previous occupation was as a tin worker furnaceman. He had also previously served for just less than two years with the Royal Navy. He remained as a Constable until retirement on 27th December 1958.

William Gregory joined Manchester City Police on 28th September 1938. His previous occupation was as a grocer. William Gregory left to join the military forces on 23rd August 1942. He re-joined Manchester City Police on 19th September 1945, serving until 24th March 1950, when he resigned voluntarily.

Arthur Davenport was born in Macclesfield, Cheshire, and was appointed to Manchester City Police on 11th August 1920, aged 23 years, 11 months.

His previous occupation is recorded as being a wood turner. He is also shown as having served in the 2/8th Battalion of the Lancashire Fusiliers. Arthur Davenport was awarded the Military Medal during the Great War.

Arthur Davenport was pensioned on 16th September 1945.

22nd December 1940

Samuel PROCTOR, Sergeant   **Manchester City Police**

King's Commendation for Brave Conduct in Civil Defence

Sergeant Proctor of the G Division, was on duty on the evening of 22nd December 1940, when he heard a shower of incendiary bombs fall on a congested industrial area.

He hastened to the scene and found that a Greaseproof Paper Works was on fire. With the assistance of four constables he helped a detachment of the A.F.S. and succeeded in preventing the fire from spreading upwind to more valuable works property.

During all the time Sergeant Proctor was engaged, enemy aircraft were flying overhead, dropping land mines and bombs in the vicinity.

HO 250 Civil Awards case: 618   L.G. 14/4/41 Issue 35104 Page 1507

FURTHER INFORMATION:

Location of incident – Grave's Greaseproof Paper Works, Higher Openshaw, Manchester.

Samuel Proctor was born at Ulverston, Lancashire, and was appointed to Manchester City Police, aged 20 years, on 5th September 1923. His previous occupation was as a ploughman. He attained the rank of Inspector, retiring on pension on 29th September 1949.

22nd December 1940

Richard BAILEY, Police Sergeant   **Manchester City Police**

King's Commendation for Brave Conduct in Civil Defence

On the night of the 22nd December 1940, a heavy high explosive crushed the dwelling houses, 154/156 Fog Lane, Didsbury.

Three persons were trapped under the wreckage at 156, Fog Lane. Police Sergeant 'D' 3, Richard Bailey went to this incident.

On his arrival, it was found that Rescue Squads had not yet arrived. He resolutely set to work, making a way through the debris to reach the three people who were trapped underneath the staircase. Crawling through the wreckage on his stomach, after considerable effort he reached the trapped persons. By his own personal courage and cheerful words, he comforted and reassured thee people until the arrival of the Rescue Squad.

In carrying out this work, Sergeant Bailey displayed uncommon initiative, courage and determination and unrelenting effort in the face of great danger of becoming trapped himself. His example was an inspiration to Air Raid Wardens and others who assisted him.

His efforts had prepared the way for the rescue of these people by the Rescue Squads.

HO 250 Civil Awards case 614   L.G. 21/3/1941 Issue 35111 Page 1643

FURTHER INFORMATION:

Richard Bailey was awarded the King's Police Medal in 1921 and commended for bravery in 1929. (See previous entry for the award of the King's Police Medal.)

Richard Bailey was born at Biddulph Park, Staffordshire, and was appointed to Manchester City Police in October 1913, aged 21 years. His previous occupation was as a miner. He left Manchester City Police on 15th September 1915 to join the Royal Garrison Artillery, reaching the rank of Sergeant. He was posted to France on 31st May 1916 and served with 136th (3rd C./Palatine) Heavy Battery.

In April 1918, whilst in France, he was admitted to hospital as wounded, suffering from the effects of poison gas. Following his discharge from the Army he re-joined Manchester City Police on 22nd January 1919. He was pensioned at the rank of Sergeant on 9th December 1941.

22nd December 1940

Frank PRENDERGAST, Police Constable   **Manchester City Police**

Basil HEXTER, 342396 Aircraftsman, 1st Class   **Royal Air Force**

King's Commendation for Brave Conduct in Civil Defence

On the evening of the 22nd December 1940 whilst an enemy air raid was in progress, Police Constable Frank Prendergast was on duty outside the Regional Commissioners Offices, Arkwright House, Manchester when he observed an incendiary bomb of the explosive type roll underneath a motor car which was parked in the street.

He immediately took steps to extinguish the bomb by putting on sand when it exploded and injured the constable's eyes necessitating his removal to hospital.

At about 22.00 hours on the 23rd December 1940, whilst an air raid was in progress the Constable was an in-patient at the Royal Eye Hospital, Manchester and with others in the shelter when a high explosive bomb fell causing damage to the shelter and a water burst. He was prominent in assisting the staff to remove patients to a safer place.

Hearing that two doctors and nurses were missing he at once commenced to search for them and was assisted by Aircraftsman Basil Hexter who was also an in-patient. Together the two men located Doctor Scott in his room trapped under the wreckage with no means of escape.

Securing an axe and a large spanner the two men hacked their way through the wall removing bricks to admit air to the Doctor who was unable to move. A Rescue Party then arrived, and the two men assisted in the final rescue of the Doctor.

Both men although suffering themselves from injuries and in-patients showed extreme courage and devotion to duty.

HO 250 Civil Awards case: 615

L.G. 21/3/1941 Issue 35111 Page 1643 (Prendergast)

L.G. 14/3/1941 Issue 35106 Page 1523 (Hexter)

FURTHER INFORMATION:

Manchester Royal Eye Hospital remains in existence, situated at Oxford Road, Manchester.

Frank Prendergast was born in Manchester and was appointed to Manchester City Police, aged 21 years, on 4th January 1933. His previous occupation was as a weaver. He served with Manchester City Police until released to serve with the Control Commission in Germany on 21st July 1946. He re-joined Manchester City Police on 9th September 1950 and was pensioned as a Constable on 10th July 1958.

Basil Hexter was born in November 1902 in Devon. He died, aged 67 years, in 1970.

22nd December 1940

Alexander Duncan WARDROP, Police Constable **Manchester City Police**

King's Commendation for Brave Conduct in Civil Defence

About 8p.m. on Monday 23rd December 1940, an incendiary bomb fell on to the premises occupied by many firms including the A.R.P. stores at 22, Lloyd Street, City.

Wardrop was informed of this and with other constables entered the premises and found the bomb was burning in the rafters of the premises occupied by the King's Roll War Disabled Soldiers Ltd, which is on the third floor.

They were unable to reach the bomb in order to put it out and Wardrop climbed on to the shoulders of another man and grasped hold of some pipes, which ran along the roofing, and with a stirrup pump, put out the bomb, which was gradually igniting the roof.

Wardrop worked under difficulties, with his face being so near to the flames coming from the incendiary and showed excellent spirit and promptitude in preventing what could have been, very probably, a serious fire, with the loss of considerable A.R.P. equipment.

HO 250 Civil Awards case: 662   L.G. 21/3/1941 Issue 35111 Page 1644

FURTHER INFORMATION:

Alexander Duncan Wardrop was born in Muirkirk, Ayr, Scotland, and was appointed to Manchester City Police on 18th April 1934, aged 20 years. His previous occupation is recorded as being a plumber. On 1st November 1942, he left to join the military forces.

He re-joined Manchester City Police on 24th August 1945, serving until 14th September 1964 when he was pensioned, retiring as a Constable. He died in 1992.

22nd December 1940

Edward RUSS, Sergeant   **Salford Special Constabulary**

British Empire Medal (Civil Division)

Throughout the raids on Salford, Sergeant Russ was continually in action. A house was demolished by a high explosive bomb and two persons in an Anderson shelter were buried under the debris. Russ obtained help to raise a mass of the wreckage and then crawled underneath and brought the two victims to safety.

He assisted at other incidents and, when a number of houses were wrecked, he gave valuable aid in the work of rescue. His disregard of danger had a very reassuring effect on the people concerned.

Sergeant Russ worked untiringly and showed great devotion to duty.

HO 250 Civil Awards case: 631   L.G. 11/3/1941 Issue 35104 Page 1505

FURTHER INFORMATION:

Location of incident – various locations in Salford, Lancashire.

Edward Russ was aged 42 years at the time of the incident and had served with the Special Constabulary of Salford Police for 2 years. His civilian occupation was as an omnibus driver.

22nd December 1940

James Buxton WILES, Police Constable 287   **Salford Police Force**

British Empire Medal (Civil Division)

During a heavy air raid Constable Wiles showed exemplary coolness and initiative.

Although blown down by blast from a H.E. bomb he searched in the debris of some demolished houses and found an Anderson shelter which had been completely buried under the wreckage. The shelter was crushed, but, after much labour, he recovered four people, three of whom have survived. After attending to the casualties, Wiles continued his search and, although the debris was burning, he rescued a woman and a dog.

Wiles showed untiring energy and devotion to duty.

HO 250 Civil Awards case: 629

L.G. 11/3/1941 Issue 35104 Page 1506

FURTHER INFORMATION:

Location of incident – Great Cheetham Street, Salford.

James Buxton Wiles was born at Buxton on 19th June 1910 and joined Salford Police on 12th November 1935. His previous occupation was as an electrician. He reached the rank of Sergeant and retired on pension on 11th November 1965. He died in 1983.

22nd December 1940

William Edward ROBINSON, War Reserve Constable   **Salford Police Force**

King's Commendation for Brave Conduct in Civil Defence

Police War Reserve Robinson was on duty patrolling the Cromwell Bridge area during the evening of the 22nd December 1940, during an intensive air raid on the City. Shortly after 7.00p.m. a large number of incendiary bombs fell on Cromwell Bridge. Robinson obtained a number of bags of sand from a nearby police box, extinguishing the bombs.

When returning the empty sand bags to the box, a large high explosive bomb fell about 50 yards away, blowing Robinson round the police box and putting the box out of action. Although suffering from shock and blast, he ran to the scene of the explosion and found five houses destroyed. Hearing screams from underneath the debris Robinson recovered one girl uninjured and took her to safety.

He then removed seven persons from an adjacent house which was severely damaged, took them into nearby cellars, calmed them down and left them as comfortable as possible. He returned to the bombed houses, started to remove debris and assisted in the recovery of five people, one being dead.

Scraping debris with his hand to release people, he was seen to be thoroughly exhausted. He later assisted in the extinguishing of a house fire at Constable 315 Andrews' house and then went to a large factory fire, assisting to run hose for the firemen. A call was received for assistance at Hope Hospital and Robinson also accompanied this party.

Towards the end of the raid, when a high explosive bomb and a parachute mine exploded in a densely populated district, demolishing a large number of houses, Robinson carried on searching the debris and materially helped in recovering two middle aged women, who were found to be dead.

During the whole of the night Robinson showed a keen sense of duty, tireless energy and an entire disregard of personal danger.

HO 250 Civil Awards case: 630   L.G. 11/3/1941 Issue 35104 Page 1507

FURTHER INFORMATION:

Location of incident – Cromwell Bridge, Salford and other locations.

William Edward Robinson was aged 37 years at the time of the incident. He had served as a War Reserve Constable for two years. His civilian occupation was as a property repairer

Report by 'A' Division Inspector W, Humphry

I beg to report that the above Special Constable reported for duty at 7.00p.m. 22.12.1940 in connection with the Air Raid 'Alert'.

He had his motor car with him and offered to use it. He was kept standing by to drive 'A' Division parties to far away incidents. During the night, he was constantly engaged taking parties of men to the Hulme, Cornbrook and Portland Street District. He was traveling through the streets during the time the Air Raid was at its worst.

His fearlessness and courage in turning out many times was a good example to all.

HO 250 Civil Awards case: 700   L.G. 28/3/1941 Issue 35117 Page 1782

FURTHER INFORMATION:

William James McClintock was aged 34 years and had been a reserve Special Constable for 6 months. His civilian occupation was as a traveller.

Copy of Police Report, dated 8th January 1941

Since joining the Special Constabulary, Beckett has regularly used his private car for Police purposes. On the night of 22nd/23rd December he attended the Regent Road Police Station on the sounding of the sirens and was on duty throughout the night.

He performed invaluable work driving parties of men to various incidents, and for a considerable time drove his Divisional Superintendent to scenes of damage. He was on the streets for the greater portion of the night and displayed particular courage and devotion to duty, regardless of all personal risk.

Whilst driving along Oldfield Road, two high explosive bombs fell about one hundred and fifty yards in front of him, the blast causing extensive damage to a large block of artisan dwellings and forcing his car onto the footway.

In spite of this he immediately drove to the dwellings, directed the persons to a nearby shelter and made a search of the damaged buildings for the possible injured occupants. On returning to the Station immediately after this experience Beckett volunteered to drive a party of constables to an incident at which persons were known to be trapped under demolished houses.

The body of a woman and two injured men were quickly recovered from the debris by the Rescue Party and, as no ambulance was then available, Beckett conveyed the injured men and dead woman to hospital in his car. By this time, he had been driving almost continuously through nine hours of heavy raiding.

These are typical examples of his eagerness to be of service through the whole of the raid.

HO 250 Civil Awards case: 632

L.G. 18/3/1941 Issue 35111 Page 1643

FURTHER INFORMATION:

William Beckett was aged 43 years at the time of the incident and had been a Special Constable for 7 months. His civilian occupation was as a fruiterer.

22nd/23rd December 1940

Thomas Edward MORRIS, Police Constable D 178   **Manchester City Police**
(incorrectly named as William Morris in the *London Gazette*)

British Empire Medal (Civil Division)

Vernon Francis DICKINSON, Police Constable D 177   **Manchester City Police**

William Reginald LOMAS, Police ConstableD 119   **Manchester City Police**

King's Commendation for Brave Conduct in Civil Defence

Dwelling houses were demolished by a H.E. bomb. Constable Morris worked his way into a cellar and rescued two women who were injured. He returned and carried out a man who was injured and unconscious.

Morris then collapsed and, although told to rest, voluntarily went out again to help in further rescue work. Throughout the night he displayed unusual courage, initiative and resource.

HO 250 Civil Awards case 698a

L.G. 28/3/1941 Issue 35117 Page 1781

Constables Lomas and Dickinson worked hard assisting at the first mentioned incident, giving invaluable support to Morris until the Rescue Squads took over.

HO 250 Civil Awards case: 698 b & c   L.G. 28/3/1941 Issue 35117 Page 1782

FURTHER INFORMATION:

Locations – 87-97 Higher Cambridge Street, 66-70 Cowcill Street and later at 282–288 Oxford Road, Chorlton-on-Medlock, Manchester.

Thomas Edward Morris was born at Chester in 1902 and joined Manchester City Police in 1927, having transferred from the Fire Brigade where he had served for nearly two years He was pensioned in 1943 as medically unfit.

(There is no record of a William Morris as having served with Manchester City Police. Within the body of the award recommendation he is later named as D178 Thomas Morris. Thomas Edward Morris served as Constable D178. This appears to confirm the incorrect name within the citation in the *London Gazette*.)

Vernon Francis Dickinson was born in Blackpool and was appointed to Manchester City Police in February 1939, aged 20 years. His previous occupation is recorded as having been a fitter. Dickenson left Manchester City Police on 12th October 1941 to join the Royal Air Force.

On 29th January 1944, Pilot Officer 170952 Dickinson R.A.F. was on board a Short Stirling four engine bomber EF246, of 1660 Conversion Flight from RAF Swinderby on a night searchlight co-operation exercise. Shortly after 2200 hours, EF246 came into the Hull area flying on a course due south at 15,000 feet and was illuminated by about 20 searchlights. The aircraft commenced violent evasive action, turning north, and diving appeared to be in distress with smoke coming from one side of the aircraft.

All searchlights were doused at 8/9,000 feet. The aircraft continued diving with smoke and flames pouring from one engine. The aircraft crashed straight into the River Humber at 2203 hours. All crew members were killed. Pilot Officer Dickinson has no known grave and is commemorated on Panel 211 of the Runnymede Memorial.

The Air Forces Memorial at Runnymede commemorates by name over 20,000 airmen who were lost in the Second World War during operations from bases in the United Kingdom and North and Western Europe, and who have no known graves.

Pilot Officer Dickinson left a widow, Annie.

William Reginald Lomas was born in Manchester in January 1914 and was appointed to Manchester City Police on 18th March 1934, aged 20 years. He remained a Constable until being pensioned as medically unfit on 8th October 1946.

Runnymede Memorial at Cooper's Hill in Runnymede, Surrey. (© C.W.G.C.)

22nd/23rd December 1940

Ernest Alfred REDFERN, Police Sergeant   **Manchester City Police**

King's Commendation for Brave Conduct in Civil Defence

During an enemy air raid on the evening of the 23rd December 1940, Sergeant Redfern was off duty, but immediately responded to the 'Alert' warning. He supervised officers at incidents resulting from incendiary bombs, and later rendered valuable assistance extricating people from a demolished house which had caught fire.

While attending to this incident Sergeant Redfern discovered that a land mine had fallen 50 yards away and he successfully caused the evacuation of the surrounding district, including some wards of Baguley Sanatorium.

The following evening Sergeant Redfern again off duty succeeded in subduing a number of fires until the arrival of other personnel, whom he greatly assisted.

HO 250 Civil Awards case: 621   L.G. 21/3/1941 Issue 35111 Page 1644

FURTHER INFORMATION:

Ernest Alfred Redfern was born at Ipstones, Staffordshire, and was appointed to Manchester City Police on 7th February 1923, aged 20 years. His previous occupation was as a joiner's apprentice. He was pensioned on 7th February 1951, having reached the rank of Inspector. He died, aged 93 years, on 26th December 1996.

23rd December 1940

William HANLON, War Reserve Police Constable   **Manchester City Police**

British Empire Medal (Civil Division)

High explosive bombs demolished several houses. Hanlon immediately attempted to release a man trapped in wreckage up to his neck, with his legs held by cross beams. He tunnelled underneath the victim, working continuously for two and a half hours, with debris falling about him, before he succeeded in effecting the rescue.

Although Hanlon sustained minor bruises, he continued to help the rescue squads in extricating other trapped people, remaining on duty for a period of forty hours.

HO 250 Civil Awards case: 617

L.G. 11/3/1941 Issue 35104 Page 1505

FURTHER INFORMATION:

Location – Rylance Street Ardwick, Manchester.

William Hanlon was aged 44 years at the time of the incident and had served as a War Reserve Constable for 16 months. His civilian occupation was as a miner.

During an air raid Constable Crann extinguished fires at a warehouse and an office and was assisting the A.F.S. at another when a high explosive bomb dropped on the building. This caused the whole of the building to collapse and become a raging inferno.

The Constable, although severely shaken by the blast, searched for and found two injured and unconscious A.F.S. men. With assistance, the Constable carried them to a nearby air-raid shelter.

Although there was grave danger from burning timber and collapsing walls, Crann returned and at once set to work to release a man who was buried. Being without tools of any description he removed the debris with his hands and after a time was able to extricate the victim and carry him to safety. The Constable then again returned to the burning building and rescued an injured and unconscious fireman.

The Constable's unselfish and brave efforts, which were carried out in the worst possible conditions, were primarily responsible for the rescue of four men who would otherwise have lost their lives.

HO 250 Civil Awards case: 1054   L.G. 27/5/1941 Issue 35174 Page 3065

FURTHER INFORMATION:

Location of incident – Warehouse in King Street, Garston; Office and Telephone Exchange, South John Street, Central Liverpool; Warehouse in Atherton Street, Liverpool.

Edward Crann was born in 1895 at Haydock, Lancashire. He joined Liverpool City Police in August 1919, having served as a gunner with the Royal Field Artillery from 2nd September 1914 to 6th January 1919. Prior to this he worked as a collier.

During his police career, he was commended by the Watch Committee on five occasions. These included a commendation for the rescue of a youth from the Mersey in August 1933 for which he also received a Bronze Medal from The Liverpool Shipwreck and Humane Society.

He was also commended for prompt action during the IRA's S-Plan offensive in connection with an explosion at Renshaw Street, Liverpool on 26th August 1939. (See separate award relating to P.C. Francis Edward Dodd for other actions relating to this campaign.)

This involved George Whittaker, a member of the I.R.A. who was seen with smoke and flames emanating from an explosive device hidden under his coat, which he threw down prior to its exploding. The man was pursued by several police constables and was seen to throw a parcel away which was later found to contain 13 sticks of gelignite, a detonator and a balloon of acid. Whittaker was later convicted for terrorist offences at Liverpool Assizes and sentenced to seven years imprisonment.

Crann served until retirement in August 1946 and he died in October 1962, aged 67 years.

Bombs demolished houses, several people were trapped. Sgt. Claydon tunnelled twenty feet and rescued two women. He then shored up the tunnel with wood and masonry and after strenuous efforts succeeded in releasing another woman who was buried beneath rubble.

The Sergeant owing to his exertions in a gas-laden atmosphere, was overcome and had to rest. He recovered and though warned of the danger of gas, returned to the tunnel and continued his rescue work. A large piece of wood was blocking the passage, he obtained a saw, crawled into the space again, and lying on his stomach sawed through the block and was able to release two casualties.

Removing more debris, he freed a child and a man and cleared a space so that others could rescue those remaining. Claydon showed exceptional courage and by his efforts ten persons were rescued.

HO 250 Civil Awards case: 1096   L.G. 6/6/1941 Issue 35180 Page 3198

FURTHER INFORMATION:

Location of incident – Adlington Street, Liverpool.

Harold Frederick Claydon was born on 30th December 1907. He joined Liverpool City Police in 1927 and was promoted to Sergeant in 1938.

He was later promoted to Inspector and in 1959 he was responsible for making safe a bomb in Sir Thomas Street, Liverpool. He retired in 1964 after 37 years' service. He died in 1991, aged 83 years.

On 27th January 1959 telephone calls were received by staff in offices in Sir Thomas Street, Liverpool – Martins Bank and The Federation of Building Trade Employers. A man with a slightly foreign accent said, 'Listen carefully. This is urgent. Leave the building at once. There is a bomb in it.' The same call was received by the Police minutes later.

Initially the office staff treated it as a hoax, but one of the people who received the call noticed a brown attaché case on the floor near to the main entrance. She picked it up and placed it on the counter. Inspector Harold Claydon and Inspector Phillips then ran into the building and tore the back off the case. They found a battery from which two wires went into a hollowed-out loaf of bread, which contained white powder. Two bottles of petrol were wired in and there was a clockwork mechanism attached which was ticking.

Inspector Claydon defused the bomb by cutting through the wires with a pair of scissors. The apparatus was later forensically examined, and the powder was identified as a commercial explosive. He was commended for this brave action.[38]

---

[38] Liverpool City Police from http://liverpoolcitypolice.co.uk/harold-f-claydon/4555749632 – Retrieved 31/5/2017

13th March 1941

James CAMERON, Constable 97 'B'   **Liverpool City Police**

King's Commendation for Brave Conduct in Civil Defence

Chief Constable's report

At about 01.30 hours on Thursday, 13th March 1941 a parachute mine fell on St. Anne's R.C. School, Chatham Place, Liverpool and did not explode until 15 minutes later, with the resultant death of two Police Constables and the serious injury of four others.

Constable 97 'B' Cameron and other Police Officers were on duty at a nearby Police Station when information was received that an unexploded bomb had dropped in the vicinity. Cameron and other officers in charge of an Acting Sergeant went to investigate and located a parachute mine protruding from the roof of the above school, the mine apparently suspended in the building. A few minutes later the mine exploded.

The Constable was serious injured, having sustained a fractured left fibula, fractured right scapula, abrasions and burns to face, and severe shock. In this condition and whilst quickly losing consciousness, he made an effort to get away from the scene to obtain aid for his comrades whom he knew were either in or near the building. He was, however not successful in doing this unaided, and was carried into a nearby Sector Post.

Although the Constable must have been suffering great pain, his one thought was for the safety of his comrades, and before lapsing into unconsciousness he was able to give exact details as the number engaged at the incident, thereby rendering their rescue easier, with the result that three, although seriously injured, were saved. Unfortunately, two were killed instantly.

HO 250 Civil Awards case: 1055   L.G. 3/6/1941 Issue 35180 Page 3201

FURTHER INFORMATION:

The two officers killed at St. Anne's R.C. School, Chatham Place on 13th March 1941[39] were:

Police Constable 214 'B' Alan Trevor, aged 37 years, of 66 Allington Street, Liverpool. Husband of Alice Trevor.

Police Constable 73 'B' Cyril Nelson Read, aged 35 years, of 6 Stopgate Lane, Liverpool. Son of Henry and Fanny Read of 13 Stanley Road, Oldfield Park, Bath. Husband of Muriel Christina Read.

Four other police officers were injured in the same incident.

James Cameron was aged 26 years and had served with Liverpool City Police for two years.

---

[39] C.W.G.C. UK, *Civilian War Dead in the United Kingdom, 1939–1945*

29th March 1941

Thomas Arthur BENN, Constable 244 'C'   **Liverpool City Police**

Leslie Walter LACEY, Constable 347 'H'   **Liverpool City Police**

King's Police and Fire Services Medal

At about 3.15a.m. on 29th March 1941, the two Constables went out on motor cycles to a house that was on fire. When they arrived, the premises were well alight, the Fire Brigade had been sent for, and the Constables were told that the occupants were trapped upstairs.

They tried to force their way through the door without success, then Constable Lacey broke a window, and followed by Constable Benn climbed through, and up to the first floor, where they found the occupier, James Campbell his wife and three children. Campbell climbed through the window and jumped to the ground, whilst Constable Lacey helped the eldest daughter through the window, lowering her by hand.

At this point the Fire Brigade arrived, and Constable Lacey was rescued from the window, which was by now on fire. In the meantime, the front door was forced, and firemen made their way upstairs, finding the bodies of Constable Benn, Mrs Campbell and two children. Mr Campbell died later in hospital.

PRO Ref: H045/18911   L.G. 12/6/1941 Issue 35184 Page 3301

FURTHER INFORMATION:

Location of incident – 73 Laxey Street, Toxteth Park, Liverpool.

The casualties from the fire were: Police Constable Benn (25), Mrs Annie Campbell (43), Annie Campbell (15), Patrick Campbell (10) and Mr James Campbell (47), who died later. Mr Campbell, in addition to being burned, sustained a broken leg when he fell from a window ledge he was holding on to. Also injured were Police Constable Lacey and Marie Campbell (18), who were burned.

The inquest was held on 11th June before the Liverpool City Coroner, Mr G. C. Mort. Constable Lacey gave evidence to the inquest whilst lying on a stretcher. A verdict of accidental death was recorded for all five persons, concluding that the fire service had done all that it could in the circumstances and praised the selfless act of Constable Benn. Superintendent D. Richie of Liverpool City Police expressed regret that only two lives could be saved and offered his sympathy to the widow and relatives of Constable Benn.

The cause of the fire was never established due to the extensive damage to the house. Irene Campbell, another family member, stated she often stayed at the house with her father-in-law, who she had heard state there was a gas leak in the kitchen which was traced to the gas meter.

Thomas Arthur Benn was born in Liverpool on 4th September 1915. He is buried at Allerton Cemetery, Liverpool (Plot NC/11/314). He was a married man and a keen rugby footballer. His father was a Sergeant with the Liverpool Police Force. He was described as being a most promising officer who had served for four years.

His brother, **John Edwin Benn**, was awarded the B.E.M. for his gallant actions at Trafford Park, Manchester, whilst a Sub Officer of the Stretford and Urmston Joint Fire Brigade on 23rd December 1940. His citation reads as follows:

Thomas Arthur Benn

Sub-Officer Benn displayed courage and coolness in dealing with a very serious situation when H.E. bombs caused casualties to firemen and civilians. He gave first-aid treatment and applied tourniquets to three badly wounded persons. The Sub-Officer then went on foot, through intense bombardment, to other fires. He showed presence of mind and devotion to duty in extremely dangerous conditions.

L.G. 11/4/1941 Issue 35152 Page 2086

John Edwin Benn was killed as a result of shrapnel wounds arising from enemy action, aged 34 years, on 12th March 1941 at Great Stone Road, Stretford. He was buried at Allerton Cemetery on 15th March 1941 (Plot NC/11/240).

Leslie Walter Lacey

Leslie Walter Lacey was born in Colchester in 1914. He died, aged 74 years, in 1988.

2nd May 1941

Thomas SMITH, Sergeant 11 'E'	**Liverpool City Police**
Thomas SCULLY, Gunner 1703207	**Royal Regiment of Artillery**
George Medal	
John MURPHY, Constable 52 'E'	**Liverpool City Police**
British Empire Medal (Civil Division)	

High explosive bombs demolished a number of houses and people were trapped under the wreckage.

Sergeant Smith aided by a broken slate and working by the faint light of a bicycle lamp succeeded in reaching them after tunnelling in a gas laden atmosphere for more than fourteen yards. The tunnel was barely wide enough for one person to crawl through and there was constant danger of it collapsing.

After dragging out a man and a woman, the Sergeant again entered the tunnel and, when within a few feet of two other people, was himself trapped by a sudden fall of debris. He was eventually extricated in a collapsed condition. Sergeant Smith showed great bravery and made possible the release of four persons.

HO 250 Civil Awards case: 1700

L.G. 23/9/1941 Issue 35285 Page 5582

The King has been graciously pleased to approve the award of the George Medal, in recognition of conspicuous gallantry in carrying out hazardous work in a very brave manner, to:

No. 1703207 Gunner Thomas SCULLY, Royal Regiment of Artillery (Liverpool).

HO 250 Civil Awards case: 1700

L.G. 23/9/1941 Issue 35319 Page 6107

John Murphy

Dwelling houses were hit by bombs and people were trapped under the wreckage. Constable Murphy succeeded in rescuing a woman and her two children from the ruins of a demolished house. Later, whilst searching the first floor of another building, he fell through to the ground floor. Despite the severe shaking he received, he continued rescue work and was responsible for the release of other trapped victims

HO 250 Civil Awards case: 1700   L.G. 23/9/1941 Issue 35285 Page 5583

FURTHER INFORMATION:

Location of incident – Chancel Street, Toxteth, Liverpool.

Thomas Scully, 9 Meyrick Road, Liverpool 11, a gunner in the Royal Artillery who had been assisting Sergeant Smith by passing debris out of the tunnel, went to the rear of the house and after removing a considerable amount of debris managed to tunnel a way to, and eventually release, the man, woman and Sergeant Smith, the latter being removed to hospital in a collapsed condition.

Although most exhausted, Scully stuck tenaciously to his task and it was largely due to his efforts that three people were rescued alive.

Thomas Smith was born in Staffordshire in 1888 and appointed to Liverpool City Police in June 1909 serving until July 1911 before resigning. His service record shows he served with the Royal Field Artillery prior to joining the police and whilst a serving officer, so it appears he may have been an Army reservist.

He is shown as having served in the RFA during the Great War until released in June 1919. He was reappointed to Liverpool City Police in August 1919. He was commended on three occasions and was promoted to Sergeant in 1925. He was also awarded the Bronze and Silver Good Conduct medals.

He was pensioned in May 1944, having completed his pensionable service. In February 1947, he joined the First Police Reserve and served until September 1951. He died, aged 76 years, in January 1964.

Thomas Scully was attached to No. 1 Troop, 322 Heavy Battery, Royal Artillery, Altcar.

John Murphy was born in 1893 and served with Liverpool City Police for 25 years before being retired and being granted a special pension as a result of being assaulted on 14th February 1943, where he was knocked unconscious, sustaining a head injury and injuries to his left ankle. He died in 1962.

2nd to 7th May 1941	
Arthur Diamond BOYD, Temporary Sergeant, 111 'H'	**Liverpool Fire Brigade**
British Empire Medal (Civil Division)	

A serious fire was caused by enemy action. Sergeant Boyd, who was in charge of a party of firemen, climbed to the apex of the roof of an adjoining building and from there directed operations. In spite of his precarious position and the danger of naphtha tanks exploding, of which he was fully aware, the Sergeant remained on the roof until the fire was under control and the building and its contents were saved.

On two other occasions during air raids Temporary Sergeant Boyd has, by his promptitude and courage, been responsible for preventing serious fires.

HO 250 Civil Awards case: 1345   L.G. 15/7/1941 Issue 35220 Page 4106/4107

FURTHER INFORMATION:

Location of incident – Bridgewater Street, Liverpool.

On the night of the 2nd/3rd May 1941, a serious fire was caused by enemy action at the premises of the African and Eastern Trade Corporation, Bridgewater Street, Liverpool, which contained large stocks of naphtha and paint.

Temporary Sergeant 111 'H' of the Liverpool Fire Brigade, who was in charge of a party of firemen, climbed to the apex of the roof of an adjoining building from where he directed operations. In spite of his precarious position, and the danger of naphtha tanks exploding, of which the Sergeant was fully aware, he remained on the roof until the fire was under control, and a considerable portion of the building and contents were thus saved.

On the night of the 4th/5th May 1941, a further fire caused by enemy action at the Welsh Chapel, Northumberland Street, presented a serious difficulty to the Fire Service. The Chapel has a high and steeply sloping roof. Temporary Sergeant Boyd made a perilous ascent, and by stripping off the slates, and with the aid of a first aid branch confined the fire to the roof. In this case his promptitude and courage was undoubtedly responsible for preventing a serious fire. Enemy aircraft were overhead all the time and the attack was intense.

Again, on the night of the 6th/7th May, Temporary Sergeant Boyd by his leadership and devotion to duty was largely responsible for saving the major portion of the important Flour and Rice Mills belonging to Messrs. W.O. and J. Wilson, South End Mills, Liverpool 8. In spite of the fact that high explosive and incendiary bombs were falling all around, Temporary Sergeant Boyd and his crew, together with the Works crew, remained at his post until the fire was under control.

FURTHER INFORMATION:

Arthur Diamond Boyd was born in Liverpool in April 1897 and, prior to joining Liverpool Police Fire Brigade, he worked as a painter. He joined the King's Liverpool Regiment on 11th May 1914, serving until 4th May 1919, being discharged holding the rank of Sergeant. In January 1927, he was awarded the Silver Medal and Letter of Appreciation from The Liverpool Shipwreck and Humane Society for the rescue of a man from the Canada Dock on 7th December 1926.

In 1941, he was transferred to the National Fire Service. He died, aged 87 years, in 1985.

2nd-9th May 1941 (and devotion to duty during war period)

Henry Donald SCOTT, District Commander   **Lancashire Special Constabulary**

British Empire Medal (Civil Division)

Throughout his service, extending over a period of 25½ years, Mr Scott has shown exceptional zeal and devotion to duty.

Since the outbreak of the war, he gave up the whole of his time and energy to the task of maintaining and increasing the efficiency of the Special Constabulary in the district under his command. Without a thought for his own safety, he visited his men in the heaviest air raids, and by his cool courage he encouraged and assisted in their difficult tasks.

During the heavy raids on the Merseyside district from May 2nd to May 9th, 1941, Mr Scott was on duty almost continuously setting his men a splendid example by being constantly in the midst of dangerous incidents, and by his fine demeanour and disregard of danger he encouraged his men and kept up their spirits to a high level.

As a result of his personal efforts the Special Constabulary in the area carried out their duties with zeal and efficiency, and Mr Scott is entirely deserving of the award which His Majesty was pleased to confer upon him.

Lancashire Constabulary award file – PLA/ACC6849

HO 250 Civil Awards case: 1480

L.G. 15/8/1941 Issue 35245 Page 4705

FURTHER INFORMATION:

Henry Donald Scott was aged 64 years at the date of the incidents. Mr Scott was a retired glass merchant.

3rd May 1941

William Henry COTTIER, Constable 14	**Bootle Police Force**
British Empire Medal (Civil Division)	
Thomas Joseph McCARTHY, G.M., Constable 27	**Bootle Police Force**
James BESFORD, War Reserve Constable 21	**Bootle Police Force**
Stanley Percival JONES, Special Constable 59	**Bootle Special Constabulary**
King's Commendation for Brave Conduct in Civil Defence	

During an air raid a house was demolished and set on fire. Constable Cottier heard a shout for help and, with his bare hands, scooped a hole in the debris.

There was room for only one man to work as the flames were creeping nearer and the heat was intense. He began to pull the victim out through the hole, but a large beam partly blocked the way. Cottier crawled under the beam and, with help, raised it sufficiently to release the man. As he got clear, the end of the beam, which was now ablaze, crashed into the hole.

HO 250 Civil Awards case: 1779

L.G. 10/10/1941 Issue 35302 Page 5838 (Cottier)

L.G. 7/10/1941 Issue 35302 Page 5839 (McCarthy, Besford & Jones)

FURTHER INFORMATION:

Location of incident – Bailiol Road, Bootle.

Report by P.C. Cottier:

I was instructed by the Chief Inspector to go to the Central Police Station, accompanied by W.R. 21 Besford and Sp. Con 59 Jones and report verbally, I reported the incidents to the Superintendent. P.C. McCarthy then offered to take me back in the Police Van and we started to return via Balliol Road. When near Dr. Buxton's house we saw that a house had been completely demolished and was blazing furiously. We stopped there and on climbing through the debris we saw the face of a man buried 2 ft. below the surface. He was completely trapped. The flames were no more than 3 ft. away from him. I tried to pull him out but was unable to owing to the debris covering him.

We then saw that a long beam protruding from the debris, which if eased up, might free the man. P.C. 27, W.R. 21 and S.C. 59, and other helpers then lifted the beam whilst I placed my back underneath it to prevent it slipping. I then got hold of one of the man's arms whilst another man took the arm on the other side, as the others tugged at the beam, we managed to drag him out.

The flames were about 18 ins. from him. He was clad only in a shirt and appeared very dazed. From what we could gather, six females were buried in the cellar but owing to the intensity of the flames we could not get near them. A Warden said he reported the incident and we decided to get the man to Hospital, which we did.

Bomb damage – Bailiol Road, Bootle. (Note remains of Anderson shelter to left of photograph.)
(© Sefton Library Services)

William Henry Cottier was aged 30 years at the time of the incident and had served with Bootle Police for five years.

Thomas Joseph McCarthy was previously awarded the George Medal for his actions at an earlier incident. (See previous entry.) At the time of this incident he was aged 29 years and had served with Bootle Police for five years. In 1968 he is reported as being a Superintendent.

James Besford was aged 39 years at the time of the incident and had served as a War Reserve Constable for two years. His civilian occupation was as a sugar boiler.

Stanley Percival Jones was aged 40 years at the time of the incident and had served as a Special Constable for five months. His civilian occupation was as a Sub-Transport Manager.

3rd May 1941

Henry James COUSINS, Plumber	**Bootle**

George Medal

Charles FRASER, Constable 48	**Bootle Police Force**

Maurice COLLINGS, Engineer
(Now Civil Defence Wardens Service)	**Bootle**

John Joseph O'GARA (Civil Defence Wardens Service)	**Bootle**

King's Commendation for Brave Conduct in Civil Defence

A high explosive bomb demolished a house and persons were trapped in a brick shelter. The top of the shelter was leaning on the bricks of the side wall which was pinning the casualties underneath. The back wall of the house had fallen on top of the shelter. Cousins crawled underneath a large concrete slab, which formed the roof of the shelter, and fixed props to take the weight.

This allowed the brickwork to be removed and the victims were then extricated alive without further suffering. Mr. Cousins was fully aware that he might be buried under the bricks and concrete but risked his life to effect this gallant rescue.

HO 250 Civil Awards case: 1512

L.G. 19/8/1941 Issue 35252 Page 4848

FURTHER INFORMATION:

Location of incident – Keble Road, Bootle.

Copy of report by P.C. Fraser

I have to report with reference to the high explosive bomb incident at 69/73 Keble Road, Bootle that Henry James Cousins, 84 Keble Road, Bootle, plumber, performed gallant rescue work in assisting me with the rescue of Francis Garrett, 45 years of 73 Keble Road, Rose Garrett, 44 years, wife, and Joan, 13 years, daughter, who were trapped in a brick shelter in their back yard. Francis Garrett, 18 years, son believed dead and John Roney, 62 years, dead were also brought out of the shelter.

The rescue was dangerous owing to the top of the shelter being pushed off and leaning on the bricks of the sidewall which was pushed over and pinning the occupants underneath. The back wall of the house also fell on top of the shelter.

Cousins at great risk to his own safety got underneath the concrete slab (top of the shelter) and put in props to take the weight which allowed the brickwork to be removed and the persons to be extricated without causing further suffering.

The Garretts were then conveyed to Hospital for treatment, and I feel sure they will be good witnesses to corroborate the good work done by Cousins.

Statement of M. Collings.

At about midnight on Saturday, May 3rd, 1941 I had just returned to the Warden's Post in Stanley Gardens from an incident when a message was received that a high explosive bomb had dropped near to No. 71 Keble Road...

I returned to the incident and went round to the back yard of No. 71. I then found that the Anderson shelter had been damaged by a high explosive bomb which had fallen just outside, and that the bricks and concrete shelter at No. 73 had been demolished. When I arrived, I found that Lee and Pilkington, and some F.A.P.[40] men were removing the last of the people.

I assisted to take the people from No. 71 to an ambulance and returned to No. 73 to see what could be done about the people in the brick shelter. I then found that Mr Cousins, P.C. Fraser and Jack O'Gara were there. Mr Cousins had decided with P.C. Fraser to tackle the job.

The sides of the shelter had been blown in, and the roof had collapsed intact onto the sections of brickworks which were pinning the occupants. The pieces of brickwork had interlocked in such a position, that some of the people were not crushed, but the roof was balanced on top of them in such a fashion that if one piece of the brickwork was removed, the lot would fall on top of them.

We propped the roof up to secure it and enable Mr Cousins and O'Gara to get underneath and remove what debris they could without disturbing the big piece. Fraser and I removed all the big pieces off the top. When Cousins and O'Gara had been under some time we found we couldn't move the people that way, so we decided to try and move the big piece off the top.

We could see Mr. and Mrs. Garrett and the little girl Joan underneath and we decided to get Mrs. Garrett out first.

Bomb damage – Keble Road, Bootle. (© Sefton Library Services)

---

40   F.A.P. – First Aid Party

While Cousins and O'Gara cleared the debris from her legs and removed her skirt, Fraser and I lifted two big pieces which were trapping her away. I then got hold of her under her armpits and lifted her straight out. I managed to lift Joan, who had been trapped underneath her, out quite easily.

Mr Garrett was sitting in a chair with his legs wound round the front legs. His chest was pinned by a section of brickwork weighing about four hundredweight. We decided to get him out next.

Mr Cousins got underneath and broke the chair to release his legs. Fraser and I then managed to move the big piece of brickwork sufficiently to allow Mr Garrett to be freed.

We then saw a youth, Frank Garrett, lying in the debris at the bottom of the shelter. The big section of brickwork was then covering but was not touching him. Fraser and I then managed with difficulty to remove this piece from the shelter altogether, but we had to stand with our legs wide apart over the hole we had made to remove the other people. We were then able to lift him out. His mouth and nose were full of debris, and O'Gara and I tried artificial respiration, but we were not successful in reviving him.

Mrs Garrett then told us there was another man underneath, but we found he was completely buried, we then removed the debris and got him out, but he was obviously dead.

All this took about three hours, and during that time, high explosive and incendiary bombs, and shrapnel were continuously falling.

HO 250 Civil Awards case: 1512   L.G. 13/1/1942 Issue 35417 Page 272

FURTHER INFORMATION:

Henry James Cousins was aged 59 years at the time of the incident and a plumber. He resided at 84 Keble Road, Bootle.

Charles Fraser was aged 46 years at the time of the incident and had served with Bootle Police for 22 years.

Maurice Collings was aged 29 years at the time of the incident and had been a part-time Warden for 7 months. His civilian occupation was as an engineer.

John Joseph O'Gara was aged 38 years at the time of the incident and had been a part-time Warden for 2½ years. His civilian occupation was as a plumber.

3rd May 1941	
Christopher John GARTLAND, Sergeant 19 'A'	**Liverpool City Police**
Herbert Frederick Collier BAKER, Constable 243 'A'	**Liverpool City Police**
John Edward Willington UREN, Constable 347 'A'	**Liverpool City Police**
Thomas TOLEN, Member A.R.P, Rescue Party	**Liverpool**
George Medal	

During an air raid a building was demolished by enemy action. Portions of the interior walls collapsed, and the outside wall was leaning dangerously inwards. Gartland, Baker and Uren, accompanied by Tolen, entered the building and after searching in complete darkness they found a firewatcher trapped and almost buried under the debris on the ground floor.

When some of the wreckage had been removed a large wooden beam, which was carrying the weight of debris of the roof and upper floor, and which was directly over the trapped man, appeared about to collapse.

Constable Uren at once got under the beam, supporting it with his shoulder. He remained in this position for a considerable time, during which the other three men worked frantically to free the victim.

The weight of the beam became too much for Uren to support, and Baker took up a position beside him. It was clear that the whole building might collapse at any moment, and the Sergeant who is a man of exceptional strength placed his arms around the man's body and with powerful and sustained effort pulled him clear of the debris.

Constable Baker then got away from the beam but owing to the great weight Uren was unable to move. The Sergeant took hold of him and snatched him away. As he did so the upper floor collapsed completely covering the place where the rescuers had been working.

During the whole of this time Tolen had been untiring in his efforts to release the trapped man, entirely regardless of the near danger.

Constables Uren and Baker, by supporting the beam for over an hour, made the rescue possible. Had they collapsed under the severe strain the rescuers and rescued would have been killed.

Sergeant Gartland who was in charge of the operation, showed initiative and leadership of the highest order with complete disregard of danger.

HO 250 Civil Awards case: 1406

L.G. 1/8/1941 issue 35233 Page 4417

FURTHER INFORMATION:

Location of incident – G. V. Pickthall Shop and Office Contractors, Cornwallis Street, Liverpool.

The rescued firewatcher was Mr Anthony McQueen.

Christopher John Gartland was born in Roscommon, Ireland, in 1895 and joined Liverpool City Police in August 1919. His previous occupation was as a kiln filler and he had served with the Royal Navy from 17th March 1918 to 20th March 1919.

He was commended on two occasions in 1923 for stopping runaway horses and was awarded with a Silver Medal by The Liverpool Shipwreck and Humane Society. He was promoted to Sergeant in 1930.

He was also commended on a number of other occasions and was commended by the Watch Committee for acting with courage in the rescue of 13 people from a dwelling house at 55 Wilbraham Street, Liverpool on 12th September 1934. For this action he was awarded a Bronze Medal by The Society for the Protection of Life from Fire.

Christopher John Gartland was pensioned on 18th September 1945 as a consequence of a knee injury sustained on duty. He died in October 1976.

Herbert Frederick Collier Baker was born in 1905 and served with Liverpool City Police for 19 years, before being granted a special pension in 1945 arising from injuries received during this incident. He died in 1953, aged 47 years.

188

John Edward Willington Uren was born in Cornwall in 1906 and joined Liverpool City Police in September 1930. His previous occupation was as a flour mill salesman.

Uren was commended by the Watch Committee for promptly and courageously stopping two runaway horses attached to a lorry at the junction of London Road and Lime Street, Liverpool on 21st December 1934. He was also awarded a Bronze Medal by the Liverpool Shipwreck and Humane Society in respect of this incident.

He was pensioned from Liverpool City Police on 19th September 1944 as a consequence of back injuries sustained during the rescue efforts on 3rd May 1941. This injury troubled him for the rest of his life and was a contributory factor leading to his death, aged 60 years, in November 1966.

Thomas Tolen was aged 36 years and had been an A.R.P. rescue worker for six months.

3rd May 1941	
Daniel John COLLINS, Sergeant 7 'E'	**Liverpool City Police**
George Medal	

A shop, with house quarters above, was demolished by a bomb. The occupier's wife and two children were trapped in the cellar by a large quantity of debris.

Sergeant Collins began tunnelling and after strenuous efforts reached the casualties. Portions of the building were continually falling, there was an escape of coal gas and the wreckage was on fire. In spite of these dangers, the Sergeant redoubled his efforts, and, with other help, the three persons were eventually released.

Collins' excellent work, performed with total disregard of his own safety, was instrumental in saving three lives.

HO 250 Civil Awards case: 1755   L.G. 30/9/1941 Issue 35293 Page 5706

FURTHER INFORMATION:

Location of incident – 94 Walton Road, Kirkdale, Liverpool.

Daniel John Collins was born in 1904 and served with Liverpool City Police for 31 years, retiring as an Inspector in 1957.

3rd May 1941	
George Robert SYMINGTON, Constable 258 'A'	**Liverpool Police Force**
Thomas Joseph GRANT, Foreman of ARP Rescue Party	**Liverpool**
Bertie KAVANAGH, Member of ARP Rescue Party	**Liverpool**
British Empire Medal (Civil Division)	

During an air raid a man and a boy were trapped beneath a demolished building. Constable Symington, together with Grant and Kavanagh, began tunnelling operations.

Enemy aircraft were overhead, and bombs fell within fifty yards of the men and demolished a nearby

building. One of the two remaining walls of the wrecked house collapsed, and Symington was buried to the thighs in debris. He remained in this position, supporting part of the wreckage with his body until, after two hours' continuous effort, the two victims were brought to safety.

All three men showed courage in effecting the rescue, being aware of the likelihood of the collapse of the remaining walls

HO 250 Civil Awards case: 1560

L.G. 2/9/1941 Issue 35264 Page 5142

FURTHER INFORMATION:

Location of incident – Cellar of property situated at Upper Frederick Street, Liverpool.

George Robert Symington was born in 1896 and served with Liverpool City Police for 27 years before being pensioned in 1946. He died in 1968, aged 72 years.

Thomas Joseph GRANT was aged 47 years and had been a member of the ARP Rescue Party for 18 months. His civilian occupation was as a labourer.

Bertie KAVANAGH was aged 34 years and had been a member of the ARP Rescue Party for 9 months. His civilian occupation was as a labourer.

3rd May 1941	
John CARSON, Sergeant 28 'B'	**Liverpool City Police**
David Charles LEWIS, War Reserve Constable 529 'R'	**Liverpool City Police**
Norman MORRISEY, Constable 100 'B'	**Liverpool City Police**
King's Commendation for Brave Conduct in Civil Defence	

Chief Constable's report

At about 23.25 hours on Saturday, 3rd May 1941, during the heaviest air raid yet experienced on Merseyside, a parachute mine fell in the back courtyard of Mill Road Infirmary, Liverpool demolishing a considerable portion and causing extensive damage to the remainder of this large building. A great number of people were trapped by debris and fires broke out.

Shortly afterwards Police Sergeant 28 'B' John Carson arrived at the Infirmary in charge of a number of Constables and after establishing contact with the Medical Superintendent, he immediately collected volunteer rescue workers and formed them into working parties for the most needed parts of the building.

The Sergeant then assisted in the general rescue of patients and his coolness, courage and organising ability were responsible for many persons trapped by debris being subsequently released. This work then continued throughout the night regardless of personal safety and he also efficiently supervised the control and regulation of hundreds of vehicles in the devastated and congested area outside the Infirmary grounds.

Constable 100 'B' Norman Morrisey, who arrived at the Infirmary with Sergeant Carson, at once went to the passage leading to the underground emergency operating theatre, where he found that the floors above had collapsed on to the theatre. A nurse was trapped underneath the debris and a Greek patient was almost buried on an operating table.

With assistance, the Constable commenced rescue work and after three or four hours of untiring and courageous effort was successful in extricating both the nurse and patient. He afterwards gave valuable assistance in the evacuation of patients.

War Reserve Constable 529 'R' David Charles Lewis was near the Infirmary when the mine fell. Immediately after the explosion he hurried into the building and with assistance succeeded in rescuing several female patients buried under debris in one of the wards.

He then worked with Constable Morrisey for several hours in effecting the release of the nurse and patient trapped in the operating theatre.

Constable Lewis who had had a trying time at an incident during a raid the previous night continued to give assistance in the evacuation of patients until he collapsed from his exertions.

The work of Sergeant Carson and Constables Morrisey and Lewis was carried out under the most difficult and dangerous conditions. During the whole of the raid, which lasted several hours after the Infirmary was hit, high explosive and incendiary bombs continued to fall in the neighbourhood and a very large fire was raging at a factory about 70 yards away. There was a considerable danger of further collapse of the building, especially where the rescue work was being carried out.

In addition to the severe structural damage the incident was serious from a point of view of casualties and the risk to a large number of patients. Seventeen members of the staff, fifteen ambulance drivers and some thirty patients lost their lives and about 70 persons were injured.

In addition to the immediate problems of fires and rescue work it was necessary to undertake the evacuation of some 350 hospital patients, which work was completed by 08.00 hours on Sunday, 4th May 1941.

HO 250 Civil Awards case: 1754   L.G. 7/10/1941 Issue 35302 Page 5839

FURTHER INFORMATION:

Mill Road Hospital was built as a workhouse for the sick poor. By 1891 it had been renamed Mill Road Infirmary. It remained a general hospital until the Second World War. The only major addition to the original institution was a new outpatients' department, which was built in 1938.

When the war ended there was a debate about whether or not the hospital should be rebuilt. When it did finally reopen in June 1947, it was not as a general hospital but as a specialist maternity hospital. In November 1993, the main part of the hospital was closed.

The building has since been demolished and the site is now occupied by modern housing.

Leonard Findlay, the Medical Superintendent of the Hospital, was awarded the George Medal for his actions following the bombing. His citation reads as follows:

Dr. Findlay displayed outstanding courage and devotion to duty when the Mill Road Infirmary was badly damaged during an air raid. Although badly shaken and severely burned he immediately organised rescue work and personally led parties of volunteers to release persons trapped under the wreckage.

He worked without ceasing throughout the night and following day and refused to have his own wounds treated until he had accounted for all his patients and staff. Under his cool and courageous direction many lives were saved, and all the patients evacuated to other hospitals.

L.G. 2/9/1941 Issue 35264 Page 5140

Miss Gertrude Riding, Matron of the Hospital was awarded the Order of the British Empire for her work during the bombing. Her citation reads as follows:

Miss Riding has been most active in the reception and treatment of air raid casualties and her loyalty and enthusiasm have greatly encouraged the Nursing Staff and contributed to the smooth running of the Hospital. When the Nurses' Home was partially demolished by a high explosive bomb, she did not hesitate, despite the danger, to make an immediate search of the premises.

Later, when the Hospital was badly damaged by enemy action, Miss Riding was seriously injured. Nevertheless, despite the fact that she was unable to see owing to an eye injury, Miss Riding was instrumental in releasing a nurse who was trapped, and she endeavoured, before she finally collapsed, to help another injured member of the staff. Miss Riding's conduct has been an example of devotion to duty and self sacrifice in the service of the Hospital.

L.G. 29/8/1941 Issue 35258 Page 4999

John Carson was born in 1904 and joined Liverpool City Police in March 1927. He rose through the ranks, reaching the rank of Chief Superintendent before retirement after 36 years' service in September 1963. During his career, he was commended on seven occasions.

He died in February 1977, aged 72 years.

David Charles Lewis at the time of the incident was aged 31 years and had been a War Reserve Constable for one year. His civilian occupation was as a commercial traveller.

Norman Morrisey was born in 1908 and served for 32 years, retiring as a Sergeant in 1963. He died in 1967.

3/4th & 7/8th May 1941	
James BLACK, Sergeant 31 'E'	**Liverpool City Police Force**
John BRYCE, A.R.P. Warden	**Liverpool**
British Empire Medal (Civil Division)	

During an air raid, houses and two surface shelters were demolished by enemy action. Warden Bryce and Sergeant Black worked untiringly and rescued sixteen people who were trapped under the shelters.

They then began to tunnel in the remains of a wrecked house. For six hours, they worked in conditions of grave danger and were eventually successful in rescuing two people.

Both men showed real courage and complete disregard of their own safety.

HO 250 Civil Awards case: 1623   L.G. 2/9/1941 Issue 35264 Page 5141

FURTHER INFORMATION:

Location of incidents – Index Street, Kendrick Street & Teulon Street, Liverpool.

Narrative by C.C.

Sergeant Black was responsible for the rescue of many people during this period and his coolness and tenacity in the face of great danger was an inspiration to all with whom he came into contact, and was responsible for restoring calm in many distressing incidents.

Black is a man of powerful build and used his strength to maximum advantage in rescue operations and he has, without any regard for his own safety, worked at many incidents until exhaustion, and in one instance temporary blindness, forced him to abandon his efforts.

It is quite true to say that many people owe their lives to his courageous actions, outstanding examples of which are the rescue of fifteen people from a demolished air raid shelter in Kendrick Street on the 8th May and the rescue of eleven persons from debris in Index Street on the 4th May.

Statement of Sergeant Black

At 01.25 hours on Thursday, 8th May 1941 information was received at Westminster Road Police Station that an enemy land mine had been dropped during an air raid which was in progress at this time at the junction of Toulon Street and Kendrick Street.

On arrival I found that Kendrick Street had been completely demolished including two surface shelters under which a number of people were trapped, attempts being made to rescue them by a number of civilians and an Air Raid Warden whom I now know to be John Bryce of 2, Bodley Street.

Warden Bryce appeared to have taken charge of the operations, prior to my arrival and was able to furnish an account of the situation which was of considerable value in deciding the action to be taken and the establishing of an Incident Post. He assisted untiringly in the rescue of these people under the demolished shelters until 02.40 hours when 16 people had been rescued, three still being trapped.

I received information that the occupiers of the dwelling house, 87 Toulon Street, namely Thomas Culshaw and his son Thomas were trapped under the debris of his home which had been demolished by the mine. Warden Bryce commenced work and succeeded in tunnelling underneath and made contact with Culshaw and his son. Bryce was working in a confined space with only sufficient room for one person, his movements were cramped and great care had to be exercised in this operation to avoid subsidences which would have meant certain death for Culshaw or himself.

At 04.45 hours he succeeded in releasing the boy Culshaw but the father was still trapped. Bryce continued in his rescue efforts unceasingly in this confined space without any regard for his own safety until Culshaw senior was rescued at 08.25 hours. For approximately six hours he worked under the conditions mentioned, the major part of the excavating was done by his hands, as no room was available to use tools.

James Black was born in 1903 and served with Liverpool City Police for 26 years, retiring as an Inspector in 1951. He died in 1970, aged 67 years.

John Bryce was aged 58 years at the time of the incident and had been a Warden for three months. His civilian occupation was as a member of the Mersey Docks and Harbour Board maintenance staff.

3/4th May 1941	
Ernest Sidney LEATHAM **Fire Watcher (Assistant Inspector, Outdoor Staff)** **Ministry of Health**	**Liverpool**
William HUNTER, Constable 327 'H'	**Liverpool City Police**
British Empire Medal (Civil Division)	

During an air raid Mr Leatham, with some colleagues was in a basement shelter when the building above was hit by H.E. bombs and set alight. Mr Leatham managed to release himself and went for help. He directed the firemen so that the trapped men should not be drowned by the water from the hoses.

Constable Hunter dug a way through the debris and located one of the men pinned down by beams. Despite the limited space the Constable removed rubble, sawed through the timber and released the casualty.

While Hunter was working, Mr Leatham was burrowing through to the other victim but was unable, owing to heavy obstruction to reach him unaided. Whilst waiting for help from the Rescue Party, Leatham salvaged valuable papers from the offices and at intervals crawled down the tunnel to the trapped man to reassure him. He was eventually released after seven hours.

Constable Hunter and Mr Leatham worked in considerable danger both from the fire which was raging overhead and from falling masonry.

HO 250 Civil Awards case: 1438   L.G. 1/8/1941 Issue 35333 Page 4421

FURTHER INFORMATION:

Location of incident – Government Buildings, Victoria Street, Liverpool.

Ernest Sydney Leatham was aged 48 years and was one of the four fire watchers on duty at the Government Buildings who were stationed on the roof. As the raid developed, the building was surrounded by flames and further bombs were falling, forcing the party to take cover in a prepared basement shelter. The man released from under beams was named W. Cleaver. The other trapped man was Mr F.B. Birdsall, the party leader, who was 42 years old and worked in the Probate Registry. He was released after 7 hours.

William Hunter was aged 33 years at the date of the incident and had served with Liverpool City Police for 14 years.

4ᵗʰ May 1941	
George Ernest WHEELER, Able Seaman	**Merchant Navy**
Mark Vincent EBEL, Sub Lieutenant	**R.N.V.R.**
George Medal	
Thomas Morton SKELTON, Inspector	**Liverpool City Police**
Bar to British Empire Medal (Civil Division)	
Harry GANNAWAY, Constable 66 'E'	**Liverpool City Police**
Sidney John GARDLER, Police War Reserve Constable 413 'R'	**Liverpool City Police**
British Empire Medal (Civil Division)	

Wheeler, Skelton, Gannaway & Gardler

During an air raid a ship in dock was hit by a bomb and caught fire. Two members of the crew were injured, and Wheeler attempted to save them. He climbed aboard the burning ship and fastened a rope to one of the men who was then hauled ashore by the police officers.

Wheeler with help, lowered the second casualty to the quay and then returned and searched the forecastle for other victims.

Stretchers were improvised from wire mattresses and both injured men were carried through a blazing dock shed to an ambulance. The Police officers who were concerned in the rescue exposed themselves to great danger whilst getting the injured men away from the ship and through the burning shed. H.E. bombs, masonry, iron girders and burning embers were falling around the rescuers who acted with outstanding courage and coolness.

HO 250 Civil Awards case: 1615

L.G. 7/10/1941 Issue 35302 Page 5838

Mark Vincent Ebel

For bravery and resource in rescuing two wounded men from burning vessel.

L.G. 31/10/1941 Issue 35331 Page 6353

FURTHER INFORMATION:

Location of incident – No 1. Canada Dock, Liverpool.

The ship which had been hit by a parachute mine was the SS *Elstree Grange*. It was moored at the north-west branch of Canada Dock. *Elstree Grange* was destroyed by the fire and later scrapped. *Elstree Grange* had a tonnage of 6,598 tons. It had been built in 1916 at Middlesbrough as the SS *Abadesa* but was renamed in 1929 to SS *Elstree Grange*. The ship was hit by the parachute mine at 01.00 hours on 4th May 1941.

S.S. "ELSTREE GRANGE."

Wheeler was a member of the crew engaged on fire watching duties when the vessel was hit by the bomb, and the vessel caught fire. On recovering after the explosion, he found two casualties who he dragged to safety. He left the ship and obtained some ropes, climbing back aboard. The ship deck was about 20 feet higher and the hull about 12 feet away from the quayside.

The two casualties he rescued were Second Officer Donald Francis Hocken, 74 Shorton Valley Road, Paignton and Chief Cook B. Long, 47 Richmond Road, Dublin.

The police officers on reaching the quay, which could only be accessed through a burning dock shed, saw Wheeler on board who requested ropes, which were obtained from a fire pump that could not reach the vessel due to the debris.

The ropes were passed to Wheeler who fastened a rope around Chief Cook Long, who was then lowered to the quayside with the assistance of the officers. He was placed onto an improvised stretcher and carried through the shed to a safer place. The shed was now a mass of flames and part of the roof gave way, showering the group with burning sparks.

Wheeler was unable to lift Second Officer Hocken unaided and Sub Lieutenant Ebel climbed a rope from the quay to the ship to assist and Hocken was lowered to the quayside. Hocken was then again carried by the group through the burning shed. The group then returned to the quay and assisted Wheeler and Ebel to leave the vessel.

Both casualties were then carried to the dock gates. This was hindered by a large bomb crater and associated debris and rubble, which impeded their progress. Two delayed action bombs were also present, which had to be passed. Whilst this took place enemy aircraft continued to drop bombs, incendiaries and parachute mines in the area and the ship's ammunition exploded continuously.

Both casualties were taken to hospital. Second Officer Hocken died of his injuries on 9th May 1941 at Walton Hospital and is buried at Liverpool (Kirkdale) Cemetery. He was 28 years old and a married man.

Able Seaman **George Ernest Wheeler** resided at 28 Baglan Street, Swansea, having signed on with the *Elstree Grange* at Swansea in February 1941.

Letter of congratulation to Sydney Gardler from Inspector Skelton.

Mark Vincent Ebel was a member of the crew of H.M.S. *Belmont* at the time of this incident. Belmont was a former US Navy destroyer, launched in 1918 and transferred to the Royal Navy under Lend Lease arrangements. *Belmont* was at Liverpool for repairs after being damaged in a collision in the Irish Sea in March 1941.

Following repairs, the vessel was engaged in convoy escort duties in the North Atlantic until torpedoed on 31st January 1942 by U-82, south of Newfoundland. There were no survivors.

Mark Vincent Ebel transferred to the submarine service in August 1941 and was lost on 24th February 1943 whilst serving as a Lieutenant on H.M. Submarine *Vandal*. This submarine, built by Vickers Armstrong, was lost four days after commissioning after joining the Third Submarine Flotilla at Holy Loch, Scotland. There were no survivors. The submarine's resting place was located in 1994 on the sea bed north of Arran. The cause of the loss of the submarine has never been established.

Mark Vincent Ebel resided at St. Lawrence, Lindfield, Sussex and his pre-war occupation was as a chartered accountant. He has no known grave and is commemorated on the Portsmouth Naval Memorial.

Thomas Morton Skelton – See entry for the previous B.E.M. award to Inspector Skelton. Skelton was also awarded the Belgian Croix de Guerre for removing high explosives from a Belgian ship which had been set on fire by incendiary bombs on 4th May 1941. (See letter written by Skelton congratulating Sidney Gardler on the award of his B.E.M.)

Harry Gannaway was born at Childwall, near Liverpool, in 1903 and joined Liverpool City Police in February 1926. In 1927, he was commended by the Watch Committee for vigilance and intelligence in a case of shop breaking.

He was pensioned in November 1958, having applied to extend his police service, which was approved for a further year. He died, aged 75 years, in 1979.

Sidney John Gardler was born in 1903 in Liverpool. It is not known when he commenced police service but in June 1938 he was serving with Liverpool City Police as a Sergeant in the Special Constabulary. His civilian occupation is recorded in the 1939 Register as being a dock worker in the fruit trade.

He served as War Reserve Constable 413 from 8th September 1939 until the Reserve was disbanded on 1st January 1946. On discharge his conduct was recorded as being 'Exemplary'. He died, aged 88 years, in 1991.

(His service papers are in the Lancashire Police Museum collection.)

4th May 1941

Percy Albert Jones GREEN, Constable 264 'E'	**Liverpool City Police**
Frederick Albert SPICER, Constable 127 'E'	**Liverpool City Police**
George Medal	
Thomas Morton SKELTON, Inspector	**Liverpool City Police**
Bar to British Empire Medal (Civil Division)	
Charles Frederick BLACKBURN, Sergeant 17 'E'	**Liverpool City Police**
Robert Henry METCALFE, Constable. 164 'E'	**Liverpool City Police**
Thomas ROUGHLEY, Constable 239 'E'	**Liverpool City Police**
Alfred WATSON, Sergeant 26 'E'	**Liverpool City Police**
William Arthur YOUNG, Constable 272 'E'	**Liverpool City Police**
King's Commendation for Brave Conduct in Civil Defence	

During an air raid a dock shed caught fire. The shed contained a cargo of army stores, including explosives. Immediately outside were railway trucks loaded with ammunition and moored alongside the quay was a motor vessel containing a similar cargo. The fire spread rapidly towards the stores and the ship.

Constables Green and Spicer gave directions for the ship to be moored on the other side of the dock, cast off the mooring ropes and then began the gigantic task of removing ammunition and stores to a safe place. A Police party arrived, and the ammunition trucks were pushed out of the direction of the fire, guns and gun limbers were dragged out of the shed and tins of kerosene and ammunition were taken away on hand trucks.

During this time, the area was a constant target for enemy bombers and burning debris fell all around the workers.

Constables Green and Spicer showed great courage and tenacity and by their efforts valuable stores and plant were saved.

HO 250 Civil Awards case: 1620   L.G. 7/10/1941 Issue 35302 Page 5837 & 5838

FURTHER INFORMATION:

Location of incident – Railway wagons and No 2. Shed, Alexandra Dock, Liverpool.

Chief Constable's report

About 00.45 hours on Sunday 4th May 1941 whilst a heavy air raid was in progress, the North No. 2 Alexandra Dock Shed caught fire. The shed contained a valuable but dangerous cargo of army stores, including heavy guns, ammunition and kerosene, whilst immediately outside the shed were eight railway trucks loaded with ammunition.

Moored alongside the quay was the Motor-vessel *'Pinto'* also loaded with ammunition. With the fire having gained a firm hold, and spreading rapidly towards the stores, and the ship, it would be difficult to imagine a more dangerous and hazardous scene.

Constables 264 'E' Percy Albert Green and 127 'E' Frederick Albert Spicer, showed courage and initiative of the highest order and immediately took stock of the situation. Directions were given to the ship's crew to moor the ship on the other side of the dock, and this was done, the Constables casting off the mooring ropes.

Telephonic communication had broken down, and lack of pressure in the hydrants rendered all firefighting equipment useless, but this did not deter the Constables in their efforts and using an electric bogie they commenced the gigantic task of recovering the ammunition and stores, to a safe place.

It became for these two men, not only a race against time, but a race against death, for had the fire reached this ammunition it would have had devastating results to all in the vicinity. Fortunately a party of men arrived, consisting of Sergeants 26 'E' Alfred Watson and 17 'E' Charles Frederick Blackburn and Constables 164 'E' Robert Henry Metcalfe, 239 'E' Thomas Roughley, and 272 'E' William Young, with Inspector Skelton in charge.

A united effort was now made in the removal of the stores. The ammunition trucks were pushed out the way of the direction of the fire, guns and gun limbers were dragged out of the shed, whilst all the time tins of kerosene and ammunition were taken out on hand trucks.

Owing to this fire and others in the neighbourhood, this dock area was a constant target for enemy bombers, and the physical and moral effort on the part of these men was fraught with every conceivable danger.

Constables Green and Spicer are worthy of the highest recognition for their courage and tenacity and to a lesser degree those who eventually came to their assistance.

T. Winstanley, Chief Constable.

Percy Albert Jones Green was born in 1902 and served with Liverpool City Police for 26 years, retiring in 1950. He died in 1963, aged 60 years.

Frederick Albert Spicer was born in 1901 and served with Liverpool City Police for 25 years, retiring in 1949. He died in 1967, aged 66 years.

Thomas Morton Skelton – See entry for the previous B.E.M. award to Inspector Skelton.

Charles Frederick Blackburn was born in Liverpool in July 1905 and joined Liverpool City Police in March 1927. His previous occupation was as an electrician. He was commended on a number of occasions during his career, one of which was for carrying out his duties after being severely assaulted on 4th September 1938 in Haddock Street, Liverpool.

He retired after 30 years police service in April 1957 and died in March 1968, aged 62 years.

Robert Henry Metcalfe was born in 1897 and served with Liverpool City Police for 31 years, retiring in 1951. He died, aged 75 years, in 1972.

Thomas Roughley was born in 1892 and served for 26 years before retiring in 1946. He died in 1961.

Alfred Watson was aged 54 years and had served with Liverpool City Police for 30 years at the time of the incident.

William Arthur Young was born in Liverpool in June 1900 and served as a Lance Corporal with the King's Liverpool Regiment from June 1918 to February 1919. He joined Liverpool City Police in 1920.

He served until 1955, having had his service extended beyond his pensionable term. He died whilst still a serving officer on 21st July 1955, aged 55 years, having completed 35 years police service.

4th May 1941	
William Alban DOBSON, Sergeant 57	**Bootle Police Force**
British Empire Medal (Civil Division)	
George Henry DALGARNO, Constable 50	**Bootle Police Force**
Thomas HAYES, Constable 2	**Bootle Police Force**
Robert John EVANS, Constable 40	**Bootle Police Force**
Leonard REES, Detective Constable 64	**Bootle Police Force**
William ERICSON, Driver 2133275	**Royal Engineers**
King's Commendation for Brave Conduct in Civil Defence	

During an air raid, a time bomb fell on a shelter and two women were trapped under the wreckage. Sergeant Dobson, who was on sick leave, took charge of the rescue operations.

As speedily as possible the broken slabs of concrete were cleared away and the two casualties extricated and removed to hospital. The Sergeant then arranged for the evacuation of the area.

Sergeant Dobson acted with promptitude and courage being fully aware that the bomb might explode at any moment.

HO 250 Civil Awards case: 1780

L.G. 17/10/1941 Issue 35310 Page 6026

William Ericson

The KING has been graciously pleased to approve of the publication of the names of the undermentioned as having been Commended for brave conduct:

No. 2133275 Driver William Ericson – Corps of Royal Engineers

HO 250 Civil Awards case: 1780

L.G. 21/10/1941 Issue 35316 Page 6089

FURTHER INFORMATION:

Location of incident – Orrell Lane, Bootle.

Report by G. Dalgarno P.C. 50.

I have to report that at about 1.50a.m. Sunday, 4th May 1941, I was on air raid duty in Captain's Lane, Orrell with P.S. 57 Dobson. We were returning from a fire at the Bennett Timber Yard near Ford Station, when several bombs fell in close proximity.

On arrival at 49 Orrell Lane (occupied by William White) we were met by P.C.s, 2 Hayes, 40 Evans and D.C. 64 Rees, and several other people, who informed us that the Anderson shelter at the rear of 49 Orrell Lane had received a direct hit, and that Mrs White and her daughter were trapped inside.

Owing to the small crater at the mouth of the shelter, and the lack of nearby damage, it was apparent that the bomb had not exploded, but had broken the concrete bed of the shelter which had trapped the two women.

Sergeant Dobson took charge of the situation, placing himself in the mouth of the shelter, and, assisted by P.C.s Hayes, Evans and Rees, and a soldier named Ericson who lived nearby, the broken slabs of concrete were cleared away from the shelter as speedily as possible under the circumstances and the two women extricated, both of them were badly injured.

Mrs White received a head wound and an ankle injury. Miss Vera White (21) sustained a compound fracture to her leg.

William Alban Dobson was born in Bolton and was 42 years old at the time of this incident. He had served for 20 years with Bootle Police. He was born in 1899 at Warrington. During the Great War he served with the Royal Flying Corps/Royal Air Force as Aircraftsman First Class with his trade being as an aero fitter. Dobson was awarded his medal by the King at an Investiture held at Buckingham Palace on 24th March 1942. William Dobson died, aged 92 years, on 16th August 1991.

Sgt. W. A. Dobson

George Henry Dalgarno was 52 years old at the time of this incident and had served for 22 years with Bootle Police. He died, aged 68 years, in 1957. Constable Dalgarno was the holder of the Silver Medal of The Liverpool Shipwreck and Humane Society for the rescue of a child from the live rail.

Thomas Hayes was 43 years old at the time of this incident and had served for 22 years with Bootle Police.

Robert John Evans was 44 years old at the time of this incident and had served for 21 years with Bootle Police.

Leonard Rees was 33 years old at the time of this incident and had served for 10 years with Bootle Police.

William Ericson was 35 years old at the time of this incident and was serving as a Driver with the 116 Road Construction Company, Royal Engineers, Farnham Park, near Bury St Edmunds. His home address was 37 Orrell Lane, Bootle.

4ᵗʰ May 1941

Elymer ANKERS, Sergeant	**Liverpool Fire Brigade**

British Empire Medal (Civil Division)

Alexander Francis Livingstone HAGGART, Lieutenant	**Home Guard**
Miss Muriel Ruth WILLIAMS, A.R.P. Warden	**Liverpool**

King's Commendation for Brave Conduct in Civil Defence

When bombs fell on a railway siding an ammunition train caught fire and the contents of the railway trucks exploded. The Fire Brigade arrived and Sergeant Ankers at once took charge of the fire fighting and rescue work.

In attempting to control the fires and remove the ammunition train from the area, he showed a complete disregard of his own safety and acted with courage and resource.

HO 250 Civil Awards case: 1399   L.G. 29/7/1941 Issue 35233 Page 4419

Williams   L.G. 29/7/1941 Issue 35233 Page 4423

Haggart   L.G. 26/8/1941 Issue 35256 Page 4935

FURTHER INFORMATION:

Location of incident – Breck Park Railway Sidings, Liverpool.

Report by Chief Constable.

At about 00.30 hours on the 4ᵗʰ May 1941, a large number of incendiary bombs fell on the Breck Park Railway Sidings, Liverpool, causing many fires in the vicinity. An ammunition train in the sidings loaded with 250lbs. bombs, caught fire and at intervals until about 06.30 hours, the contents of the railway trucks exploded with devastating effect on the surrounding neighbourhood. During the whole of this time, Sergeant Ankers of the Liverpool Fire Brigade, Mr Alexander Francis Livingstone Haggart, who holds the rank of Lieutenant in the Home Guard and Miss Muriel Ruth Williams, a lady warden, displayed great courage in the manner in which they performed their duty.

Sergeant Ankers was calm and resourceful and acting as leader in the operations, he was an inspiration to all who assisted him. In attempting to control the fires and remove the ammunition train from the area, he showed a complete disregard for his own safety.

Lieutenant Haggart and Miss Williams were conspicuous for the way in which they helped to evacuate people from the area and although Lieutenant Haggart was injured and bombs fell very close to Miss Williams during the time they were engaged, both held tenaciously to their tasks and only ceased when the danger had abated.

Enemy aircraft were overhead until about 03.00 hours.

The railway sidings were situated in the Tuebrook area of Liverpool, south of Townsend Lane. The location is now occupied by Darmonds Green Avenue and other roads comprising modern housing.

At the time of the incident an ammunition train in the sidings containing wagons laden with 250lb. bombs and gun cotton were set alight and began to explode. Railwaymen present at the location had attempted to fight the fire without success and had already begun to uncouple wagons before the arrival of Ankers, who arranged for a locomotive from Edge Hill to attend to remove the wagons. Whilst awaiting the arrival of the locomotive, Ankers made efforts to control fires in the shattered houses around the sidings.

The locomotive arrived and the train was moved with explosions continuing to occur in the sidings.

Ten railwaymen of the London Midland and Scottish Railway was awarded gallantry awards, namely George Roberts was awarded the George Medal, Peter Kilshaw and James Edward Rowland were each awarded the British Empire Medal (Civil Division) for their work in uncoupling wagons. Seven other railwaymen were awarded the King's Commendation for Brave Conduct for shunting and removing wagons from this location.

L.G. 11/11/1941 Issue 35344

The explosions destroyed or damaged approximately 1,000 houses, rendering the occupants homeless. One A.F.S. fireman was injured and died later from his injuries. Large numbers of the houses on Pennsylvania Road, Worcester Drive and Missouri Road (situated adjacent to the east of the railway track) are described as having been damaged and set on fire.

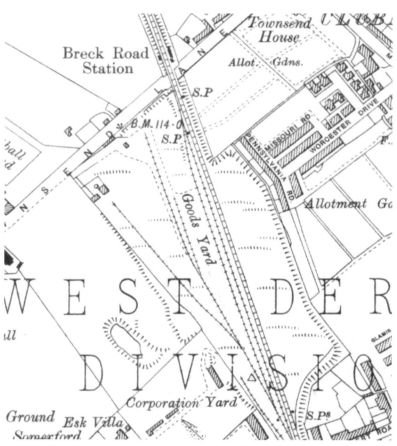

Ordnance Survey – Lancashire CVI.NE published 1933.

Elymer Ankers was born in December 1897 at Hay, Denbighshire, Wales. He joined Liverpool Police Fire Brigade on 4th November 1921. His previous occupation was as a blacksmith. In August 1932, he was promoted to Sergeant. On 14th May 1935, he was awarded 15s. by the Watch Committee for acting very creditably for rescuing a number of horses from a burning stable at 63 Pembroke Place, Liverpool on 27th April 1935. He was also awarded a Bronze Medal by the R.S.P.C.A. for his actions at this incident.

In 1941, he was transferred to the National Fire Service, becoming a Company Officer. He was pensioned at the rank of Station Officer in 1951. He died, aged 74 years, in 1971.

Alexander Francis Livingstone Haggart was born in 1898 at West Derby, Liverpool. During the Great War he served with the Royal Army Medical Corps, The Royal Fusiliers and the Machine Gun Corps. He served in France from July 1915. He was garage proprietor and a Lieutenant in 'A' Company, 86th County of Lancashire (Liverpool) Home Guard at the time of the incident. He died in 1972 at Liverpool.

Muriel Ruth Williams was 36 years old at the time of the incident and was a part-time lady warden. She had been a warden for 1½ years. Her occupation was as a fruiterer. She died, aged 70 years, in 1975.

<table>
<tr><td>

4th/6th May 1941

Thomas CALLAGHAN, Acting Sergeant

British Empire Medal (Civil Division)

</td><td>

Wigan Fire Brigade

</td></tr>
</table>

Sergeant Callaghan displayed courage and resource when fighting fires caused by enemy action. Once, when a fire spread to a dynamo room the engineers were unable to switch off the electric current. Sergeant Callaghan was made aware of the danger of serious shock, but he insisted on taking over the hose and he quelled the fire.

He showed qualities of leadership and, while he took risks himself, he was constantly mindful for the safety of the men around him.

HO 250 Civil Awards case: 1664   L.G. 16/9/1941 Issue 35277 Page 5400

FURTHER INFORMATION:

Location of incident – Head Post Office, Victoria Street, Liverpool.

Thomas Callaghan and other members of the Wigan Fire Brigade were deployed to Liverpool during this time.

Thomas Callaghan joined Wigan Fire Brigade in 1939 and, apart from nine months whilst in the National Fire Service, served at Wigan for all his service. In 1951 and 1955 he was commended by the Wigan Watch Committee for devotion to duty. He retired in 1969, having served as Deputy Fire Chief for ten years and died in 1973.

<table>
<tr><td>

5th May 1941

Fred CROSBY, Constable 940

British Empire Medal (Civil Division)

Henry Abel BATES, Timber Worker

King's Commendation for Brave Conduct in Civil Defence

</td><td>

Lancashire Constabulary

Seaforth

</td></tr>
</table>

Constables Crosby and Rylance were in the Police Motor Patrol Yard at about 1.15a.m. on May 5th, 1941, when a stick of bombs fell on Barrage Balloon site – No. 26 close to the yard.

Crosby and Rylance ran at once to the site, where they found that Corporal Clegg R.A.F., who was at the time working the winch, was very badly injured. They gave him what First Aid they could, then noticed that the tarpaulin sheet which was covering a stack of hydrogen cylinders was on fire, Crosby and a firewatcher named Bates assisted by one of the R.A.F. personnel, dragged the tarpaulin away. It was then seen that one of the cylinders, which had been punctured by bomb splinters, was also on fire. Realising the extreme danger if other cylinders caught fire, Crosby ran to the Police Station yard, obtained a rope and without any hesitation, assisted by Bates, fastened the rope to the burning cylinder and dragged it away to the railing separating the Balloon site from the Police yard.

Crosby then entered the Police yard, connected up a hose and extinguished the flames. Some of the cylinders were full, and there is no doubt that, had it not been for the prompt, resourceful and extremely courageous conduct of Crosby and Bates both of whom showed a complete disregard for danger. A very serious state of affairs might have arisen, the other cylinders might have exploded, in which case a number of people would certainly have lost their lives.

HO 250 Civil Awards case: 1054 Lancashire Constabulary award file – PLA/ACC6849

L.G. 23/9/1941 Issue 35285 Page 5580

Ordnance Survey – XCIX.13 (Bootle Cum Linacre; Litherland; Seaforth; Waterloo) published 1939.

FURTHER INFORMATION:

Location of incident – Barrage Balloon site no. 26, Lime Grove, Seaforth.

Barrage Balloon site 26 was situated adjacent to the Police Motor Patrol Branch garages at Peach Grove, Seaforth, at the easterly end of Lime Grove.

Corporal 855242 John Clegg of the Royal Air Force (Auxiliary Air Force), 921 Balloon Squadron was killed. He was aged 31 years and was the son of Albert and Margaret Clegg of Liverpool and the husband of Jennie Clegg. Clegg is remembered on the memorial at Birkenhead (Landican) Crematorium.

Henry Abel Bates was aged 47 years and was employed as a timber worker, residing in Seaforth.

Fred Crosby was born in Tarbock, near Widnes, Lancashire, in 1906 and was appointed to Lancashire Constabulary on 30th July 1929.

He served at Royton, Bury, Ulverston, Brierfield Reedley, Seaforth, Ormskirk, Leigh and Prescot. A significant part of his career was as a police motorcyclist and motor patrol officer and was engaged on the Home Office Motor Patrol scheme.[41] During his career he was commended on five occasions. He served until July 1954, when he retired as a result of ill health. He died, aged 69 years, in 1975.

7th May 1941

Paul CATTERALL, Acting Sub-Officer   **Bolton Fire Brigade**

British Empire Medal (Civil Division)

Sub-Officer Catterall was in charge of a contingent of men sent to a town to deal with fires, the result of enemy action. Under his leadership the crews remained steadfastly at their posts of duty in spite of the fact that large numbers of incendiary and high explosive bombs were showered around them. He displayed calm courage and devotion to duty in exceptionally dangerous and harassing circumstances and showed keen interest in the welfare of the men in his charge, giving first aid and arranging for the despatch of the injured to hospital.

FURTHER INFORMATION:

Sub-Officer Catterall was in charge of a group of 79 men dispatched to Liverpool in response to a regional call for assistance. The men were drawn from the Bolton, Bury, Worsley, Farnworth, Wigan and Horwich Fire Brigades.

In addition, three Bolton A.F.S. firemen, Edwin Aspinall Hitchon (deceased), George Longmate, and Stanley Emmason were awarded the King's Commendation for Brave Conduct. Paul Catterall had been a been a member of Bolton Fire Brigade for nine years, stationed at the Central Fire Station in Bolton.

Regional aid provided to Liverpool amounted to 220 pumps and 2,262 men.

HO 250 Civil Awards case: 1275   L.G. 7/7/1941 issue 35210 Page 3896

7th May 1941

James TARBUCK, Constable 15 'H'   **Liverpool City Police**

British Empire Medal (Civil Division)

High explosive bombs demolished many houses and trapped a number of people.

Constable Tarbuck who was off duty, was engaged in extinguishing an incendiary bomb on the roof of a building. He was blown to the ground by the blast of the bomb and injured his left kneecap.

Despite his injury, he immediately went to the incident and organised a rescue party of volunteers. Under his direction and leadership ten people were rescued alive from the debris. During these operations, the district was subjected to a very heavy bombardment.

Although in considerable pain from his injured knee Constable Tarbuck worked with courage and untiring devotion to duty.

HO 250 Civil Awards case: 1348   L.G. 1/8/1941 issue 35233 Page 4421

---

[41] See entry for Stanley Dobson for an explanation of the scheme.

FURTHER INFORMATION:

Location of incident – 63-69, Moses Street, Liverpool.

James Tarbuck was born in 1905 and served with Liverpool City Police, retiring in 1957 at the rank of Sergeant. He died, aged 84 years, in 1989.

7/8th May 1941

Albert Edward FALLON, Constable 1954   **Lancashire Constabulary**

British Empire Medal (Civil Division)

Early in the extensive Merseyside Raids which lasted from May 2nd till May 9th, 1941 the telephone system was disorganised, and the Seaforth Division of the Lancashire Constabulary became dependent on wireless transmission for communication with Headquarters and other Police Divisions. Constables Fallon and Smith were sent from Bolton Division in a wireless car and were stationed in the yard of the Police Station, which is about half a mile from the Gladstone Docks at Liverpool.

On the night of May 7th, shortly before midnight a very heavy raid was experienced, showers of incendiary bombs fell near the Police Station and Smith left Fallon in the car, while he went to assist with the resultant fires.

As the raid became fiercer the Superintendent of the Division visited Fallon and told him to take whatever cover he could during intensive bombing, as he was in a very exposed position in the car. Fallon, however, said he was all right and wished to carry on. He was able to keep the County and Divisional Headquarters informed of the position in Liverpool, Bootle and Litherland and fully realised the very vital part he was playing in the organisation.

At about 1.20a.m. May 8th, an extremely heavy bomb fell directly on to the rear of the Police Station, about 15 yards from the wireless car. Fallon at the time was returning on foot to the car after delivering a message. The bomb splinters punctured the car in about 90 places, and a piece struck Fallon's right arm shattering the elbow, while he was slightly injured in the left wrist. Fallon was driven against the wall and covered with debris. He struggled to his feet, his right arm was useless, and blood was pouring from it.

The houses of the Superintendent and the Street Inspector, also the garages were destroyed, and the stables were set on fire. Fallon went back to the car to carry on with his transmission but found that the wireless was out of action.

While he was making his way to the Police Station to report this, and receive attention for his injuries, another bomb fell nearby, and the blast again blew him to the ground. He reported what had happened, and was at once given First Aid, a tourniquet was applied to his arm. When the Superintendent saw him again, he was quite undaunted, and eager to return to his duty, but the Superintendent saw what a serious condition he was in and insisted on sending him away for medical attention.

Fallon was taken to the Royal Southern Hospital, Fazackerley, where he was given an immediate blood transfusion and had his minor injuries dressed, after which his right arm had to be amputated.

All through his period of duty, and afterwards when faced with a permanent incapacity Fallon showed amazing coolness and courage, and unflinching devotion to duty. His example is an inspiration to the whole Force.

Lancashire Constabulary award file – PLA/ACC6849

HO 250 Civil Awards case: 1479   L.G. 25/8/1942 Issue 35683 Page 3769

(See entry for P.C. Fred Crosby for map showing the location of Seaforth Police Station.)

Albert Edward Fallon was born in February 1910. He was appointed to Lancashire Constabulary in May 1930. He served at Lonsdale, Rossendale, Garstang, Manchester, Bolton and Leigh Divisions. He retired as a Police Sergeant in November 1956 and died in 1975, aged 65 years. At the time of his death he was residing in Leigh.

8th May 1941

Charles Leslie CAIRNS, Constable 62	**Bootle Police Force**

British Empire Medal (Civil Division)

William ROUTLEDGE, Foreman Burner	**Bootle**
George Stanley ALEXANDER, Motor Driver	**Bootle**
Stanley CHALLIS, Auxiliary Fireman	**Bootle Auxiliary Fire Service**

King's Commendation for Brave Conduct in Civil Defence

During an air raid a shelter together with its occupants was blown into the rafters of a house. Under the leadership of Police Constable Cairns rescuers climbed to the damaged roof and lowered the victims to the ground.

During this time, adjacent houses were on fire and bombs dropped nearby shaking the roof, which was in a very dangerous condition. The Constable fell through on two or three occasions but recovered himself and carried on until the rescue work was completed.

It was due to the initiative and energy of Police Constable Cairns that the rescues were achieved.

HO 250 Civil Awards case: 1405

L.G. 1/8/1941 Issue 35233 Page 4419

FURTHER INFORMATION:

Location of incident – 14, Leicester Road, Bootle.

Report of P.S. 7 Grayson:

I have to report re the H.E. bomb incident at 14 Leicester Road, that I have interviewed witnesses and have obtained the following signed statements. In addition to P.C. 62 Cairns, there were four other men working on the roof of the damaged house, viz: - William Routledge, George Alexander, Stanley Challis and a soldier who I have not been able to trace. P.C. Cairns in particular, was prominent throughout this very dangerous work, as will be seen from the statements which show he took full charge of the Rescue Party and by his cool efficient and courageous work, inspired confidence in those working with him.

The dwelling house, 14 Leicester Road, is an 8 bedroomed, two storey building. There were 7 of the Roberts family in the Anderson shelter at the rear of the house when the bomb fell. They were all blown into the rafters of the roof together with the shelter. By the untiring efforts under very dangerous conditions of P.C. Cairns and the men working with him, they were all brought down, four of them still alive. It was necessary to improvise, and raincoats and mackintoshes were used to support some of the injured persons, who were then lowered down by clothes lines, which were collected from adjoining yards on to doors which were used as stretchers.

Alexander is also worthy of special mention, as his left arm is partially paralyzed, and he was working with only one sound arm.

(Sgd) A. J. Grayson P.S. 7. Bootle Borough Police.

Charles Leslie Cairns was born in September 1908 at Bootle. He died, aged 73 years, in 1981.

William Routledge was a 37-year-old foreman burner residing at Sefton Villas, Bootle.

George Stanley Alexander was aged 31 years and was employed as a motor driver.

Stanley Challis was aged 28 years and was a member of the A.F.S. and his civil occupation was as a soldier. It is stated that he was the holder of the India Service and Palestine Medals.

2nd June 1941	
Edward IRWIN, Fireman (Constable) 12	**Salford Fire Brigade**
British Empire Medal (Civil Division)	
Fred Hall SMITH, Leading Fireman	**Salford Auxiliary Fire Service (now National Fire Service)**
King's Commendation for Brave Conduct in Civil Defence	

When the Nurses Quarters of the Salford Royal Hospital were hit by a H.E. bomb, Fireman Irwin helped to rescue two nurses buried under the debris. He searched amongst the wreckage and located another nurse who was trapped.

In order to reach her he had to remove a considerable amount of debris and then crawl under the wreckage through a small hole. The nurse was tightly trapped by a heavy girder and tons of masonry on her left arm.

Although there was constant danger of the further collapse of the building Irwin remained with her and attempted to make her comfortable until he was relieved by a fully equipped rescue party.

HO 250 Civil Awards case: 1810

L.G. 18/11/1941 Issue 35351 Page 6692

FURTHER INFORMATION:

Extract of Superintendent's report:

Having been informed by the rescued nurses that others were trapped, Fireman Irwin and Leading Fireman Smith continued to search amongst the debris and succeeded in locating another nurse who was trapped by girders and debris. In order to reach this nurse they had to remove a considerable amount of debris, and then crawl under the wreckage through a small hole. The nurse was tightly trapped by a heavy girder and tons of debris on her left arm and the firemen found it impossible to release her. She was conscious, and they remained with her attempting to make her comfortable.

The trapped nurse was Doris Tyson. Sadly, she died before she could be extricated from the rubble. Doris Tyson was the 19-year-old daughter of Joseph and Beatrice Tyson of Edmondson Street, Ulverston, Lancashire.

Fourteen probationer nurses were killed at Salford Royal Hospital that night.

Arising from the rescue operations a number of other gallantry awards were presented to Rescue Party members and to Dr Wyse, the Resident Surgical Officer of Salford Royal Hospital. (Barlow, Aspin, Edwards, Wyse – Case Number 1577 and Walker – Case Number 1703 – WW2 Civil Defence Gallantry Awards.)

Both Irwin and Smith were recommended for the award of the George Medal.

Edward Irwin was born in St Helens and was appointed to Salford Police in 1923. He served until 1945 when he was pensioned due to an injury received on duty prior to the war.

Fred Hall Smith was aged 33 years and had been a member of the A.F.S. for twelve months. His civilian occupation was as a cycle and radio dealer.

2nd June 1941

Albert COOK, War Reserve Constable 'A' 161   **Manchester Police Force**

King's Commendation for Brave Conduct in Civil Defence

On the 1st June 1941 Cook was on night patrol and about 2.30a.m. 2.6.1941 he successfully dealt with a small fire that occurred at the Saxone Shoe Shop, 3/5, Oldham Street, City, as a result of an incendiary bomb.

He then noticed a larger fire on Oldham Street spreading to the Central Hall and endangering the Waverley Hotel. He got the people out of the Hotel, had the windows shut, and seeing the Fire Brigade heavily engaged at the Central Hall suggested to an officer of the A.F.S. that a hose playing from the top of the Waverley Hotel would prevent the fire from spreading.

He obtained a rope from the A.F.S. Officer and obtained the assistance of three soldiers. He then hauled a hose onto the roof of the Hotel and commenced to play the hose on the Central Hall fire. He got a second hose on the roof and was then joined by a detachment of the A.F.S.

It would appear from statements taken that Cook has displayed a great amount of energy and a high sense of duty. Three soldiers who were with him thought his work was remarkable.

HO 250 Civil Awards case: 1572   L.G. 26/8/1941 Issue 35258 Page 5003

FURTHER INFORMATION:

Albert Cook joined the Police War Reserve on 7th May 1941 and, due to undertaking his training, had performed only five nights police duty. He was aged 37 years and his civilian occupation was as a commercial traveller. The three soldiers involved were Lance Corporals Hadfield and MacFarlane and Corporal Hartley.

2nd June 1941

Bernard KYTE, War Reserve Constable 'B' 41   **Manchester City Police Force**

British Empire Medal (Civil Division)

Incendiary bombs fell on a Gas Works, damaged two of the gas holders and caused the escaping gas to ignite. Constable Kyte climbed to the top of the gas holders in turn, each a height of 45 to 50 feet from the ground and, with assistance, succeeded in stopping the escape of gas.

During this time, enemy planes were overhead and bombs were exploding nearby but Kyte continued to work until the flames were extinguished. He showed courage and determination in dangerous circumstances.

HO 250 Civil Awards case: 1756

L.G. 10/10/1941 Issue 35302 Page 5839

FURTHER INFORMATION:

Location of incident – Gas Works, Gould Street, Manchester.

Bernard Kyte at the time of the incident was aged 35 years and was a professional musician living at 1 Haley Street, Cheetham. He had been a War Reserve Constable for six months.

2nd June 1941

Philip DIXON, Police Sergeant   **Manchester City Police**

James TAYLOR, Senior A.R.P. Warden   **Manchester**

British Empire Medal (Civil Division)

During an air raid a high explosive bomb exploded only 50 yards from Sergeant Dixon and Warden Taylor.

Although badly shaken, both men rushed to the scene of the incident, where they found that the bomb had demolished some houses. Together they searched for people who were trapped and performed this duty with such courage and skill that before the rescue squads arrived they had succeeded in releasing thirteen people.

The rescues were carried out whilst bombs continued to fall nearby but both men worked with complete disregard of their own safety.

HO 250 Civil Awards case: 1571   L.G. 26/8/1941 Issue 35258 Page 5002

FURTHER INFORMATION:

Location of incident – Ferneley Street, Manchester.

Philip Dixon was born at Southwick, Durham and was appointed to Manchester City Police on 9th May 1923, aged 23 years. His previous occupation was as a seaman, having served in the Royal Navy for just over 7½ years. He served until 22nd February 1951 and retired as a Police Sergeant.

James Taylor was aged 41 years and had been an ARP Warden for 28 months. His civilian occupation was a labourer.

20th August 1941

Robert William DAVIS, Constable 289　　　　　　　　　　**Lancashire Constabulary**

King's Police and Fire Services Medal

At about 2p.m. on August 20th, 1941, George Dawson, aged 66 years, a labourer employed by the Chorley U.D.C. was working in a sewer manhole endeavouring to clear a stoppage in the inlet pipe of the sewer by means of draining rods. The compartment is 11 feet deep, about 3 feet square in section with an entrance at the top of 17 inches by 15 inches, after inserting his rod into the blocked pipe, a pocket of sewer gas was released with the result that Dawson was soon overcome by the gas.

Another of the Council workmen was watching from the surface when Dawson collapsed, he called to a passer-by, who in turn went for help to the Police Station. Davis who was on duty at the time, arranged for a doctor to be sent for, and immediately went himself to the scene. Here he found Dawson lying unconscious at the bottom of the manhole compartment in about two feet of stagnant sewage. He called for a rope, and, putting on his respirator started to go down the manhole.

While he was doing this, he was warned by a colliery fireman named Martin that his respirator was no protection against carbon monoxide which was the gas he would encounter at the bottom of the manhole. In spite of this Davis did not hesitate, but went down, raised Dawson and called for a rope, which he attached to Dawson with one hand at the same time supporting him with the other arm. Dawson quite unconscious was drawn up with great difficulty through the small aperture at the surface, during which time Davis remained below. As soon as the hole was clear, Davis tried to climb up the ladder, but he was in such an exhausted condition, due to the foul gas and his great exertions, that he was only just secured and dragged out in time. His face and lips had lost their colour and were turning blue, but fortunately he quickly recovered under medical treatment.

Dawson after artificial respiration had been applied, recovered, but, in the opinion of the doctor who attended him, he was only rescued in time, and had it not been for the very prompt action on the part of Davis, Dawson must inevitably have lost his life.

Among the remarks of the Chairman of the Bench at Croston, Mr. R. Lathom, on the extremely gallant conduct of Davis, is the following: *'This was a most gallant act on the part of Police Constable Davis, and the Bench are proud to think that a member of the Force is willing to risk his life to save a comrade. We have read of many thrilling rescues in bombing raids, and we think the action of Davis worthy to rank with some of the bravest of them.'*

Lancashire Constabulary award file – PLA/ACC6849　　　　　L.G. 30/12/1941 Issue 35399 Page 55

FURTHER INFORMATION:

Location of incident – Town Road, Croston, Lancashire.

George Dawson lived at 110 Station Road, Croston. Sergeant Bannister and Special Constable Marsden assisted by hauling the men from the manhole. (*Lancashire Evening Post*, 26/8/1941)

Robert William Davis was born at Skerton, Lancaster on 21st August 1904. He was appointed to Lancashire Constabulary on 26th April 1926, giving his previous occupation as being a motor driver. He served at Leigh, H.Q. and Chorley Divisions. On promotion to Sergeant in 1946 he was transferred to Accrington. During his career he was commended on four occasions and was awarded £10 and the Merit Badge for his actions on 20th August 1941. He retired on 29th October 1953 and died, aged 76 years, in 1980.

27th August 1941

Thomas William BEESTON, Constable 82   **Blackpool Borough Police**

King's Commendation for Brave Conduct

When rescuing a child from a fire caused by a crashed aircraft.

L.G. 15/12/1942 Issue 35828 Page 5519

On the 27th August 1941, a collision occurred between two Royal Air Force aircraft operating over the Promenade at Blackpool. Both fell to earth with one machine crashing through the roof of the Central Railway Station and the other on Reads Avenue some distance away.

When the two aeroplanes collided, Constable Beeston was on duty in a street nearby, and upon seeing the machines falling he telephoned for ambulances and fire engines to be sent, and then ran towards the Central Railway Station.

Upon arrival there, he found the entrance ablaze and someone said to him, *'There's a kiddie there'*. The Constable, on looking towards the train indicator, saw a girl of five years of age lying at the edge of the flames.

She was helpless and just waving her arms about. Without hesitation Beeston dashed into the flames, grabbed the child by her clothing and commenced to drag her away, but in doing so the clothing gave way. He made another attempt, succeeded in removing the child from the flames and took her to a nearby chemist's shop.

Beeston sustained burns to his right hand and his face was scorched, necessitating his being absent from duty for nine days.

HO 250 Civil Awards case: 2030

Smoke rises from the Central Station following the crash. Blackpool Tower is to the left of the photograph.
(© Blackpool Gazette)

The child rescued by Constable Beeston was five-year-old Jean Zeun. She died the following day in the Victoria Hospital. Her father, Victor, was killed outright at the station and her mother, Alice Mary Zeun, died in Victoria Hospital on 3rd September. All were on holiday in Blackpool and lived in London. Her father was a London A.R.P. ambulance driver.

Mr Abraham Miller, a witness, stated he, *'saw P.C. Beeston pick up the child and carry it to safety, whilst he was doing this another explosion occurred as if a petrol tank had burst. The flaming debris was scattered all about the station entrance, over P.C. Beeston and the child... I witnessed the whole of this P.C.'s courageous conduct and consider it one of the most courageous acts I have witnessed. Whilst working as a Home Guard in London I witnessed many brave acts.'*

T. Hill witnessed the incident and *'saw a policeman rush in and drag out a small child. The child's clothes were a mass of flames.'*

Constable Beeston was commended and awarded the Merit Badge by the Watch Committee along with a gratuity of 10 guineas.

Police War Reserve Constable J.E.K. Harrison, Special Constable W. Jackson and Mr James Gallimore were also commended and awarded gratuities of five guineas for services during the identification of the casualties.

Five soldiers were also commended by the military for their actions that day. Two entered the sea to reach one of the aircrew and another rescued several people at the station.

The remaining two soldiers were involved in recovery operations at Reads Avenue to recover the body of the pilot of the aircraft from the ruins.

Interior of the Central Station
(© Blackpool Gazette)

The Mid-air collision

Blackpool in the Second World War was home to thousands of servicemen and was a major centre for the training of aircrew.

Squires Gate during the war was a busy airfield housing No. 3 School of General Reconnaissance, which, for a time, operated twin engine Blackburn Botha aircraft to train aircrew for Coastal Command. In 1941, 256 Squadron were also based at Squires Gate with Boulton Paul Defiant night fighters, flying in defence of the cities and ports of North-West England. On the afternoon of Wednesday 27th August 1941, three

Defiants were flying over the sea, a little west of Blackpool Tower, at an altitude of about 2,000 feet Some 500 feet below them, was one of three of S.G.R.'s Botha's.

Blackburn Botha (Public domain)

Boulton Paul Defiant (Public domain)

Ruins of 97 Reads Avenue, Blackpool.

P.C. John William Ashfield in the Police Station yard saw the Defiants break formation and, one by one, dive towards the Botha as if making a mock attack and then level out afterwards.

Two of the fighters completed the manoeuvre successfully, but as the third Defiant began its dive the Botha suddenly banked to the right and the diving fighter struck the Botha amidships, cutting it in two and itself losing a wing.

The Botha immediately went into a dive. Seconds later it crashed through the roof of the entrance hall of the Central Station, showering aviation fuel over the platforms below, which erupted into a massive fire.

The Defiant came down on a private house at 97 Reads Avenue. The impact destroyed the house but remarkably the occupants emerged unscathed.

All the aircrew perished along with eight civilians on the ground. Seventeen others on the ground were hospitalised with five later succumbing to their injuries.

The dead at the station that day included John Sheldon, aged 45 years, a Constable with the West Riding Constabulary from Scholes, Cleckheaton.

The Central Railway Station was demolished post war and the site is now occupied by the 'Coral Island' amusement arcade complex. The house, 97 Reads Avenue, was demolished and never rebuilt.

In 2009, a commemorative plaque was unveiled at Blackpool North Railway Station remembering the incident and the actions of P.C. Beeston and others that day.

Thomas William Beeston was appointed, aged 19 years, to Blackpool Borough Police as Constable 82 on 7th August 1928. He served at Blackpool for the whole of his service apart from a period between 9th June 1941 to 23rd June 1941 when he served with Birkenhead Police on a voluntary exchange. He was commended on nine occasions during his service prior to his retirement on 11th August 1953. He died in 1968 whilst residing in Blackpool.

Aircraft debris (© Blackpool Gazette)

Memorial wall at Blackpool North Station. (Author's collection)

Mid-air collision 1935

This was not the first mid-air collision which had taken place over Blackpool.

On 7th September 1935, a collision occurred between a Westland Wessex, a high wing three-engine light transport aircraft and an Avro 504N single engine biplane. The Avro was split in two by the propeller of the Westland. The Avro and its three occupants fell to the ground and lost their lives. Fortunately, no persons on the ground were injured. The Wessex was able to land safely at Squires Gate Airfield.

Both aircraft were part of a group of aircraft which had taken off earlier from Squires Gate to take part in a formation flying display over Blackpool.

The pilot of the Avro was Captain Hugh William Patrick Stewart (29) of Chichester who had previously been in the Royal Air Force and the Royal Canadian Air Force. He had in excess of 1,700 hours flight time, having flown for 11 years. The two passengers were two sisters – local women Lillian (33) and Doris Barnes (30) who lived at Gloucester Avenue, Blackpool. Both sisters had flown previously and had received complimentary tickets for the flight.

At the inquest it was revealed that Stewart had attempted to join the formation from below, which was not the normal practice, and would not have been visible to the pilot of the Wessex.

The Coroner recorded verdicts of death by misadventure on the casualties.

Burnt wreckage of the Avro 504N on Swainson Street, Blackpool – 7/9/1935.

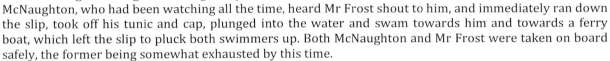

3rd July 1943

Donald Neil McNAUGHTAN, Constable 66   **Lancashire Constabulary**

King's Police and Fire Services Medal

At about 12.40p.m. on 3rd July 1943, Constable McNaughton was near the Ferry Slip at Knott-End-on-Sea, when he saw Mr T.W. Frost of Green Bank, Hibbert Lane, Marple, Cheshire, who was staying at the Bourne Arms Hotel, enter the sea for a bathe.

Mr Frost swam towards Fleetwood and appeared to be making for a post on the sea breaker on the north side of the River Wyre and about 150 yards from the end of the Ferry Slip. When he reached the post, the strong current swept him over the breaker into the River Wyre and further out from the shore.

Mr Frost, in difficulties owing to the current, made several attempts to reach the Ferry Slip, but when he was about 30 or 40 yards away became exhausted and was in great danger of being swept towards the centre of the river. McNaughton, who had been watching all the time, heard Mr Frost shout to him, and immediately ran down the slip, took off his tunic and cap, plunged into the water and swam towards him and towards a ferry boat, which left the slip to pluck both swimmers up. Both McNaughton and Mr Frost were taken on board safely, the former being somewhat exhausted by this time.

The tide at the time was high and the water was about 12 feet deep at the place where the rescue was effected, and there was a strong current running.

There is no doubt that Mr Frost would most probably have drowned had it not been for the very courageous act of McNaughton, who although not a particularly strong swimmer and just recovering from illness, did not hesitate to plunge into the very dangerous water with most of his clothes on, kept his head admirably, and thoroughly deserved the high award which has been granted to him.

Lancashire Constabulary award file – PLA/ACC6849   L.G. 31/12/1943 Issue 36309 Page 47

FURTHER INFORMATION:

NOTE: There are two spellings of this officer's surname. The London Gazette lists it as being McNaughtan and the officer's record sheet shows it as being spelt McNaughton.

Donald Neil McNaughton was born at Lakeside, Ulverston, Lancashire on 13th May 1917.

He was appointed to Lancashire Constabulary on 26th September 1938, having had previous service in the Metropolitan Police for 312 days. His previous occupation was as a motor driver. He served at Manchester, H.Q., Kirkham and Garstang Divisions until 12th November 1944.

He was commended and complimented for rendering first aid, which probably resulted in the saving of life in 1939 and was awarded The Royal Humane Society Testimonial on Parchment for his actions in July 1943.

He died, aged 54 years, in 1972.

26th October 1943

Tom WILLIAMSON, Constable 267 'E'   **Liverpool Police Force**

British Empire Medal (Civil Division)

Two horses which were harnessed tandem fashion to a lorry loaded with 7 tons of bacon were suddenly startled and set off at a gallop towards the gate leading from a dock to the street.

On one side of the road along which the horses galloped was the dry dock. In front, directly in the path of the runaways, hundreds of dockers were leaving their work and assembling in queues to enter the canteens.

Constable Williamson, on duty at the Dock Gate, heard the sound of the galloping horses and lorry, ran to meet them, seized the reins of the leading horse and by holding on managed to turn the team to the off side in a southerly direction thus avoiding the gateway and the crowd of dockers who could not possibly have cleared had the runaways continued.

As the Constable turned the leading horse it fell, one of the chains caught round his ankle, he was thrown to the offside and both his feet were trapped between the two horses when the shaft horse also fell., He lost consciousness and was taken to hospital suffering from injuries to the head, body and legs.

Williamson showed great courage without regard for his own safety. In addition to the probability of being trampled on by the horses or run over by the lorry, had the team swerved to the near side he might have been thrown into the dry dock.

His action no doubt prevented serious injury to those present.

HO 250 Civil Awards Non War case: 7   L.G. 9/6/1944 Issue 36559 Page 2810

FURTHER INFORMATION:

Location of incident – No 2 Gladstone Dock Avenue, Liverpool.

At the time of the incident, Tom Williamson was aged 53 years. The lorry and horses were owned by J. Nall & Co Ltd., 1 Tithebarn Street, Liverpool, and driven by Thomas Heaton. The lorry was laden with 65 bales of bacon, weighing 7 tons, and had travelled a distance of about 150 yards before Constable Williamson stopped them.

Thomas Heaton stated that it was around 12.50p.m. and he was about 10 yards away from the lorry when there was a report of gunfire, which startled the horses before he had time to do anything.

20th February 1944

Joseph BARTON, Constable 343 'A'   **Liverpool City Police**

British Empire Medal (Civil Division)

A fire broke out in a dwelling house. Police officers were informed and hurried to the scene. They found the door open and the house full of smoke and were told that all the occupants were out except an elderly man who occupied a room on the second floor.

Constable Barton ran through the hall and up the stairs and, on reaching the first floor landing, found the smoke *so* thick that it was only possible to ascend the second flight by crawling.

He found the bedroom ablaze and saw the man lying unconscious on the floor near the door. He dragged him out of the room to the staircase but the Constable himself was now fast becoming affected by the smoke and it was only with great difficulty that he was able to pull the man to the first floor landing. With help, he then managed to carry the man out of the house.

Constable Barton showed courage and devotion to duty.

HO 250 Civil Awards Non War case: 20.

L.G. 9/1/1945 Issue 36884 Page 281

FURTHER INFORMATION:

Location of incident – 6 Rathbone Place, Liverpool.

At 21.05 hours on Sunday 20th February 1944, fire broke out at 6 Rathbone Place, Liverpool. Sergeant 3 'A' Paton and Constable 'A' 343 attended the house. They found the door open and the house full of smoke and were told all the occupants were out except for 74-year-old John Eddie Dickson who occupied a room on the second floor.

Constable Barton ran through the hall and to the first-floor landing and to the second flight by crawling. He dragged the unconscious Dickson to the first-floor landing where he was assisted by Sergeant Paton to carry the man outside, where artificial respiration was applied and Dickson was taken to hospital. Despite being much distressed by his efforts Constable Barton, after resting for a while, continued his duty.

Mr Dickson lived for only twelve hours after the rescue but this did not detract from the gallantry of Constable Barton, who was 42 years old, and had 18 years police service.

Before the arrival of Constable Barton, three residents had made attempts to reach Dickson but were driven back by smoke and flame.

Constable Barton was granted £5 and the Merit decoration. He was awarded the Silver Medal and Certificate of Thanks by the Liverpool Shipwreck and Humane Society.

Mr H. McVeigh, the occupier of 6 Rathbone Place, stated that he believed it was practically suicide to go onto the top landing and that for the Constable to succeed in rescuing the man was a very brave act. Mr McVeigh believed the cause of the fire to have been due to Mr Dickson reading in bed by candlelight and that he may have fallen asleep, knocking the candle over, setting the bedclothes on fire. Mr McVeigh commented that the Constable *'is worthy of the highest recognition.'*

26th May 1944

Charles MOORE, Sergeant 1844   **Lancashire Constabulary**

King's Police and Fire Services Medal

Late on the night of 26th May 1944, Sergeant Moore was in Little Lever, when he heard a woman screaming.

He ran 200 yards along an old colliery wagon road to where he saw a man and a woman struggling. He saw the man strike the woman several times on the neck and chest, and as he reached them he saw that the woman was bleeding profusely from wounds to the neck and chest.

Sergeant Moore seized the man, who immediately stabbed him in the arm. The man tried to run away, but the Sergeant grabbed him and a violent struggle took place in which he was struck several times by the knife causing several deep wounds.

The Sergeant overpowered the man, and pinned him down, but he was losing the use of his right arm, and

with the aid of two civilians, the man was disarmed and arrested.

Lancashire Constabulary award file – PLA/ACC6849

HO 250 Civil Awards Non War case: 17

L.G. 29/12/1944 Issue 36866 Page 107

FURTHER INFORMATION:

At Manchester Assizes on 27th July 1944, William Cocks (49) of Second Avenue, Bolton, appeared charged with wounding with intent to murder Mrs Ruth Martindale and wounding with intent to do grievous bodily harm to Sergeant Moore.

The court heard that Mrs Martindale had two children and was living apart from her husband. She became friendly with Cocks, who worked with her at a local factory. When she wanted to break off the association and she refused to let him spend the night at her house, Cocks struck her and in the struggle with Sergeant Moore struck him with a penknife.

The jury found him guilty of wounding with intent to inflict grievous bodily harm on both charges and Mr Justice Stable sentenced him to three years penal servitude on each charge to run concurrently. The judge congratulated Sergeant Moore and his prompt action.

Charles Moore was born at Woore, Shropshire, in 1896. In 1911, he was working as a gardener. During the Great War he served in the R.A.M.C. (Royal Army Medical Corps) for three years and 271 days.

He was appointed to Lancashire Constabulary on 6th December 1920, stating his previous occupation as being a gardener, resident at Brindle, near Chorley. He served at Ashton-under-Lyne, Bury and Warrington Divisions and on promotion to Sergeant in February 1935 he transferred to Bolton Division, serving at Little Lever. Arising from the incident of 26th May 1944, he was awarded the Merit Badge and £10. Previously to this he had been commended on three occasions

He served until 31st March 1947, being pensioned on account of his injuries. He died in 1952. His widow was awarded a special pension as it was adjudged by the Chief Medical Officer that the injuries he received in this incident contributed to his death.

12th October 1944

James BIRCHENOUGH, Constable   **Southport Borough Police Force**

Vere Rogers NICHOLAS, Sergeant   **Southport Borough Police Force**

King's Commendation for Brave Conduct

When rescuing a boy from drowning.   L.G. 13/7/1945 Issue 37181 Page 3678

FURTHER INFORMATION:

Location of incident – Sea off Birkdale, Liverpool.

At 9a.m. on Wednesday 11th October 1944, the Liverpool fishing smack *Venture* left for a fishing trip on the Mersey. On board were Hugh Unsworth (27) and Jimmy Jones (15). Unsworth had been a fisherman for fourteen years and Jones for just three days.

The vessel was reported missing that evening when it failed to return to port. Also reported missing was another vessel, the *Gypsy Queen*. The New Brighton lifeboat was launched and unsuccessfully searched Liverpool Bay twice in the night for both vessels. The *Gypsy Queen* successfully returned to port the following morning. Nothing, however, was known about the *Venture*.

In the evening of Thursday 12th October, an exhausted Unsworth made his way into Birkdale Police Station, having swum to shore from the vessel, which was grounded on sandbanks offshore opposite the Palace Hotel at Birkdale. Jimmy Jones remained on the *Venture* as he could not swim.

It transpired that the fishing trip went without incident until about 4p.m. on the Wednesday when the rudder broke in strong winds and high waves and the vessel then drifted helplessly in Liverpool Bay until about 5.30p.m. the following day when it grounded and Unsworth swam to shore. Whilst drifting, they sent off distress signals without success. The Lytham lifeboat was contacted but in the event was not needed.

Police officers rushed to the shore. Constables Nicholas and Birchenough plunged through the waves for half a mile to reach the vessel, sometimes up to their necks in the water, taking turns to carry Jones to safety on their backs. Jones and Unsworth were both taken to Southport Hospital for treatment for exposure and exhaustion and later released. Constables Nicholas and Birchenough suffered no ill-effects and were on duty the following day.

Both officers were awarded The Royal Humane Society Certificate and presented with scrolls and cheques from the Southport Marine Fund, a charity established in 1817 for making rewards to people for saving or attempting to save life at sea.

Information contained within award recommendation papers:

His Majesty's Inspector of Constabulary made the following comments within the supporting papers for the award relating to the location of the rescue:

'The whole nine miles of Southport foreshore is dangerous from the fact that each incoming tide alters the position and height of sandbanks and produces quicksand; the Birkdale area where this rescue took place is the most dangerous part.

Experienced local shrimp fishermen, who use horses and carts in the water, from which to fish, have frequently disappeared – horse, cart and man – in unexpected quicksand.

In November 1940 [sic], a Liverpool pilot boat ran ashore close to where the present incident occurred. The vessel was only about 150 yards from terra-firma. Twenty two of the pilots attempted to swim or wade ashore. They were all drowned.

The police officers who reached the boy, James Jones, would be well aware of the risk they were taking.'

It was also stated within the award application that Constable Nicholas was a non swimmer and Constable Birchenough was only a mediocre swimmer. It was stated that the tide was coming in rapidly and that the sea was choppy.

HO 250 Civil Awards Non War case: 45

Loss of the pilot boat *Charles Livingston* in 1939

The Number 1 pilot boat was the S.S. *Charles Livingston*, a steam ship which was 145 feet in length and 28 feet in breadth. The vessel was owned by the Mersey Docks and Harbour Board, Liverpool. It had been built for the Docks and Harbour Board by Ferguson Brothers (Port Glasgow) Ltd. and launched on 15th December 1921.

The *Charles Livingston* left Liverpool at noon on November 24th 1939, as first duty pilot boat to cruise outside the Bar and board inward-bound vessels, with Pilot A.M. McLeod as 1st Master and Pilot Ernest

Bibby as acting 2nd Master. Her crew consisted of 10 apprentice pilots, referred to as boat hands, two engineers, two firemen, a steward, a cook and two mess room boys. At the time of the incident she also had on board 11 pilots and 2 officers of the Examination Service for the Port of Liverpool.

On the morning of 25th November 1939, the vessel ran aground in poor weather at around 3.30am off the Ainsdale coast. A radio distress call was made but the location of the vessel was incorrectly given. Distress flares and rockets were launched. Life boats in the area were launched to the incorrect location and failed to locate the vessel. The weather worsened, and the boat was driven further onshore, with water breaking over the vessel, resulting in the loss of the life boats and flooding the interior and sweeping members of the crew away.

Police officers were able to see the vessel from the beach, describing it as being 500 to 600 yards away. Attempts were made to launch the Ainsdale Lido motor lifeboat from the shore six times. It overturned twice, and it was impossible to make any headway in the heavy seas.

At the Court of Enquiry held in April 1940, the Pilot in charge of the vessel at the time, Pilot Ernest Bibby, was censured for neglect and incompetence. Inspector Smithson and Sergeant Baddeley of Southport Police, along with members of the public, were praised for their attempts to launch the boat from the shore.

Four members of the Blackpool and Lytham Lifeboat were awarded medals by the R.N.L.I. for saving lives during the rescue. Four members of the crew of the *Charles Livingston* were given awards by the Carnegie Hero Fund.

In May 2014, a memorial to the crew of the *Charles Livingston* who lost their lives was unveiled at Marine Promenade, New Brighton, Merseyside.

The *Charles Livingston* was salvaged and rebuilt as an examination vessel before, returning to service as a pilot boat until 1951. Following that, the vehicle was used as a sealer in Hudson Bay. The vessel was deleted from Lloyd's Register in 1960.[42]

Vere Rogers Nicholas was 34 years of age at the time of the incident. He was born in December 1910 in Swansea and was a pupil at Aberdare Boys' County School. He was appointed to Southport Borough Police

---

[42] http://www.clydeships.co.uk/view.php?ref=23901#v – Retrieved 25/4/2018

on 7th September 1934 and served until 6th September 1964, retiring at the rank of Inspector, having completed 30 years' service. He died, aged 89 years, in 2000 in Swansea.

James Birchenough was 32 years old at the time of the incident. He died, aged 88 years, in 2001.

James Jones had previously been rescued when he was nine years old from Sefton Lake, where he nearly drowned. He lived at 14c Dingle House, Liverpool.

Hugh Unsworth was a married man and had previously been a merchant seaman. He lived at 49c Dingle House, Liverpool.

> **14th February 1945**
>
> **John Jackson LONGSTAFF, War Reserve Constable 958 'R'**   **Liverpool City Police**
>
> **British Empire Medal (Civil Division)**

A laden horse drawn lorry was stopped at the top of a steeply sloping floating roadway leading down to a ferry goods stage to enable the driver to put on the drag chain before entering the roadway. The horse suddenly moved forward before the drag chain was in position and careered down the roadway. The steep incline, together with full load of some three tons caused the lorry to quickly gather momentum.

Constable Longstaff ran and caught hold of the bridle on the nearside in an attempt to stop the horse but could not control it. The Constable, however, hung on to the bridle but stumbled and was dragged practically the whole length of the roadway, some 500 feet.

Having regained his feet Longstaff continued to pull the horse to the nearside in an attempt to get the front wheel of the lorry against the iron rail, which separates the foot walk from the carriageway, and so check the speed.

The Constable's determined efforts were rewarded when he succeeded in bringing the horse to a standstill on the last section of the roadway. Had the horse not been checked it would have no doubt plunged into the river and endangered the lives of persons on the landing stage.

Constable Longstaff showed courage and devotion to duty.

HO 250 Civil Awards Non War case: Un-numbered

L.G. 1/2/1946 Issue 37455 Page 807

FURTHER INFORMATION:

Constable Longstaff was also awarded the Silver Medal and Certificate of Thanks by The Liverpool Shipwreck and Humane Society.

30th September 1946	
Raymond WINDLE, Constable 2196	Lancashire Constabulary
Harry SIMMONS, Constable 2430	Lancashire Constabulary
Arnold ROTHERHAM, Constable 2270	Lancashire Constabulary
King's Police and Fire Services Medal	

At about 6p.m. on 30th September 1946, a ten-year-old boy, Jack Ives of Walmersley Road, Bury, fell into a flooded culvert, and was swept underground. His six-year-old friend ran for help, and a lorry driver, Mr. Thomas Lee of Beswick, Manchester, tried to rescue the boy without success.

The boy was stuck halfway along a 375 foot long flooded culvert 25 feet below ground at Pigslee Brow in Bury. He had been attempting to jump a 4 feet wide culvert when he slipped and fell and was swept into the 6 feet wide culvert pipe, the water pressure of which was running through at a rate of 123,000 gallons a minute. He managed to get a foothold halfway along the culvert just above a 5 feet waterfall.

Constables Simmons and Windle attended the scene, and first attempted to reach the boy from the culvert exit, but the rush of water was too great.

Constable Windle and Mr. Lee found a manhole at the junction of another culvert which was bringing in a further 62,000 gallons of water a minute into the mains pipe. Roped together they descended the 25 feet to the culvert level and Mr. Lee attached himself firmly to the bottom of the iron rungs and paid out the line while Constable Windle struggled to keep a foothold in the rushing water. Three attempts were made but finally abandoned.

A message was sent to Divisional Headquarters in Tenterden Street for more rope and an empty oil drum which was attached to one end of the new rope and floated down the culvert. In the meantime, young Jack was shouting to let them know he was still safe.

When the drum reached the lower end of the culvert the rope was secured at both ends and, using it to drag themselves along Constables Simmons and Rotherham dragged themselves upstream to an underground waterfall, where with a great effort they were able to climb iron stanchions set in concrete.

Constable Simmons clung to these with a torch in his hand so that Constable Rotherham had enough light to locate the boy who was trapped on a bend of the culvert, but alive and able to breath. He took the boy, and they both went downstream with the torrent, over the waterfall, and out of the culvert, where they were rescued. They had been in the water for over two hours.

All of them made their way to safety and were rushed to Bury Infirmary suffering from shock.

Lancashire Constabulary award file – PLA/ACC6849

L.G. 4/2/1947 Issue 37872 Page 613

FURTHER INFORMATION:

Raymond Windle was born at Kilnhurst, Rotherham, Yorkshire, in February 1914.

He was appointed to Lancashire Constabulary on 1st July 1937, stating his previous occupation as being an electrical engineer. He served until 1st September 1962, retiring as a Chief Inspector. He died, aged 67 years, in 1981.

Raymond Windle

Harry Simmons was born at Pemberton, near Wigan, Lancashire, in March 1917.

He was appointed to Lancashire Constabulary on 26th February 1938, stating his previous occupation as being a motor driver (haulage). He served in the Army during World War 2. He served until 5th February 1952.

Harry Simmons

Arnold Rotherham was born at Pemberton, near Wigan, Lancashire, in July 1916.

He was appointed to Lancashire Constabulary on 31st July 1937, stating his previous occupation as being a stock keeper. During World War 2 he saw military service with the Army. He served until 1st September 1967. He died, aged 80 years, in 1996.

Thomas Lee lived at Lanfair Street, Beswick, Manchester.

Arnold Rotherham

All three officers and Mr Lee were awarded the Humane Society Bronze Medal and Certificate for their actions that day.

8th March 1947

William Binch THORLEY, Constable 544   **Lancashire Constabulary**

King's Police and Fire Services Medal

At about 7.45a.m. on 8th March 1947, Constable Thorley was driving a police car, when he saw a car which had been reported stolen, travelling towards him.

He stopped the vehicle, and the driver told him that he had just recovered the vehicle from police, and that he was the part owner of it. Not being entirely satisfied with answer, the Constable sent a radio message to verify this.

In the meantime, he followed the driver to Preston, where the driver said he worked. As he arrived at the yard, Constable Thorley was informed by radio that the vehicle was still on the stolen list, and the man was to be arrested.

As he went to arrest him, the man ran off, and after about 250 yards, stopped, turned, and aimed a short-barrelled revolver at the Constable, and fired a shot which hit him on the left arm. The man fired two more shots before jumping on a bus and escaping. He was arrested later in London.

Lancashire Constabulary award file – PLA/ACC6849   L.G. 2/9/1947 Issue 38062 Page 4154

FURTHER INFORMATION:

Location of incident – Starchhouse Square and other locations in Preston, Lancashire.

At Preston Magistrates Court on 23rd March 1947, James Heaton (25) of no fixed abode, appeared charged with attempted murder, using a revolver to resist arrest, robbery with violence, garage breaking and theft of a suitcase at King's Cross Railway Station.

The court was told that Heaton, along with another man, Christopher Cowell, attacked crippled 68-year-old Miss Lucy Coward, a boarding house keeper, at her house at 25, Fishergate Hill, Preston on 1st February and stole cash (£6. 7s.) and other items from a bag tied around her waist.

Heaton was arrested in London on 12th March by P.C. Joseph Thomson, a L.N.E.R. Constable who stopped him at King's Cross Railway Station. When questioned, Heaton gave a false name and ran off. He was chased and after a tussle he was detained. At the police office Heaton suddenly jumped up and made towards the door. Heaton attempted to pull a fully-loaded revolver from his pocket, but the hammer of the gun caught in the pocket lining and he was overpowered. He was committed for trial at Liverpool Assizes.

On 19th April 1947, Heaton was sentenced to 14 years penal servitude for the offences after the shooting with intent to murder had been withdrawn. Heaton was told by the judge, *'A man who goes about with a lethal weapon and is prepared to use it whenever he thinks it expedient is not fit to be at liberty.'*

Heaton gave evidence that he purposely aimed well away from P.C. Thorley to deter him from following and at Kings Cross he was taking the revolver from his pocket to hand it to the police.

It was revealed that Heaton had a number of previous convictions and had been sentenced to seven years penal servitude at the age of 19 after a jail breaking episode at Blackpool and had been released on licence in August 1946.

It was further stated that Heaton was a dangerous criminal who would resort to violence to achieve his own ends.

In August 1940, Heaton, whilst a serving soldier with the East Kent Regiment, was remanded in custody for trial at Preston Sessions and was temporarily held in cells at Blackpool Police Station whilst enquiries were made about him there. At 9.30p.m. on 10th August, P.C. Charles Parr was called to Heaton's cell and was later found unconscious with head injuries. Heaton had escaped, taking the cell keys with him.

P.C. Parr had been hit with an iron bar removed from equipment used to measure a prisoner's height in the police station. How this bar came into Heaton's possession was not established. P.C. Parr had a broken jaw and a depressed skull fracture, which required emergency surgery. Parr was in hospital for six weeks and 3 days after the assault.[43]

After escaping, Heaton immediately broke into a house on Weymouth Road, Blackpool, stealing clothing and a revolver. At the house, he left his military battledress and the cell keys behind. He remained at large for four days before being arrested at Hanley in Staffordshire.

Also involved in the theft from Miss Coward was Christopher Cowell (30), Haydock Street, Preston, who  was sentenced to five years penal servitude at Manchester Assizes on 10th March 1947 for his part in the offence. Cowell sought leave to appeal, which was refused with the judge stating the sentence imposed was not a day too long. Cowell had 18 previous convictions.

William Binch Thorley was born at Sale, Cheshire, in 1914.

He was appointed to Lancashire Constabulary on 30th April 1934, stating his previous occupation as being a plasterer. He served at Wigan and Lancaster and then at various Divisions as a traffic patrol motorcyclist, working on the Home Office Motor Patrol Scheme.[44]

---

[43] **Constable 76 Charles Richard Parr** was appointed to Blackpool Borough Police, aged 24 years, on 19th November 1926. In addition to his other injuries his record indicates he also had partial paralysis of his right arm. Due to his injuries he was unable to return to work for a period of 180 days and on his return, he worked as a summons and warrant officer for the remainder of his career. He retired on 18th November 1956 and died in November 1964.

[44] See entry for Stanley Dobson for an explanation of the scheme.

In 1951, on promotion to Sergeant, he was transferred to Manchester Division. During his career he was commended on three occasions and awarded the Merit Badge on two occasions.

He served until 1st May 1959, retiring as a Police Sergeant. He died, aged 71 years, in 1985.

17th March 1947

Francis Henry JONES, Constable 104 'H'   **Liverpool City Police**

James RATCLIFFE, Constable 106 'H'   **Liverpool City Police**

King's Police and Fire Services Medal

At 9.35p.m. on 17th March 1947, Constables Jones and Ratcliffe were sent to the Seamans Club, in Upper Stanhope Street, Liverpool.

They were told that a man named Cassidy had shot at another man and had then run off up the street. The Constables immediately went after him, with Constable Ratcliffe driving the police car. When they reached Percy Street, Constable Jones got out of the car as the man turned, took deliberate aim at Constable Jones and fired but missed. Constable Ratcliffe swung the police car towards the man, and the man aimed at a car shouting *'I'll shoot!'*

The man changed position, and Constable Jones jumped on him, whereupon the man lost a grip on the revolver. The man broke away, but after a further short chase he was arrested.

L.G. 2/1/1948 Issue 38167 Page 84

FURTHER INFORMATION:

Location of incident – Percy Street, Huskisson Street and Upper Parliament Street, Liverpool.

Cassidy was already known to Constable Jones as being a man of violent disposition and was nicknamed 'Two gun Cassidy'. The man who was shot at was Michael Lasese (native of Lagos, West Africa), a resident of Hatherley Street, Liverpool. The gun was recovered and was found to be an American made .38 five-chambered revolver containing 4 live rounds and one spent round. One round was in the firing position and three others in a position for continuous fire.

Cassidy appeared at the Manchester Assizes in July 1947, where he was convicted of using a revolver with intent to resist arrest. He was sentenced to 18 months imprisonment.

After sentencing, the judge called the officers forward and said, *'I am sure the Jury would not like to part with this case without complimenting the Police Officers, and especially the officer Jones, the extraordinarily courageous way they handled with this case. It is alright sitting here hearing the story. But it is not so funny when you are face to face in the streets of Liverpool with a formidable looking gentleman with a revolver in his hand. I think the Police Officers both did admirably.'*

Francis Henry Jones joined Liverpool City Police in September 1934 and at the time of the incident was 33 years of age.

James Ratcliffe was born at Kingston upon Hull in 1904 and joined Liverpool City Police in June 1928. His previous occupation was as a turner. He was commended by the Watch Committee for prompt action in

---

the rescue of a woman from a house and shop at 79 Park Hill Road, Liverpool on 17th July 1933. He also received a Letter of Thanks from The Liverpool Shipwreck and Humane Society.

In addition to the award of the King's Police Medal, he was awarded £10 by the Watch Committee and the Merit decoration. He was promoted to Sergeant in June 1948.

On 8th February 1959, he was compulsorily pensioned on account of his age. He joined the 1st Police Reserve on 16th February 1959 and served until 3rd March 1972, when he was retired on reaching the age of 65 years.

28th July 1947

Joseph Stanley WAPPETT, Constable 217 'A'   **Liverpool City Police Force**

King's Commendation for Brave Conduct

For rescuing a man from drowning.

L.G. 28/5/1948 Issue 38306 Page 3250

FURTHER INFORMATION:

Silver Marine Medal and Parchment to Police Constable 217 'A' Joseph Stanley Wappett, Liverpool City Police, for having rescued James John Royden from drowning in the River Mersey, at the rear of George's Landing Stage, near No. 2 Bridge, on 28th of July 1947.

At approximately 4:10p.m., Wappett was on duty at the Princes Landing Stage, when he was informed that a man was in the river at the rear of George's Stage. Hurrying to the scene, Wappett saw a man, Royden, struggling in the water, about midway between the Landing Stage and river wall.

Discarding his tunic and helmet the Constable jumped down on to a pontoon, then dived into the water, and swam to the man, who was, by this time, lying face downwards having ceased to struggle, whereupon Wappett seized hold of Royden, turned him on his back, and swam with him towards the stage, but before he could reach safety, Royden partly recovered consciousness, and commenced to struggle violently, with the result the Constable had great difficulty in continuing to tow the drowning man, and support him at the same time.

A lifeboat, moored some yards from the rear of the stage, was eventually reached, and Wappett endeavoured to gain hold of its side, but owing to Royden's weight and the height of the boat's side, he was unable to do so, consequently that along with the man's struggles, caused the Constable to strike his head on the side of the boat.

Though exhausted, however, Wappett managed to pull Royden to a mooring rope, and, holding on to this, supported him until help arrived, and both men were hauled on to the stage. They were later removed to hospital and detained.

Previous award

Bronze Medal and Certificate of Thanks to Police Constable 217 'A' (Joseph Stanley Wappett), for courageously stopping a runaway horse attached to a Cheshire Lines parcel van in Church Street, on 12th of September 1924.

(Information courtesy of The Liverpool Shipwreck and Humane Society.)

Joseph Stanley Wappett was born at Kirkby Stephen, Westmorland, in October 1895 and joined Liverpool City Police in February 1920. His previous occupation was as a grocer and soldier. He served with the Border Regiment as a Private from 5th January 1915 to 21st January 1920.

During his Police career, he was commended on five occasions. He was also awarded the Merit Decoration in respect of his rescue of Royden on 28th July 1947. In October 1950, he was compulsorily retired on reaching the age limit. He was appointed to the 1st Police Reserve in 1951 and in 1968 his service was terminated due to his age. He died, aged 77 years old, in February 1973.

14th October 1947

Ernest ATKINSON, Constable 1271   **Lancashire Constabulary**

King's Police and Fire Services Medal

At 9.50p.m. on 14th October 1947, Constable Atkinson went to examine a house in a lonely lane at Rixton, near Warrington, near to a breakers yard. The occupants of the house were away, and the Constable saw a broken window in the kitchen. He shone his torch inside and saw a man pointing a revolver at him. The Constable stepped to one side, and the man jumped from the window and ran across the back lawn of the house.

Constable Atkinson decided to head him off at a fence, when he heard a shot fired. As he reached the bottom of the garden, Constable Atkinson heard a second shot fired. The man then ran through the car breakers yard and hid among the derelict vehicles. However, after a search, the man had escaped. He was arrested some time later.

Lancashire Constabulary award file – PLA/ACC6849

L.G. 6/4/1948 Issue 38255 Page 2218

FURTHER INFORMATION:

Location of incident – Chapel Lane, Rixton, Warrington.

On 2nd December 1947, at Manchester Assizes, Thomas Barnes Bird pleaded guilty to charges of using a firearm to resist arrest, burglary and armoury breaking. A plea of not guilty to shooting with intent to murder was accepted by the prosecution.

At the scene of the incident, a glove and loaded revolver were found and later the other glove and another loaded revolver were found at his home. It was stated that Bird was a dangerous man who put his military training to criminal use. Bird cycled 54 miles to break into the armoury at Sealand Aerodrome and steal eleven revolvers and a rifle.

When his wife found the revolvers, she made Bird throw them into a pit, but he later recovered some of them. At his home, a rubber truncheon was found, along with a list of 15 addresses of shops, a club, a cinema and a bank. When questioned, Bird stated these were to be *'obvious sources of income'*.

Sentencing him to twelve years penal servitude, the judge commented that he did not accept any of the shots went near the officer and added, *'It was only by the intervention of Providence that you did not hit the officer'.*

The judge commended the behaviour of Constable Atkinson, saying his actions in continuing the pursuit was worthy of the highest praise and hoped it would be brought to the notice of the Chief Constable.

Ernest Atkinson was born at Bolton, Lancashire, in November 1901. He was appointed to Lancashire Constabulary on 29th June 1925, stating his previous occupation as being a plate moulder. He served as a Constable at Fulwood, Colne, Old Trafford, Lytham, Adlington, Leigh and Padgate as a Foot Patrol Officer.

In addition to the King's Police Medal he was awarded £10 and the Merit Badge. He retired on 1st May 1954 and died on 22nd July 1969.

13th June 1948

Charles Lathom POTTER, Constable 133   **Blackpool Borough Police**

George Swan WRIGHT, Constable 19   **Blackpool Borough Police**

King's Commendation for Brave Conduct

For services when arresting an armed criminal.

L.G. 15/3/1949 Issue 38561 Page 1328

FURTHER INFORMATION:

Godfrey Gordon Eastwood, aged 24 years, of Dickson Road, Blackpool, went to a house armed with an automatic pistol and held up the housekeeper, Anthony John Baxter. A violent struggle took place, resulting in Eastwood being arrested and placed before Blackpool Court, where he was remanded in custody.

It was stated that Eastwood had recently been discharged from the Navy and had been out with friends and had too much to drink and did not know what he was doing.

It is recorded on the officer's record sheets that both officers were commended by the Justices at Blackpool Magistrates Court for keen attention to duty displayed at 12.15a.m. on 13th June 1948, when they arrested Godfrey Gordon Eastwood, who was armed with a pistol, on charges against the Larceny Act 1916, Offences Against the Person Act 1861 and Firearms Act 1937.

Both officers were commended by the Watch Committee, awarded the Merit Badge and given a monetary award.

Charles Latham Potter was born at Blackpool in September 1914. He was appointed to Blackpool Borough Police on 1st April 1937 as Constable 133.

During his career, he was commended on seven occasions and was awarded the Rhodes Marshall Trophy in 1960. He was promoted to Sergeant on 6th May 1949 and retired after 30 years police service on 24th June 1967. He died, aged 61 years, in March 1976.

George Swan Wright was born in Avonbridge, Stirlingshire, Scotland, in March 1911. On being appointed to Blackpool Borough Police on 31st October 1933 as Constable 19, his stated previous occupation was a soldier, having served with the 2nd Battalion of the Scots Guards from 27th November 1930 to 21st October 1933.

When he was appointed to Blackpool Borough Police he was an Army Reservist for a period of a further nine years. He was recalled for military service from 1st December 1939 to 2nd January 1946.

During his career, he was commended on six occasions and was promoted to Sergeant in 1951 and Inspector in 1959. He retired on 30th October 1963 after 30 years police service and died in March 1968.

5th December 1948

Leslie MAULT, Constable 136 'C'   **Liverpool City Police Force**

King's Commendation for Brave Conduct

For attempting to rescue a man from drowning.

L.G. 10/5/1949 Issue 38607 Page 2300

FURTHER INFORMATION:

Silver Marine Medal and Parchment to Police Constable 136 'C' Leslie Mault, Liverpool City Police, for having rescued Edward Melhuish from the South East Brunswick Dock, Liverpool, on 5th of December 1948.

At approximately 4a.m., whilst on duty at the North East Toxteth Dock Gate, Constable Mault was informed that a man (Melhuish) had fallen into the South East Brunswick Dock, and was in imminent danger of drowning.

Hurrying to the scene, Mault saw Melhuish, who was then apparently unconscious, floating away towards the middle of the dock. Discarding his great coat, helmet and tunic, the Constable slid down a rope, held by onlookers, and swam to Melhuish, who had then floated about 12 yards out.

The Constable grasped the drowning man and swam with him towards some small boats moored 20 yards or so away. On reaching the first boat, he clung on to the side with his right arm, whilst supporting the unconscious man with his left.

Men on the dock then called to the Constable to hold on and, casting off the moorings, they hauled the boat towards an iron ladder in the dock side. On reaching this, two men descended into the boat and, pulling both Mault and Melhuish aboard, rowed across to steps on the west side of the dock.

An ambulance was quickly summoned and Melhuish removed to hospital, where on examination by a doctor, he was found to be dead. Constable Mault was off duty for 8 days, suffering from the effects of immersion.

The fact that Melhuish did not live, does not in any way detract from the Constable's gallantry, which was in keeping with the best traditions of the Police Service. On a cold winter morning he was informed of this incident and, without thought for his own safety, immediately entered the water and got the deceased man out of the dock.

(Information courtesy by the Liverpool Shipwreck and Humane Society.)

Leslie Mault was born in 1922 and served with Liverpool City Police for 25 years, retiring in 1972 as a Sergeant. In 1970, he was served as a training officer at the Liverpool Police Training School at Mather Avenue and was the Secretary of the Police Comrades Association. He was awarded the British Empire Medal (Civil Division) in the New Year Honours list of 1971. (L.G. 31/12/1970 Issue 45262 Page 26)

He died, aged 73 years, in 1995.

17th February 1950

John Robert LEACH, Constable 863   Lancashire Constabulary

King's Police and Fire Services Medal for Gallantry

Constable Leach was in Trafford Park, Manchester, at 1.15a.m. on 17th February 1950, when he became suspicious of a lorry, with four persons in the cab. The driver ignored the Constable's signal to stop, and as the lorry passed, Constable Leach jumped on the back, and saw rolls of cloth and a large parcel in the back.

The driver realised the Constable was hanging on and tried to dislodge him by erratic driving. Finally, the vehicle came to a stop, and Constable Leach seized the driver, who called on his accomplices for help. All four men set upon the Constable knocking him to the ground, and kicking him in the head and body, until he was almost unconscious.

As the men walked away, Constable Leach, suffering from severe bruising, and exhausted, got hold of the driver again, but this time his friends did not respond to his call for help, and he was detained. Two of the others were arrested later. The lorry and its contents had been stolen.

Lancashire Constabulary award file – PLA/ACC6849   L.G. 25/8/1950 Issue 39002 Page 4321

Awarded 'William Garnett' Cup.

FURTHER INFORMATION:

On 11th May 1950, three men were convicted at Manchester Assizes of assaulting P.C. Leach and of taking a lorry without the owner's consent and receiving garments and cloth knowing they were stolen. They were all sentenced to four years imprisonment.

The men were George Morland Derbyshire (36), butcher of Lloyd Street, Chorlton-on-Medlock; Reginald Hugh Nuralli (41), engineer of Bickley Street; and Alfred Meehan (29), private hire car proprietor of Stockton Street, both in Moss Side. The fourth man had not been traced.

In evidence, Leach said he clung on to the tailboard of the lorry for 600 yards in spite of attempts to dislodge him. He saw Nuralli, Meehan and another man and pulled the driver, Derbyshire, from the cab. After being attacked he feigned unconsciousness but managed to seize and hold onto the driver, Derbyshire.

The judge, Justice Lynksey, said that Constable Leach had behaved with great gallantry and requested his commendation be brought to the notice of the authorities.

John Robert Leach was born at Churchtown, Garstang, Lancashire, in August 1918. He was appointed to Lancashire Constabulary on 4th October 1937 and served until 30th June 1968, retiring as a Chief Inspector. He joined the Army on 20th August 1942.

Constable Leach was previously awarded the British Empire Medal in April 1941 for gallant conduct, rescuing people trapped in demolished buildings during air raids in Manchester in December 1940. Arising from this incident, Inspector Thomas Edward Holliday was awarded the George Medal and four of his other colleagues were also awarded the British Empire Medal. (See previous entries.) He died, aged 85 years, in 2003.

11th July 1950

Frank ROSE, Constable 159 'H'   **Liverpool City Police**

George Medal

Constable Rose was on motor patrol duty with another officer when they were told that about ten minutes earlier a child had fallen into the Leeds and Liverpool Canal at a point where it is crossed by a road bridge.

The officers drove to the bridge and Constable Rose saw the arms of the child above the surface of the water. The canal at this place is about 60 feet wide and is a mass of driftwood, oil and other refuse.

Although only a moderate swimmer Constable Rose climbed onto the wall of the bridge, jumped 18 feet to the canal bank and dived into the water fully clothed except for his cap and tunic.

To locate the child, who was floating beneath the surface, the Constable had to dive and swim under the refuse. While doing this he was in danger of being rendered unconscious by a blow from one of the many blocks of wood or other heavy obstacles.

He managed to reach the child and raising him above the surface brought him to the canal bank. Constable Rose, who was exhausted, could only with difficulty support the unconscious child until they were both taken from the water.

Despite his own condition he at once began artificial respiration on the child but collapsed almost immediately. He recovered and with the child, was driven to hospital in the police car.

During the journey, he continued the artificial respiration and as a result of his efforts the child's breathing was restored. The Constable and the child, who eventually recovered, were both admitted to hospital suffering from shock and exposure.

In carrying out this gallant rescue Constable Rose seriously endangered his own life and acted in the highest traditions of the police service.

L.G. 9/5/1951 Issue 39167 Page 1280

FURTHER INFORMATION:

Location of incident - Boundary Street Bridge, Everton, Liverpool.

Frank Rose resigned from Liverpool City Police on 23rd December 1950. He had previously served with the R.A.F. between 1943 and 1945.

20th December 1950

John Finlayson SLIDDERS, Constable 168   **Liverpool City Police**

King's Commendation for Brave Conduct

For rescuing a man from drowning.

L.G. 9/3/1951 Issue 39167 Page 1283

FURTHER INFORMATION:

Police Constable Slidders jumped 16 feet from the quayside into the water of the West Prince's Dock, Liverpool to rescue a man from drowning. He swam with the man to the piles supporting the quay where he was able to fasten a rope around the man who was pulled onto the quay.

At the time of the incident he was 45 years old had been with Liverpool City Police for 25 years including 4 years on dock duty. It was reported that he was still suffering from a leg injury sustained when he was injured by an incendiary bomb in 1940.

(*Liverpool Daily Post*, 14/3/1951 and *Police Review*, 23/3/1951)

Later incident

On 2nd November 1954, at Liverpool Assizes, David Sebi Agyeman Darku, a 32-year-old West African seaman, was convicted of the wounding of Constable Slidders and another officer.

Both officers went to Darku's home with a warrant for his arrest. Standing in the doorway, Darku said, *'Don't come in here or I will kill you'*. Slidders saw Darku raise an axe above his head and made a grab for it. The axe caught Slidders between the fingers and struck the side of his jaw, breaking it. His colleague jumped to his aid, dodging a blow from the axe.

Darku was sentenced to seven years imprisonment.

Whilst serving his sentence at Winson Green Prison, Darku attacked a prison officer with a metal bar. He appeared at Birmingham Assizes on 12th July 1956, charged with attempted murder. In a legal first, Darku gave evidence at the trial as to his fitness to plead. The jury failed to agree and a second was empanelled, finding him unfit to plead to the charge. Dr Percy Coates said Darku was suffering from paranoid schizophrenia and had already been transferred to Broadmoor. Mr Justice Finnemore ordered that Darku be detained at Her Majesty's pleasure.

John Finlayson Slidders was born in August 1905. He served with Liverpool City Police for 31 years before retiring on medical grounds in June 1957. He died in 1974.

17th April 1951

John Charles BEAVERSTOCK, Detective Sergeant 91   **Liverpool City Police**

Isaac Joseph GILLBANKS, Detective Sergeant 88   **Liverpool City Police**

King's Commendation for Brave Conduct

For services when arresting an armed murderer.

L.G. 21/9/1951 Issue 39341 Page 4990

FURTHER INFORMATION:

On Monday, 16th April 1951, Lillian Beryl Beech (24 years) and her mother Lillian Harris Parr (55 years) were found shot dead at a house at Underley Street, Wavertree, Liverpool.

Mrs Beech's husband Walter Richard Beech (29 years) an ex ships steward had been released from prison five months previously having served most of a five year sentence for armed housebreaking and was suspected to having been the killer.

The next day Sergeant's Beaverstock and Gillbanks who were making routine checks of public houses and cafes in the area spoke with Beech in the parlour of the Princes Park Hotel, Upper Stanhope Street, Liverpool approximately a mile and a half from the scene of the crime.

'He was evasive' said Sergeant Beaverstock, and *'suddenly he pointed a gun and said, 'Stand back or you'll get it.' The next second he had shot himself through the head.'*

At the inquest held on 2nd May the Jury concluded that Beech had killed his wife and mother-in-law and had taken his own life. The Coroner said there was no evidence to show the state of Beech's mind. He was *'a cool customer and killed these women with malice aforethought.'*

John Charles Beaverstock was born in 1906 and served with Liverpool City Police for 28 years, retiring as an Inspector in May 1957. He died, aged 89 years, in 1995.

Isaac Joseph Gillbanks was born in 1905 and served with Liverpool City Police for 33 years before retiring as a Sergeant in 1960. He died in 2004.

17th May 1951

Peter BATTERSBY, Sergeant 12 'D'   **Liverpool City Police**

King's Commendation for Brave Conduct

For rescuing a boy from drowning.

L.G. 16/11/1951 Issue 39387 Page 6055

FURTHER INFORMATION:

Location of incident – Leeds and Liverpool Canal near Lightbody Street, Liverpool.

Sergeant Battersby was on duty in the afternoon of 17th May 1951, when he was informed that a boy had

fallen into the canal. Along with two other officers he ran to a bridge over the canal near where the incident had happened.

He could not see the boy but noticed bubbles on the surface of the water. He climbed over the railings at the side of the bridge and dropped about 18 feet onto the tow path. He then dived into the water at the point where the bubbles had been seen and located the boy lying in the mud on the canal bed and brought him to the surface. Sergeant Battersby applied artificial respiration until the arrival of the ambulance. In carrying out the rescue he incurred considerable risk from objects which may have been adhering to the canal bed.

After changing his uniform, he went back on his beat. The child involved was Charles Wignall, of 7 St. Martins Cottages. (*Liverpool Echo*, 2/11/1951)

Peter Battersby was born in June 1905 and served for 25 years with Liverpool City Police and retired in 1956. He died in 1974, aged 69 years.

29th September 1951	
Joseph GLAISTER, Constable 304 A	**Liverpool City Police**
King's Commendation for Brave Conduct	

For rescuing a man from drowning.

L.G. 8/2/1952 Issue 39465 Page 851

FURTHER INFORMATION:

Bar to the Silver Marine Medal, which he already holds, and Parchment to Constable 304 A Joseph Glaister, Liverpool City Police, for having rescued a man from drowning in the River Mersey, at the rear of George's Stage, on 29th of September 1951.

At approximately 1.05p.m.. whilst on duty at Prince's Stage Barrier, Constable Glaister was informed by a passer-by that someone was in the water at the rear of George's Stage, near the floating roadway. He ran to the scene and, discarding his helmet and tunic, climbed over the guard chains. Observing a man struggling in the water, and in danger of being swept under the Stage, the Constable immediately jumped in to the rescue. The drowning man was then between two pontoons and was being gradually drawn below the surface.

Constable Glaister swam towards him and just managed to grasp the back of his collar before he was carried under the Stage. He then swam backwards with the man to the open and there grasped hold of a lifebelt. He then pushed him to the side of the Stage where both men were hauled to safety.

Constable Glaister's action in jumping into the river, a distance of about 11 feet, during a strong ebb tide, and thereby running a grave risk of being sucked under the Stage, from where there would be little hope of rescue, called for the highest praise.

Details of previous award

Silver Marine Medal and Parchment to Police Constable 304 A Joseph Glaister, Liverpool City Police, for the rescue of John Fazenfield from drowning in the River Mersey, at the rear of George's Landing Stage, on the 18th June 1948.

At approximately 11:40p.m. whilst on duty at the Prince's Stage, Glaister heard shouts for help coming from the rear of George's Stage. Running in the direction of the cries, the Constable climbed over the chains at the rear of the stage, on to a pontoon, then crossed a greasy wooden plank to another pontoon under No. 3 Bridge, and there saw Fazenfield in the water holding on to a rubber fender made fast to the side of the pontoon.

Laying down on his stomach, Glaister gripped the drowning man, who was in a state of exhaustion, and held on to him until the arrival of two other Constables. All then assisted to haul Fazenfield out of the water.

There is little doubt that Fazenfield owes his life to the prompt manner in which Glaister located him, and the efficiency displayed in bringing him ashore. He has only one arm and could not have retained his hold much longer. The tide was strong ebb and he would quickly have been washed under the stage and drowned.

(Information courtesy of the Liverpool Shipwreck and Humane Society.)

Joseph Glaister was born in 1901 and served with Liverpool City Police for 32 years, retiring in 1956. He died in 1984, aged 83 years.

1952	
William James BRADLEY, Greaser	**Mersey Docks and Harbour Board**
William Walter GREENWAY, Constable 202 'C'	**Liverpool City Police**
Queen's Commendation for Brave Conduct	

For services when rescuing a mentally deranged woman from drowning.

L.G. 25/7/1952 Issue 39609 Page 4069

16th November 1952	
Fred ELSBURY, Detective Constable	**Rochdale Borough Police**
Annie SWEENEY Mrs., Packer	**Rochdale**
Queen's Commendation for Brave Conduct	

For services when two people were rescued from a burning house.

L.G. 6/2/1953 Issue 39774 Page 833

FURTHER INFORMATION:

Location of incident – Bertha Road, Rochdale.

During the early hours of November 16th 1952, Mrs Annie Sweeney was awakened by the smell of burning

and, looking through her bedroom windows, saw flames in the living room of the house next door, occupied by Miss Mary Ann Greenhalgh, who is an invalid, and her brother, Mr Frank Greenhalgh.

Mrs Sweeney shouted through the letter box and had a message sent to the Fire Station. She then awakened Detective Constable Fred Elsbury, who lived nearby. The front door was opened by Mr Greenhalgh, who was affected by the dense smoke.

The staircase was blazing, making it impossible for Mrs Sweeney to go to the aid of Miss Greenhalgh, who was upstairs. Detective Elsbury tried twice to no avail but on the third attempt managed to reach the landing and found Mr Greenhalgh lying on the floor unconscious and Miss Greenhalgh in a state of collapse at a bedroom door. Detective Elsbury manged to get Miss Greenhalgh halfway down the stairs, passing her into the care of Mrs Sweeney. He then returned upstairs and carried Mr Greenhalgh downstairs, handing him to firemen who had arrived at that time.

Mrs Sweeney was later awarded £5 5s. and Detective Fred Elsbury was congratulated by the Watch Committee in carrying out his duty so ably.

Fred Elsbury joined Rochdale Borough Police in 1939 and had been attached to the C.I.D. for four years at the time of this incident. (*Rochdale Observer*, 14/2/1953)

Fred Elsbury was born on 13th December 1916 at Sedgefield, Durham. In 1939, he was living as a lodger at 40 Sedgley Avenue, Rochdale. He died, aged 74 years, in June 1991.

24th August 1953	
John Desmond HUGHES, Constable	**Liverpool City Police**
Queen's Commendation for Brave Conduct	

For rescuing a girl from drowning.

L.G. 8/1/1954 Issue 40071 Page 294

FURTHER INFORMATION:

Location of incident – River Mersey, Prince's Landing Stage, Liverpool.

The rescue took place at 11.18p.m. on 24th August, when the Constable ran for a distance of 50 yards along the stage before jumping down six feet onto the pontoon and then leaping into the water in full uniform except for his helmet. On coming to the surface, the Constable managed to grasp the girl's scarf and eventually her clothing. In the darkness he lost his sense of direction but struggled towards some people who were shouting to him and subsequently managed to catch hold of a lifebelt to avoid being swept under the landing stage. He continued to support the girl, while they were both assisted from the water.

P.C. Hughes was 25 years old and only a moderate swimmer.

Deaths from falling through ice – 1954

Twenty-two children and one adult died in Lancashire in January 1954, arising from incidents at frozen ponds. On 30th January 1954, which later became known as 'Black Saturday', the weather conditions improved with a rise in temperature, which was accompanied by bright sunshine, tempting children to venture onto the ice. Warnings were issued for children not to go onto the ice and police patrolled canal banks and areas of open water.

Within the *London Gazette* of 18th June 1954, in addition to the officers and civilians detailed, a number of others were commended by the Queen for their services when accidents occurred on frozen ponds. In total, nine Queen's Commendations were made.

These included **Philip Smithies**, who was thrown into the water when he went onto the ice to rescue his five-year-old son, also named Philip, at Lea, Preston. Mr Smithies, a non-swimmer, kept his son's head above the water until he lost consciousness. He drowned but his son was saved. **Charles Highton M.M. Croix de Guerre**, a craneman, and **Philip Hunt**, a textile manager, both also fell into the water whilst trying to assist Mr Smithies and his son.

The widow of Mr Smithies was later awarded a Memorial Certificate and a weekly award by the Carnegie Hero Trust. Mr Highton and Mr Hunt were also awarded honorary certificates from the Trust.

At Rawtenstall, nine-year-old Lynne Fitzjohn ran onto the ice, chasing a dog and drowned after falling into the water when the ice broke. Her mother entered the water in a rescue bid but had to be brought to the side by **Harry Dennis**, aged 17, a neighbour who jumped into the pond a second time and recovered the child's body.

Peter Seddon M.M. was also commended after rescuing two brothers, nine- and ten-years old, after they fell through the ice at Leigh. Mr Seddon of Laxley Crescent, Leigh, was awarded the Military Medal for rescuing casualties under fire in Burma in World War 2. (Note – Mr Seddon's name is also spelt as Sleddon in some press reports.)

All of those commended were presented with the awards at Knowsley Hall by Lord Derby on 25th October 1954.

30th January 1954

Andrew WHIGHAM Constable 2301	**Lancashire Constabulary**
Brian SWINDLEHURST Constable 2741	**Lancashire Constabulary**

Queen's Commendation for Brave Conduct

For services, when accidents occurred on frozen ponds in Lancashire.

L.G. 18/6/1954 Issue 40211 Page 3687

FURTHER INFORMATION:

At 2p.m., on Saturday 30th January 1954, Constable Whigham, accompanied by Police Cadet Swindlehurst, was cycling home along Cop Lane, Penwortham, after completing his duty, when he was told that two boys had fallen through thin ice into a nearby pond.

After removing part of their outer clothing, Whigham and Swindlehurst walked on the ice towards the two boys, but before they reached them, the ice broke, and they were both thrown into the water. Eventually,

they each took hold of a child and swam to the edge of the hole in the ice, but they were unable to lift the children out or get out themselves as the ice continued to break when any weight was put on it, and the water was too deep to allow them to stand.

Other persons had gone for a ladder to help in the rescue, but owing to exhaustion and cold both Whigham and Swindlehurst were forced to release their hold on the boys before this arrived. Whigham made two surface dives in a further effort to recover the body of one of the boys, and afterwards he made sure that Swindlehurst was taken from the water before himself.

Both boys unfortunately died.

(G.O. 3/1955 21st January 1955)

The boys who lost their lives were Ian McElfratrick (6) and Andrew Stewart (7), both of Penwortham.

Both officers were highly commended by the Chief Constable and awarded £5. Both were also awarded the Royal Humane Society Testimonial on Vellum.

Andrew Whigham was born at Rishton, Lancashire, in 1913. He was appointed to Lancashire Constabulary on 31st July 1937, his previous occupation was as a machine operator.

He served at Warrington, Rochdale, Wigan, Headquarters and Lonsdale Divisions and he retired on 1st June 1968. He died, aged 90 years, in 2004.

Andrew Whigham

Brian Swindlehurst was born at Preston. He joined Lancashire Constabulary as a Police Cadet and was appointed as a Constable in Lancashire Constabulary in 1957. He carried out 2 years National Service with the Royal Military Police prior to his appointment to the Constabulary. He left the Constabulary in 1964.

30th January 1954

James ABBOTT, Constable **Lancashire Constabulary**

Eileen HOOTON, Mrs, Housewife **Hindley**

Queen's Commendation for Brave Conduct

For services, when accidents occurred on frozen ponds in Lancashire.

L.G. 18/6/1954 Issue 40211 Page 3687

FURTHER INFORMATION:

On Saturday 30th January 1954, Mrs Eileen Hooton attempted to rescue Wilfred Edward Crompton, aged 9 years, who had fallen through the ice on a mill lodge in Hindley.

A five foot hole was apparent, and she ventured onto the ice with a clothes prop and found the child under the ice. He came to the surface and at that moment the child's mother arrived, rushing onto the ice, which broke throwing both women into the water. Mrs Hooton grasped Wilfred, but he was too heavy and slipped from her grip. Mrs Hooton was pulled out by rope by rescuers.

P.C. Abbott arrived and stripped, entering the water, and after several dives found the child about twenty feet from the side. The ice was one-inch thick.

Both were commended by the South West Lancashire Coroner, Mr C. Bolton, for their actions that day.

James Abbott was born in 1931 and joined Lancashire Constabulary in May 1952. His previous occupation was as a farm worker. He served at Wigan, Leigh, Rochdale, Fylde, Blackpool, Preston and Bolton Divisions. He was promoted to Sergeant in 1959 and Inspector in 1964. On Force re-organisation in 1974 he was transferred to Manchester Police. He died, aged 69 years, in 2001.

Mrs Eileen Hooton of Cowburn Street, Hindley, was a mother of five and had an adopted son. She was a non-swimmer.

30th January 1954

Thomas WADESON, Sergeant 751   **Lancashire Constabulary**

Queen's Commendation for Brave Conduct

For services, when accidents occurred on frozen ponds in Lancashire.

L.G. 18/6/1954 Issue 40211 Page 3687

FURTHER INFORMATION:

Sergeant Wadeson dived through the hole in the ice on a pond at Lowton near Leigh in an attempt to rescue Brendan Else (9) of St. Nicholas Road, Lowton, after he had fallen through one-inch thick ice about 15 feet from the edge of the pond. Sergeant Wadeson was unable to find the child and had to be taken from the water due to the extreme cold. Witnesses describe him as being blue and almost paralysed by the cold. He was taken to a house where he changed and then went on with the rescue attempts.

Sergeant Wadeson was commended by the South West Lancashire Coroner, Mr C. Bolton, for his actions that day.

Thomas Wadeson was born at Bolton in 1912 and was appointed to Lancashire Constabulary on 30th April 1934. He served at Bury, H.Q. and Leigh Divisions. He was promoted to Sergeant in 1953 and posted to Leigh Division. He returned to Headquarters on promotion to Inspector in 1958 and to Chief Inspector in 1960. He retired in 1964 and died, aged 68 years, in 1981.

31st May 1955

Norman Robert FLEMING, Rigger

Doris Elizabeth QUINE, Policewoman

Mersey Docks and Harbour Board

Liverpool City Police

Queen's Commendation for Brave Conduct

For rescuing a man from drowning.

L.G. 23/9/1955 Issue 40592 Page 5417

FURTHER INFORMATION:

The rescue took place at the Liverpool Landing Stage. The rescued man was Frank Connolly, aged 60 years, of Huyton. (*Liverpool Echo*, 28/9/1955)

2nd July 1955

Patrick Joseph GRAY, Fitter

George Frederick ROSKELL, Constable

Liverpool

Liverpool City Police

Queen's Commendation for Brave Conduct

For rescuing a woman from drowning.

L.G. 16/12/1955 Issue 40659 Page 7151

FURTHER INFORMATION:

On the evening of 2nd July 1955, a woman tried to commit suicide by throwing herself in the River Mersey. A Mr Patrick Gray swam to assist the woman but became exhausted in the strong tide. P.C. Roskell went to his assistance and grasped the woman. Despite her continued struggles, a strong tide and rough water, P.C. Roskell was able to bring the woman to safety.

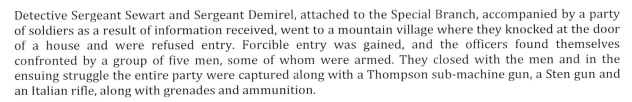

The QUEEN has been graciously pleased to approve the immediate award of the Colonial Police Medal for Gallantry to Detective Sergeant Alan Sewart, Sergeant Talat Souleiman Demiral and Constable Timour Mehmet of the Cyprus Police Force.

L.G. 20/8/1957 Issue 41155 Page 4927[45]

Awarded the Colonial Police Medal for Gallantry whilst serving as a Detective Inspector with the British Police Unit in Cyprus for his action in apprehending a party of armed terrorists.

(W.O. 6/9/1957)

FURTHER INFORMATION:

Location of incident – Kannavia, Cyprus.

Detective Sergeant Sewart and Sergeant Demirel, attached to the Special Branch, accompanied by a party of soldiers as a result of information received, went to a mountain village where they knocked at the door of a house and were refused entry. Forcible entry was gained, and the officers found themselves confronted by a group of five men, some of whom were armed. They closed with the men and in the ensuing struggle the entire party were captured along with a Thompson sub-machine gun, a Sten gun and an Italian rifle, along with grenades and ammunition.

Further skilled and astute interrogation by the officers led to the arrest of other terrorists (including five wanted men) and the recovery of arms, ammunition, explosives and documents. Both officers had been previously awarded the Meritorious Service Award. (TNA - FCO 141_3543)

This was a pre-planned operation arising from information received. Sewart went to the village to arrest five suspects and was accompanied by a party of ten soldiers and an officer. Talat Demirel was acting as his interpreter.

The party travelled towards the village in a bus which broke down near the crest of the mountain at Troodos. Two army trucks and drivers were obtained by the officer from a nearby Army depot, enabling the operation to continue. At the time the weather was bitterly cold and the roads were covered with snow. At the village soldiers were stationed at the front and back of each of the five houses, which were searched in turn and the suspects detained. It was at the final house that this incident took place.

During the arrest, two of the terrorists received minor wounds from a single shot fired by the army officer during the incident. The terrorists were members of a mountain terrorist group who had moved into the house for winter and had been previously involved in ambushes and murders. Later, an underground hide was discovered at the house which contained dynamite in a deteriorated and unstable state. It was decided it could not be safely removed and was exploded in situ, destroying the hide along with the house.

(With thanks to the Sewart family for this additional information and photograph.)

---

[45]   The Colonial Police Medal awarded to Constable Timour Mehmet was sold at DNW Auctions on 2nd March 2003 for £720.

https://www.dnw.co.uk/auction-archive/past-catalogues/lot.php?auction_id=48&lot_id=84948 – Retrieved 1/6/2017

Alan Sewart was born at Bolton in 1928 and was appointed to Lancashire Constabulary on 4th April 1949. He had previously served with the Royal Army Ordnance Corps from 1946 to 1949. Sewart served two periods of service with the British Police Unit in Cyprus, in 1956/57 and in 1958. He rose through the ranks, retiring as a Superintendent in 1981.

During his career he served at Bolton, Ashton-under-Lyne, Bury, Chorley and Headquarters Divisions. He also served at the District Police Training Centre at Bruche, Warrington and as Deputy Commandant at Newby Wiske District Police Training Centre in North Yorkshire. Newby Wiske later became the Headquarters of North Yorkshire Police, until 2017 when it relocated to a purpose built facility.

Alan Sewart became a published author of over 30 crime novels. He died aged 69 years.

Sergeant **Talat Souleiman Demiral** was aged 35 years and had served for 12 years with the Cyprus Police Force. He came from Limassol.

Constable **Timour Mehmet** received his award for a separate unrelated incident.

The Cyprus Emergency 1955—1959

The island of Cyprus is situated in the eastern Mediterranean and prior to 1878 formed part of the Ottoman Empire. In 1878, the United Kingdom took over the governance of the island as a protectorate as part of the Cyprus Convention. The Sultan ceded the administration of Cyprus to Britain in exchange for guarantees that Britain would use the island as a base to protect the Ottoman Empire against possible Russian aggression.

In 1914, at the start of the First World War, Cyprus was annexed as Britain and the Ottoman Empire were at war. In 1925, it was made a Crown Colony, remaining so until 1960.

EOKA (National Organisation of Cypriot Struggle), a nationalist organisation, was established in the 1950s with the objective of the ending of British control and achieving *enosis* – the union of Cyprus with Greece.

On the 1st April 1955, EOKA launched a military campaign with simultaneous attacks on the British controlled Cyprus Broadcasting Station in Nicosia and other targets. After this, EOKA confined its actions to sabotaging military installations, attacks on military convoys and patrols, and the assassination of British soldiers and local informants.

To assist the Cyprus Police, volunteers were sought from UK police forces, with officers being seconded to the British Police Unit in Cyprus. Fifty-three Lancashire Constabulary officers, mainly men but also a number of women officers, were seconded to the British Police Unit. A number of officers, such as Alan Sewart, served more than one attachment with the unit.

A number of officers who served in Cyprus also received gallantry awards later in their careers and rose to senior rank. One such officer was Joseph Mounsey, who received the British Empire Medal for his service as a Sergeant with Special Branch in Cyprus. In 1971, he was responsible for the arrest of Frederick Joseph Sewell, the murderer of Superintendent Gerald Richardson, and played a leading part in the investigation of the Moors Murders committed by Ian Brady and Myra Hindley.

EOKA's activity continued until December 1959, when a cease-fire was declared which led to the end of the emergency on 16th August 1960, when Cyprus attained independence after the Zürich and London Agreement between the United Kingdom, Greece and Turkey. The UK retained the two Sovereign Base Areas of Akrotiri and Dhekelia.

16th June 1957

Thomas Arthur LOCKETT, Constable   **Manchester City Police**

George Medal

Thomas FISHER, Wholesale Newsagent   **Manchester**

British Empire Medal (Civil Division)

One night, about 10.15p.m. when the last customers of a public house had left, the licensee was suddenly confronted by a man who pointed a pistol at him and demanded money.

The licensee was forced to walk backwards into a yard behind the public house, where the man threatened to shoot him unless he opened a gate leading to a narrow street. The gunman then ran off.

Constable Lockett was walking towards the back of the public house and Fisher was a few yards away. They saw the man running towards them. The Constable tried to grab the man as he passed, but he evaded the Constable's grasp. Lockett ran after him and when only two yards away the gunman turned and fired at him. The bullet struck a wall, but Lockett was not hit, and he continued the pursuit, caught the man, knocked him to the ground and wrested the gun from him. In the meantime, Mr. Fisher had joined in the chase.

He was about 20 yards away when the Constable first tried to grab the gunman and clearly saw him shoot at Constable Fisher, however, closely followed the chase and by the time Lockett had caught the man, Fisher was there to help to prevent him breaking away.

L.G. 22/11/1957 Issue 41237 Page 6681

FURTHER INFORMATION:

Location of incident – Nicholas Street, Manchester.

The masked gunman, Patrick O'Donovan (22) of Rathmines Road, Dublin, was sentenced to seven years imprisonment at Manchester Crown Court for using an automatic pistol with intent to resist arrest and for assaulting a licensee whilst armed and with intent to rob.

The jury sent a message to the judge that they wished to commend P.C. Lockett; the judge added his own commendation to that expressed by the jury.

Thomas Arthur Lockett was born at Altrincham and was appointed, aged 28 years, to Manchester City Police on 5th June 1950. His previous occupation was as an engineer. He served until 10th May 1965 when he transferred to Kent Constabulary.

Constable Beattie was on night duty in a police patrol car when a call was received that a man was threatening to throw himself from scaffolding erected outside a hospital. The Constable drove to the hospital and there saw a man standing on the scaffolding some 55 feet above ground level.

It was a dark night, raining heavily with a strong wind blowing. Beattie shouted to the man to come down, but he replied that he was going to jump. The Constable immediately went to the second floor of the hospital and found a casement window which opened on to the scaffolding. The nearest foothold was below the bottom of the window and about 2 feet away from the building face. Beattie climbed out, managed to grasp a scaffolding tube and swung down to a narrow board on the scaffold. The plank was only about 9 inches wide and was laid loosely across the wet scaffolding. The man was standing about 25 feet away.

The Constable talked to him in an effort to dissuade him from jumping and slowly made his way along the slippery scaffolding to within two or three feet of the man who then backed away, still threatening to jump. Eventually Beattie managed to catch hold of the man's coat with one hand while he held on to the scaffolding with the other. The man, who was hysterical and frightened, commenced to struggle but the Constable held on to him and waited for assistance.

On the arrival of the Fire Service an escape ladder was erected but the man's condition was such that he was a danger to himself and his helpers and he had to be taken to safety through a nearby window of the hospital.

Constable Beattie showed great courage in climbing on to the scaffolding under such adverse weather conditions to deal with a man displaying suicidal tendencies.

L.G. 11/4/1958 Issue 41361 Page 2371

Constable Beattie shows his medal to his family watched by Lord Derby who made the presentation. (Liverpool City Police Annual Report – 1958)

FURTHER INFORMATION:

Location of incident – Liverpool Ear, Nose and Throat Hospital, Myrtle Street, Liverpool.

Constable Beattie was also presented with a Certificate of Merit and an inscribed gift by the Watch Committee.

He died, aged 72 years, in 2000.

30th March 1958

Arthur Graham Ferguson COLLINS, Superintendent   **Liverpool City Police**

Queen's Commendation for Brave Conduct

For services when an aircraft crashed into the River Mersey.

L.G. 17/10/1958 Issue 41528 Page 6427

FURTHER INFORMATION:

On the 30th March 1958, a two seat DH.82A Tiger Moth Biplane G-ANSA was approaching Speke Airport when it plunged into the Mersey.

The former R.A.F. aircraft belonged to the Merseyside & North Wales Flying Club and was engaged on a half hour training flight. Present in the aircraft was the Flying Club owner Mr Jack Green (38) and a student pilot Mr Arthur Hobin (32). The crash was witnessed by hundreds of people on the foreshore and at the airport.

The New Brighton life boat was launched, and other vessels were directed to the area. Members of the airport fire crew with assistance from two unknown civilians waded waist deep through the mud to launch an inflatable rubber dinghy towards part of the aircraft which could be seen protruding from the water.

Mr Hobin managed to escape from the cockpit and was swept down river towards Widnes by the strong current and was picked up by the rescuers in the dinghy.

Superintendent Collins of the Liverpool Police Traffic Department stripped on the foreshore and swam out to the aircraft but was unable to see anyone in the cockpit and as other help was nearby he returned to the shore caked with slime and mud. He was taken to the Airport and later returned to the scene of the incident after drying out. The body of Mr Green was later recovered after having drowned in the cockpit of the aircraft.

Coxswain Stonall of the New Brighton lifeboat stated that they found the aircraft capsized about 500 yards from the shore with its wings, undercarriage and tail sticking out of the water.

Tow ropes were attached, and the aircraft was towed to shore by boat where it was dragged out with the assistance of the crowd numbering about 200. Mr Hobin was detained at Sefton General Hospital with face and leg cuts, bruises and suffering severely from the effects of immersion and shock.

The accident to this Tiger Moth resulted from flying into the flat calm surface of the River Mersey in poor hazy visibility whilst on approach to Liverpool/Speke Airport.

It would seem that the delineation of the horizon between sea and sky was not easy to perceive and the pilot was misled by the 'glassy calm' waters of the River Mersey, and the mist and sea fog. He therefore was unsure of the aircraft's altitude above mean sea level (a.m.s.l.) and the fact that the aircraft was slowly descending to zero feet.

The DH.82A Tiger Moth Coupe G-ANSA involved in the crash,
pictured at Coventry (Baginton) Airport on 20th August 1955. (© RuthAS)

FURTHER INFORMATION:

Arthur Graham Ferguson Collins was born in 1910 at Liverpool and joined Liverpool City Police in April 1931. His previous occupation was as a clerk. In addition to the Queen's Commendation, Collins was awarded a Certificate of Merit and £10 by the Watch Committee in recognition of this incident. He had been previously commended for consistently good work whilst on plain clothes duties in April 1934. He served until retirement in 1965, having been promoted to the rank of Chief Superintendent in 1961. He died in January 1991, aged 80 years.

1st December 1958

Roland Hugh HUGHES, Motor trader   **Heald Green, Cheshire**

Archibald VERTH, Constable   **Manchester City Police**

British Empire Medal for Gallantry (Civil Division)

Mr. Hughes was driving his motor car one evening when he saw a man between the front iron gates and the door of a gunsmith's. He saw the man break the glass panel of the door and enter the shop. Hughes drove on until he met Constable Verth in an adjoining street.

He told him what had happened and took him back by car to the shop.

The Constable shone his torch through the broken panel and saw a man standing behind the counter at the rear of the shop. The Constable called on him to leave the shop, but the man applied a light to an object which he was holding and threw it at the Constable.

It struck the ground near to the gate where it exploded with a loud report. Constable Verth's clothing was damaged but he was not injured and immediately started to climb the gate. As he did so the man lit another object. The Constable shouted a warning to Hughes, pushed him out of range and at the same time jumped away. There was a further explosion within the doorway of the shop. The Constable sent Mr. Hughes to summon assistance by telephone. In the meantime, two further objects had been thrown into the road. There were explosions and damage was caused to the shop premises.

The intruder then came out of the shop and commenced to climb the iron gates. Verth ran forward and closed with him, Hughes had returned by this time and although he saw that the man was armed with an axe, he immediately went to help the Constable in the struggle. The shop was on fire and ammunition was exploding but the man was overcome and taken into custody.

L.G. 23/5/1958 Issue 41396 Page 3327

FURTHER INFORMATION:

Location of incident – Withy Grove, Manchester.

The offender, Brian Hay (23) of Miller Street, Heywood, appeared at Manchester Crown Court on 9th January 1958.

Hay pleaded guilty to breaking into the gunsmith's shop at Withy Grove, Manchester and stealing 500 rounds of ammunition, causing gunpowder to explode with intent to injure a policeman and to having in his possession at home explosive substances with intent to destroy or damage buildings.

On arrest Hay was found to have in his possession four unexploded bombs made out of grease guns and firework powder. He said, *'I only used the bombs to cause a diversion while I stole a pistol'*.

Hay was sentenced to eight years imprisonment. (*The Manchester Guardian*, 10/1/1958)

Archibald Verth joined Manchester City Police on 4th January 1952, aged 22 years. His previous occupation was as a railway fireman. He died, aged 74 years, in 2008.

Roland Hugh Hughes died, aged 81 years, in 2007.

12th December 1958	
James O'DONNELL, Detective Inspector	**Blackburn Borough Police**
Queen's Police Medal for Gallantry - Posthumous Award	
John COVILL, Constable	**Blackburn Borough Police**
Peter HALLIWELL, Constable	**Blackburn Borough Police**
John HARRISON, Inspector	**Blackburn Borough Police**
Jack RILEY, Constable	**Blackburn Borough Police**
Queen's Commendation for Brave Conduct	

O'Donnell   L.G. 14/8/1959 Issue 41790 Page 5065

Covill, Halliwell, Harrison & Riley

For services when apprehending a man armed with a shotgun.

L.G. 11/8/1959 Issue 41789 Page 5064

FURTHER INFORMATION:

The Brewery Street Siege

At about 11.35p.m. on Friday 12th December 1958, Mr Harry Barker, a taxi-driver, drove to Blackburn Borough Police Headquarters at Northgate and reported that he had just dropped off a fare in Brewery Street, Blackburn. As he was reversing on the street he heard a woman shout, *'He's going to shoot, he's got a gun'*. He then saw a man standing outside a house with a gun in his hands.

Constables Halliwell, Covill (both in plain clothes) and Riley immediately went to the scene and entered Number 8 Brewery Street, which was a two-up, two-down house with a communal back yard.

There were seven persons present in the kitchen, including Henry King who was holding the others at gunpoint with an automatic shotgun.

The house was owned by Mr and Mrs Bullen, the parents of Sheila King, the wife of 27-year-old Henry King. She was in the house with her parents and their other daughter Pauline, Pauline's boyfriend James Bett and a neighbour, Blanche Cowell. Sheila's six-month-old son David was also present. King and his wife Sheila had separated a number of times and for the previous three weeks she had been living apart from him with her parents.

Pauline Jean Bullen, James Bett, Robert Bullen and his wife Alice Bullen. (© Talbot Archive)

Henry King had gone to the house at about 10.00p.m. after having spent the day drinking, entering the house with a shotgun. Henry King had made the occupants stand in the kitchen. To prove that the gun was loaded he had earlier fired the gun into the ceiling. King then told his wife to put her coat on as they were going to church, so they could renew their marriage vows.

Sheila King handed her baby to her father who put him in a pram, which he wheeled into the front room. Blanche Cowell then managed to leave the house to raise the alarm. King then threatened to kill himself.

It was at this time that the taxi driver, Mr Barker, heard a shout from her and made his way to the Police Station to raise the alarm. Mrs Cowell contacted the police from a police box and another neighbour also telephoned the police.

As Constable Covill entered the kitchen he said to King to put the gun down, but King fired the shotgun without warning, hitting the Constable in the groin. Constables Riley and Halliwell immediately dragged their injured colleague out of the kitchen and into the front room. As this was taking place, Sheila King said something to Henry King and another shot rang out. Sheila King had been shot in the back and fell to the floor.

The other occupants of the room managed to leave the house, with King shouting, *'If anyone comes in here they'll get one!'* The baby remained in the front room and a neighbour, Frederick Dugdale, dashed into the room and pulled the pram and baby out. King asked for a priest who was summoned. The priest attended but was a Roman Catholic priest. King said he wanted a Protestant priest. Police reinforcements in the charge of Detective Inspector O'Donnell arrived. After being made aware of what had taken place, he went to the kitchen door and spoke with King who he knew and asked to enter the room, which was now in darkness. Inspector O'Donnell entered the room along with Inspector Harrison.

A brief time after Inspector O'Donnell entered the room, mention was made by King that he would make a statement, whereupon the Detective Inspector took out his notebook and a pencil. He held the notebook in his left hand and the pencil in his right hand. In order to pacify King, he agreed to write down any statement which he cared to make. King spoke in an incoherent manner, saying something about Inspector O'Donnell not writing. O'Donnell then turned in his direction and, without the slightest warning or provocation, King raised the gun and shot O'Donnell in the lower chest. He then pointed the gun at Inspector Harrison, who jumped through the open doorway into the front room and took up a heavy dining chair to defend himself.

Officers outside the front door of 8 Brewery Street, Blackburn.
(Note – man on right appears to be holding a gas mask in his left hand.) (Author's collection)

Henry King being led away from court. (© Talbot Archive)

At this time Inspector O'Donnell was shuffling on his buttocks through the doorway into the front room. He was obviously badly hurt and in great pain. He was taken from the house by Inspector Harrison and rushed to the Blackburn Royal Infirmary, where an emergency operation was performed on a gunshot wound in the left side of the lower part of his chest, and for severe lacerations to the large and small intestines. During the afternoon of that day, Inspector O'Donnell's condition deteriorated, and despite a further emergency operation which was carried out, he died at about 11.45p.m. A post-mortem examination revealed the cause of death to be shock and haemorrhage from a gunshot wound to the lower left chest and abdomen.

Other officers had arrived at Brewery Street, including the Chief Constable, Superintendent Rogers and Captain William Whalley, who had been brought from Fulwood Barracks with three tear gas grenades. Lieutenant Colonel Lake, Officer Commanding the 4th East Lancashire Regiment, attended, bringing with him three rifles and ammunition. The Chief Constable had also brought four small arms to the scene. These weapons were placed in the possession of a sergeant and constables proficient in their usage who were placed in strategic positions. Two Lancashire Constabulary dog handlers were also deployed to assist Blackburn Police.

At 2.15a.m. it was decided that the siege should be ended. Orders were now given for the police to enter the house by force. Two tear gas grenades were thrown through the rear window. A shot was heard from the kitchen and King shouted that he had shot himself. A police dog was sent in, closely followed by armed police officers. When the police got to the room he was laid on the floor. King was wounded on the left side of his chest. King was taken to Blackburn Royal Infirmary and detained for treatment to his injuries.

He was released from hospital after three days and appeared before Blackburn Magistrates charged with the murder of Sheila King (20 years) and Inspector O'Donnell (48 years) and the attempted murder of John Covill. When charged with the murder of Inspector O'Donnell, he replied, *'He was a good man'*. He made no reply when charged with the murder of his wife or the attempted murder of Constable Covill. He was remanded to the Assizes at Manchester.

He stood trial at Manchester Crown Court in March 1959. During the trial evidence was presented about his mental state. A defence witness gave evidence that he considered King was of low average intelligence and was suffering from a 'split mind' and was insane at the time of the killings. Other evidence was given that whilst a serviceman in Germany King had suffered from mental issues.

Dr Gray, a senior medical officer at Walton Prison, disputed this opinion and stated that King was not suffering from any abnormality which would substantially impair his mental responsibility. King had told him that *'I said to Inspector O'Donnell I was born on a thirteenth and I am going to die on a thirteenth. I am going to kill myself. I said to him to get out as he was not writing. It came to me that they were trying to get me. He raised his arms as though to knock the gun out of my hands and I shot him.'*

Dr Benedict Finkleman, the Superintendent of the Rainhill Mental Hospital, told the jury that King was sane and responsible for his actions that night. He said that although King was a psychopath, he was not a paranoid schizophrenic.

King was found guilty of manslaughter after a three-day trial and was sentenced to life imprisonment. During sentencing, Mr Justice Elwes said, *'This is a bad a case of manslaughter as I have heard. The behaviour of the Inspector was in the best traditions of the police force and I would also like to mention Constable Covill, who went into the room in an attempt to disarm him and was shot.'* He also mentioned Constable Riley and Inspector Harrison and expressed sympathy with Mrs O'Donnell and her family.

FURTHER INFORMATION:

James O'Donnell was born in Bolton, Lancashire, on 7th April 1911. He enlisted in the Irish Guards in September 1929. In September 1932, he left the Army and was transferred to the Army Reserve. He was appointed to Blackburn Borough Police as Constable 99 on 30th September 1932.

He became a Detective Constable on 12th October 1936. O'Donnell was recalled to the Army and left to re-join the Irish Guards on 4th December 1939, returning to Blackburn Police on 3rd December 1945.

He was promoted to Detective Sergeant 15 in December 1947 and to Inspector in July 1955, in charge of the C.I.D. During his career he was commended on six occasions.

Military career 1939-45

James O'Donnell was recalled to the colours on the outbreak of hostilities in 1939 and was advanced to Lance-Sergeant and accompanied a composite battalion of the 2nd Irish Guards to the Hook of Holland in May 1940. Amongst other duties, the Battalion oversaw the evacuation of the Dutch Royal Family.

But, as described in *The History of the Irish Guards in the Second World War*, by Major D.J.L. Fitzgerald, M.C., the Germans were fast approaching:

'It was the first heavy air raid on the Battalion in the area. Flights of bombers roared over the village, bombing and machine-gunning. The Battalion had been expecting this all day, but they could offer no effective opposition.

The anti-aircraft gun posts came into action at once. They were necessarily in very exposed positions, but they fired continuously throughout the raid. Lance-Sergeant J. O'Donnell's A./A.[46] post was particularly exposed, but he stood to his gun, pumping a steady stream of tracer, till he collapsed badly wounded by machine-gun bullets... This air-raid killed seven Guardsmen and wounded twenty-three.

Three of the casualties were wounded some distance from the R.A.P.[47] [including O'Donnell]. *A local doctor treated them and then, with the best intentions, drove them to hospital in The Hague, where, unfortunately, the Germans collected them.'*

M.M. London Gazette 21 February 1946:

'In recognition of gallant and distinguished services in the Field.'

Bar to M.M. London Gazette 6 June 1946:

The original recommendation states:

'O'Donnell was captured at The Hague on 15 May 1940 and spent the greater part of his imprisonment in Poland. He was wounded and in hospital at the time of his capture, but unsuccessfully tried to evade the Germans through the American Legation. After a short period in hospital he was sent to Thorn where he escaped in August 1940 by posing as a member of a working party. He was recaptured the next day.

In February 1942, he allowed himself to be caught out of bounds so that he should be sent to a working

---

[46] A.A. (Anti-Aircraft)

[47] R.A.P. (Regimental Aid Post)

party for punishment. He was sent to a farm, but his preparations were noticed, and he was returned to the Stalag. During August 1942, he slipped away from his guard when working outside the camp and started walking to Warsaw disguised as a Pole. After four days, he was recaptured.

In February 1943 he climbed the wall at Fort 13 but was quickly recaptured. By May of the same year he had obtained a passport, clothing and money. He hid close to the main gate, and when it was dark, climbed over the wall and railings. He caught a train for Danzig, but the forged passport did not satisfy an official on the train. O'Donnell was then confined indefinitely in Fort 16 but managed to find Poles who were prepared to help him.

He escaped in November 1943 by bluffing the guard and spent the next ten days in Thorn trying to obtain a satisfactory passport. He was recognised and recaptured by a Gestapo official who had caught him on a previous attempt. At this stage, O'Donnell was guaranteed his passage to England if he agreed to collaborate with the Germans for six months. By February 1944, he was ready for another escape. He and one companion hid in a load of Red Cross boxes which were being sent to a Stalag nearby. With the help of a Pole, they were hidden in a room attached to the German Officers Mess but, having failed to obtain forged papers, they decided to travel by train to Gotenhafen. They were discovered near Marienburg.

When clothing was being moved from Fort 15 to Thorn in May 1944, O'Donnell hid in one of the sacks and escaped. He put up in a working camp so that he could forge papers and then set out for Danzig on foot. He was recaptured several days later.

Later that year, the camp was under orders to move and he managed to pass into the German compound and climb over the perimeter wire. On this occasion, he was free for four days. Whilst on the march in April 1945, he escaped from the column and joined our troops in Bergen.'

Returning to the U.K. from Bergen on 23rd April 1945, he was placed back on the Army Reserve and, after further medical treatment, re-joined the Blackburn Borough Police.

DNW Auctions Lot 608 12/12/2012

'His sense of duty was of the highest order and his loyalty to his colleagues, superiors and subordinates alike was something to be experienced to be believed. He was a great man. I personally will miss Inspector O'Donnell terribly and I can pay no greater tribute than that expressed to me by a well-known criminal, who said, "Jim O'Donnell was fair in all things.".'

Deputy Chief Constable J. M. Rodgers

Medal group - James O'Donnell, (L-R) The Queen's Police Medal for Gallantry, Military Medal and Bar, 1939-45 Star, British War Medal – James O'Donnell's medals were sold for £16,000 on 12th December 2012.

(© DNW Auctions)

James O'Donnell is remembered with a memorial plaque placed within Blackburn Police Station.

The O'Donnell Trophy was instituted by Blackburn Borough Police in honour of James O'Donnell and to recognise the most gallant deed of year.

One recipient of the trophy was Sergeant Henry Martindale Bullock, awarded in 1965. Bullock was also awarded the British Empire Medal. (See later entry.)

In 2003, the trophy was resurrected as a way of remembering the past as the Force moved into new, £7.3 million headquarters at Greenbank, Blackburn.

The trophy was presented jointly that year to four officers for the arrest of a mentally ill and armed killer. The trophy was presented by Jack Covill in a room at the police station named after James O'Donnell on 1st February 2003. Since then the trophy has been awarded on a number of occasions.

The funeral procession of Detective Inspector James O'Donnell, Blackburn Cemetery,
led by Chief Constable Bibby.

John (Jack) Covill was born in Blackburn in 1928 and was appointed to Blackburn Borough Police on 14th February 1949. He had previous military service with the Royal Army Ordnance Corps (R.A.O.C.) from November 1946 to March 1949.

He was promoted to Sergeant in 1969 and, after amalgamation with Lancashire Constabulary, to Inspector in 1970. He retired on 14th December 1977 and died, aged 85, in 2013.

John Harrison was born in Blackburn in 1908 and joined Blackburn Borough Police on 1st August 1930. On joining, his previous occupation is recorded as being an omnibus conductor. He joined the C.I.D. in 1940 and was promoted to Uniform Sergeant in 1949 and to Patrol Inspector in 1953. He retired from Blackburn Police on 25th September 1960 after 30 years' service and was commended on four occasions.

Peter Halliwell was born in 1921 and joined Blackburn Borough Police in January 1947 after having served as a Sergeant with the R.A.F from 1938 to 1946. During the war he served in India and Burma. After a short period of police service he left to re-join the R.A.F. He served with them for a further 4 years before being reappointed to Blackburn Police in December 1951. He left Blackburn Borough Police in 1960 and took employment working for several Blackburn funeral directors. He died, aged 72 years, in 1994.

Jack Riley was born in Blackburn in September 1921. During the Second World War, he held the rank of Able Seaman in the Royal Navy, serving from November 1941 to January 1946. He served aboard H.M.S. *Teazer* R23 from 7th August 1943 until 11th January 1945. *Teazer* was a 'T' class destroyer which saw service in the Mediterranean during World War 2.[48]

He was appointed to Blackburn Borough Police on 23rd October 1950 and was promoted to Sergeant in 1969. After amalgamation with Lancashire Constabulary he rose to become an Inspector in 1974 prior to his retirement. He died in 1999.

HMS *Teazer* (R23) (Public domain)

The officers were presented with their commendations by Lord Derby at Knowsley Hall on 21st October 1959.

Brewery Street, Blackburn was situated approximately 400 yards from the Blackburn Borough Police Station at Northgate, Blackburn. Brewery Street was a cul-de-sac, accessed from St. Paul's Street.

Brewery Street no longer exists, having been swept away during slum clearances. The location where Number 8 stood now forms part of the car park for Blackburn College, with University Close now situated on the approximate site of Brewery Street.

---

[48] https://www.maritimequest.com/warship_directory/great_britain/pages/destroyers/hms_teazer_f23 _as_jack_riley_collection_page_1.htm – Retrieved 13/4/2018

Presentation of Commendations at Knowsley Hall on 21st October 1959. L-R Peter Halliwell, John Harrison, Jack Covill, Jack Riley and Chief Constable Richard Bibby. (Author's collection)

Rear of 8 Brewery Street, Blackburn.
(Note – broken windows where tear gas bombs were thrown into the house.) (© Talbot Archive)

22ⁿᵈ August 1959

William McLOUGHLIN, Sergeant	**Salford City Police**
Graham SMITH, Constable	**Salford City Police**
Thomas SYKES, Foreman Joiner	**Pemberton, Wigan**

Queen's Commendation for Brave Conduct

For services when a boy fell into a sewage sedimentation tank.

L.G. 11/12/1959 Issue 41894 Page 7938

FURTHER INFORMATION:

Thomas Sykes, a joiner, was working at the sewage works when he was told by a boy that his friend had fallen into a sewage tank. He sent for the police and stripped and repeatedly dove into the tank but could not reach the bottom.

Sergeant McLoughlin and Constable Smith attended. P.C. Smith and Mr Sykes dove into the tank but failed to locate the boy. Sergeant McLoughlin obtained a 15-feet ladder and they forced themselves down into the bottom of the tank, which was described as 12-feet deep, containing 500,000 gallons of concentrated liquid, described as disgusting and dangerous. Working entirely by touch one of them caught hold of the child's leg and the boy was brought to the surface and artificial respiration was started but efforts to revive him failed.

The child was John Edward Borg, aged 7 years old, of Peabody Street, Weaste, Salford, who was said to have climbed onto the top of the concrete wall of the tank, which was protected by barbed wire and either slipped or overbalanced falling in.

All three of the rescuers were warmly commended by the Coroner.

In addition to the risks taken by the men there existed a possibility that the sewage could have contained organisms which could cause typhoid or waterborne diseases. (*The Guardian*, 26/8/1959)

FURTHER INFORMATION:

Graham Smith retired as an Inspector and died, aged 74 years, in August 2013.

Salford Wastewater Treatment Works is situated at Pacific Way, Salford, on the northerly side of the Manchester Ship Canal to the west of MediaCity, Salford.

5th November 1960

Walter Brian MURPHY, Detective Constable 160   **Preston Borough Police**

British Empire Medal for Gallantry (Civil Division)

Edward TILL, Farm labourer   **Preston**

Roy Anthony WILSON, Farm labourer   **Preston**

Queen's Commendation for Brave Conduct

Two police officers went to a farm and saw a youth who was recognised as an absconder. This youth was carrying a .410 shotgun and on seeing the police officers he immediately turned to run away but, in doing so, fell over a dog. He got to his feet, cocked the gun, levelled it at the officers and threatened to shoot if they approached any nearer. The officers walked towards him and he turned and ran away across some fields.

He was pursued by Detective Constable Murphy, and in the course of the chase the youth stopped twice and threatened to shoot the officer. In spite of this Murphy, disregarding the possibility of any personal danger, relentlessly pursued his quarry and eventually succeeded in disarming and arresting him. On examination, the gun was found to be cocked with a live cartridge in the chamber.

L.G. 25/4/1961 Issue 42334 Page 3062

Edward Till and Roy Anthony Wilson

For helping in the arrest of a youth armed with a shotgun.

L.G. 25/4/1961 Issue 42334 Page 3063

FURTHER INFORMATION:

Location of incident – Rough Hey Farm, Fulwood, Preston.

Detective Sergeant Fred Studholme and Detective Constable Murphy went to the farm to make enquiries. Two youths were in the farm yard when their car pulled up, one armed with a .410 shotgun. The one armed with the gun turned and attempted to run off and fell over a dog and on getting to his feet raised the gun at the officers and the officers heard a click.

Sgt. Studholme told him to put the gun down and he said, *'Stay where you are, or I'll shoot'*. The officers moved towards him and he ran off. Sgt. Studholme detained the other youth and D.C. Murphy ran after the gunman followed by the two workers from the farm, Edward Till and Roy Anthony Wilson. After running for some distance and threatening his pursuers twice he eventually stopped and levelled the gun at the hip at them. They spread out and advanced and when D.C. Murphy neared him he threw the gun down and said he would *'give in'*.

Walter Brian Murphy was born in Preston, Lancashire, and joined Preston Borough Police in 1956. D.C. Murphy was presented with his award by Lord Derby on behalf of Her Majesty the Queen at Knowsley Hall, Prescot, on 20th June 1961. D.C. Murphy was also awarded the Kay Taylor Trophy for the most meritorious deed of 1960. He was pensioned on 1st April 1985, having attained the rank of Chief Inspector within Lancashire Constabulary. He died in 1992.

7th December 1960

Robert Edward ANDREWS, Constable 133   **Warrington County Borough Police**

Maurice Murray CARO, Constable 28   **Warrington County Borough Police**

Queen's Commendation for Brave Conduct

For services when three men broke into a garage.

L.G. 21/4/1961 Issue 42334 Page 3062

FURTHER INFORMATION:

Constables Caro and Andrews were making a routine check at the Black Bear Garage, Knutsford Road, Warrington. Constable Caro went to the rear of the premises and Constable Andrews went to the side. Constable Caro discovered the garage had been broken into at the rear and on entering he saw three men. They came towards him, each armed with an iron bar. One man struck him with a bar on the shoulder and face then all three attacked him. He was knocked to the floor whilst one held him down and all struck him. At this stage Constable Andrews came to the assistance of Constable Caro, fighting the men off. Constable Caro managed to get up and draw his truncheon. In the violent fight which followed one man was detained and the two others escaped. The detained man was John Joseph Oates from Kirkby, Liverpool. The other two men, Jack Farrimond and James Lundon, both of no fixed abode, were arrested the following morning, waiting for a Liverpool bus at Bridge Foot.

All three were charged with garage breaking and feloniously wounding two constables.

Constables Caro and Andrews attended Warrington Infirmary to have their wounds stitched. Constable Caro required 39 stitches to wounds to his head.

All three defendants appeared at Liverpool Crown Court and were sentenced to ten years, eight years and four years imprisonment. Judge Laski, presiding, said that he thought the two officers deserved *'a generous commendation for their courage and initiative, which was of the highest order'*.

Both were later commended by the Warrington Watch Committee and the Chief Constable for their devotion to duty.

Robert Edward Andrews was a native of East Ham, London and had served in the Merchant Navy for several years before joining Warrington Borough Police in April 1960 and served until 1962. He died in 2011. His Queen's Commendation and award papers were presented by his son to The Museum of Policing in Cheshire in 2018.

Maurice Murray Caro joined Warrington Borough Police in April 1956 after serving in the Royal Navy from 1949 to 1956. He served with Warrington Borough Police until November 1962 when he transferred to the Buckinghamshire Constabulary, which later became part of Thames Valley Constabulary (later renamed to Thames Valley Police) after amalgamation in 1968.

He initially served in uniform at High Wycombe and then as a Detective Constable at Burnham and Slough. He was promoted to Detective Sergeant in 1967 and Uniform Inspector in 1967 at Wolverton and Buckingham, followed by Chief Inspector at Aylesbury in 1969. He then served for ten years as Detective Chief Inspector at Aylesbury. He was promoted to Superintendent at Slough in 1980 and became Detective Superintendent for the Southern Crime Area in 1982. In 1985, he returned to Aylesbury Police Division as 2nd i/c and retired in 1987. During his career he was commended on a number of occasions by Chief Constables and Judges.

(With thanks for additional information provided by Mr Maurice Caro and The Museum of Policing in Cheshire.)

2nd March 1961

William HARRISON, Sergeant 2394   **Lancashire Constabulary**

British Empire Medal for Gallantry (Civil Division)

John McCARTHY , Detective Constable 111   **Lancashire Constabulary**

Queen's Commendation for Brave Conduct

An emergency call was received by the Police that a man who had been drinking heavily was in possession of a loaded shotgun and threatening to use it.

The house was visited by a Constable who, from outside, saw the man in the living room holding the shotgun. The Constable tried to persuade him to surrender the gun, but he refused and threatened to shoot. The Constable summoned assistance and was quickly joined by Sergeant Harrison and a Detective Constable. The Sergeant knocked on the door of the house, but the man refused to admit him and again threatened to shoot.

Some ten minutes later he came out of the house still holding the shotgun and whilst pointing it towards the officers he walked towards them and stopped about five yards away. Sergeant Harrison eventually persuaded him to return to the house and he did so but kept the gun pointed towards Harrison and the Detective Constable who followed him into the house. Inside the house the man sat on a chair and placed the gun across his knee keeping his right-hand forefinger on the trigger, as if about to shoot.

The Sergeant sat in a chair opposite him about six feet away and continued to engage him in conversation. After some time, he succeeded in getting into a position where he was able to grab the gun barrel with his left hand and at the same time he grabbed the man's right hand which was on the trigger. The gun was fired but the shot narrowly missed the Sergeant's legs and entered the carpet a few feet away. The Sergeant succeeded in forcibly taking the gun away and the man was arrested.

L.G. 22/9/1961 Issue 42471 Page 6964 (Harrison) & 6965 (McCarthy)

FURTHER INFORMATION:

Location of incident – 5 Parsonage Street, Church, Lancashire.

On 28th April 1961, John Winston Duxbury (26), a television engineer of Parsonage Street, Church, appeared before the County Sessions at Preston charged with having a gun with intent to damage property and a weapon with intent to endanger life.

Duxbury was convicted of having the weapon with intent to damage property but was acquitted of having the weapon to endanger life.

The court was told that Duxbury threatened to blow the officers' heads off. Duxbury said he had never intended to shoot anyone and that he had been drinking that night. *'I said I would blow the policemen's heads off but it was only a threat. I would never have shot.'*

Duxbury was bound over for three years. (*The Guardian*, 29/4/1961)

William Harrison

William Harrison joined Lancashire Constabulary and was posted to Kirkham Division on 19th February 1939. He served at Manchester Division before being posted to Bolton as a temporary Sergeant in February 1955.

On being promoted to a substantive Sergeant on 3rd April 1955 he was posted to Accrington, where he served until his retirement in 1963.

John McCarthy was born in Wigan on 10th May 1915 and was appointed to Lancashire Constabulary on 1st March 1937. His previous occupation was as a motor driver. He served at Lower Blackburn, Warrington, Kirkham and Accrington Divisions.

On 20th August 1942, he left for military service, returning to Lancashire Constabulary on 11th November 1945. John McCarthy retired on 1st September 1963. He died, aged 83 years, in 1998.

John McCarthy

5th June 1961

Percy BOWERS, Detective Constable   **Manchester City Police**

Queen's Commendation for Brave Conduct

For attempting to rescue a man from drowning.

L.G. 22/9/1961 Issue 42471 Page 6965

FURTHER INFORMATION:

On 5th June, a man was reported to be in the River Irwell in the city centre. At this point the river is bounded by walls 36-feet high. Detective Constable Bowers swam to the man and fastened him to a rope and lifebelt, which had been thrown into the water, so that he could be pulled to a landing stage. Detective Constable Bowers then had to swim about 60 yards to a ladder fixed to the wall. The river is 110 feet wide and nine to ten feet deep at the point where the rescue took place. Detective Constable Bowers knew he had to enter the water from a considerable height and face quite a strong current, and if the drowning man had become obstructive it would have been almost impossible for others to come to his assistance owing to the height of the sheer walls.

Percy Bowers was born in Hyde and was appointed, aged 29 years, to Manchester City Police in January 1951. His previous occupation was as a painter and decorator.

He served for fifteen years and four months before he died on 19th May 1966 whilst still in service.

Robert CARSWELL, Constable 180 'M'	**Liverpool City Police**
Thomas Owen DAVIES, Constable	**Mid-Wales Constabulary**
Robert William ROBERTS, Constable	**Shropshire Constabulary**
Arthur Rees ROWLANDS, Constable	**Gwynedd Constabulary**

George Medal

John Francis Ivor BENNETT, Constable	**Mid-Wales Constabulary**
Geoffrey Seymour EDWARDS, Sergeant	**Mid-Wales Constabulary**

British Empire Medal for Gallantry (Civil Division)

Following a series of burglaries in the surrounding countryside an intensive search was made for the criminal who was known to be dangerous. At about 3a.m. Constable Rowlands, who was patrolling in the vicinity of some lonely cottages, suddenly came upon the criminal who was carrying a sawn-off shotgun.

The man pointed the gun straight at Rowland's face and threatened to shoot him. Although only two yards away from the pointed gun the Constable advanced unflinchingly towards the man, at the same time trying to reason with him. As Rowlands moved forward the criminal fired at point-blank range, full into his face.

The Constable was terribly injured but in spite of the agonising pain, being blinded in both eyes, his face covered by multiple wounds, and losing much blood, P.C. Rowlands remained conscious on his hands and knees and tried to voice an alarm. His mouth and teeth had been smashed by the gunshot, but he did not spare himself and was able to provide an accurate description of his attacker.

Constables Roberts and Carswell took up the chase and followed a trail through a valley until Roberts saw the criminal, still holding the gun, run for cover of some bushes. Roberts immediately ran after him and fearlessly approached although threatened by the gun.

When only a few yards separated them, the criminal fired but the Constable ducked, and the shots smashed into the boughs above his head. The man then ran off and Roberts followed. Meanwhile Carswell had gone ahead with a police dog in an attempt to cut off the escape. He released the dog which ran towards the armed man. When the dog was a few yards away the gunman shot it in the head.

Carswell attempted to reach the man who threatened to shoot him and as the Constable came forward fired directly at him. Carswell threw himself to one side and the shots flew over his head. The gunman then jumped on a bicycle which was lying nearby and rode away. Constable Davies, who had been in the front of the chase, made a final effort to capture the mad gunman. He jumped into a police car and caught up with him on a small bridge.

The car hit the rear wheel of the bicycle and threw the rider off but he regained his feet and withdrew the shotgun from its holster. Before he could fire it, Constable Davies threw himself at his legs and brought him down. There followed a terrific struggle during which the deranged man tried to fire the gun into the Officer's stomach but help came from Sergeant Edwards and Constable Bennett, who had been prominent throughout the chase, and the man was eventually subdued.

L.G. 2/2/1962 Issue 42590 Page 994

FURTHER INFORMATION:

Location of incident – North Wales.

At approximately 3a.m. on 2nd August 1961, Constables Williams and Rowlands were carrying out checks at Dovey Bridge, Machynlleth, Montgomeryshire, checking people and cars following cases of housebreaking. Constable Rowlands was the village policeman at Corris, Merioneth.

A man was sighted crossing the bridge and both officers made an unsuccessful search for the man by car. P.C. Rowlands was dropped off near to Dovey Cottages. It was in this area where he challenged the man who came out of the shadows at the back of a cottage near the bridge and was shot, blinding him for life.

Presentation by the Chairman of the Watch Committee, Alderman A.B. Collins, MBE, JP to P.C. Carswell of the Certificate of Merit for exceptional and meritorious performance of duty.
(Chief Constable's Annual Report, 1958)

Following his wounding, a large-scale search was instigated with surrounding forces providing officers as part of mutual aid. Liverpool City Police provided a Sergeant and eight officers and their dogs to assist in the search. Part of this team was Constable Robert Carswell and his Police dog 'Derry'.

Five days later, on 7th August 1961, the man was sighted in the village of Aberllefenni, Merioneth (approximately 7-8 miles away from the initial incident.) Police arrived, and a police dog handled by P.C. Roberts (Shropshire Constabulary) picked up a scent and tracked to a farm where the man was sighted, leading to the incidents described in the citation. The man was brought off the bicycle and arrested by the officers with the assistance of a forestry worker.

The arrested man was Robert Boynton, aged 48 years, of no fixed abode. He appeared at Caernarvon Assizes and was convicted of attempting to murder three police constables, one of which was Arthur Rowlands, who was blinded. He was also convicted of two charges of larceny and one of house breaking.

After conviction, Dr William John Grey, Senior Medical Officer at Walton Prison, Liverpool, told the court he had formed the opinion that Boynton was suffering from mental illness, namely paranoid schizophrenia, and that he needed hospital treatment for his own protection and the protection of others.

The court was told that in 1946 he had been certified insane and had escaped from Exminster Mental Hospital (situated near Exeter in Devon) and that he had remained on the run for the statutory period, meaning that no action could be taken. He had been arrested on a number of occasions after that, both in the UK and in Poland, and was repatriated to the UK from Munich in 1959. Following this he was sentenced to three years imprisonment in 1951.

Boynton, who conducted his own defence at the trial, asked that 138 other offences should be taken into account, comprising breaking and entering and larceny offences.

Judge Hinchcliffe ordered that Boynton be detained at Broadmoor with his discharge restricted for 30 years. He died, whilst still detained there, in 1994.

The judge commended the officers who he described as showing *'fearless and conspicuous courage'* in undertaking the apprehension of an armed man. A German forestry contractor, Sigfried Siegler, was also commended for his part in the arrest.

Police Dog 'Derry' recovered from his injuries and continued in service with Liverpool City Police until his retirement.

Constables Rowlands, Carswell, Davies and Roberts received their awards from Her Majesty the Queen at Buckingham Palace on 6th March 1962.

Arthur Rees Rowlands died on 2nd December 2012, aged 90 years of age. Following his shooting he worked as a voluntary police switchboard operator and became a keen advocate of Guide Dogs for the Blind, working for the Gwynedd Guide Dogs Association. He helped to raise many thousands of pounds for the charity and took to visiting schools to show children what it means to be without sight.

13th December 1961

John WALLWORK, Sergeant 2388	**Lancashire Constabulary**
John Jack FLEMING, Police Constable 225	**Lancashire Constabulary**

Queen's Commendation for Brave Conduct

For apprehending a drunken man armed with a shotgun.

L.G. 22/6/1962 Issue 42712 Page 5104

FURTHER INFORMATION:

At 6,20p.m. on Wednesday 13th December 1961, a call was received by Sergeant Wallwork from James Briggs of 8 Warwick Avenue, Cleveleys, regarding a disturbance at his home.

On arrival at this address, the Sergeant was informed that the cause of the trouble was the conduct of Francis Robert Briggs, aged 23 years, the son of the complainant, whom it was stated caused trouble when he had been drinking. The Sergeant interviewed Francis Briggs and as a result Briggs voluntarily left the house.

At 11.12p.m., an emergency call was received from James Briggs regarding the conduct of his son who had returned home a little while earlier, much the worse for drink. Sergeant Wallwork and Constable Fleming visited the house, 8, Warwick Avenue, Cleveleys, again and were informed that Francis Briggs had returned home between 10.30p.m. and 11p.m. and had again caused trouble and demanded to know where his double-barrelled shotgun was hidden. After much argument and, owing to Francis Briggs' attitude, his father brought the gun from where it had been hidden upstairs.

Briggs pointed the gun at his parents and told them to get out. Briggs senior took his wife and daughter to a neighbour's house and, whilst on their way, saw Francis Briggs smash the dining room window and discharge one of the barrels of the gun. Francis Briggs then fired a second shot and his father decided to call the police again and, as he went to the telephone, a third shot was fired. A fourth shot was fired just before the arrival of the police.

On the arrival of the officers, Francis Briggs was leaning out of the broken front windows of the house with the shotgun pointed at them. As the officers went along the garden path, Briggs was asked by Constable Fleming to put the gun down. Briggs said, *'Get away or I'll get you'*. The Sergeant and Constable moved to another position, but Briggs continued to point the gun in their direction. An unknown person shouted to Briggs to come out and then he then jumped through the window of the house and ran towards a lorry which was parked nearby.

Briggs then approached the two officers with the gun chest high and shouted for his sister to come out of the adjoining house, which she did and walked a few paces along the garden path towards her brother. At the same time, the Sergeant and Constable walked forward and Briggs said, *'Keep away or I'll shoot you. I won't touch Mary'*.

Constable Fleming then jumped at Briggs from the front, knocking the gun away to his left side. At the same time, Sergeant Wallwork grabbed the gun and threw it to one side and after a short struggle Briggs was arrested. On examination, the gun was found to be loaded in both barrels and, on being cautioned, Briggs said, *'I don't think I'm right in the head, I could have shot you if I'd wanted'.*

At the Lancashire County Intermediate Sessions, Preston, on Wednesday 21ˢᵗ February 1962, Briggs was charged with being in possession of a firearm with intent to endanger life.

He was acquitted of the charge, the defence being that he had consumed 16 pints of beer and was too drunk to know what he was doing. At the conclusion of the case, the Learned Chairman, W. H. Openshaw, Esq., made the following statement:

'I have discussed this with my colleagues and we think we should commend to the Authorities the conduct here of Sergeant Wallwork and Constable Fleming. Undoubtedly, whatever the defendant's intentions were when they disarmed him, they had every reason to suppose that they were in grave physical danger themselves, and their conduct is highly commendable.

Many other people in this case acted with courage, but we think these two Police Officers were outstanding in the way they behaved and we hope that someone will draw these remarks to the attention of the appropriate Authorities.'

(W.O. 3/1963)

Awarded 'William Garnett' Cup.

Presentation of the William Garnett Cup to P.C. Fleming and P.S. Wallwork.
(Note – Queen's Commendation emblems next to medal ribbons on tunics.)

FURTHER INFORMATION:

Both officers were presented with the awards on Monday 17ᵗʰ September 1962, by Lord Derby on behalf of Her Majesty at Knowsley Hall.

John Wallwork was appointed to Lancashire Constabulary on 6ᵗʰ November 1937, after having previous service with the Royal Artillery for 6 years and 230 days. He was recalled to the Army on 1ˢᵗ December 1939 for war service and was reappointed on 13ᵗʰ September 1945.

He served at Bury, Rossendale, Bolton, Seaforth and Fylde Divisions and was promoted to Sergeant on 22ⁿᵈ February 1952. He retired in 1966.

John Jack Fleming was appointed to Lancashire Constabulary on 13ᵗʰ September 1948.

He served at Manchester, Bury and Fylde Divisions before moving on promotion to Sergeant on 3ʳᵈ December 1962 to Ashton-under-Lyne and later to Oldham and Bolton Divisions. He retired in 1973.

27ᵗʰ December 1961
Alan ASHWORTH, Constable 107   **Rochdale Borough Police**
British Empire Medal for Gallantry (Civil Division)

Two children were playing on an ice-covered mill pond when the ice gave way and both fell through into the water.

Constable Ashworth, who was in a police car, received information and was driven to the scene within 1½ minutes from the time of the call. On the way, he took off his tunic and cap. On arrival, he plunged into the pond and swimming through the water and thin ice, managed to find the children. When he reached them both were unconscious.

Taking hold of them by their clothing, he struggled towards the opposite bank, breaking the thin ice by his own weight as he went along.

When the ice became too thick to break he lifted the children on to it and they were picked up by other police officers.

L.G. 21/9/1962 Issue 42789 Page 7510

FURTHER INFORMATION:

The children involved in this incident were Eric (8) and Kristine Porter (10). Despite warnings from his sister, Eric ventured onto an ice-covered mill pond, situated between Newbold Street and Albert Royds Street, Rochdale, in an attempt to recover an umbrella.

The ice cracked as he neared the item and he sank into the water. Kristine, seeing this, went into the water to assist but was dragged underwater by her waterlogged coat. This was witnessed by a neighbour, Mr Arthur Whitehead, through his kitchen window, who immediately rang the police before rushing to the pond with rope to attempt a rescue.

Before he could attempt this, the police car arrived and P.C. Ashworth entered the water. When P.C. Ashworth reached the children, only the top of Eric's head was visible and Kristine was on her back. Both were unconscious. Both were brought to the side by P.C. Ashworth, where they were given artificial respiration before being taken to Rochdale Infirmary, where they were discharged later that day suffering no ill effects. From falling into the water to reaching the hospital just eight minutes elapsed. (*Rochdale Observer*, 30/12/1961)

Alan Ashworth was born at Rochdale and joined Rochdale Borough Police in April 1960. His previous occupation was as an engine fitter with Rochdale Passenger Transport Department.

In addition to the award of the B.E.M., he was also commended by the Watch Committee, awarded the Rochdale Borough Silver Medal for Conspicuous Gallantry and awarded The Royal Humane Society Testimonial on Vellum. He was also presented with the Gracie Fields Trophy, which was presented to Rochdale Borough Police to celebrate its centenary, to be awarded to officers for work of exceptional merit.

He was also commended in 1966 and 1968 by the Chief Constable for good police work. He retired as a Sergeant and died, aged 80 years, in 2014.

14th June 1962

Walter Alan BONNER, Constable 53 'T'	**Liverpool City Police**

British Empire Medal for Gallantry (Civil Division)

David Jack DEMAIN, Clerk	**Liverpool**
Brian FELTON, Constable 338 'A'	**Liverpool City Police**
Harold William LEWIS, Constable 250 'A'	**Liverpool City Police**

Queen's Commendation for Brave Conduct

A man entered a bank, grasped hold of the only customer, a woman, pressed a revolver into her temple and threatened to kill her unless money was handed over. The cashier fearing for the safety of the customer pushed over a bundle of five-pound notes.

The man grabbed the money and ran out of the door brandishing the revolver. The alarm was sounded, and two policemen and members of the Bank staff went in pursuit of the gunman. As his pursuers turned a corner after him the gunman turned as he ran and fired one shot at them. No one was hurt, and the chase continued.

Others joined in the chase and more shots were fired. Constable Bonner was driving a police motor cycle when he heard a shot and the sound of people screaming and shouting. He saw the man running with the revolver in his hand being chased by the constables and others. Constable Bonner then accelerated his machine and drove it straight at the man whom he hit and knocked to the ground. The motor cycle fell over and Constable Bonner jumped on top of the criminal and held him until the other Police Officers arrived and took him into custody.

L.G. 25/9/1962 Issue 42789 Page 7510

David Jack Demain, Constables Brian Felton and Harold William Lewis:

For services when an armed man attempted to rob a bank.

L.G. 25/9/1962 Issue 42789 Page 7511

Ronald Abdullah Lawrence Naif (20 years), unemployed, of Thackeray Street, Liverpool, pleaded guilty at Liverpool Crown Court to armed robbery, using a revolver to resist arrest and shooting with intent to resist arrest and was sentenced on 28th June 1962 to fourteen years imprisonment. Naif, who was said to have two previous convictions which involved the use of guns, was told by Judge Laski, *'You are a danger in a civilised community'*.

It was stated that Naif entered the Whitechapel Branch of the National Provincial Bank wearing a trilby hat pulled down and dark glasses pressed the loaded revolver to the head of a woman customer, forcing the cashier to hand over £1,000. He ran out of the bank and was pursued by the police, bank staff and members of the public, firing three times before being brought down by P.C. Bonner on his motorcycle. It was said that Naif, a moslem, was fanatical about the war taking place in Algeria (1954-1962) and maintained he wanted to send the money to a political party opposed to the O.A.S.

The O.A.S. or **Organisation Armée Secrète** (meaning **Secret Army Organisation**) was a right-wing French dissident paramilitary organization during the Algerian War (1954–62). The O.A.S. carried out terrorist attacks, including bombings and assassinations, in an attempt to prevent Algeria's independence from French colonial rule.

Constables Bonner, Lewis and Felton were awarded the Certificate of Merit for Exceptional and Meritorious Performance of Duty by the Watch Committee.

P.C. Brian Felton was awarded a British Empire Medal for Gallantry in 1965 – see later entry.

1963	
Joseph James LEE, Constable 244 'A'	**Liverpool City Police**
British Empire Medal for Gallantry (Civil Division)	

In the early hours of the morning a seaman fell from the George's Landing Stage at a point near to the Seacombe Ferry berth and was swept by the force of the ebbing tide beneath the Princess Landing Stage.

He could not swim but managed to grasp the Staging and shout for help. The cries were heard by Constable Lee and a Sergeant and two other men. Lee removed part of his clothing for immediate action and with one of the others made his way to a point just south of the Floating Roadway and climbed down onto a Pontoon.

By the beam of a hand torch directed between the water and the under part of the Stage, they saw the man hanging on to the Stage with both hands. Constable Lee lowered himself into the water and a rope was tied under his armpits.

A lifebelt with a rope attached was thrown into the water alongside the Constable. The Constable then ducked beneath the Staging, there being only about 18 inches between the water and the Stage at this time, and pulled himself along sideways towards the immersed man, whose head he could see some 15 to 20 yards away, towards the centre of the Stage.

Lee edged himself along until he could reach the man with his left hand and gripping him commenced to make his way back. The men at the other end of the rope pulled slowly and firmly until both rescuer and rescued were pulled clear of the Stage.

L.G. 23/4/1963 Issue 42974 Page 3562

FURTHER INFORMATION:

Constable Lee was awarded the Certificate of Merit for Exceptional and Meritorious Performance of Duty by the Watch Committee.

An accident occurred in the extension of a ventilation shaft and it was reported that an injured man was lying at the bottom of the tunnel shaft 150 feet from the surface, having fallen there from a moveable hanging wooden platform which was suspended 30 feet from the bottom of the shaft.

Constable Gardner went to the scene and decided to descend the shaft by the quickest possible method. This was by means of a steel bucket 3 feet in diameter and four feet in depth, which was suspended over the centre of the shaft by a surface crane.

Gardner was lowered to the bottom of the shaft. He found the injured man lying on two duck boards suspended across the sump which contained 18 inches of mud and water. Both his legs were fractured, and his arms were dislocated, and Gardner realised it would be very difficult to remove him to the surface. He called for assistance and Murphy came down in the bucket with special equipment. In view of the cramped conditions, both men stepped into the sump.

Two boards were placed over the rim of the steel bucket, but it was impossible to secure them to the bucket in any satisfactory way, and it was obvious that the injured man would have to be accompanied to the surface in order to steady this improvised stretcher, and also to negotiate it past the various obstructions. Gardner and Murphy therefore both climbed on to the bucket.

As it ascended the bucket had a tendency to swing, being built on a hinge for tipping purposes and there was considerable danger of the three men being tipped out of the bucket to the bottom of the shaft. The surface was reached after about 30 minutes and the injured man conveyed to hospital.

L.G. 19/7/1963 Issue 43062 Page 6275

FURTHER INFORMATION:

Location of incident – Mersey Tunnel, Liverpool.

The injured workman was John Carr (reported as Kerr in some newspapers), aged 48, of Spencer Street, Everton. He sustained leg and facial injuries and was detained at hospital.

Constable Gardner was awarded the Certificate of Merit for Exceptional and Meritorious Performance of Duty by the Watch Committee.

Constable Hughes was called to the quay side of the River Wyre where he saw a woman and two boys in the water. He immediately removed his outer clothing, jumped into the river and pushed a lifebelt, which had been dropped from the quay, towards the woman and the children.

Hughes manoeuvred the lifebelt and brought it within the woman's grasp but the two little boys were unconscious and due to the extremely choppy nature of the water, the Constable had great difficulty in supporting them on the lifebelt. Under difficult conditions he had to retrieve one or other of the two children who were being constantly washed away. At this point, Constable Lewis arrived and he immediately jumped into the river to help Hughes.

Together they managed to support the woman and the two children and to get close to the sea wall, but there were no steps available, the wall was almost vertical and as the level of the water was about fourteen feet from the top of the wall, it was impossible for the Constables to remove the woman and the children from the water. A pleasure boat which was about 400 yards away was hailed and the Constables with some difficulty were able to hand up the boys into the boat. By this time both officers were almost exhausted, but they managed to get the woman into the boat before being pulled in themselves.

L.G. 27/9/1963 Issue 43118 Page 8069

Awarded 'William Garnett' Cup.

FURTHER INFORMATION:

Location of incident – Wyre Estuary, Dockside, Fleetwood.

The alarm was raised by a railway signalman at Fleetwood at 9a.m. From his signal box he saw a woman holding hands with her 23-month-old twins on the estuary wall of the River Wyre. He saw the woman go to the parapet edge two or three times with the children and then jump into the river, pulling the children with her. The signalman immediately went to the scene and saw the woman floating in the water, still holding each child.

P.C. Hughes, who was on duty in Dock Street, heard the signalman shouting for help and ran about 150 yards to the quayside where he removed his outer clothing and boots before jumping into the river.

At the time of the rescue the tide was about half an hour to high water. There was an easterly wind and the water was very rough. The Constables jumped fourteen feet from the quayside into the water, which was ten feet deep. Both children were unconscious when pulled into the boat and were revived by artificial respiration by the officers. The mother and children were taken to Fleetwood Hospital and were discharged some 24 hours later. (*Lancashire Constabulary Journal*, April 1964)

Both officers were highly commended by the Chief Constable and awarded £10. They were also awarded the Liverpool Shipwreck and Humane Society Bronze Medal and Certificate and the William Garnett Cup for the most gallant act of 1963.

Both officers were presented with the British Empire Medal by the Lord Lieutenant, Lord Derby, on behalf of Her Majesty at Knowsley Hall on Friday 3rd January 1964.

Arwyn Hughes joined Lancashire Constabulary in October 1961 and served at Fleetwood and Prestwich, Manchester. He transferred to Gwynedd Constabulary in September 1966.

Thomas Raymond Lewis

Thomas Raymond Lewis was born at Kelsall, Cheshire, in 1914, and was appointed to Lancashire Constabulary as P.C. 2107 in October 1937. His previous occupation was as a farmer and he lived at Walkden when appointed. He served at St. Anne's, Manchester and Wigan with his final posting at Fleetwood Division.

During his career, he was commended three times by the Chief Constable, one incident involved the attempted rescue of a child from a disused pit lodge in the Wigan area in 1946, as well as for the incident at Fleetwood. He was pensioned due to ill health in 1964 and died in 1967.

<table>
<tr><td colspan="2">

21st July 1963

Hubert Noel PITCHER, Detective Sergeant   **Warrington County Borough Police**

Kenneth Paul COTTON, Constable 96   **Warrington County Borough Police**

John MALE, Constable 91   **Warrington County Borough Police**

Queen's Commendation for Brave Conduct

</td></tr>
</table>

For services when arresting an intoxicated man armed with a shotgun.

L.G. 3/3/1964 Issue 43261 Page 1982

FURTHER INFORMATION:

Police were called to a house in Warrington where 21-year-old Fred Cartledge, a tractor driver, resided with his wife and brother-in-law. A violent argument between the couple took place after he returned home in a bad mood after a previous argument and he had been drinking.

Assistance was sought from the neighbours and eventually his wife and brother-in-law went to a telephone kiosk to call the police. As they did so, Cartledge produced a shotgun and fired over their heads.

Detective Sergeant Pitcher and Constable Male arrived in a police car. Cartledge was standing on the footpath and, as the car slowed down, he pointed the gun towards the officers. He told the officers, *'If you put your head out of that window, I'll blow your head off'*, and kept the gun pointed at the car. Sergeant Pitcher tried to talk sense to the man, but he threatened to shoot the officer. Constable Cotton arrived on a motorcycle but was told by Cartledge, who pointed the gun at him, to *'Keep going'*.

Eventually, Sergeant Pitcher persuaded Cartledge to talk and he agreed to get into the car. There he was overpowered, and the gun taken from him. The gun proved not to be loaded, for in the struggle the hammer clicked after the trigger was pulled. Cartledge, however, had eight live cartridges in his possession.

Cartledge appeared at Liverpool County Sessions where he admitted using a firearm to resist arrest and was sent to prison for three years. The Chairman told him, *'People in this country who use firearms to resist arrest particularly when they produce them in fear of the Police will receive such sentences as will indicate to them and anyone else similarly minded, that their conduct will not be tolerated.'*

Hubert Noel Pitcher was born in 1915 at Weaverham, Cheshire, and served briefly with Warrington Borough between 1935 and 1936, before resigning. He was reappointed in 1939, seeing service with the Royal Air Force between 1943 and 1945. He retired in 1967 and died, aged 84 years, in 2000.

Kenneth Paul Cotton was born at Warrington in 1923 and was appointed to Warrington Police on 28th May 1950. His occupation is shown as being a paper board machinist.

He had previously served with the Royal Artillery from 1943 to 1946. He is recorded as serving at

Kenneth Paul Cotton

Hubert Noel Pitcher

Warrington as a Borough Officer and with Lancashire Constabulary. On reorganisation he was transferred to Cheshire Constabulary. He died in 1988, aged 65 years.

John Male was born in 1928 in Warrington and served with Cheshire Constabulary from March 1952 to December 1957 before transferring to Warrington Borough Police, serving until June 1966. John Male died in December 2002.

14th February 1964

Graham David PRIEST, Police Cadet   **Liverpool City Police**

William John SASS, Police Cadet   **Liverpool City Police**

British Empire Medal for Gallantry (Civil Division)

Cadets Priest and Sass were on duty at a Pier Head when they were told that a woman was drowning in the river. They ran to the top of a bridge and saw the woman in the water between the river wall and a floating Landing Stage, being swept by the strong current towards a second bridge.

Priest immediately discarded his police raincoat, tunic and boots, and dived into the river while Sass ran down the bridge to the Landing Stage, where he threw off his greatcoat, seized a lifebelt, and dived into the river. Both Cadets swam towards the woman. Priest reached her first and, turning her on to her back, supported her in the water.

The woman commenced to struggle and Priest had a great deal of difficulty in retaining his hold until the arrival of Cadet Sass, who had released the lifebelt because of its impeding action. The Cadets and the woman were then carried by the strong flood tide towards the second bridge.

A boat was rowed out towards them but they had drifted down river past the bridge for a distance of approximately 90 yards before it reached them. The woman was then lifted into the boat and the Cadets held on to the sides while it was rowed to the steps near a third bridge.

This part of the river is notorious for its treacherous and dangerous currents, and water flowing behind the Landing Stage is turbulent and heavily contaminated by slime and waste oil.

L.G. 14/8/1964 Issue 43411 Page 7078

FURTHER INFORMATION:

Location of incident – River Mersey, Pier Head, Liverpool.

The person rescued was Mrs Winifred Mathieson, aged 65 years, of Dundale Road, Liverpool.

Both cadets were appointed to the regular force on 11th September 1964. Constables 660 'K' Priest and 661 'K' Sass were awarded the Certificate of Merit for Exceptional and Meritorious Performance of Duty by the Watch Committee.

A man climbed on to the parapet of the 12th floor of a building and threatened to jump into the street. The Police and Fire Brigade were called and Superintendent White and Constable Adams made their way to a ledge about six feet away from the parapet.

Adams made several attempts to get on to the parapet occupied by the man but each time he did so the man moved away and appeared about to throw himself from the building.

The Superintendent and the Constable made repeated efforts to persuade the man to come down but without success and it was apparent that no direct approach could be made to seize him owing to the extreme danger of falling into the street 150 feet below.

The Police Officers were joined by Mr. Matthews who talked to the man who then moved his position slightly. Immediately Matthews, followed by Superintendent White and P.C. Adams, leapt across on to the small ledge and caught hold of the man by his arms and tried to pull him back. There was a struggle and all were in danger of falling off the parapet. Still struggling the man was pushed on to another ledge and other helpers, wearing safety belts, were then able to reach him and pull him through a window into the building. (*The Guardian*, 24/3/1964)

L.G. 24/7/1964 Issue 43393 Page 6407

FURTHER INFORMATION:

Location of incident – Sunlight House, Quay Street, Manchester.

The man removed from the building was Mr Ralph Wright, aged 30, married, of Lichfield Avenue, Reddish, Stockport.

Sunlight House is a 14-storey steel and concrete building situated in Manchester City Centre. It was opened in 1932 and was the headquarters of Joseph Sunlight's property business. It was the city's tallest building until the 1960s.

Frank White was born at Sale, Cheshire, and was appointed to Manchester City Police, aged 21 years, on 11th March 1938, stating his previous occupation as being a soldier. He had served for 3 years and 9 months with the Grenadier Guards. As a reservist he was recalled to the colours on 3rd December 1939.

He returned to Manchester City Police on 19th February 1941 but resigned on 5th August 1942 to re-join the military forces. After the war he returned to Manchester City Police, rising through the ranks to Chief Superintendent before retirement in May 1968. He died in October 2000.

Allan Shelton Cotton was born at Manchester and joined Manchester City Police, aged 26 years, in October 1950. His previous occupation was as a joiner. He retired as a Sergeant in May 1981 and died in July 2000.

9th August 1964

Thomas COOGAN, Lorry Driver **Middleton, Lancashire**

Christopher Anthony JONES, Police Constable **Manchester City Police**

Queen's Commendation for Brave Conduct

For rescuing a drunken and violent man who had climbed on to scaffolding on the face of a building in the course of erection.

L.G. 2/4/1965 Issue 43619 Page 3452

FURTHER INFORMATION:

On 9th August 1964, P.C. Jones saw a man about 60 ft. above the ground on the scaffolding of a building under construction. The man was under the influence of drink and threatened to jump. Making his way to the top of the building, P.C. Jones jumped from the parapet to a wooden platform six feet lower down and seized the man round the body. The full weight to the man, who had released his hold on the tubing, was supported by P.C. Jones on the outside of the scaffolding. With the assistance of a civilian, P.C. Jones dragged the struggling man to a platform, where he was held until the Fire Brigade arrived.

13th August 1964

Joseph DORAN, Constable 241 'D' **Liverpool City Police**

Eric JOHNSON, Motor Driver **Bootle**

Queen's Commendation for Brave Conduct

For rescuing a family from a fire at a hotel.

L.G. 29/1/1965 Issue 43565 Page 1159

FURTHER INFORMATION:

On 13th August 1964, P.C. Doran noticed smoke issuing from the ground floor windows of a nearby public house. After summoning the Fire Brigade, he ran to the house and tried to arouse the occupants. Joined by two civilian passers-by,

P.C. Doran forced the bar door and entered to find the ground floor in smoke and flames. Crawling across the floor of the bar he and the civilians broke open a locked door leading to the residential quarters. Owing to the heat and smoke. one of the civilians was forced to leave but P.C. Doran and his companion, Mr Johnson, went upstairs and roused the licensee and his wife. They then continued to the children's room and carried the two children out on to the landing, where they found the parents, and succeeded in leading the whole family to safety in the street. Both P.C. Doran and Mr Johnson had to be given medical treatment afterwards.

Constable Doran was awarded the Certificate of Merit for Exceptional and Meritorious Performance of Duty by the Watch Committee.

Possible later award

Parchment each to George William Bennett, Henry Savage, Police Sergeant 2035 Joseph Doran and Police Constable 4876 Robert Thomas Glynn, Merseyside Police, for having rescued a young woman who was attempting to commit suicide by jumping into the river from the south boom at Liverpool Landing Stage, on 12th of February 1980.

(Information courtesy of the Liverpool Shipwreck and Humane Society.)

31st August 1964

Douglas ADAMSON, Detective Constable	**County Borough of Bolton Police**
Harry RIDYARD, Detective Constable	**County Borough of Bolton Police**

Queen's Commendation for Brave Conduct

For effecting the arrest of an armed and dangerous man.

L.G. 13/11/1964 Issue 43491 Page 9817

FURTHER INFORMATION:

Detective Constables Adamson and Ridyard approached a man armed with a .22 air rifle after he had shot at three persons in the street. As they approached him, he shouted, *'I'll shoot the lot of you'*, and when they were about two yards away he fired at D.C. Ridyard at point blank range. The officers rushed him, and a struggle ensued, with D.C. Adamson being jabbed in the mouth with the butt of the gun. It required six officers to overpower the man.

Appearing at Bolton Quarter Sessions on 17th September 1964, Winston Edge, of Wellington Street, Bolton, pleaded guilty to assaulting the two detectives and possessing an air rifle when the assaults were committed and guilty to possessing an offensive weapon.

Edge told the court that the gun went off accidentally and was not loaded. *'I had an argument with a man in our house and I was shooting the gun to frighten him. I only fired two pellets in the air.'*

Sentencing Edge to three years imprisonment, Mr Russell, the Assistant Recorder, stated, *'You behaved like an animal. But for the outstanding bravery and courage of the officers one shudders to think what might have happened that night'.*

Edge told the court that he had consumed nine or ten pints that night and was half drunk at the time.

Detective Constables Adamson and Ridyard were presented with their Commendations by Lord Derby, the Lord Lieutenant, at a ceremony at Bolton Town Hall. (*Bolton Evening News*, 1/9/1964 & 18/11/1964)

Douglas Adamson was born in County Down, Ireland, in 1929, and was appointed to Bolton Police on 18th April 1957. His previous occupation is shown as being a joiner. He served with the Royal Navy from 1950 to 1956. He was promoted to Temporary Sergeant on 16th October 1967 and Substantive Sergeant on 12th April 1968. Bolton Borough Police was amalgamated with Lancashire Constabulary on 1st April 1969.

He served at Bolton for his service apart from two years when he served as an instructor at the No. 1 District Police Training Centre at Bruche. He returned to Bolton Division in 1973 and, on reorganisation, was transferred to Greater Manchester Police. He was commended twice whilst serving with Bolton Police. He died in 1986, aged 56 years.

Douglas Adamson

Harry Ridyard was born at Little Hulton in April 1934 and was appointed to Bolton Borough Police Force on 25th April 1955. Bolton Borough Police was amalgamated with Lancashire Constabulary on 1st April 1969. He had previous military service, having served with the Royal Armoured Corps as a Trooper from April 1953 to March 1955.

In addition to his Queen's Commendation in 1964, he had been commended by the Chief Constable in 1956 and 1962. He was promoted to Sergeant in March 1967 and to Inspector in August 1971.

He remained at Bolton for the whole of his service with Bolton Borough and Lancashire Constabulary and was transferred to Manchester Police on reorganisation on 1st April 1974. He died, aged 57 years, in 1992.

Harry Ridyard

19th September 1964

John FRIEL, Joiner   **Kirkby, Lancashire**

Colin Edward JOHNSON, Police Cadet   **Liverpool City Police Cadet Corps**

Queen's Commendation for Brave Conduct

For rescuing a woman in grave danger of drowning in the River Mersey.

L.G. 29/1/1965 Issue 43565 Page 1160

FURTHER INFORMATION:

At 8.45a.m. on 19th September 1964, Mr Friel, a 43-year-old father of three children, and Cadet Edwards were at the Liverpool Landing Stage when a woman's shouts were heard in the water near to the Birkenhead Ferry's berthing point. Mr Friel dived into the water and was soon followed by Cadet Johnson.

Despite stormy conditions they succeeded in bringing the 37-year-old Liverpool woman back to the landing stage and safely ashore. (*Liverpool Echo*, 3/2/1965)

Cadet Johnson was awarded the Certificate of Merit for Exceptional and Meritorious Performance of Duty by the Watch Committee.

21st November 1964

William James CLARKSON, Constable 191 'A'	Liverpool City Police
Robert DICK, Driver	Liverpool Corporation Passenger Transport
Leslie Wyn EDWARDS, Constable 136 'M'	Liverpool City Police
Brian FELTON, Constable 338 'A'	Liverpool City Police
Harold William LEWIS, Constable 250 'A'	Liverpool City Police

British Empire Medal for Gallantry (Civil Division)

A woman who had been suffering from a nervous disorder, and had been drinking heavily during the evening, was seen to climb over the railings of a river wall and jump into the river.

She was wearing a heavy fur coat. Constables Felton and Clarkson who were on duty nearby, ran along the river wall and saw the woman floating in the water about 10 yards away. Both Constables took off their uniform caps, jackets and boots, and jumped into the water, the surface of which was then about 20 feet from the top of the wall. The water and the side of the river wall are heavily contaminated at this point with mud, slime and waste oil.

The officers swam to the woman and supported her in the water. They were then joined by Mr. Dick, who had jumped into the water shortly after the officers. He assisted in supporting the woman who commenced to scream and struggle violently. They swam with her to the wall and eventually found a ringbolt attached to the wall about 4 feet from the surface of the water, which they grasped, and supported the woman between them. A crowd of persons, many of whom were of the hooligan element, gathered at the top of the wall. Some of them shouted and jeered at the rescuers, threw cups and other missiles and poured hot tea on them, which had been obtained from a nearby coffee stall.

Constable Clarkson was struck by a cup, but fortunately was not injured. Constable Edwards saw his colleagues struggling with the woman in the water. He removed his jacket and boots and then jumped into the water to help support the struggling woman. Constable Lewis, hearing shouts and screams, went to the south side of the river removed his jacket and boots and dived in from the landing stage. He swam to the river wall and assisted in supporting the woman.

There is little doubt that but for the action of Constables Felton, Clarkson, Edwards, Lewis, and Mr. Dick, this unfortunate woman would have drowned. They entered a tidal river on a cold night and risked their lives by continuing to retain their hold on her, despite her maniacal efforts at self-destruction, and in the face of the shameful conduct of a number of hooligans, whose actions could well have prevented her rescue.

In spite of the fierce struggles of the drowning woman and the considerable obstruction caused by the actions of hooligans, they persisted in their rescue efforts and with great courage and tenacity retained their hold upon her.

L.G. 25/6/1965 Issue 43698 Page 6205

FURTHER INFORMATION:

Location of incident – River Mersey, Pier Head, Liverpool.

The person rescued was Ruth Tucker, aged 20 years, of Victoria Square, Liverpool, who was detained at hospital suffering from shock and the effects of immersion.

Also assisting in the rescue was Thomas Neville, a ferry hand, who rowed out in a boat against the strong ebb tide. Extra police had been on duty at the pier head due to rowdyism by teenagers.

All officers were awarded the Certificate of Merit for Exceptional and Meritorious Performance of Duty by the Watch Committee.

P.C. Brian Felton had been previously awarded a Queen's Commendation for Brave Conduct in 1962 – see previous entry. He was promoted to Sergeant in 1971.

4th December 1964

Henry Martindale BULLOCK, Sergeant 2   **County Borough of Blackburn Police**

British Empire Medal for Gallantry (Civil Division)

The police were called to a block of flats in course of erection where a man was seen seated on tubular scaffolding on the tenth floor with his feet dangling in mid-air threatening to jump if anyone came near to him.

Sergeant Bullock entered the flats and mounted the steps to the tenth floor. It was apparent that the man had got into his precarious position by walking along a plank and out on to the steel scaffolding.

At this time the man was about four feet past the end of the wooden plank, but still sitting on the steel bar. Sergeant Bullock knelt on the plank as near as possible to him and for the next fifteen minutes engaged him in conversation. The Sergeant crawled nearer and suddenly grabbed hold of the man's left arm. There was a struggle but the Sergeant succeeded in pulling him from the steel scaffolding, on to the wooden plank and finally into the building.

L.G. 2/4/1965 Issue 43619 Page 3451

FURTHER INFORMATION:

Location of incident – Lark Hill Flats, Blackburn, Lancashire.

The rescued man was James Battersby (21), a motor mechanic, of Rockcliffe Street, Blackburn.

Three 14-storey tower blocks were constructed as public housing at Larkhill, Blackburn. They were the first multi-storey flats to be built in Blackburn. Each block consisted of 27 one-bedroom flats and 53 two-bedroom flats.

Two of the blocks, Ribble House and Pendle House, were demolished in 2000. The third, Bowland House, underwent a £2.3 million refurbishment and is now owned by a housing association.

Henry (Harry) Martindale Bullock was born at Blackburn in 1913. He was appointed to Blackburn Police on 5th March 1939 as Constable 71. He had previously served with the West Riding of Yorkshire Constabulary from 1937 to 1939.

He was promoted to Sergeant 2 on 14th January 1954, retiring after 30 years' service on 14th September 1967. He died in 1981. During his career, he was commended on five occasions and was awarded the James O'Donnell Trophy on 8th January 1965 for his part in this incident. He had previously been commended on 9th September 1964 by the Chief Constable for his part in a similar rescue of a 17-year-old girl who was threatening to commit suicide by jumping from the top section of a mill fire escape in August 1964. (*Blackburn Times*, 9/4/1965 & 11/12/1964)

Sergeant Harry Bullock, pictured in April 1965 with Larkhill Flats, the scene of the incident, in the background. (© Talbot Archive)

19th February 1965

Raymond George BUCK, Constable 10   **Lancashire Constabulary**

British Empire Medal for Gallantry (Civil Division)

A call was received by the Police to the effect that a man was threatening his wife and three children with a shotgun.

On arrival at the house Police Constable Buck found that four other Constables had also answered the call. Looking through the window the officers could see the man pointing a single barrelled shotgun at the front door.

Police Constable Buck entered the house followed by the other officers and was confronted by the man holding the shotgun, which was both loaded and cocked. Police Constable Buck continued to move slowly towards the man, who backed away until he was almost against the wall.

By that time the Constable was within three feet of him and made a dive at the man knocking the gun sideways, keeping a grip on the gun and finally succeeding in throwing the gun away. The gun was cocked and contained a live cartridge in the breech. Although he knew the danger of being shot Buck took the lead in disarming an armed man.

L.G. 6/8/1965 Issue 43734 Page 7567

Awarded 'William Garnett' Cup.

Location of incident – Bury, Lancashire.

At the time of the incident P.C. Buck was attached to Bury Group Traffic Patrol.

It was established that the man had taken about 20 Purple Heart tablets and consumed six pints of beer. At the Quarter Sessions, the chairman commended the conduct of the police in the case and in particular the conduct of P.C. Buck

Raymond George Buck was born in May 1934 at Preston, Lancashire, and was appointed to Lancashire Constabulary as P.C. 10 in October 1955.

He served at Leigh, Nelson, and as a Traffic Patrol Officer at Bury, Manchester and Bolton. He was commended by the Chief Constable on 13th October 1962 for courageous conduct in entering a canal during the hours of darkness and rescuing a man with suicidal tendencies.

On Force reorganisation in April 1974, he was transferred to Manchester Police. He died, aged 79 years, in 2014.

18th March 1965

Thomas Henry LUCAS, Constable   **Warrington County Borough Police**

British Empire Medal for Gallantry (Civil Division)

In the early hours of the morning a Constable saw a man standing on the parapet of a bridge. As the officer approached, the man jumped off the bridge into the River Mersey.

The Constable immediately summoned help and taking a lifebelt ran some distance down river. From here he lowered the lifebelt to the water level. The man was seen in the water floating down in mid-river.

In the meantime, several other police officers arrived on the scene including Constable Lucas. He divested himself of his uniform ran barefoot about thirty-two yards until he was slightly ahead of the floating man and then entered the water and swam diagonally towards the centre of a bridge.

He was able to grab the floating man, and at the same time take hold of the lifebelt which had been lowered. Various other ropes were obtained, and one was lowered to the two men in the water. With help from several people both on the bridge footpath and on the river bank, the men were pulled to the side of the river and lifted from the water.

The River Mersey at the scene is nothing more than an open sewer. The water was filthy and covered with a foam. The street lighting did not give much illumination to the river and valuable assistance was given by lorry drivers turning their headlights on to the water.

L.G. 15/10/1965 Issue 43793 Page 9769

FURTHER INFORMATION:

The incident occurred at 3.10a.m. on 18th March 1965. P.C. Lucas entered the Mersey from Marshall Gardens. P.C. Lucas was assisted by P.C. Lodge, who also entered the water to assist. The man rescued from the Mersey was James Crookes, who was attempting suicide.

P.C. Lucas had previously been involved in another incident, approximately 12-18 months before, where he had entered the Mersey in response to reports of a child in the water, which proved not to be the case and the incident was fabricated. Following that incident he spent four months in hospital after becoming seriously ill several days later after contracting suspected meningitis from the water of the Mersey.

Thomas Henry Lucas was born in January 1929 at Padgate, Warrington, and was appointed as Constable 38 to Warrington County Borough Police on 10th August 1952. His previous occupation is recorded as being a printer's assistant and soldier.

He had served as a Guardsman with the Scots Guards from 1946 to 1952. For his actions on 18th March 1965 he was presented with the Bronze Medal and Certificate by the Liverpool Shipwreck and Humane Society and commended by the Chief Constable and Watch Committee and awarded £10.

He served with Warrington County Borough Police and then as a Traffic Officer, based at Stretford with Lancashire Constabulary from 1st April 1969 until reorganisation on 1st April 1974, when he was transferred to Cheshire Constabulary. He died, aged 76 years, in 2005.

22nd April 1965

John VALLELY, Sergeant   **Barrow-in-Furness Borough Police**

Queen's Commendation for Brave Conduct

For services when apprehending two armed youths.

L.G. 10/8/1965 Issue 43734 Page 7568

FURTHER INFORMATION:

At about 2a.m. on 22nd April 1965, two youths seen by a beat Constable in suspicious circumstances were stopped and questioned. Two other Constables also came up, as one of the youths was known to the police and gave a false name and address. A radio call was made to Headquarters.

Sergeant Vallely then arrived in a police van and whilst he was questioning one of the youths, the other suddenly produced a pistol and, pointing it at the police, threatened them as he backed away. Sergeant Vallely immediately grappled with the youth and after a struggle overpowered and disarmed him.

Later the youth said: *'I don't know whether the gun was loaded or not but I pulled the trigger just in case it was.'* He was sent to Borstal by the Recorder at Barrow Quarter Sessions.

Sgt. Vallely was commended for his courage by the Recorder, Mr Godby Shorrock, who said: *'I wish to express my great admiration for the conduct of the officers in this case in particular that of Sgt. Vallely.'* (*North West Evening Mail*, 11/8/1965 & *Barrow News*, 13/8/1965)

For services when arresting an offender who was hiding on the sloping roof of a building.

L.G. 15/10/1965 Issue 43793 Page 9767

FURTHER INFORMATION:

The incident took place on the rooftop of a building at Albert Square, Manchester, where an offender was arrested.

The officers were called to a five-storey city centre office where a man was believed to have broken in. The offices were searched for around two hours before the man was spotted on the roof, 60 feet from the ground. They chased the man over the rooftop before he jumped over a parapet wall and slipped on a sloping roof and became trapped in the guttering overhanging the 60-foot drop. The officers climbed down the slippery roof without regard for their own safety and pulled the unconscious man slowly back to the roof ridge where others were able to assist. (*Police Review*, 22/10/1965)

Police Constable Irvine and another Constable were on duty in a police van when they saw a man carrying a large square object which he put into the back of a car. The officers were suspicious that this was stolen property and decided to interrogate the man.

Constable Irvine started up the engine of the van and drove diagonally across the road towards the car. As they did so the car drove straight at them and Irvine had to swerve to avoid a collision.

A chase ensued and eventually Constable Irvine managed to get the police van in front of the car which stopped. The man got out and ran down a nearby entry closely followed by Irvine. The Constable caught the man who immediately attacked him. Irvine felt a blow in his chest which forced him down to his knees. He retained a grip on the man with his left hand and put his right hand to his chest where he felt the handle of a knife which was sticking into him.

He pulled the knife out of his chest and the pain this caused made him drop the knife. His assailant went for the knife again and there was a struggle which resulted in Irvine regaining possession of the knife. The other Constable then came to his assistance and the man was overcome and arrested.

In spite of the serious and painful nature of his injury, Constable Irvine was so devoted to duty that he plucked the weapon from his body and held on to his struggling prisoner until such time as he was able to hand him over safely to the custody of other officers.

L.G. 15/10/1965 Issue 43793 Page 9767

Location of incident – Entry off St. Bees Street, Moss Side, Manchester.

Appearing at Manchester Crown Court on 23rd July 1965, Constable Irvine's assailant, James Ronald Walsh (36) of Plymouth Grove, Chorlton-on-Medlock, was sentenced to thirteen years imprisonment.

He pleaded guilty to wounding Constable Irvine with intent to commit grievous bodily harm, breaking into a doctor's home and stealing property valued at £200.

Constable Irvine was praised by the judge for his devotion to duty. The knife used to stab Ken Irvine is with the Greater Manchester Police Museum.

17th October 1965

Brian David WAUGH, Sergeant 63 C.I.D.	**Liverpool City Police**
Reginald McFALL, Constable 171 C.I.D.	**Liverpool City Police**
John William ROOKE, Constable 236 C.I.D.	**Liverpool City Police**

Queen's Commendation for Brave Conduct

For disarming and arresting a violent criminal.

L.G. 16/8/1966 Issue 44084 Page 9040

FURTHER INFORMATION:

During inquiries into the activity of absconders the police learned of the whereabouts of a youth listed as an absconder since August 17th 1965, when he had failed to return to a Borstal institution after a period of home leave.

The youth was known to be violent and arrangements were made for a party of police officers to arrest him in the early hours of Sunday morning. On October 17th 1965, Sergeant Waugh and Constables McFall and Rooke went to the house where the youth was staying but they were unable to get in until 10.20a.m. when they found the youth sleeping in a first-floor room.

He admitted being an absconder and was taken into custody with Constable McFall holding his right arm. As the party reached the street the youth tried to break away from Constable McFall's hold and struggled violently. He then took from his pocket what looked like a revolver and fired it twice at Sergeant Waugh and Constable Rooke. Constable McFall kept hold of the youth's right arm and the other officers closed in to restrain the youth who continued to struggle violently and fired the weapon again at Constable Rooke until he was disarmed.

On examination the weapon was found to be a Perfecta starting pistol of German manufacture, loaded with a clip of .22 blank cartridges but incapable of firing bullets. The police officers were not to know that the weapon was not a lethal firearm and their action in disarming a violent, armed criminal showed a total disregard for their personal safety in accord with the best traditions of the police service. (*Liverpool Echo*, 17/8/1966)

All officers were awarded the Certificate of Merit for Exceptional and Meritorious Performance of Duty by the Watch Committee.

All the officers were stationed at the Prescot Street Divisional CID office.

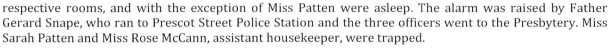

7th November 1965

Joseph Gerard TOWNSEND, Inspector   **Liverpool City Police**

Donald CHALKLEY, Sergeant 12 'B'   **Liverpool City Police**

Eric LEACH, Sergeant 15 'B'   **Liverpool City Police**

Queen's Commendation for Brave Conduct

For services when rescuing a woman from a burning house.

L.G. 1/4/1966 Issue 43942 Page 3934

FURTHER INFORMATION:

Location of incident – Sacred Heart R.C. Presbytery, 2 Hall Lane, Kensington, Liverpool.

The Sacred Heart Presbytery was a building of three floors and the fire occurred in the staircase well in the basement. It was detected by Father Thomas Burrowes, who was in his room on the first floor at about 12.25a.m. At the time of the fire the entire household of five priests and two housekeepers were in their respective rooms, and with the exception of Miss Patten were asleep. The alarm was raised by Father Gerard Snape, who ran to Prescot Street Police Station and the three officers went to the Presbytery. Miss Sarah Patten and Miss Rose McCann, assistant housekeeper, were trapped.

Sergeant Leach immediately went to the first floor, showing a complete disregard for his personal safety. He found Miss Patten in the passageway lying on her side against a wall. He dragged her to the landing down several stairs and then was unable to endure any longer the heat and fumes, even with his face pressed to the floor. Sergeant Leach was forced to withdraw.

Sergeant Chalkley met Sergeant Leach inside the building and was told there was a woman *'somewhere'*. Sergeant Leach joined his colleague in a further effort to reach Miss Patten, but both were beaten back, unable to breath. Sergeant Chalkley ran to the kitchen to get wet cloths but Sergeant Leach commented, *'We must get them out'*, and went back up the staircase. Inspector Townsend found Sergeant Chalkley and Father Gerard Snape in the kitchen, soaking towels. The Inspector then rushed to the first floor where he met Sergeant Leach, and because of his distressed condition, Sergeant Leach was told to retire. He replied, however, *'I can't go out, sir because there are people trapped up there'*.

Inspector Townsend took off his coat, wrapped it about his head, and went in search of Miss Patten. He was beaten back, but on receiving a wet towel he made a further attempt and found Miss Patten lying unconscious on the stairs. He succeeded in dragging her some way towards safety then had to retreat to the first floor, exhausted, and finally collapsed. Father O'Brien helped him to the fresh air, and when he had partly recovered, Inspector Townsend went back to assist in the rescue. He re-joined Sergeants Leach and Chalkley, who had returned using wet towels and, as a result of their combined efforts, Miss Patten, a heavily-built woman, was dragged to the safety of the first floor. Although the three police officers again made their way to the top floor they finally discovered that Miss McCann had been brought to safety from the window of her room by way of a Liverpool Fire Brigade escape ladder.

Bur for the timely and courageous action of the three police officers the outcome of the fire would have been far more serious. (*Liverpool Echo*, 6/4/1966)

All officers were awarded the Certificate of Merit for Exceptional and Meritorious Performance of Duty by the Watch Committee.

Joseph Gerard Townsend was promoted to Superintendent (Grade 1) in February 1971 and retired in September 1979. During his career he was awarded two merit decorations, one award for outstanding police work in the Lesley Hobbs murder case in 1962, and another for this incident.

24th May 1966

John Graham WIGGINS, Constable 165 'C'   **Liverpool City Police**

Queen's Commendation for Brave Conduct

For helping to rescue children from a fire in a dwelling house.

L.G. 14/7/1967 Issue 44366 Page 7895

FURTHER INFORMATION:

Location of incident – 17, Mulgrave Street, Toxteth, Liverpool.

Constable Wiggins was on motor scooter patrol when he saw a woman leaving the burning building with two children. After calling the Fire Brigade by radio he dashed into the burning house, and only penetrated the smoke to the first floor up two flights of stairs by placing a glove over his face. On hearing a child's cries, he forced a door and carried out the young boy.

He handed the boy to the people in the street and dashed back into the blazing house. On reaching the first floor again he had to crawl up two further flights of stairs to the second floor. By this time the smoke was dense and blinding and the heat was fierce. Nevertheless, he groped his way around other rooms in search of another child. He heard crying and eventually picked up the baby girl. He placed a blanket over the child for protection before making his way again to the street.

Constable Wiggins returned a third time to the burning house to satisfy himself that everyone had been taken to safety and, when he reached the street, he was exhausted and overcome by the rescue operations.

Constable Wiggins joined the police in May 1954 and had been commended on six previous occasions. His father served with Liverpool City Police for 27 years. (*Liverpool Echo*, 19/7/1967)

Constable Wiggins was awarded the Certificate of Merit for Exceptional and Meritorious Performance of Duty by the Watch Committee.

4th July 1966

Robert MOORES, Sergeant 916   **Lancashire Constabulary**

Roger HUGHES, Constable 2939   **Lancashire Constabulary**

British Empire Medal for Gallantry (Civil Division)

Detective Sergeant Moores and Detective Constable Hughes received information that a man, who had failed to answer his bail on a charge of receiving stolen postal orders was about to keep an appointment with an acquaintance at a garage.

The man was also wanted in several other parts of the country for crime, including the theft of motor cars. It was known that he possessed a firearm which he would use to avoid arrest.

The two officers went by car to the garage and saw the criminal seated in the driving seat of a stolen car. Moores positioned the police vehicle across the

front of the car whilst other police positioned their vehicle immediately behind it. Hughes went to the driver's door of the stolen car and Moores to the front passenger door which were both locked.

On the driver's side, the window was down, and Hughes grappled with the wanted man and tried to stop the car engine but was unsuccessful. Moores joined in and a violent struggle ensued. The man managed to throw himself backwards across the driver's seat and lifted up a sawn-off shotgun and pointed it at Hughes. Although the muzzle of the gun was only a matter of two feet away from his face, and he could see it was the intention to shoot, Hughes lunged forward and grabbed the end of the barrel with his left hand trying to force it away from his face and body.

At the same time Moores tried to make the man release his grip of the weapon. Moores managed to push Hughes head down below the level of the gun as it was fired. Hughes was shot in the palm of his left hand but managed to wrench the gun away whilst Moores continued the struggle.

Despite their efforts, they were unable to retain hold of the man who drove his vehicle violently backwards and forwards. He managed to ram the police vehicle out of his way and drove off at a fast speed. He was arrested three days later. Moores and Hughes showed exceptional courage and outstanding devotion to duty in their efforts to arrest a desperate criminal in possession of a loaded gun.

L.G. 30/3/1967 Issue 44279 Page 3586

Awarded 'William Garnett' Cup.

FURTHER INFORMATION:

Location of incident – Moscow Drive, off Queens Drive, Stoneycroft, Liverpool.

On 31st October 1966, Henry James Sealby, aged 32, appeared at Liverpool Crown Court and was sentenced to eleven years imprisonment. Sealby's plea of not guilty to shooting with intent to murder D.C. Hughes was accepted.

He entered guilty pleas for wounding with intent to cause grievous bodily harm, carrying a firearm to resist arrest, feloniously receiving 1,017 postal orders, stealing a Lotus Cortina car, and stealing two revolvers, two air rifles, a shotgun and other property from a Scarborough gunsmith.

Sealby asked for 26 other offences, including forgery, housebreaking, theft and store breaking, to be considered.

Sealby had been arrested in Leeds after D.C. Alan Roberts stopped a car with an unusual registration plate. Driving the car was Sealby and on the passenger seat was a loaded revolver.

Before sentencing, Mr. Justice Fenton Atkinson said to him, *'It is only by the mercy of providence that you did not kill this officer, and for a man who discharges a firearm at a policeman who is trying to arrest him, the punishment must be severe.'*

Both officers were presented with the British Empire Medal by Lord Derby, the Lord Lieutenant, on behalf of Her Majesty on 15th May 1967 at Knowsley Hall.

Robert Moores was born at Hulme, Manchester, in August 1922 and joined Lancashire Constabulary on 8th March 1948. He had served with the R.A.F. from 1941 to 1946.

He was promoted to Sergeant in 1959 and Inspector in 1968, rising to Chief Inspector in 1970 and Superintendent in 1972. He served at Bury, Ashton-under-Lyne, Widnes, Rochdale, H.Q. and St Helens.

During his career with Lancashire Constabulary, he was commended by the Chief Constable on six occasions. Robert Moores was transferred on amalgamation to Merseyside Police. He died, aged 84 years, of age in 2006.

Robert Moores

For preventing a youth from throwing himself off a bridge.

L.G. 14/2/1967 Issue 44248 Page 1711

FURTHER INFORMATION:

Sgt. Twyford was on duty at 11.30p.m. when he saw a youth sitting with his legs over Salthouse Railway Bridge.

With P.C. W. Jackson Lawrence of the British Transport Police, he went onto the bridge by the signal box on the bridge's westerly side.

As Sgt. Twyford approached, the youth said, *'I'm going to let go'*, and climbed down the girders and disappeared from view, holding on by his fingertips. Sgt. Twyford ordered the police van to be placed on the road 21 ft. under the bridge.

Then he climbed on to the bridge and, lying flat on his stomach, grasped the youth by the wrists and managed to hold on to him until assistance came from P.C. Lawrence. If Sgt. Twyford had lost his balance he could have been pulled over the bridge. (*Barrow News*, 17/2/1967)

FURTHER INFORMATION:

Salthouse Railway Bridge is situated on the A5017, Salthouse Road/Roose Road, Barrow-in-Furness.

Police officers were summoned by radio to a dwelling house where a man had discharged a firearm at a police officer. On arriving at the house, the police officers, led by Sergeant Moore, went to an attic room in which the man had locked himself.

Sergeant Moore, after asking the man to open the door, broke it down and was confronted by the man who was holding a pistol in his left hand and a knife in his right. The Sergeant kicked the pistol from the man's hand and closed with him. In doing so he was stabbed in the stomach.

Another officer then attempted to disarm the man but was stabbed in the right hand and right leg and fell to the floor. In spite of his injuries Sergeant Moore again closed with the man and held him from behind until he was overpowered by other police officers.

L.G. 19/5/1967 Issue 44316 Page 5729 – Moore

Anthony George Lowe Grisdale

For services when assisting in the arrest of an armed man.

L.G. 19/5/1967 Issue 44316 Page 5730 Grisdale

FURTHER INFORMATION:

Location of incident – Fernleaf Street, Moss Side, Manchester.

It is reported that prior to 2.20a.m. an officer was talking to a man at the front door of Ayeetey's property when Ayeetey came downstairs armed with a pistol and a knife. When the officer asked what was going on, Aryeetey fired on him and closed the door.

The offender, Charles Barrow Aryeetey (46), appeared at Manchester Court on 17th November 1966, charged with wounding Police Sergeant Moore with intent to murder him and of wounding Constable Grisdale with intent to cause grievous bodily harm. It was described that it required four officers to overpower Aryeetey, who was a very large man.

He was committed to the Crown Court for trial. (The outcome of the proceedings is not known.) (*The Guardian*, 18/11/1966)

12th December 1966	
Lawrence Stanley CLARKE, Constable	**Manchester City Police**
Michael Joseph HANNIGAN, Constable	**Manchester City Police**
Queens Commendation for Brave Conduct	

For services when a mentally disturbed man threatened to throw himself off the roof of a building over 200 feet high.

L.G. 19/5/1967 Issue 44316 Page 5730

FURTHER INFORMATION:

Location of incident – Albert Bridge House, Bridge Street, Manchester.

The police officers attended after the man had been sitting on the edge of the lift housing of Albert Bridge House, Bridge Street, Manchester. After Constable Hannigan had attracted the man's attention, Constable Clarke grabbed the man and brought him down. The man was later admitted to hospital. (*Manchester Evening News*, 24/5/1967)

19th December 1966

Francis Anthony BARTNIK, Maintenance Engineer	**Blackpool**
John Dugdale BROWN, Sergeant	**Blackpool Borough Police**
Derek Peter TAYLOR, Constable	**Blackpool Borough Police**

The British Empire Medal for Gallantry (Civil Division)

William Derek HANDLEY, Maintenance Foreman	**Widnes**

Queen's Commendation for Brave Conduct

A small boat used to transport men and materials to and from a drilling rig platform offshore, sank as a result of engine failure caused by rough seas, throwing the four occupants into the water. They were carried by the wind and tide past the end of a pier to a jetty where they were flung against the stanchions.

Constable Taylor, who was on the jetty, threw life belts and with the help of other men on the pier, secured and then threw over a scrambling net. Taylor saw one man in the water who was almost unconscious and having difficulty supporting himself.

He immediately climbed down the pier stanchions, grabbed the man and climbed back up the ironwork to the pier rail. Still without a life belt or life line, Constable Taylor again climbed down the ironwork and had hold of another of the men in the water when a huge wave struck him, knocking him off balance into the sea amongst the pier ironwork. He surfaced on the other side of the pier, climbed up the ironwork and was taken to hospital.

Another of the men in the water was able to fasten a rope around himself and was assisted out of the water by Bartnik, who climbed down the stanchions. A third man was reluctant to leave go of the pier tie bar to which he was clinging. Bartnik made several attempts to reach him but was beaten back by the rough seas. An attempt was made by Sergeant Brown to rescue this man.

He went down the scrambling net and with someone holding his left hand the Sergeant entered the water and took hold of the man. He managed to pull him along a cross member until his head and shoulders were clear of the water but then a huge wave submerged them both and the Sergeant lost his grip but he again went into the water and was dragging him clear when two more waves hit them and the man was torn from his grasp and washed away under the pier.

The weather and sea conditions were appalling and there was always the danger of the rescuers particularly the police officers who entered the water, being buffeted against the pier stanchions and severely injured.

L.G. 19/5/1967 Issue 44316 Page 5728

William Derek Handley, Maintenance Foreman, Widnes.

For attempting to rescue a man from drowning in a heavy sea.

L.G. 19/5/1967 Issue 44316 Page 5730

Preserved DUKW at Eden Camp Modern History Theme Museum, Malton, North Yorkshire. (Public domain)

FURTHER INFORMATION:

Location of incident – Sea off North Pier, Blackpool.

The vessel involved in this incident was a DUKW 6-wheel amphibious vehicle. This type of vehicle was of American manufacture and was used extensively by the Allied forces in the Second World War and afterwards. It was one of a pair of such vehicles in use at the offshore rig.

The DUKW was returning from the Bedford X rig, carrying four men. The rig was situated ¾ mile offshore and was at the sea end of the sewage outfall scheme being built by Blackpool Corporation. The sewerage scheme was almost completed.

The four men were washed towards the North Pier where three were rescued. The three men rescued were Mr Joe Davies, aged 48, of Thames Ditton, Surrey; Mr Keith Wilson, aged 26, of Park Avenue, Clitheroe; and Mr Michael Roper, aged 30, of Kingston-upon-Thames. The fourth man was Mr William Webb, a 42-year-old tunnel inspector, employed by Blackpool Corporation of Ashton Road, Blackpool. He was washed away from Sergeant Brown's grasp and drowned.

At the time of the incidents all four of the boat occupants were wearing heavy clothing to counter the cold conditions on the day and were wearing life jackets.

The DUKW was never recovered and the other DUKW was not used for further transport to and from the rig.

Sergeant Brown, Constable Taylor and Mr Bartnik were later presented with their awards by Lord Derby at a ceremony held at Knowsley Hall.

(With thanks to John D. Brown and Derek Taylor for additional information provided.)

John Dugdale Brown was appointed to Blackpool Borough Police in 1953. He had been twice awarded the Rhodes Marshall Trophy for the most meritorious act of the year. This included the actions of December when he and P.C. Taylor were jointly awarded the trophy and for a previous incident, along with Sergeant Heyworth, for his part in the rescue of two boys from the sea in 1962. He was awarded a testimonial from The Royal Humane Society and had three other commendations for police work before this incident. John Brown retired in June 1983 at the rank of Superintendent and was 2nd i/c at Blackpool Division of the Lancashire Constabulary.

Derek Peter Taylor was appointed to Blackpool Borough Police in 1955. He had previously served as a Police Cadet from 1951 to 1953. Along with Sergeant Brown, he was jointly awarded the Rhodes Marshall Trophy. He retired in 1984.

Francis Anthony Bartnik was Polish and came to Britain in 1940, having escaped from a Romanian P.O.W. camp. He served with the Royal Air Force for the remainder of the war and also saw service with the Polish and Free French Air Forces. He commented, *'I never expected anything like this. All that worries me is that we could not save the man's life.'* He died in Blackpool, aged 86 years, in 2002.

William Derek Handley was a maintenance foreman, aged 27 years, residing at Foster Street, Widnes. He was fishing from the jetty of the North Pier at the time of the incident. He went down the scrambling net with Sergeant Brown and assisted him in his efforts to rescue Mr Webb.

15th June 1967

Christopher Matthew DAVIES, Student	**University of Liverpool**
Edward GROGAN, Motor Driver	**Liverpool**
William MARSHALL, Constable 105 'M'	**Liverpool and Bootle Constabulary**

Queen's Commendation for Brave Conduct

For rescuing a man from a burning house.

L.G. 10/05/1968 Issue 44585 Page 5456

FURTHER INFORMATION:

Location of incident – 60 Russell Street, Liverpool.

At about 2.30p.m. on 15th June 1967, Constable Marshall, a dog handler, was on duty when he saw smoke coming from the three-storey house at Russell Street. Entering the building, he groped his way through the smoke and found 69-year-old John Clague, who he carried outside, and an ambulance was called.

Constable Marshall went back into the burning house, making his way to the rear where he found a wooden shed on fire alongside a stable, where he found a horse and a dog. Releasing the animals, he led them to safety from the rear of the property.

In the meantime, the Liverpool Fire Brigade arrived, where they carried out a search of the building using breathing apparatus after being told a young girl might have been trapped on the upper floor. They searched for some time before they were assured there was no one else on the premises. One fireman was taken to hospital after sustaining a burn to his face. The fire was extinguished after about half an hour, but considerable damage had been done.

Constable Marshall was awarded the Certificate of Merit for Exceptional and Meritorious Performance of Duty by the Watch Committee.

William Marshall was injured on Sunday 6th July 1981, during rioting in Toxteth. Whilst bending down to assist a wounded colleague he was struck on the back by a large piece of concrete. He shrugged off the injury and, despite feeling unwell, he continued working. He was admitted to hospital but was released. On 9th July, he went on holiday to Spain with his family. Whilst there he collapsed and was rushed to hospital. Doctors in Spain discovered he had lost the use of one kidney and the other had been damaged as a result of the blow to his back. He spent the following nine weeks in hospital in Spain before returning home. Fund raising allowed a dialysis machine to be provided at his home and he was able to return to work. He died suddenly in 1986. (*Liverpool Echo*, 29/7/1981 & 4/7/1986)

8th August 1967	
James Gerald FORREST, Constable 2482	**Lancashire Constabulary**
Queen's Commendation for Brave Conduct	

For services during floods at Wray in Lancashire.

L.G. 10/05/1970 Issue 44585 Page 5456

About 5.15p.m. on Tuesday, 8th August 1967, a violent thunderstorm developed over the Roeburndale and Wray areas and torrential rain began to fall. The River Roeburn swelled to such an extent that it ripped whole trees from its banks and swept them down towards the village of Wray, where they were hurled against the Wray Bridge.

The bridge, although damaged, withstood the flood but the trees built up a dam to a height of eight feet above the bridge level. This created such a volume and depth of water that the river violently changed its course, destroying houses that were built on the banks and damaging many more, and Meal Bank Bridge, Wray, was in danger of collapsing.

When P.C. Forrest arrived on the scene, he saw that the flood had demolished four cottages near Wray Bridge and that the water was about 20 feet deep at the bridge and appeared dammed by trees. The houses were all flooded on both sides of the Main Street at varying depths to half way up the bedrooms at the bottom of the hill. P.C. Forrest was personally responsible for the rescue of four elderly people trapped in a house, by climbing on to the roof of an outbuilding and encouraging and assisting the occupants to make a hazardous descent.

He was then informed that the occupant of another of the cottages, a 74-year-old man, had not been seen and was believed to be still in his house. The officer made his way to the house, which was flooded up to bedroom level and in danger of collapsing and gained access into a bedroom by climbing over a mass of debris and trees. He found the occupant lying on his bed with water level to the mattress. The house had been struck by a tree which had removed the front bedroom window and part of the wall. He carried the man from the house, through the window, to a ladder at the rear of the house, where he was removed to safety.

Throughout these incidents, P.C. Forrest showed initiative and courage at considerable risk to his life, and by his example and fortitude he was an inspiration to the voluntary helpers who assisted him in the rescue operations.

By his leadership, organisation, and complete disregard for his own personal safety, he ensured that there was no loss of life in the village and prevented an already serious situation from developing into one with more disastrous consequences.

(W.O. 3/1967 – 19/1/1968)

Awarded 'William Garnett' Cup.

FURTHER INFORMATION:

In addition to his Queen's Commendation, P.C. Forrest was commended by the Chief Constable. Two other officers were also commended by the Chief Constable for their actions during the floods. They were P.S. 1724 Smith, who was commended for early appreciation of the situation and summoning assistance before all lines of communication with the area was lost, and P.C. 2752 Clowes, for his assistance to trapped residents and during the clear up operations at Farleton.

5th January 1968	
Keith PARK, Constable 247	**Bolton Constabulary**
Donald Thomas TAYLOR, Sergeant 27	**Bolton Constabulary**
Queen's Commendation for Brave Conduct	

For rescuing a man who was in danger of drowning.

L.G. 10/05/1968 Issue 44585 Page 5456

FURTHER INFORMATION:

Chief Constable's Annual Report, County Borough of Bolton, 1968

BY HER MAJESTY THE QUEEN

The Queen's Commendation for Brave Conduct was awarded to Sergeant 27 D.T. Taylor and Constable 247 K. Park for their courageous efforts in rescuing a man from the icy waters of Doffcocker Lodge on the 5th January 1968. The operation involved a swim of more than 200 yards for each officer and both had to be assisted in turn by their colleagues before the rescue was completed. The Presentation was made by Lord Derby at Knowsley Hall on the 5th July 1968.

BY THE ROYAL HUMANE SOCIETY

For their part in the above mentioned rescue operation at Doffcocker Lodge, Constable 139 A. J. Sharpe and Constable 68 Haydn Mathews were awarded respectively, a Testimonial on Vellum and a Testimonial on Parchment.

Doffcocker Lodge, Bolton is a former mill lodge created in 1874. It is 20 to 30 feet deep and is now a local nature reserve.

A 999 call was received at the Central Police Station, stating that a man had been seen going into the water and swimming. Constable Park and Sergeant Taylor arrived at the scene and swam out to the 60-year-old man in the icy lodge, who was 200 metres from the bank. As they reached him, Constable Park was affected by the cold and got into difficulties. P.C. James Sharpe swam out with a rescue line while P.C. Haydn Mathews waded in, holding the end of the line. Constable Sharp brought P.C. Park to the bank and then swam back out to assist Sergeant Taylor with the man. Two youths were also praised by the police for wading into the lodge to assist the men out.

Following the incident, Sergeant Taylor, P.C.s Park and Sharpe were taken to hospital for treatment for exposure and later released. The man was detained at hospital. His identity is not known.

Commenting on the award, Sergeant Taylor said, *'It's an award for the whole team. If it hadn't been for P.C. Sharpe neither of us would be here now.'* PC Park said, *'It's all in the line of duty. To go in was an awkward decision. Self-preservation seems to lose itself after that.'*

In addition to Constable Park and Sergeant Taylor, other officers assisted in the rescue, namely Constables 139 James Sharpe, 68 Haydn Mathews and 241 Laurence Whitehead. All officers were later commended by the Chief Constable and the Watch Committee.[49]

Keith Park was appointed to Bolton Police in 1965. He left Bolton Police in 1969.

Donald Thomas Taylor was born at Warrington in 1921 and was appointed to Lancashire Constabulary as Constable 845 on 8th October 1951. His previous occupation was as a registered forester.

He had also served as a Sergeant in the Royal Artillery from January 1939 to March 1946. He served at Bolton Division as a Foot Patrol Officer, Traffic Officer and a Crime Patrol Officer. He was commended twice by the Chief Constable.

On 17th August 1964, he transferred to Bolton Borough Police and was appointed Temporary Sergeant and then Substantive Sergeant on 16th October 1967. On amalgamation with Lancashire Constabulary in 1969, he was issued with the Lancashire collar number 4027. On Force reorganisation in 1974, he was transferred to Manchester Police. He died, aged 65 years, in 1987.

1st June 1968

Michael John TORKINGTON, Constable   **Manchester and Salford Police**

British Empire Medal for Gallantry (Civil Division)

At 1.30a.m. Constable Torkington was patrolling in a police vehicle when he was approached by a man who complained to him that he had been robbed while visiting a house nearby.

The officer told the man to go back to the house and he followed him there. After repeated knocking the door was opened by the occupant of the house who denied any knowledge of the incident.

Constable Torkington took down the names and addresses of both parties and began to explain the position to the complainant who without warning struck the officer in the face with his right fist. He then removed a knife from his pocket and stabbed the Constable in the stomach.

---

[49] *Duty Bound – A History of Bolton Borough Police 1839-1969*, page 136 and Chief Constable's Annual Report 1968.

The officer grappled with the man and received a stab wound to the left cheek. The man broke away and ran off pursued by Torkington. He caught up with him and a further scuffle occurred during which the officer received two stab wounds to his left shoulder. The man again broke free and the pursuit was continued. After a short chase, there was another scuffle and the officer was stabbed in the left cheek close to the ear. Torkington who was now exhausted and weakened from loss of blood was forced to give up the chase.

He had called for assistance over his personal radio and other police officers arrived. Torkington was conveyed to hospital where he received an emergency operation.

His notebook was found, and this led to the home of the man where he was arrested.

L.G. 25/2/1969 Issue 44796 Page 2086

FURTHER INFORMATION:

Location of incident – Fairlawn Street, Moss Side, Manchester.

21ˢᵗ July 1968

Joseph HANCOX, Constable 346 'D'   **Liverpool and Bootle Constabulary**

British Empire Medal for Gallantry (Civil Division)

Constable Hancox was informed that a woman had fallen in the water between a pier head wall and a floating landing stage. He ran to the scene and was then told that the woman was in the water beneath the floating stage, where she had been carried by the current.

The Constable climbed down on to a pontoon and plunged into the water. The tide was on the ebb and a fast current was flowing. He swam underneath the floating stage, where the water is very turbulent due to the suction caused by the rise and fall of the pontoons.

It is also very dark, making it difficult for a rescuer to distinguish objects. Hancox eventually located the woman but as he approached her she sank beneath the surface of the water. When he reached the spot where she had sunk, she floated back to the surface and he was able to grasp her.

She was then apparently unconscious. He supported her in the water and swam with her, against the ebbing tide, back to the pontoon. Several men then climbed down and the woman was lifted on to the stage. She was taken by ambulance to hospital where after treatment she recovered.

The action of Constable Hancox in the rescue of the woman, taken with complete disregard for his own personal safety, was in accord with the best traditions of the police service.

L.G. 23/12/1968 Issue 44751 Page 13801

FURTHER INFORMATION:

At the time of the incident Joseph Hancox was 31 years of age and had been a police officer for six years. He received treatment for exposure and for abrasions caused to his right arm caused by barnacles. He described the water as being polluted with oil and sewage. (*Liverpool Echo*, 27/12/1968)

For arresting a man armed with a shotgun.

L.G. 15/7/1969 Issue 44896 Page 7292

FURTHER INFORMATION:

At 12.10a.m. on December 23rd 1968, 35-year-old Alan Roberts was ejected from the Las Vegas Club, King Street West, Wigan, by the manager, Mr Duffy, and one of his staff. As he was being thrown out, he shouted, *'If you put me out, I'll shoot you.'*

The manager disregarded the remark for Roberts had made similar threats on other occasions. A little while after the incident, the club officials were startled when a shot shattered one of the windows. Mr Ryder, a barman, was only a few feet away from being killed.

P.C. Brandon Hilton saw Roberts in Marsden Street walking towards him and was carrying a single-barrelled shotgun. Roberts pointed the gun at him and said, *'Go away. Please go away or I'll shoot you.'* The officer backed away and called for assistance.

P.C. Frank Peach, a Panda car driver, who was in the vicinity, heard the call and hurried to the scene. He drove his car down the Queen's Hall Passage, where he saw Roberts in the beam of the headlights. Roberts raised the gun, but Peach drove past him and got out. Roberts told him, *'Be careful! This is loaded! I have no quarrel with you cops. I will kill Duffy and McFarlane. They've beaten me up.'* The officer took the gun from Roberts, who smelled strongly of drink and arrested him. It was later discovered that the gun and cartridges had been stolen from Oliver Somers' shop in Mesnes Street, Wigan.

The offender, Alan Roberts (35), appeared at Wigan Quarter Sessions on 3rd March 1969, where he entered guilty pleas to breaking into a sports shop and stealing a gun and 55 cartridges. He also admitted possessing a firearm with intent to injure and using a firearm to resist arrest.

The court was told that Roberts, of Laithwaite Road, Pemberton, had previous convictions dating back to 1950. Medical evidence indicated that the accused showed signs of mental illness and had attempted suicide on more than one occasion. The Recorder made a restriction order for Roberts to be detained in the Psychiatric Unit at Billinge Hospital for an unspecified time.

After passing sentence, the Recorder, Leslie Rigg, addressed the following remarks to P.C. Peach:

'You must have known – it must have been communicated to you, I think, that this man you were going to approach had already discharged the shotgun which he had in his possession. No doubt you also knew that he had already threatened to kill another officer who had approached him. You knew it was a situation of very considerable danger to yourself. When you approached this man, the gun was pointed at you, but notwithstanding that you closed with him and disarmed him. In my view your conduct is deserving of the highest possible commendation.'

At the time of the incident P.C. Peach was serving with Wigan Borough Police but when his award was gazetted in July 1969, Wigan Borough Police had been amalgamated with Lancashire Constabulary.

Frank Theodore Peach was born at Nottingham in July 1937. He joined Wigan Borough Police on 5th July 1956, having had previous service as a Police Cadet with Bedfordshire Police from 12th August 1953 to 4th July 1956.

In 1968, he was commended by Wigan Magistrates for courage and determination in the pursuit of a motor cycle at fast speeds, resulting in the conviction of the rider for motoring offences.

On 5th March 1969, he was commended by the Wigan Chief Constable in addition to his Queen's Commendation for Brave Conduct in the arrest of Alan Roberts who pointed a loaded shotgun at him.

Following amalgamation with Lancashire Constabulary in 1969 he continued to serve at Wigan.

P.C. Frank Peach (Note the Wigan Borough Police lapel badges.)

On reorganisation on 1st April 1974, he was transferred to Greater Manchester Police. Whilst a member of Greater Manchester Police he gained promotion to Inspector in 1977, moving to Bolton Division, but continued to live in Wigan. He died, aged 48 years, in 1985.

7th August 1969

Edward McDonald GREENWELL, Constable 221 'A'	**Liverpool and Bootle Constabulary**
David James SMITH, Constable 174 'D'	**Liverpool and Bootle Constabulary**

Queen's Commendation for Brave Conduct

For arresting an armed man.

L.G. 13/02/1970 Issue 45042 Page 1958

FURTHER INFORMATION:

Location of incident – Red Cross Street, Liverpool.

Constables Greenwell and Smith were on duty in a Police Land Rover when they were called to Red Cross Street where a group of youths were reported to be firing guns.

Constable Greenwell saw a raised arm and a flash as someone fired at the Land Rover. Both officers got out of the vehicle and Constable Greenwell dived at the man, bringing him to the ground where a struggle took place between the man and both officers before he was arrested. (*Liverpool Echo*, 18/2/1970)

13th August 1969

Harold Powell JONES, Police Constable 112 'T'   **Liverpool and Bootle Constabulary**

Alan William WOOD, Police Constable 111 'F'   **Liverpool and Bootle Constabulary**

Queen's Commendation for Brave Conduct

For arresting two men armed with knives.

L.G. 13/02/1970 Issue 45042 Page 1958

FURTHER INFORMATION:

Location of incident – Menlove Avenue & grounds of Abbot's Lea School, Beaconsfield Road, Liverpool.

Constable Wood (35) disturbed two men breaking into a house on Menlove Avenue. Whilst struggling with one of the men the other stabbed him twice in the back, in the chest, arm and hand. Constable Wood was in hospital for 11 days with a punctured lung and was off duty for three months. Constable Jones (42) came to his assistance and arrested both men after a struggle in the grounds of Abbot's Lea Special School. (*Liverpool Echo*, 18/2/1970)

23rd December 1969

Stanley BOOTH, Constable   **Manchester and Salford Police**

Jeffrey Richard OWEN, Constable   **Manchester and Salford Police**

Queen's Commendation for Brave Conduct

For preventing a mentally deranged man from throwing himself from the roof of a five-storey building.

L.G. 12/5/1970 Issue 45097 Page 5342

FURTHER INFORMATION:

Location of incident – Long Millgate near Victoria Station, Manchester

Constables Booth and Owen struggled for twenty-five minutes to prevent a man from throwing himself from the building sixty five feet from the ground. At one stage P.C. Booth was in danger of being dragged from the rooftop by the man until P.C. Owen threw himself across his colleague's legs and managed to drag both back to safety. Both officers were then almost flung off the roof several times by the struggling man as they tried to take him towards a fire brigade ladder.

PC Owen was 34 years old with ten years police service and had been commended by the Chief Constable on three previous occasions. P.C. Booth was 27 years old and had four years' service. He had also been previously commended by the Chief Constable. (*The Guardian*, 15/5/1970)

For rescuing a child who was in danger from an articulated vehicle which was out of control.

L.G. 17/07/1970 Issue 45154 Page 8032

FURTHER INFORMATION:

Constable Taylor was on school crossing duty on Childwall Valley Road, Liverpool, a busy main road, while it was dark and raining heavily. She was standing in the middle of the road and, as she was certain the road was reasonably clear, she signalled some children to cross. The driver of an articulated vehicle saw the signal and began to apply the brakes, then realising his trailer was skidding and would 'jack knife', sounded his horn to warn of the danger.

The W.P.C. calmly motioned the children back but eight-year-old David Cassidy of Wellgreen Road, Gateacre, ran past her into the path of the vehicle. She ran to him and pulled him clear of the front offside wheel and carried him to safety.

Constable Taylor had served with Liverpool Police for twenty years. She was presented with her commendation by Lord Rhodes, Lord Lieutenant of Lancashire, at Liverpool Town Hall. (*Liverpool Echo*, 26/11/1970)

At about midnight a Constable heard shouting and splashing coming from between a river wall and a floating landing stage and saw a man in the water being carried along on an ebbing tide.

Throwing a lifebelt, which the man ignored, the Constable blew his whistle for assistance and was joined by Constable Smith. In spite of the low temperature and the dangerous currents, Constable Smith discarded his tunic and shoes, dived into the river and swam towards the man.

Taking hold of him Constable Smith then began an arduous swim from beneath a boom to an unmanned launch. The Constable tried to haul the man aboard the launch, but on account of the man's condition, the turbulence of the water and his own exhausted state the unconscious man slipped from his grasp and disappeared below the surface.

Constable Smith immediately submerged to try and locate the drowning man. When the tide is ebbing in this part of the river, the suction and the current between the pontoons of the floating landing stage are extreme and there are additional hazards such as underwater chains.

Unfortunately, the Constable's efforts were in vain, weakened by the cold and exhaustion, he was forced to abandon his search after twice facing the dangers of an intensively cold ebbing tide in a particularly dangerous area.

L.G. 17/07/1970 Issue 45154 Page 8030

For services when arresting a man armed with a loaded firearm.

L.G. 25/10/1971 Issue 45505 Page 11568

FURTHER INFORMATION:

The officers were on plain clothes duty when they were called to a public house in Westminster Road, Liverpool, when an informant pointed out a man sitting with his back to the wall with both hands in his jacket pockets. The informant had alleged that the man had a loaded gun. P.C. Greener, standing 2 feet from the seated man, produced his warrant card and told the man who he was.

The man pulled out a revolver and pointed it at the officer's stomach. P.C. Greener closed with the man, grabbing his right hand and at the same time bringing his knee into the man's groin. There was a violent struggle in which both officers were involved, both were injured.

After some time, they subdued the man but then another man came to try to wrest the prisoner away in spite of warnings from the officers. Eventually a woman was persuaded to telephone for police assistance.

Alfred Frederick Skillen (29), of Knock Road, Belfast, appeared at Liverpool Crown Court charged with possessing a loaded firearm and for using it to resist arrest and having no firearms certificate. Skillen pleaded not guilty and said someone must have put the gun in his pocket in the public house. He was convicted and sentenced to three years concurrent imprisonment for the possession of the firearm and using it to resist arrest and three months concurrent for having no firearms certificate.

A second man, Vincent O'Farrell (34), of Embledon Street, Toxteth, was also charged with obstructing a police officer in the execution of his duty.

23rd August 1971	
Gerald Irving RICHARDSON **(Deceased), Superintendent**	**Lancashire Constabulary**
Carl WALKER, Constable 3932	**Lancashire Constabulary**
George Cross	
Ian HAMPSON Constable 4018	**Lancashire Constabulary**
Andrew HILLIS, Constable 3950	**Lancashire Constabulary**
Patrick JACKSON, Constable 3847	**Lancashire Constabulary**
Kenneth MACKAY Sergeant	**Lancashire Constabulary**
The George Medal	
Edward GRAY, Inspector	**Lancashire Constabulary**
Edward HANLEY, Constable 3804	**Lancashire Constabulary**
British Empire Medal for Gallantry (Civil Division)	
Stephen Drummond REDPATH, Inspector	**Lancashire Constabulary**
Queen's Commendation for Brave Conduct	

Following an armed robbery at a jeweller's in Blackpool, Constable Walker, having been directed to the scene by radio, arrived to see the bandits running towards a Triumph Estate car.

All the men succeeded in getting into the car and a shotgun was pointed through the window at P.C. Walker; the car was then driven away followed by the Constable. A chase at high speeds then ensued; at several stages Constable Walker lost contact briefly with the Triumph but came upon it stationary in a blind alley.

All the occupants were out of the car, the Constable remained in his Panda car which he parked at right angles to the alley, thus blocking the exit.

The men then climbed back into the Triumph which was reversed at a fast speed down the alley into the side of the Panda car. As the car drove away from the alley Constable Hampson arrived on the scene in his Panda car.

He saw Constable Walker sitting in his car, in a shocked condition, and he followed the Triumph. The bandits' car was driven in a fast and dangerous manner through various streets and Constable Hampson during the whole of this chase remained five to ten yards behind the Triumph relaying his position to Blackpool Central by personal radio.

The Triumph suddenly screeched to a halt and Constable Hampson pulled up about five or six yards behind it. One of the gunmen ran back to the Panda car and shot the Constable through the passenger door window of the Panda car.

The Constable, who was badly wounded in the chest, fell from the car into the roadway but managed to raise himself, reached his radio transmitter and gave his position to Control Room.

A number of police cars were now in the area and Constable Walker, who had resumed the pursuit in his damaged Panda car saw the Triumph and positioned his Panda at a junction to block its route.

As he did so Constable Jackson in a Panda car, and Constable Hillis in a C.I.D. car, drove either side of his Panda, trapping the Triumph between them. Constable Jackson collided with the offside of the Triumph and Constable Hillis with the front nearside.

All the gunmen climbed out of the Triumph. Constable Jackson was thrown across the front seat of his Panda car by the force of the collision and the driver of the Triumph threatened him and then ran towards an alley to the next street.

Constable Hillis got out of his police car and saw the five men who were then retreating from the crashed car. The officer ran towards them and the driver of the Triumph pointed a pistol at him and fired two or three shots from a distance of about six feet but did not hit him.

Triumph getaway car and Police vehicles – Clifford Road, Blackpool.

Constable Hillis raised his arm in front of his face and when at this stage one of the robbers broke away, he ran after him and caught him after a violent struggle. In the meantime, another police car had arrived at the scene with Inspector Gray, Inspector Redpath and Superintendent Richardson. Inspector Redpath got out of the car and then the officers saw three of the gunmen, running towards an alley.

Inspector Redpath ran after them. Inspector Gray with Superintendent Richardson drove into the next road in an effort to head them off. The three men were by now running along the alley, followed by Constables Walker and Jackson and when Constable Walker was about ten yards from the bandits the driver of the Triumph turned and fired a shot at him.

The officer carried on running towards him, and when the man reached the end of the alley he turned to face the Constable and fired a second time at a distance of about six feet he fired a third time and hit him in the groin. The man pointed the gun at Constable Walker again, looked at the officer who was clutching his injured leg, then turned away towards a Ford Transit delivery van which was parked outside a butcher's shop.

The man jumped into the driving seat of the butcher's van, and two of the men ran to the back of the van and jumped in just as Inspector Gray and Superintendent Richardson arrived on the scene in their police car; the butcher's van moved off rapidly.

Constable Jackson got into the police car with Superintendent Richardson and Inspector Gray, who then drove off in pursuit of the butcher's van which attempted to turn into an alley, collided with a garden wall and stopped.

The police car stopped behind the van and Inspector Gray went to the rear of the van, attempting to keep the doors closed and trap the men inside. Superintendent Richardson and Constable Jackson ran to the front passenger door and saw that the front of the van was empty, the driver having clambered out and run to the rear of the van.

Triumph getaway car and Police vehicles – Clifford Road, Blackpool.

Stolen Triumph getaway car.

The Superintendent and the Constable then went to the rear of the van just as the doors burst open and the men appeared and jumped out; two of the men ran off down the alley. Superintendent Richardson and Inspector Gray tried to talk the driver into surrendering his gun; but he continued to threaten the officers, turned round and ran off. The Police Officers ran after him, Superintendent Richardson leading, followed by Inspector Gray. A few yards into the alley Superintendent Richardson caught hold of the gunman.

The man turned, thrust his gun into the Superintendent's stomach and fired. Before Inspector Gray could reach them the man fired a second time as Superintendent Richardson was falling to the ground. The man then escaped in a stolen van.

Superintendent Richardson was taken to Blackpool Victoria Hospital where he died later the same morning. The other two bandits were seen by Sergeant Mackay and Constable Hanley, who had just arrived in the area in a C.I.D. car. These officers, still in their car, entered the pursuit and caught up with the two fugitives, one of whom levelled his pistol at Sergeant Mackay's head as the C.I.D. car drew alongside him.

Stolen crashed Ford Transit butchers van.

The Sergeant swung the driver's door open and it struck the man, knocking him off balance. The police car stalled and Constable Hanley, who was getting out of the passenger door, stumbled and fell. Both men ran off with Constable Hanley and other officers chasing them on foot. Sergeant Mackay re-started the police car and drove after them, he quickly overtook the men and they turned round, one, who was only about six feet from the front of the car, levelled the revolver at Sergeant Mackay and pulled the trigger, but the gun did not fire.

Front of stolen Triumph showing shotgun and holdall containing jewellery.

The Sergeant drove the car directly at the two men knocking them off balance, he knocked them off their feet several times by driving at them, he then got out of the police car and ran towards one of the men. During the chase through the alleys the men had run almost all the way back to the butcher's shop where Constable Walker had been shot.

Inspector Redpath, who was still outside the butcher's shop, saw them emerge from the end of the alley, running directly towards him. Sergeant Mackay was immediately behind one of them and closing on him. The Inspector saw that he was carrying a revolver but he stood his ground waiting for him to come closer.

The Sergeant then crash-tackled the man and brought him to the ground with his arms sprawled out in front of him, immediately in front of Inspector Redpath, who kicked the gun out of his hand. Constable

Hanley, who was chasing the other man, knocked him down and arrested him.

Throughout the pursuit which followed the robbery, all the police officers concerned were aware that they faced the threat of death or serious injury but gave no thought to their own safety in their efforts to effect the arrest of armed and dangerous criminals.

L.G. 13/11/1972 Issue 45826 Page 13433

FURTHER INFORMATION:

The gang members involved on Monday 23rd August 1971 comprised Frederick Joseph Sewell, 38, a Brixton businessman, who operated a car dealing business and owned property; Charles Henry Haynes, 38, who owned a night club in King's Cross; John Patrick Spry, from Streatham; Dennis George Henry Bond, 43, from Clapham, who had just served seven years for armed robbery; and Thomas Farrell Flannigan, 43, from Hackney. The gang had four weapons: a sawn-off single-barrelled 12 bore shotgun, a .32 Star automatic pistol and two .38 revolvers.

The gang drove to Blackpool from London in three cars, two stolen cars, namely a green coloured Triumph 2000 estate car and a Ford Capri both fitted with false number plates. The third vehicle was a Rover 2000 owned by Sewell. The Triumph was to be the bandit vehicle and the others getaway cars. Sewell stayed in a rented flat at 27 Cocker Street, Blackpool, with his common-law wife, Irene Jermain, and the others found accommodation at a boarding house.

The jeweller's targeted was Preston's, situated at The Strand, Blackpool. The Strand is a narrow street running parallel with Blackpool Promenade within sight of Blackpool Tower. On the morning of the incident the gang boarded the Triumph and travelled to the shop with Haynes remaining in the vehicle as driver.

On entering the shop, which had just opened, the staff were threatened and forced to move to the back of the shop.

The manager, Joseph Lammond, managed to slip into the repair room, closing the door, and had activated a silent alarm which sent a message to the Police Station.

The gang began collecting jewellery from the displays. Passing the shop at this time was Sub-Officer Ronald Gale from the Fire Brigade who intervened to attempt to stop the robbery. Gale was threatened with the shotgun pushed into his stomach and hit over the head, rendering him unconscious.

The robbers left the shop with jewellery valued at £106,000, running towards the Triumph. Malcolm Serjantson, a window cleaner, gave chase and threw a brush at one of the robbers which, despite hitting him, failed to stop him. The gang got into the Triumph, which led to the pursuit through the streets of Blackpool described in the citation.

The three persons arrested on the day of the incident were:

- Dennis George Henry Bond
- John Patrick Spry
- Thomas Farrell Flannigan.

Spry was responsible for the shooting of P.C. Hampson on Clevedon Road, Blackpool. Frederick Sewell, responsible for shooting Superintendent Richardson and P.C. Walker, made good his escape. Sewell returned to the rented flat in Blackpool where he was later joined by Haynes, who had also escaped.

Memorial plaque to Supt Richardson at Lancashire Police H.Q.
(Author's collection)

They later left Blackpool in the Rover 2000 with Irene Jermain driving. Haynes was in the front passenger seat with Sewell hiding in the boot. They travelled north to Windermere before driving east and joining the M1 motorway, travelling south to London.

Superintendent Richardson's body lay in an open coffin for a day whilst thousands paid their respects. On 26th August, a civic funeral was held at St. John's Church, where he had been married fifteen years earlier. An estimated 100,000 people lined the streets for Gerry Richardson's funeral cortege through to Layton Cemetery.

Charles Henry Haynes was subsequently arrested at Stoneleigh, Warwickshire, on 26th August 1971, the same day of the funeral. His daughter was competing at an equestrian event at this location.

Sewell, who had shot Superintendent Richardson and wounded P.C. Walker, remained on the run during which time he was Britain's most wanted man. He was arrested after 45 days in hiding in Holloway by Lancashire Detective Superintendent Joe Mounsey and a team of officers.

Sewell said to Superintendent Joe Mounsey after his arrest, *'The job went wrong from the start. I shall see him every day of my life. He just kept on coming. He would not go back. He was too brave. He should not have dived at me.'*

Sewell was taken back to Blackpool and, with the other gang members, tried at Manchester Crown Court.

Spry was convicted and sentenced to 20 years for the manslaughter of Superintendent Richardson, 25 years for the attempted murder of P.C. Hampson, 15 years for conspiracy to use firearms to prevent arrest and 15 years for the jewel robbery to run concurrently.

Haynes, Bond and Flannigan were sentenced to 10, 15 and 13 years for their part in the robbery.

Naming of Gerry Richardson Way, May 2018.
(L-R Maureen Richardson, Ian Hampson G.M. and Kenneth Mackay G.M., Q.P.M.)

Sewell was convicted and sentenced to 20 years imprisonment for the murder of Superintendent Richardson, 25 years for the attempted murder of P.C. Walker, 15 years for conspiracy to use firearms to prevent arrest and 15 years for the jewel theft with the sentences to run concurrently. He was sentenced to life imprisonment with a recommendation that he serve a minimum of thirty years.

In sentencing Sewell, Mr Justice Kilner Brown said, *'It was a deliberately horrifying course of conduct which eventually led to your pulling the trigger deliberately twice and causing the death of Superintendent Richardson. It is necessary not only to sentence you in relation to your own part and on your own character but also as a warning than any man who shoots down a police officer in the course of his duty must expect the severest punishment which is permitted to the courts.'*

Sewell was released, aged 68 years, in 2001, reportedly having made a million pounds from property deals whilst in prison.

Five other persons were convicted of assisting Sewell following the robbery. Eugene Francis Kerrigan was convicted and sentenced to five and a half years imprisonment for providing clothing and £5,620 in cash to Sewell. Panaylotis Nicou Panaylotou was sentenced to four years imprisonment and Miss Nitsa Stavrou to 30 months imprisonment after conviction for providing him with accommodation.

Mrs Irene Jermain, who had driven Sewell and Haynes from Blackpool to London after the robbery, entered guilty pleas and was sentenced to 15 months imprisonment. Mrs Barbara Palmer (mother of Sewell's daughter) also charged with assisting Sewell, was given a suspended sentence of nine months imprisonment after pleading guilty.

Gerald Irving Richardson G.C. (pictured as Chief Inspector – Blackpool Borough Police)

Superintendent **Gerald Irving Richardson G.C.** is the highest ranking British police officer to have been killed on duty in modern times.

He was born in November 1932 in Blackpool and was one of two children, the son of a painter and decorator and he attended Blackpool Grammar School. He became a Police Cadet with Blackpool Borough Police in 1949. In 1951, he joined the Royal Corps of Military Police for his two years National Service, serving for most of his service at the Supreme Headquarters Allied Powers – Europe (S.H.A.P.E.) near Paris.

He returned to Blackpool Police in 1953, rising rapidly through the ranks, taking charge of Blackpool Central Division as Temporary Superintendent in 1968.

Following amalgamation with Lancashire Constabulary in 1969, he took charge as Superintendent of Blackpool Central Sub-Division.

At the time of his death he had been married to his wife Maureen for 15 years and had no children of his own but was deeply involved in the welfare of young people. In addition to the George Cross, Superintendent Richardson was posthumously awarded many honours, including the Medal of the American Federation of Police.

Following his death, the Superintendent Gerald Richardson Memorial Youth Trust was founded in 1974 by the Rotary Club of Blackpool North and has so far helped over 16,000 young people who live, or work within 15 miles of Blackpool Town Hall. This work continues to this day.

Superintendent Richardson's George Cross is displayed at the Lord Ashcroft Gallery, Imperial War Museum, London.

In 2015, the **Gerald Richardson Memorial Trophy** was inaugurated by the Lancashire Constabulary Branch of the Police Superintendents' Association of England and Wales (P.S.A.E.W.). The trophy is awarded annually in his memory, to recognise excellence in leadership, staff welfare, quality of service or the development of the organisation.

Superintendent Richardson's grave and memorial – Layton Cemetery, Blackpool. The memorial reads:
FOR JUSTICE and LAW GOOD MEN MUST DIE BUT DEATH CANNOT KILL THEIR NAMES
(© Anthony Rae)

On 23rd August 2016, on the 45th anniversary of his death, a memorial garden was opened at Blackpool Aspire Academy with the re-dedicated memorial stone to Superintendent Richardson being unveiled by Mrs Maureen Richardson.

In May 2018, the access road to the new multi-million pound Blackpool Police Station on Clifton Road, Blackpool, was officially named Gerry Richardson Way. Present at the official unveiling were Gerry Richardson's widow, Maureen, Ian Hampson G.M. and Ken Mackay G.M., Q.P.M.

Carl Walker G.C. was born in March 1934 in Kendal, Westmorland (now Cumbria). He was the son of a paper mill worker and the middle child of seven. He left school at 15 years of age and went to work as an apprentice joiner. Aged 18, he began his National Service, spending two years in the RAF Police.

After completing his National Service, he joined the Lancashire Constabulary in 1953 as a Constable. He married two years later, and the couple went on to have a son. After 18 months, Walker left the police and moved back to Cumbria.

After returning to work as a joiner, he also spent time working in an asbestos factory, before returning to the police, joining Blackpool Borough Police in 1959.

He rose to the rank of Inspector in 1976. Still troubled by the effects of his gunshot wound, he was medically discharged in 1982.

Ian Hampson G.M. joined Blackpool Borough Police in February 1965 and, following the incident in 1971, was promoted to Sergeant, serving at Blackpool, the Task Force and within the Commerce Branch. He was promoted to Inspector in 1984, serving at St. Anne's, Detective Inspector at Blackpool South and with the Regional Crime Squad before retirement in 1996.

Andrew Hillis G.M. was born in Kilmalcolm, Renfrewshire, Scotland, in 1933 and joined Blackpool Borough Police in May 1959. His previous occupation was as a joiner and he had served as a gunner in the R.A.F. from 1951 to 1953. He was promoted to Sergeant in September 1971. He served at Blackpool and on No. 1 District Task Force and the Regional Crime Squad from May 1975. He died, aged 50 years, in December 1983 whilst still a serving officer.

Patrick Jackson G.M. was born in 1943 at Accrington, Lancashire, and joined Blackpool Borough Police in August 1963. His previous occupation was as a clerk. In July 1964, he was commended by the Chief Constable for keen observation and attention to duty leading to an arrest.

Patrick Jackson was again to be threatened with a gun following a robbery at a jeweller's shop on Market Street, Blackpool, on 1st June 1990. Two men made off on a motorcycle after threatening staff and customers, making off with £107,000 worth of jewellery. Patrick Jackson became involved, following in a Police Landrover, the motorcycle stopped and the shotgun was pointed at him before the robbers made off. A further officer was later also threatened with the shotgun. The gunman eventually gave himself up after holding two elderly women hostage at a house on Woburn Road, Blackpool. He was later sentenced to fourteen years imprisonment. Two other members of the gang later also pleaded guilty to robbery charges.

Patrick Jackson died, aged 66 years, in 2009.

Kenneth Mackay G.M., Q.P.M. was a native of Bury and joined Burnley Borough Police as a Police Cadet, serving from 1952 to 1954 before performing National Service in the RAF for two years. He returned to Burnley Borough Police in 1956, serving with them for the following 9 years.

He became a member of Blackpool Borough Police in February 1967.

He was awarded the Queen's Police Medal in 1991. (L.G. 30/12/1991 Issue 52767 Page 26.) He retired from Lancashire Constabulary in 1995 as Chief Superintendent in charge of Blackpool Division.

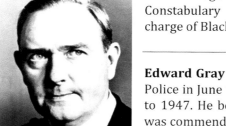

Edward Gray B.E.M. was born in Eccles in 1922 and joined Blackpool Borough Police in June 1947, having served as a pilot with the Royal Air Force from 1943 to 1947. He became a Sergeant in 1959 and an Inspector in 1967. In 1967, he was commended by the Chief Constable in connection with a difficult fraud case, resulting in 39 charges being preferred. He was promoted to Superintendent in September 1971. He died, aged 68 years, in 1990.

Edward Hanley B.E.M. was born in 1934 and joined Blackpool Borough Police in September 1955, aged 21 years. His previous occupation was as a clerk. He had served with the Army from 1952 to 1955 and on appointment remained an Army Reservist until 1959.

In July 1964, he was awarded a certificate from the Society for the Protection of Life from Fire for distinguished conduct at the scene of a fire at North Promenade, Blackpool on 17th January 1964. He was also awarded the Rhodes Marshall Trophy in connection with this incident. He died, aged 48 years, in 1982.

Stephen Drummond Redpath was born in 1934 at Windgates. Fifeshire. He joined Blackpool Borough Police on 18th August 1956. His previous occupation is recorded as having been as a locomotive fireman. He also saw military service in the Royal Air Force from 1952 to 1954. He was promoted to Sergeant in 1969 and Inspector in 1970 and was pensioned on 1st December 1983. He died, aged 65 years, in 2000.

Ronald Gale was a Blackpool man and had served with the Fire Brigade for 18 years. He was born in 1930 and attended Tyldesley School, Blackpool. After two years National Service with the Royal Air Force he joined Blackpool Fire Brigade in 1953. In 1962, he was commended for bravery when he rescued a 22-year-old man from a blazing flat at South Shore, Blackpool.

At the time of the robbery, Sub-Officer Gale was making his way to a fire prevention inspection at North Shore, Blackpool. He died, aged 79 years, in 2010.

L-R Carl Walker, Ian Hampson, Pat Jackson, Ken Mackay, Andrew Hillis, Edward Gray, Edward Hanley and Stephen Redpath.

311

Constable McDonald was on duty at the barrier on the Prince's Landing Stage when a man, who had earlier discharged himself from the Psychiatric Ward of a hospital, removed his clothing and jumped into the River Mersey.

The Constable immediately shouted to a colleague and then dived into the water and managed to grasp hold of the drowning man about six yards from the quayside. The officer had taken a lifeline with him which he threw to his colleague who had to lie flat on the stage in order to pull the two men in. The rescued man became hysterical, but although Constable McDonald felt himself being sucked under the stage, and despite the man's struggles he succeeded in maintaining his hold on him.

Constable Collins arrived at this point and on seeing the difficult situation immediately plunged fully clothed into the river and managed to reach the two men and give assistance. Meanwhile other policemen had gone in search of a boat and had engaged the assistance of a Customs and Excise launch.

A rope was lowered to the men and a lifebelt placed over the rescued man, but by this time Constable McDonald had been in the water for some time and was exhausted and the Police Inspector in charge of the rescue operations gave instructions for him to be lifted out of the water. The other two men were too heavy to be lifted out in this way.

The Customs and Excise launch had by now arrived at the scene and a rope was tied round the man who was hauled on board, Constable Collins then let go of the life line, but due to the oily state of his body and clothing he slipped and was in danger of being sucked under the launch by the tide, but a man who was on a ladder which had been lowered over the side of the stage managed to grab one of his arms and a policeman on the launch grasped his tunic and he was pulled from the water.

All three men were taken to hospital. At the time of the rescue the tide was ebbing, the speed of the ebb current was in the region of six knots and conditions were *'choppy'*.

It is almost certain that the man would have drowned but for the prompt action of these two Constables, and in continuing the long and strenuous struggle against the elements to rescue him at considerable risk to their own lives they showed determination and courage of a very high order.

L.G. 10/4/1972 Issue 45642 Page 4294

For arresting and disarming a man who had shot and wounded a woman and two policemen.

L.G. 20/2/1973 Issue 45911 Page 2357

FURTHER INFORMATION:

Late on the night of Sunday 4th June 1972, police officers went to a house in Wigan in order to interview a man regarding a previous occurrence. On entering the house, a disturbance ensued as a result of which P.S. Still and P.C. Dean went to the scene together with their dogs and waited outside the house.

As the man was being questioned, he grabbed a double-barrelled shotgun and, after voicing certain threats, fired in the direction of the officers, wounding an Inspector, two Constables and the man's own sister.

At this stage, P.S. Still and P.C. Dean were still outside the house and took the dogs from the dog van and ran into the doorway of the house. The man was still in possession of the shotgun, which was still loaded with a cartridge in the second barrel.

P.C. Dean released his dog and, as the dog tackled the man, P.C. Dean grabbed the barrel of the gun and a violent struggle ensued. P.S. Still and P.C. Dean were successful in overcoming the man and disarming him, but this was made doubly difficult by the presence of a friend of the offender who attempted to free him from their grasp.

The actions of the two officers were especially commendable in that they knew they were dealing with a violent, armed, man who moments earlier had shot and wounded other persons and it was obvious that they themselves were in great danger.

Awarded 'William Garnett' Cup.

(W.O. 207 – 2nd March 1973)

Location of incident – Roberts Street, Wigan.

Four officers were wounded that night. Inspector James Lyon and Constable Peter Mercer were both taken to hospital. P.C. Mercer (23) was detained in the intensive care department at Wigan Hospital with wounds to his face, neck and chest. Inspector Lyon (46) was allowed home after treatment for an arm wound. The other wounded officers were Constables Terence Dunn and Glynn Winstanley, who both received minor injuries.

On 6th October 1972, at Liverpool Crown Court, Eric Lewis Catterall, aged 37 years, a general dealer, pleaded guilty to attempting to murder the officers and having a firearm with intent to endanger life and was jailed for seven years.

Sergeant Still and Constable Dean were attached to the No. 3 District Task Force, both having served at Wigan previously.

1972

Arthur DENT, Inspector   **Lancashire Constabulary**

British Empire Medal for Gallantry (Civil Division)

Acting on information received, Inspector Dent, with other officers, went to a house where a man was believed to be in possession of a firearm and stolen jewellery.

The Inspector arranged for the back of the house to be covered and then went to the front entrance, knocked on the door and asked for admission.

By the time he was able to enter the door there was no trace of the man, but on a further search of the house and backyard the man was seen standing on the wall dividing the gardens and was holding a revolver with which he threatened to shoot the Inspector.

The officer moved towards the wall with the object of disarming the man who, at the same time, had jumped back into the yard and was still pointing the revolver and threatening him. The officer then tried to get the gun from the man who hit him viciously across the face with the barrel of the revolver.

Inspector Dent closed with the man grabbing hold of the hand in which the gun was held, there was a fierce struggle and with the help of two constables who had by then arrived on the scene, the man was overpowered and arrested.

During the encounter, the Inspector received fractures to his upper and lower jaws, severe damage to his teeth and lacerations to his mouth, all of which needed hospital treatment. It is considered that Inspector Dent displayed courage and devotion to duty in arresting a violent armed criminal.

At the time, he did not know whether the gun was loaded or not and despite severe facial injuries he closed with the criminal and, with the eventual help of others, arrested him.

L.G. 29/6/1972 Issue 45715 Page 7861

FURTHER INFORMATION:

Arthur Dent was stationed at Bury and, at the time of this incident, was the Divisional Immigration Liaison Officer. His attacker was sentenced to seven years imprisonment on charges of burglary, malicious wounding and possessing a firearm to resist arrest.

He had been previously commended by Bury Magistrates following the arrest of a youth who lunged at him with a knife. Ronald Gallagher (19) pleaded guilty to assaulting Constable Harry Davies and Inspector Dent and causing damage to a police raincoat.

Arthur Dent served two tours of duty seconded to the British Police Unit in Cyprus in 1956 and 1958.

1973	
Ian Charles METCALFE, Constable	**Manchester and Salford Police**
British Empire Medal for Gallantry (Civil Division)	

Constable Metcalfe who was on patrol duties was directed to attend an emergency call. On arrival at the house he and two other policemen were confronted at the front door by a man armed with a rifle, air pistol and an axe.

The man was apparently mentally deranged and had an Alsatian dog with him which was under his control. As Constable Metcalfe and the other officers went towards the man he released the dog and incited it to attack the officers.

Constable Metcalfe, however, continued to approach the man who raised his rifle and fired at the Constable, the shot missed the officer; then with the rifle trained on him he followed the man into the house. At this time, the man had an index finger on the trigger of both guns, but despite this the officer closed with him and managed, after grappling with him, to disarm him; with the assistance of the other officers he was finally overpowered.

Constable Metcalfe showed extreme courage in tackling an obviously dangerous man. His devotion to duty is displayed by his actions in following the man into the house with a gun trained upon him immediately after a loaded firearm had been discharged at him.

L.G. 20/2/1973 Issue 45911 Page 2356

1973

George ALLOTT, Chief Inspector   **Manchester and Salford Police**

Jack Picton BUTLER, Sergeant   **Manchester and Salford Police**

Queen's Commendation for Brave Conduct

For arresting and disarming an Army absentee.

L.G. 20/2/1973 Issue 45911 Page 2356

FURTHER INFORMATION:

Having escaped from the custody of Gwent Constabulary, a soldier, absent without leave in Manchester, suddenly produced a pistol from his clothing and aimed at the officers.

Chief Inspector Allott immediately punched him in the face, while Sergeant Butler grabbed his wrist and forced him to drop the gun. The soldier then produced a second gun but again was disarmed. (Later the weapons were found to be starting pistols, but at the time of the incident this was not known.)

June 1974

Barry JOLLY, Constable   **Merseyside Police**

Arthur Reginald MOSS, Inspector   **Merseyside Police**

Queen's Commendation for Brave Conduct

For services leading to the arrest of an armed and violent man who, under the influence of drink and drugs, threatened to kill them.

L.G. 5/6/1975 Issue 46591 Page 7287

Location of incident – Billinge.

Officers were called to an address in Billinge where a man in his twenties went berserk and armed himself with a pellet firing pistol and an axe. The man had smashed up the house but Constable Jolly, who lived nearby, was called and managed to get the man's mother out safely, despite having the axe thrown at him.

Other officers arrived and were fired at, one being hit. More pellets hit a police car and the frenzied man lashed at the wall with the axe and stabbed himself in the stomach and arm with a knife. Inspector Moss arrived and tried to reason with the man and disarm him and was fired at. Eventually, Constable Jolly got in by subterfuge, distracting the man and opening the way for the other officers to overpower him.

The man later appeared before Judge Lyons at Liverpool Crown Court where the two officers and their colleagues, Constable Terry Birchall and Sergeant James Anderson, were highly praised by the judge for their *'great courage and great compassion in difficult and provoking circumstances'. (Liverpool Echo, 9/6/1975)*

10th August 1974

Bryan Peter BRADSHAW, Constable   **Greater Manchester Police**

Queen's Commendation for Brave Conduct

For services leading to the arrest of an armed man who had robbed a Sub-Post Office.

L.G. 18/3/1975 Issue 46520 Page 3622

Constable Bradshaw was off duty and was returning home with his wife after a shopping trip to Wigan. As he was travelling down Darlington Street he saw a woman lying in the doorway of the Post Office. He leapt from his car and chased a man he saw running away with a gun in one hand and bank notes in the other, whilst chasing him he was threatened three times that he would be shot.

Eventually the raider was cornered in a works yard where he was disarmed. The raider was later jailed for six years at Manchester Crown Court.

Judge Joseph Zigmond said, *'His conduct cannot be praised too highly for he was in constant and maybe awful danger when this man threatened to shoot him when they were at arm's length of each other.'*

At the time of the incident, P.C. Bradshaw (25) had been a policeman for three years.

His Queen's Commendation for Brave Conduct was presented in June 1975 by the Lord Lieutenant of Greater Manchester, Lord Downward. (*Leigh Journal*, 20/3/1975 & 26/6/1975)

18th March 1975

Brian EDWARDS, Constable 2024   **Merseyside Police**

Queen's Commendation for Brave Conduct

For rescuing a baby from the path of a runaway heifer.

L.G. 17/2/1976 Issue 46827 Page 2432

FURTHER INFORMATION:

Location of incident – Honey's Green Lane, Knotty Ash, Liverpool.

In March 1975, a heifer escaped from the Stanley Abattoir, Prescot Road, Liverpool, and remained loose for two hours before being shot by a police marksman.

The animal ran towards 59-year-old Gertrude Jones and her grandniece, 11-month-old Michelle Gough. Constable Edwards snatched Michelle from her pram and was struck in the face by one of the animal's hooves. A police spokesman said, *'Witnesses said that but for his courageous action the child would have suffered serious injury.'* (*Liverpool Echo*, 18/3/1975 & 17/2/1976)

Police Review 27/2/1976

For rescuing a baby from the path of a charging heifer which had escaped from an abattoir. The officer received injuries to the face and was later detained in hospital suffering from concussion, amnesia and photo-phobia.

Chief Constable's Annual Report 1976

Constable 2024 Edwards, 'C' Division and Constable 3434 Reynolds, Traffic Department were presented with the 'Award of Merit' for their courageous actions whilst protecting members of the public from a dangerous animal which escaped from Stanley Abattoir, Prescot Road, Liverpool.

24ᵗʰ March 1975

Derrington Stephen ELLERSHAW, Constable   **Greater Manchester Police**

Javed Mahmood MALIK, Labourer   **Manchester**

Queen's Commendation for Brave Conduct

For saving the life of a child trapped in the rubble of a collapsed building.

L.G. 17/2/1976 Issue 46827 Page 2432

P.C. Derry Ellershaw, aged 22, and Mr Javed Malik received the award for rescuing 15-month-old Rachel Coburn in Wilmslow Road, Fallowfield.

Rachel was trapped by her legs under a couch which was held down by a heavy beam after falling 20 feet through the floor of her home when it collapsed into shop premises.

Mr Malik who had been waiting in a nearby doctor's waiting room, was first on the scene. P.C. Ellershaw arrived a few minutes later and they climbed in through a broken window. With sparks coming from broken wires and electrical appliances and bits of masonry still falling on them they crawled to where the baby was trapped. Completely disregarding their safety, the two men lifted the beam clear. Rachel was unhurt.

P.C. Ellershaw said, *'I never thought about the danger. It's just something you have to do when you are wearing a uniform. We went under all the rubbish together and between us we managed to dig her out.'*

P.C. Ellershaw stated that there were two other men also trying to help but their identities were not known.

May 1975

George Harold GIBSON, Sergeant   **Greater Manchester Police**

Queen's Commendation for Brave Conduct

For services in restraining and disarming an armed man who had threatened him with a pistol to obstruct him during his duty.

L.G. 27/7/1976 Issue 46973 Page 10279

William Cooper (68) a pig farmer of John Street, Simister, Prestwich, Manchester thought he was a victim of *'persecution by bureaucracy'* following the introduction of new regulations covering animal diseases.

Mr Cooper's hatred built up after having his farm inspected on six occasions in a ten-month period.

Appearing at Manchester Crown Court on 7th July 1975, Mr Cooper pleaded guilty to attempting to murder the Inspector, Mr Clifford Sharples, during a visit in May.

Mr Cooper had previously refused to allow Mr Sharples to collect samples of waste food and had been fined £25 for obstructing the Inspector and had built up an intense hatred of him. On the next visit, Mr Sharples attended the farm with an assistant and Sergeant Gibson.

Whilst Mr Sharples was taking samples, Mr Cooper took out a revolver and fired from a distance of three or four yards. The shot missed and Mr Sharples was able to duck before the weapon was fired again. Sergeant Gibson tackled Mr Cooper and during a struggle a third shot was fired before the man was disarmed.

Sentence was deferred by Mr Justice Crichton who said, *'If you undertake to move well away from the area then I would feel safe in making a suspended sentence. But I do emphasise that somebody other than Mr Sharples should carry out the official duty at that farm until they have found a house in Norfolk.'* (*The Guardian*, 8/7/1975)

1st July 1975

Emlyn Arthur WATKINS, lately Inspector   **Greater Manchester Police**

George Medal

In the early hours of the morning of 1st July 1975, three armed men entered a restaurant on the outskirts of Manchester and several shots were fired, wounding a waiter. The gunmen then fled from the restaurant and the proprietor called for police assistance.

Inspector Watkins was alone and unarmed in a police car when he received details of the incident over his personal radio. About a quarter of a mile from the restaurant he saw two men walking towards the City, he stopped the men and questioned them.

He became suspicious because they were allegedly returning to an address, but he knew they were in fact walking away from their destination. The Inspector left his car and told the men he was not satisfied with their explanation and, as he walked towards them, one of the men drew a revolver and threatened him. Undeterred, Inspector Watkins told him to hand over the gun and as he continued to advance towards the gunman the second man produced a gun and fired at the Inspector. The officer went forward again and both men began shooting at him. One of these shots hit him in the abdomen at close range and so seriously wounded him that he is now unfit for police duty. The gunmen then fired several shots at another police car which had arrived in the vicinity and then fled. They were later arrested.

Inspector Watkins displayed outstanding bravery and devotion to duty when alone and unarmed. He continued to advance towards these armed and dangerous men until he was shot and seriously wounded.

L.G. 30/9/1976 Issue 47027 page 13305

FURTHER INFORMATION:

Location of incident – Rusholme, Manchester.

The offenders were part of an active Provisional I.R.A. (Irish Republican Army) cell who had access to arms and explosives. Two of the three offenders were captured at the location and nearby and a third escaped. Other members of the

(G.M.P. Museum)

cell were captured in Liverpool following events where other Merseyside officers were shot and wounded.

Constables Brown, Harris and Keir received the Queen's Commendation for Brave Conduct for this incident. (See next entry.)

Emlyn Watkins died, aged 84 years old, in 2010. He was a widower and lived in Worsley. At 14 he was working as an Air Raid Warden and at 17 he joined the Royal Air Force, serving in the war as a Radio Operator.

Paying tribute, Don Brown, one of three Manchester Constables commended for their bravery in arresting two of the gunmen after Emlyn was shot, said: *'It was a privilege to know and to have worked with Emlyn. His actions enabled an I.R.A. squad to be captured and so saved many lives.'*

G.M.P. Chief Constable Peter Fahy said: *'He was a thoroughly professional police officer and his death reminds us of the courage of those who fight terrorism and of all those who have been injured or killed in terrorist attacks in this country.'*

1ˢᵗ July 1975

Donald James BROWN, Constable	**Greater Manchester Police**
Richard Thomas HARRIS, Constable,	**Greater Manchester Police**
Alastair Andrew KEIR, Constable	**Greater Manchester Police**

Queen's Commendation for Brave Conduct

For services leading to the arrest of two terrorists.

L.G. 30/9/1976 Issue 47027 page 13307

FURTHER INFORMATION:

(See previous entry relating to this incident.)

The offenders involved in the shooting of Inspector Watkins were chased towards St. Gabriel's Convent Hostel grounds in Oxford Place, Rusholme, Manchester, where one of the offenders, Paul Norney, was detained.

The others made off and Noel Gibson was captured nearby in Hathersage Road. The third offender, Stephen Nordone, made good his escape and later met up with Brendan Dowd and Sean Kinsella and were involved in the following incidents.

9th July 1975

Geoffrey BYRON, Inspector   **Merseyside Police**

Thomas Edward DAVIES, Chief Inspector   **Merseyside Police**

Nicholas DORAN, Sergeant 1626 'A'   **Merseyside Police**

Queen's Commendation for Brave Conduct

For services in incidents leading to the arrest of three terrorists.

L.G. 1/10/1976 Issue 47027 Page 13307

FURTHER INFORMATION:

On Wednesday 9th July 1975, three members of the Provisional IRA, Brendan Dowd, Sean Kinsella and Stephen Nordone, were stopped in a vehicle by police in Liverpool after driving through a red traffic light signal.

Sgt. Nick Doran and P.C. John Taylor came out of the nearby Hope Street Police Station to assist other officers, and as they got to the kerb, one of the I.R.A. unit went down on one knee, took aim and fired at the two police officers. The bullet hit the ground in front of Sgt. Doran and ricocheted into his face, injuring him slightly. The men then ran off.

The investigation led to the incident on 10th July involving Inspector Lea and Sergeant Davies. (See next entry.)

10th July 1975

Thomas William DAVIES, Sergeant   **Merseyside Police**

John Frederick LEA, Inspector   **Merseyside Police**

Queen's Gallantry Medal

Following a shooting incident on 9th July 1975, when three policemen were fired upon, enquiries revealed that the three gunmen responsible were terrorists.

The following day, as a result of information received, the whereabouts of the gunmen became known. A squad of police officers, thirteen of whom were armed, were sent to the scene. Inspector Lea, Sergeant Davies and another officer were members of the armed support group which followed the senior officers who made the initial entry into the three-storey house. They positioned themselves on the landing outside the door of a top-floor flat at the front of the house.

It was then discovered that the terrorists were not, as expected, in the top-floor flat and, at the same time, Inspector Lea and Sergeant Davies heard men's voices coming from the first-floor flat. They shouted that they were Police officers and Sergeant Davies kicked at the door while Inspector Lea put his shoulder to it. Almost immediately a shot was fired from inside the room and Sergeant Davies was wounded in the abdomen, but before he fell to the ground he managed to fire a single round. Regardless of the danger, Inspector Lea managed to pull Sergeant Davies out of the line of fire.

Inspector Lea then shouted to the men to lay down their arms and surrender, only to be told that they had 500lbs. of explosive in the flat and if the police tried to enter they would blow up the house. Inspector Lea remained where he was and continued repeatedly to call to the occupants of the flat to come out with their hands up although he could hear the sound of automatic weapons being loaded.

After some time, the men called that they were coming out, the door opened, and the three terrorists appeared with their hands above their heads. Inspector Lea told them to keep their hands up and walk out of the house; they were then arrested. A subsequent search of the premises occupied by the terrorists revealed a number of arms including a light machine gun, a Sten sub-machine gun, hand guns, ammunition, timing devices, detonators, and electrical equipment capable of causing an explosion and 500lbs. of explosive.

Inspector Lea and Sergeant Davies displayed outstanding gallantry, devotion to duty and a complete disregard for their own safety when they fearlessly exposed themselves to great danger to bring about the eventual arrest of these three dangerous criminals.

L.G. 1/10/1976 Issue 47027 Page 13306

FURTHER INFORMATION:

Location of incident – Oxford Road, Waterloo, Liverpool.

On 11th May 1976, five Irishmen – Brendan Dowd (27), Sean Kinsella (29), Stephen John Nordone (20), Paul Gerrard Norney (18) and Noel Gibson (23), after a ten-day trial, were sentenced following conviction at Manchester Crown Court. The men faced fifty-five charges concerning conspiracy to murder, conspiracy to cause explosions, and counts of attempted murder and possession of firearms and explosives.

Dowd and Kinsella were sentenced to three life sentences and a total of 129 years imprisment, Nordone received three life sentences and a total of 192 years imprisment, five life sentences and 66 years imprisment for Norney and two life sentences and 111 years for Gibson. Throughout the trial the men refused to recognise the court and were found by a separate jury of being *'mute of malice'*. They were not represented and offered no defence.

Mr Justice Cantley praised the zeal and bravery of named and unnamed police officers in Manchester and Liverpool who risked their lives to capture these *'dangerous and disgusting men'*. An example of the bravery was the conduct of former Inspector Emlyn Watkins of the Greater Manchester Police, who was shot in the stomach by two of the men. Equally admirable, he said, was the bravery of the task force of policemen who raided the units flat in Oxford Road, Liverpool. They went there knowing the great personal danger they were facing.

24th July 1975

Trevor BRADSHAW, Sergeant   **Greater Manchester Police**

Queen's Commendation for Brave Conduct

For services leading to the arrest of an armed man who had attempted to hi-jack an aircraft.

L.G. 27/7/1976 Issue 46973 Page 10279

FURTHER INFORMATION:

Trevor Bradshaw was commended for the arrest of 21-year-old Paul Young, who boarded a Boeing 737 aircraft at Manchester Airport with a replica .38 revolver after having been rejected by his girlfriend.

Once on the plane he pointed the gun at a teenage girl, ordered a man to *'Keep still or I'll blow your head off'* and told the cleaning staff to leave the plane, which had landed for refuelling. Detective Sergeant Bradshaw and Detective Constable Robert Gregory, both unarmed Special Branch officers, boarded the plane. Sergeant Bradshaw pretended to close the aircraft door and then lunged at Young. He and D.C. Gregory overpowered Young.

Paul Young appeared at Manchester Crown Court on 27th November 1975, charged with intending to unlawfully take an aircraft, unlawfully possessing the replica gun and using it with intent to resist arrest. He pleaded guilty and was sentenced to three years imprisonment.

Judge Arthur Prest commended the unarmed officers and said, *'We would like to thank you for what you did, you have gained the distinction which the public has come to expect of our police officers.'* (*The Guardian*, 28/11/1975)

3rd July 1977

John Stuart WILSON, Constable 5865   **Lancashire Constabulary**

Queen's Gallantry Medal

During the evening of 3rd July 1977, Constable Wilson and another police officer had detained a man in connection with a burglary. The man was placed in the rear of the officer's patrol car, but during the drive to the police station he suddenly produced a knife and attacked Constable Wilson who was the driver of the car.

Constable Wilson, who was stabbed in the neck, stopped the car while his colleague turned in the front passenger seat to grapple with the man. As Constable Wilson began to get out of the car he received two further stab wounds in his right side and the other officer was temporarily incapacitated by wounds to the head and arms. Another policeman arrived at the scene and was attacked and thrown to the ground by the assailant who had escaped from the police car.

The man then stabbed the officer several times and continued to make knife thrusts at his head and body. Constable Wilson, although bleeding profusely from his wounds and with his right lung collapsed by a knife thrust, unhesitatingly went to his colleague's assistance, thereby diverting the attacker's attention. Fortunately, another police officer arrived at the scene and the assailant concentrated on him. Constable Wilson again went to the aid of this officer in spite of bleeding heavily from the neck and mouth. The knifeman then ran away and as he made good his escape Constable Wilson collapsed. The attacker was arrested shortly afterwards having deliberately crashed head on into a police car, seriously injuring the driver.

Constable Wilson displayed devotion to duty, persistence and courage of a very high order in going to the aid of his fellow officers despite being badly wounded. There is no doubt that, but for his tenacity, even more serious injuries could have been inflicted on his colleagues.

L.G. 16/2/1979 Issue 47773 Page 2290

FURTHER INFORMATION:

Location of incident – Church Street and collision at Ribbleton Lane, Preston, Lancashire.

Seven officers were injured in this incident, including John Stuart Wilson. The other officers were P.C. Frank Roger Williams (30), stab wound to neck; P.C. Christopher David Selwood Hives (20), stab wounds to head and arms; P.S. Stanley Roberts (50), multiple injuries from the car crash; W.P.C. Catherine Helen Gregson, lacerations and bruising from the car crash; P.C. Brian Marsh (22), head injury from the crash; and P.C. David John Aston, bruising.

Michael John Lawrenson, aged 22 years, of Deepdale Road, Preston, was charged the following day and remanded in custody. The charges comprised causing grievous bodily harm to Sergeant Stanley Roberts, wounding John Stuart Wilson, P.C. Christopher David Selwood Hives, P.C. Frank Roger Williams with intent to do grievous bodily harm and assaulting P.W. Helen Gregson and P.C. Brian Marsh. Lawrenson was convicted and jailed for 13 years.

John Stuart Wilson holds the distinction of being the only Lancashire Constabulary officer to be awarded two national gallantry awards and being the holder of the William Garnett Cup twice.

(See later entry for the award of the Queen's Commendation for Brave Conduct.)

Awarded 'William Garnett' Cup for 1977 jointly with P.C. Helm.

24th November 1977

George Kenneth POWER, Constable **Merseyside Police**

Queen's Gallantry Medal

Pauline McMILLAN, Housewife **Huyton, Liverpool**

Sheila Ann SMITH, Constable **Merseyside Police**

Queen's Commendation for Brave Conduct

During the late evening of the 24th November 1977, a fire believed to have been caused by a small boy, broke out in the upper floor of a house with the result that he and a six-month-old baby were trapped in separate bedrooms.

A neighbour alerted by the children's mother, succeeded in getting into the boy's bedroom, but was beaten back by the intense heat; she tried twice more to get inside the room only to be driven back. Other unsuccessful attempts to rescue the children unfortunately, although well intentioned, had resulted in broken windows which had increased the intensity of the fire.

By the time Constable Power and another officer arrived at the scene the fire had increased, the floorboards and carpet in the room were burning and thick black smoke billowed out. The fire had spread to the ceiling above the landing, the wooden loft entrance was well alight, and they could hear a child screaming.

Constable Power, closely followed by his colleague, ran into the house and up the stairs. The officer with Constable Power entered the front bedroom to search for a child but was driven out by the heat and smoke. Constable Power then entered the room and after feeling his way, found the baby which he handed to the other officer who took it to safety and then returned to the landing to help her colleague.

Regardless of the now appalling condition in the back bedroom Constable Power entered the room. The fire had been fanned to greater intensity by draught from the broken windows and the heat was fierce. The officer fought his way through the smoke and flames to rescue the now badly burnt child from the bunk bed in the furthest corner of the room. Both Officers then left the house with the boy.

Constable Power displayed outstanding courage, determination and a total disregard for his own safety when, in spite of worsening conditions, he rescued both children and succeeded where the rescue attempts of others had failed.

L.G. 16/2/1979 Issue 47773 Page 2289

McMillan & Smith

For services in attempting to rescue two small children who were trapped in a blazing house.

L.G. 16/2/1979 Issue 47773 Page 291

FURTHER INFORMATION:

Location of incident – 9 Fincham Crescent, Huyton.

This incident took place during the Firefighters' National Strike from November 1977 to January 1978, whilst emergency cover was provided by the Army. Both officers were awarded the Force Merit Badge by the Police Committee.

George Kenneth Power Q.G.M. was born in Liverpool and joined the police as a Cadet at Stratford-upon-Avon but transferred to the Liverpool and Bootle Constabulary in 1968, being sworn in as a Constable in 1969. He served as a uniformed officer and as a firearms officer in the C.I.D. and Vice Squad as well as a Police Federation Representative. He retired in 1990 as a result of an injury received during a training exercise.

As well as the Force Merit Badge, he received a number of Chief Constables' and Judges' commendations and was awarded two Letters of Commendation by The Liverpool Shipwreck and Humane Society.[50]

28th November 1977

Denis HENAGHAN, Sergeant 2663   **Merseyside Police**

The Queen's Gallantry Medal

Charles Graham LAMBERT, Lieutenant   **The Queen's Regiment**

Queen's Commendation for Brave Conduct

During the early hours of the 28th November 1977, a fire developed in a dwelling house where two small children were asleep in a first floor front bedroom. The Fire Brigade was summoned but only emergency firefighting facilities were available and two Army pumping appliances, escorted by two police cars, were despatched. The living room, hall and staircase were a blazing inferno when the services arrived at the scene.

Sergeant Henaghan attended and with a member of the Army team, was joined by another fireman and climbed a ladder to the first floor bedroom window with the intention of rescuing the children and their grandfather, who had earlier made a rescue attempt and was believed to still be in the house.

At this stage conditions were extremely hazardous, the door leading to the upstairs landing was jammed as the bedroom ceiling had collapsed. The Sergeant used an axe to break down the door and was confronted with the fiercely burning landing and upper staircase. With Sergeant Henaghan using a hose to reduce the blaze, they managed to work their way to the head of the stairs where they found a man's body.

The landing then collapsed and Sergeant Henaghan fell to the hallway below, fortunately he was uninjured and returned again to the upper floor via the ladder. At this point, however, all personnel were ordered to withdraw because of the dangerous state of the building.

Sergeant Henaghan displayed bravery and devotion to duty of a high order when without regard for his personal safety, he entered the building three times despite the fact that it was burning fiercely, and the internal structure was collapsing.

L.G. 11/9/1979 Issue 47951 Page 11479

---

[50] *For Exemplary Bravery – The Queen's Gallantry Medal*, Page 605

Location of incident – Bulwer Street, Everton, Liverpool.

This incident took place during the Firefighters' National Strike from November 1977 to January 1978, whilst emergency cover was provided by the Army.

Sergeant Henaghan was also awarded the Award of Merit by the Police Committee.

Arising from this incident, Lieutenant Charles Graham Lambert (499989), The Queen's Regiment, was awarded the Queen's Commendation for Brave Conduct. Lambert was born in Liverpool and had previously been a member of the Territorial and Army Volunteer Reserve before being commissioned into the Queen's Regiment in February 1977. (*Liverpool Echo*, 16/5/1978).

(L.G. 5/6/1978 Issue 47560 Page 6842)

19th December 1977

Robert HELM, Constable 324   **Lancashire Constabulary**

Queen's Gallantry Medal

During the early hours of 19th December 1977, Constable Helm was called to a fire in an old terraced house.

On arrival, he found the premises filled with dense smoke and the ground floor in flames. The house was in total darkness and he was unable to see without the aid of his hand torch. He told one man to leave the house and was then informed that the building was divided into bedsitting rooms and that some of the tenants were still in their rooms.

The officer immediately went up the stairs, forced open one of the doors and carried the occupant down into the street. By this time the flames had intensified and the whole building was filled with smoke, but Constable Helm re-entered the house where he found another man on a landing whom he guided through the smoke down the stairs to safety.

The officer again returned to the house and entered a room on the first floor where he found another man who appeared too terrified to move; he had to force the man from the room and down into the street. Constable Helm was by now suffering from the effects of the smoke and fumes and was obliged to rest for a short time, but after recovering slightly he went back into the hallway and kicked open the door of one of the ground floor flats; he was met by a sheet of flame and forced to leave the house. He then tried to crawl on his hands and knees back to the flat, but the room was a mass of flame and he was finally forced to leave the premises.

Constable Helm displayed courage and devotion to duty of a high order when he risked the possibility of being trapped by fire and fumes to effect the rescue of the three men who would otherwise have died in the flames.

L.G. 16/2/1979 Issue 47773 Page 2288

FURTHER INFORMATION:

Location of incident – 7 Stanley Place, Preston.

One man died in the fire – he was Kenneth King (45). His body was found slumped over a fire, by firefighters using breathing apparatus. Mr King was reported to have had a history of heart trouble and it was thought he may have collapsed onto the fire. The flat was gutted by the inferno, which was thought to have been burning for some time before the alarm was raised.

At the inquest, Her Majesty's Coroner addressed P.C. Helm and said, *'You did a wonderful job and it is no discredit to you that you did not get to the deceased. You risked your life in doing so, I think that the public owe you a great deal of gratitude.'*

This incident took place during the Firefighters' National Strike from November 1977 to January 1978, whilst emergency cover was provided by the Army.

Robert Helm Q.G.M. joined Lancashire Constabulary as a Police Cadet and was appointed as a Constable, serving as a uniformed officer until 1980 when he joined the Criminal Investigation Department. He was promoted to Inspector in 1995 and Superintendent before retirement in 2006. He was awarded the Queen's Police Medal for Distinguished Service in 2005. (L.G. 11/6/2005).

Awarded 'William Garnett' Cup for 1977 jointly with P.C. Wilson.

28th December 1977

Geoffrey Gerald LEVER, Constable 25	**Lancashire Constabulary**
Elizabeth Dianne BARTRAM, Constable 6110	**Lancashire Constabulary**

Queen's Commendation for Brave Conduct

For services leading to the arrest of a distraught man who was armed with a home-made bomb.

L.G. 16/2/1979 Issue 47773 Page 2290

FURTHER INFORMATION:

At 9.30p.m. on Wednesday 28th December 1977, a telephone call was received at Skelmersdale Police Station from a G.P.O. operator to the effect that a man had called them from a telephone kiosk in Ormskirk Road, Skelmersdale, stating that he was in possession of a bomb. D.C. Lever and W.P.C. Bartram responded to the call individually. D.C. Lever arrived at the location first in a police car, being joined shortly afterwards by W.P.C. Bartram. There was no one in the kiosk so the officers made a search of the vicinity and a few minutes later they saw a man walking along the Ormskirk Road. D.C. Lever approached the man, whom he knew, and asked him if there was anything wrong, only to be rebuked and verbally abused by him.

Suddenly, and without warning, the man pulled a bottle from under his coat and, brandishing this in his hand, he jumped on to the bonnet of the police car. He stated that the bottle was a bomb and threatened to blow up himself, the car and anyone else who got in his way. Both officers could see that the bottle contained a white substance and that a form of fuse was hanging from its neck. The man then held the bottle out and made a striking motion with his free hand as if to light the fuse, at which point W.P.C. Bartram approached the man and stopped some ten feet from him, as it appeared that he intended to detonate the device. D.C. Lever got out of the police car, whereupon the man backed away, but continued to threaten both officers with the bottle

The man then began to strike the top of the bottle and, feeling that it might explode, both officers pleaded with him to desist. In an endeavour to calm him down and, if possible, to divert his attention, D.C. Lever offered him a cigarette and, whilst doing so, he managed to grab hold of the man's arms. A violent struggle ensued, at one stage of which the man managed to free one of his arms and attempted to strike the bottle again. W.P.C. Bartram went to the assistance of D.C. Lever, wresting the bomb from the man's grasp and removing it to safety. D.C. Lever then overpowered and arrested him.

Subsequent forensic examination of the bottle and its contents confirmed that it was in fact a home-made bomb, capable of detonation by flame or impact. It contained sodium chlorate, sugar and sodium chloride, plus pellets of single-based nitrocellulose propellant and included in the mixture was an assortment of screws, marbles and other metal objects.

The actions of D.C. Lever and W.P.C. Bartram in this incident were in the highest traditions of the Police Service, preventing as they did what could have been a serious incident involving possible loss of life and damage to property and at the conclusion of the resultant case at Preston Crown Court, in which the man was sentenced to five years imprisonment, Mr. Justice Sellers commended the conduct of D.C. Lever and W.P.C. Bartram in this matter.

(W.O. 266 – 22nd March 1979)

Jointly awarded 'William Garnett' Cup.

16th June 1979

Thomas Dobson MAWDSLEY, Constable   **Mersey Tunnel Police Force**

Queen's Commendation for Brave Conduct

For overpowering an armed and unstable man who had commandeered a private car at gunpoint and forcibly abducted the owner.

L.G. 2/10/1980 Issue 48327 Page 13803

FURTHER INFORMATION:

In the afternoon of Saturday 16th June 1979, Dorothy Penkman, a Liverpool school teacher, parked her car at a city centre car park. Whilst locking her vehicle she was confronted by Paul Lawford Eagle (24 years) of Kensington, Liverpool, who had a handgun. He ordered her back into the car and told her to drive him through the Mersey Tunnel.

After a while Miss Penkman stopped the car and refused to take him any further. Eagle 'doubled up' and asked to be taken to a hospital. Miss Penkman told him she would take him to hospital in Liverpool. On route Miss Penkman stopped the car at the Tunnel Police post at the Birkenhead entrance to the Queensway Tunnel. Miss Penkman told P.C. Mawdsley what had taken place and he observed Eagle reach into the back of the car and pick up a handgun from the back seat.

Whilst Eagle was attempting to get out of the car, Constable Mawdsley dived through the open driver's door and tackled him. Both fell out of the car, with Eagle holding the gun in his right hand. Constable Mawdsley grabbed the hand, preventing Eagle using the gun. At this moment an off-duty Merseyside police officer, who was passing, stopped to assist and Eagle was arrested. The gun was later found to be unloaded.

Eagle appeared at Liverpool Crown Court on 17th September 1979, where he pleaded guilty to kidnapping Miss Penkman, falsely imprisoning her, carrying a firearm with intent to commit an offence and having no firearms certificate. Eagle was remanded in custody for psychiatric reports. The court was told that Eagle had made a lengthy statement, saying he was upset at failing to kill himself and intended to provoke someone to kill him by creating a siege which would end in a shootout.

P.C. Mawdsley was commended by Judge Temple for his part in grappling with and disarming Eagle. During the struggle, P.C. Mawdsley sustained a neck injury and was off duty for 24 days. At the time of the incident P.C. Mawdsley was 46 years old and had been a Tunnel Policeman for nine years. (*Liverpool Daily Post*, 18/9/1979)

Eagle was later sentenced to three years' probation and a condition of residence order with Eagle agreeing to take outpatient treatment when required. (*Liverpool Echo*, 28/11/1979)

The Mersey Tunnels Police is answerable to the Mersey Passenger Transport Authority rather than the Home Office. Officers are appointed as Constables under Section 105 of the County of Merseyside Act 1980 and sworn in by a Justice of the Peace.

They are responsible for policing the Kingsway and Queensway Tunnels, the approach roads and marshalling areas. The Force was formed in 1936 and, as of 2017, had an establishment of 51 officers.

17th December 1979

Richard Andrew FAWCETT, Constable 5953   **Merseyside Police**

Thomas Paul William SINCLAIR, Constable 5168   **Merseyside Police**

Queen's Commendation for Brave Conduct

For services leading to the rescue of two men who were trapped by heat, flames and smoke during a large fire in a shopping precinct.

L.G. 3/10/1980 Issue 48327 Page 13803

FURTHER INFORMATION:

On the evening of 17th December 1979, a fire broke out in the Market Hall of St. John's Precinct, Liverpool. Within minutes of the fire being reported, one whole level of the market complex was completely ablaze, trapping a security man and caretaker on a smoke-filled higher level.

The first police officers on the scene attempted to rescue the two trapped men but were beaten back by the heat and smoke. After a few minutes, all contact with the trapped men was lost, and Constables Sinclair and Fawcett immediately entered the blazing complex from Elliot Street. The smoke and heat were intense, and it was impossible to walk into the building, so both officers crawled along the floor to search for the trapped men. Visibility was less than three feet, but after a few minutes search the security man and caretaker were found near to the entrance of the Market Hall.

After reassuring both men, the officers began to escort them from the premises but after only a few feet both men became so weak that they were unable to move. Constable Sinclair grabbed hold of the security man and his colleague, the caretaker, and they started to drag them across the floor. As the conditions became worse, the strength of both officers began to fail but they managed to hold out until they reached safety. Both officers had crawled a distance of over 370 feet to reach the trapped men in what was described as absolutely atrocious conditions.

The caretaker said of his rescuer, '*The bobby that got me out was tremendous. I reckon this saved my life because I don't think I would have got out.*' The security man also praised Constable Sinclair, saying, '*He acted above and beyond the call of duty. He was choking, absolutely exhausted. I can't thank him enough.*'

Both officers were also awarded the Force Merit Badge by the Police Authority.[51]

---

[51] Liverpool City Police from http://liverpoolcitypolice.co.uk/queens-commendation/4558081392 – Retrieved 31/5/2017

27th December 1979

John Stuart WILSON Q.G.M., Constable 5865　　　　**Lancashire Constabulary**

Queen's Commendation for Brave Conduct

For services leading to the rescue of a mentally unbalanced woman from a dangerous river in severe weather conditions.

L.G. 3/10/1980 Issue 48327 Page 13803

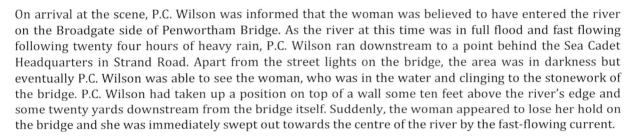

FURTHER INFORMATION:

At 12.10a.m. on Thursday 27th December 1979, a telephone call was received at Preston Police Station to the effect that a woman had been seen to climb over a fence and walk towards the River Ribble on the Broadgate side of Penwortham Bridge. The message was relayed to patrols and P.C. Wilson, who was on foot patrol on Church Street, Preston, responded to the call by obtaining a lift from a passing traffic patrol vehicle.

On arrival at the scene, P.C. Wilson was informed that the woman was believed to have entered the river on the Broadgate side of Penwortham Bridge. As the river at this time was in full flood and fast flowing following twenty four hours of heavy rain, P.C. Wilson ran downstream to a point behind the Sea Cadet Headquarters in Strand Road. Apart from the street lights on the bridge, the area was in darkness but eventually P.C. Wilson was able to see the woman, who was in the water and clinging to the stonework of the bridge. P.C. Wilson had taken up a position on top of a wall some ten feet above the river's edge and some twenty yards downstream from the bridge itself. Suddenly, the woman appeared to lose her hold on the bridge and she was immediately swept out towards the centre of the river by the fast-flowing current.

P.C. Wilson promptly used his personal radio to inform Preston Control of the woman's position and that he intended entering the river to attempt to rescue her. He quickly discarded his uniform greatcoat and tunic, and, without hesitation or thought for his personal safety, immediately jumped down the ten feet to the bank and swam out towards the woman.

He was able to take hold of her and swim back to the river bank where he was assisted by other officers who had arrived at the scene to lift her on to the bank, from where she was subsequently taken to hospital. Due to the dangerous state of the river, considerable physical strength, swimming ability and tenacity were required to reach the woman and bring her back to the bank.

P.C. Wilson's actions in entering the swollen river in conditions of near darkness were in the best traditions of the Police Service and showed courage of the highest order. P.C. Wilson was a joint winner of the William Garnett Cup in the year 1977 and this is the first occasion that the same officer has been presented with the trophy for a second time.

(W.O. 319 – 27th March 1980)

(See previous entry relating to the award of the Queen's Gallantry Medal.)

Awarded 'William Garnett' Cup.

1980

Oliver Charles BAILEY, Constable Greater Manchester Police

Barry Joseph POLLITT, Constable Greater Manchester Police

Queen's Commendation for Brave Conduct

For services leading to the rescue of the driver and passenger who were trapped and unconscious in a blazing car whose petrol tank was ruptured and in imminent danger of exploding.

L.G. 28/3/1980 Issue 48143 Page 4793

FURTHER INFORMATION:

Constables Bailey and Pollitt went into action after a vehicle they were following crashed into a wall in the grounds of Monsall Hospital and burst into flames.

Ignoring the danger, the two officers dashed to the blazing wreckage and dragged the trapped youths to safety. Because all doors were locked or jammed on impact, Constable Bailey smashed a window with his fist to open one from the inside. Constable Bailey dragged the passenger out, then went back to help his colleague free the driver. While bringing the man out there were two explosions. After the rescue the two officers evacuated a nearby building. (*Manchester Evening News*, 28/3/1980)

5th August 1980

Philip Quintin HARRISON, Constable 1167 Lancashire Constabulary

Kim Patricia WRIGHT, Constable 6196 Lancashire Constabulary

Queen's Commendation for Brave Conduct

For services leading to the arrest of two violent and dangerous criminals.

L.G. 1/10/1981 Issue 48752 Page 12502

FURTHER INFORMATION:

During the evening of Tuesday 5th August 1980, a robbery took place at an off licence shop in the Merseyside police area and the four men responsible made off in a Ford Escort van.

About 11.00p.m. that night, a Police Constable on duty in Skelmersdale stopped the van, only to be seriously assaulted by its four occupants who made good their escape in the vehicle. Within minutes, two other police officers had again stopped the van but were attacked by the four occupants who were armed with hammers, lino knives and iron bars. Both officers were badly dazed by the ferocity of the attack and the four men ran off.

Police Constable Harrison and Woman Police Constable Wright were making their way towards the scene, having received a radio message for assistance, when they saw one of the men running away from the location of the assault. Both officers gave chase and caught the man as he was attempting to climb a garden fence. Constable Harrison forced the man to the floor and, despite violent resistance, was able to hold him down whilst Woman Police Constable Wright tried to put handcuffs on him.

She was unable to do so because of the man's extremely violent attempts to escape and at this stage a second man arrived on the scene, attacked Constable Harrison, and dragged him from the man on the floor.

A desperate fight then ensued between the men and the police officers, during which W.P.C. Wright was beaten by one of the men who had picked up Constable Harrison's truncheon and who only ceased the assault on her when it appeared she was unconscious. Both men then attacked Constable Harrison with a hammer and his own truncheon, beating him severely about the head and shoulders and breaking one of his fingers.

One man then ran away from the scene and Constable Harrison, despite having been reduced to a state of semi-consciousness, was able to detain the other man and hold him to the ground. Woman Police Constable Wright, although suffering from the effects of the violent assault on her, continued to assist P.C. Harrison until the arrival of other officers, who were successful in restraining the man and effecting his arrest.

Both Constable Harrison and Woman Police Constable Wright had to be taken from the scene by ambulance to hospital where they were found to have serious injuries, as a result of which both officers were off duty for a period of almost three months.

(W.O. 372 – 2nd April 1981)

Jointly awarded 'William Garnett' Cup.

19th February 1981

Ian Charles THOMPSON, Constable 6086   **Merseyside Police**

Queen's Commendation for Brave Conduct

For services in tackling and disarming a man who had entered a hospital and threatened to murder a nurse.

L.G. 2/10/1981 Issue 48752 Page 12503

Constable Thompson and a colleague Alan Norbury were at Alder Hey Children's Hospital, Liverpool when screams were heard from nurses. When they raced to the department they found Nurse Susan Kerr on the floor with an armed man above her threatening to shoot her. Constable Thompson started trying to calm the man down and eventually 21-year-old Susan managed to creep away.

Constable Thompson said, *'This confused the gunman who started to scream all sorts of threats. I was made to kneel down in front of him whilst he held the gun at my head. I knew I had to play for time while my colleague was putting out a call for assistance.*

The noise of the radios confused the man and he ordered me to switch mine off. I decided it was now or never, so I brought my hand to my chest to turn it off, then grabbed the gun with my right hand and with my left overpowered him and got him to the floor.'

At Crown Court the gunman James Anthony Francis (33) admitted threatening to kill the nurse and Constable Thompson. The court heard that the man's 10-year-old child had died of cancer at Alder Hey and at one stage he told the police he blamed the hospital for his daughter's death. He was sentenced to three years' probation. (*Liverpool Echo*, 2/10/1981)

Constable Thompson was later presented with the Award of Merit and an inscribed gift by the Merseyside Police Committee.

4th June 1981

David Walter RILEY, Detective Constable   **Lancashire Constabulary**

Queen's Commendation for Brave Conduct

For services in overpowering and detaining an armed man who fired on him at short range in an effort to evade arrest.

L.G. 24/9/1982 Issue 49119 Page 12412

FURTHER INFORMATION:

Search warrants were executed to search for drugs at houses at Victoria Road, Walton-le-Dale, Latham Street and Avenham Colonnade, Preston, on Thursday 4th June 1981.

At 7a.m. that day, shots were fired as police entered the premises at Victoria Road. It is described that Detective Constable Riley was only inches from the man when the weapon containing CS gas was fired at him. Despite being temporarily blinded, he lunged at the man, throwing him to the ground. No resistance was encountered at the other premises. A total of seven men were detained during the raids and two firearms and substances were recovered.

At the date of the incident, D.C. Riley had served with Lancashire Constabulary for nine years and had joined the Drug Squad in 1980. (*Lancashire Evening Post*, 4/6/1983)

Chief Constable's Annual Report 1981, Page 13

D.S. 3036 Cook, D.C. 431 Riley – Highly commended for bravery. The officers displayed great courage and determination in approaching a drugs dealer who had twice discharged a tear gas gun at them. Despite one officer being temporarily blinded they closed with the man, disarmed him and effected his arrest. Awarded £25.

4th July 1981

Raymond DAVENPORT (Deceased), Constable 5951   **Merseyside Police**

Queen's Commendation for Brave Conduct

For services in attempting to arrest the driver of a stolen car.

L.G. 12/8/1983 Issue 49446 Page 10723

FURTHER INFORMATION:

Raymond Davenport was fatally injured attempting to retrieve the keys from a stolen vehicle, which had come to a halt in Roe Street in Liverpool City Centre. The offender drove off, dragging him along for 200 yards before colliding with a bus shelter.

P.C. Raymond Davenport was 35 years of age at the time of his death. He left a widow and a thirteen-year-old daughter.

At Liverpool Crown Court on 18th March 1982, Jeffrey Jaycock and Mark Kelly both from Old Swan, Liverpool, were cleared of the murder of P.C. Davenport but were convicted of his manslaughter and were jailed for nine years.

The judge told the men they were responsible for the death of a gallant police officer who was doing his duty. *'You set out on the journey of lawlessness, the kind of thing that is a menace to this country. It was a needless crime, pointless and senseless.'*

Three women passengers in the rear of the vehicle entered guilty pleas at Liverpool Magistrates Court for allowing themselves to be carried in a car which had been taken without consent and were fined £50.

On 16th January 1984, Jaycock and Kelly's appeal was heard at the Court of Appeal in London. Kelly was acquitted after Lord Lane judged his conviction was not safe or satisfactory. His co-accused, Jeffrey Jaycock, who had been the driver, had his appeal dismissed.

5th January 1983

Patrick Richard ABRAM, Constable 253   **Lancashire Constabulary**

Queen's Commendation for Brave Conduct

For services in attempting to rescue a drowning man in rough seas during severe weather conditions.

L.G. 9/8/1984 Issue 49834 Page 10916

FURTHER INFORMATION:

At about 1.50p.m. on Wednesday 5th January 1983, Alistair Anthony, a holiday maker to Blackpool, was in company with his father on the Middle Walk opposite to Wilton Parade, Blackpool, together with their dogs.

Alistair Anthony threw a ball for his dog. The ball bounced off the Middle Walk onto the Lower Walk and then over the wall into the sea.

The dog gave chase and disappeared down the steps at that point, leading to the foreshore.

Alistair Anthony undressed and entered the sea in an effort to save his dog. Because of tidal and weather conditions he was propelled northwards towards Gynn Square, by which time, despite the use of two lifebelts, he was in obvious distress.

An emergency call was passed to the police and a response to the scene was immediate, with W.P.C. Angela Bradley, Police Constables Colin Morrison, Gordon Connolly and Pat Abram reaching the slade at Gynn Square almost simultaneously.

They were faced with an unknown situation and, as is the usual practice, had first to make a quick assessment of the emergency and the dangers. They left their police vehicles and rushed to the slade from

Gynn Square where, from a vantage point, it was obvious to them that Alistair Anthony was in the water in difficulties.

The decision that was then made was crucial, but it was made without any thought for their own safety, only with the intention of rescuing Mr Anthony. The sea is often deceptive but at this stage Mr Anthony appeared near enough to the slade to be rescued and saved if immediate action was taken.

With the prevailing weather conditions at that time it was dangerous for anyone to be on the slade, as there was the possibility that they could be engulfed by waves and washed into the sea. However, Police Constables Connolly and Abram immediately part-stripped and Police Constable Abram entered the water with a lifebelt around his waist attached to a line.

Sea conditions at Blackpool on the day of the tragedy.

The first attempt to rescue Mr Anthony failed and he entered the water a second time, assisted by his colleagues who were walking along the lower slade, attached to the line to him. Due to the roughness of the sea these officers were swept into the water but then still continued in their attempt to rescue Mr Anthony but, regrettably, to no avail.

Tragically, W.P.C. Bradley, P.C. Connolly and P.C. Morrison lost their lives in this rescue attempt, as did Mr Anthony.

P.C. Abram was pulled out of the sea unconscious, but thanks to some prompt medical attention at the scene he recovered some time later.

(W.O. 534 – 26th April 1984)

P.C. Abram was awarded the 'William Garnett' Cup, which was also posthumously awarded to W.P.C. Bradley, Constable Connolly and Constable Morrison.

Memorial to the lost officers with the Emergency Services Memorial in the background – Blackpool
(© Anthony Rae)

A fifth officer, P.C. Martin Hewitson, is reported to have twice waded chest deep into the sea to attempt to rescue P.C. Abram and P.C. Morrison.

The inquests held in February 1983 recorded verdicts of death by misadventure. The court heard that at the time of the incident a south to south west wind was blowing at 18 knots, gusting to 25 knots (21.29 mph.) and the high tide was well above normal. The sea temperature was estimated to be only 5°C.

Coroner Mr John Budd commended several other police officers but singled out PC Abram for special praise. He said, *'I consider the conduct of P.C. Abram who entered the sea twice and fought with tigerish tenacity, deserves and shall receive my highest commendation.'*

Memorial plaque at Lancashire Police H.Q.
(Author's collection)

Emergency Services Memorial, Blackpool. (© Anthony Rae)

The events of that day are remembered each year at the seafront at Blackpool when a service of remembrance is held at the scene of the incident, where a memorial plaque is situated near to the Emergency Services Memorial near Gynn Square, Blackpool.

Angela Bradley
W.P.C. 6133

Gordon Alexander Connolly
P.C. 562

Colin Morrison
P.C. 1956

Angela Bradley was born in Lancaster and was 23 years old. She had been twice commended by the Chief Constable, once for bravery and was due to be commended for a previous sea rescue. She had served in Blackpool since April 1978, following her appointment in November 1977.

Gordon Alexander Connolly was born in Dunfirmline and was 24 years old. He married his wife, Bernadine, in April 1982. Their son was born six months after his death. He had served at Blackpool Central Station since May 1977, following his appointment in December 1976. He had been commended by the Chief Constable and was due to receive a further commendation for the arrest of a man flourishing what turned out to be an imitation revolver.

Colin Morrison was born in Blackpool and was 38 years of age, having been appointed in August 1963. He was married to Hilary in September 1967 and had four children, two boys and two girls. He had nineteen years' service, having been a Police Cadet and had worked at Chorley, Police H.Q. and as a Traffic Patrol Officer at Blackpool from October 1972.

In October 1983, Chief Constable Brian Johnson honoured 19 members of the Emergency Services for their part in the rescue, who were presented with Commendation Certificates. They included five members of the Fleetwood R.N.L.I. lifeboat crew who battled to reach the scene of the incident, four members of the Ambulance Service, four members of the Fire Brigade and the crew of the R.A.F. helicopter crew who attended from R.A.F. Valley. Also commended was Dr John Frankland, a G.P. from Lancaster, who was passing and stopped and was part of the team who resuscitated P.C. Abram after he had been pulled unconscious from the sea.

The Gordon Connolly Memorial Award Cup is presented annually in Blackpool to a police officer or police staff member who, through good police work, has brought about a significant arrest and prosecution.

The officers are commemorated on the memorial wall at Blackpool Police Station with a plaque and photographs.

Memorial wall at Blackpool Police Station, Bonny Street, March 2018. (Author's collection)

11th March 1983

John EGERTON (Deceased), Constable 'K' 3056   **Greater Manchester Police**

Queen's Commendation for Brave Conduct

For services leading to the arrest of an armed man who had broken into and entered factory premises.

L.G. 5/12/1983 Issue 49561 Page 16131

FURTHER INFORMATION:

Constable John Egerton, aged 20 years, and Constable David O'Brien were in the yard premises of Dynamic Plastics, Emlyn Street, Farnworth, near Bolton, searching for an intruder.

P.C. Egerton radioed that he had disturbed the intruder in the yard. He caught Arthur Edge siphoning petrol from a car in the factory yard. Nothing further was heard and P.C. O'Brien searched for P.C. Egerton and found him in the yard, having been repeatedly stabbed.

Edge was later convicted of his murder at Liverpool Crown Court on 29th September 1982 and received a life sentence. Edge served 18 years and was released in 2000.

Mr Justice Farquharson praised the Constable's courage and devotion to duty. He told Edge, who denied murder but was found guilty by a jury: *'You cruelly and cold-bloodedly ran down a young officer on the threshold of his career.'*

A plaque was unveiled at Bolton Police Station by the then Chief Constable, Sir James Anderton, and John Egerton's family and colleagues in 1983. The plaque is inscribed with his name and the phrase 'HE SIMPLY WANTED TO DO THE JOB', the words used by the Chief Constable at the funeral.

Students of the Police Training Centre at Bruche, Warrington, presented the John Egerton Trophy to Greater Manchester Police in order it should be awarded to the officer who performs the bravest act of the year. This trophy is awarded annually by Greater Manchester Police.

Plaque unveiled at Emlyn Street, Farnworth in 2012. (Author's collection)

1986

John Paul O'ROURKE, Constable   **Greater Manchester Police**

Queen's Commendation for Brave Conduct

For tackling and disarming a man who threatened him with an automatic pistol.

L.G. 3/10/1986 Issue 50673 Page 12803

FURTHER INFORMATION:

Location of incident – Longsight, Manchester.

Her Majesty the Queen graciously awarded her Commendation for Brave Conduct to Constable John Paul O'Rourke, 'O' Division (Manchester) for his actions when he pursued and arrested a man who, during the pursuit, tried to discharge a loaded firearm at the officer on three occasions and, in the ensuing struggle, injured him with a screwdriver.

The firearm when later examined, was found to be a 7.65 mm self-loading pistol containing 9 rounds of live ammunition, one round being in the breach. The firing pin was faulty but when replaced enabled the pistol to be test fired. The man was sentenced to 4 years imprisonment at Manchester Crown Court.

(G.M.P. Annual Report 1986)

11ᵗʰ March 1986

William Armistead FRYERS, Constable   **Lancashire Constabulary**

Neil Howard SMITH, Constable   **Lancashire Constabulary**

Queen's Commendation for Brave Conduct

For services leading to the arrest of an armed and violent man.

L.G. 5/8/1987 Issue 51021 Page 9975

FURTHER INFORMATION:

Location of incident – Curwen Avenue, Heysham, Lancashire.

Officers were called to a domestic incident at a house in Heysham where a man had attacked his wife. P.C. Smith entered the property through the front door and P.C. Fryers and P.C. Hutchcraft went to the rear of the property.

As he made his way to the bathroom, P.C. Smith was confronted by the woman, closely followed by her husband. P.C. Smith took hold of the woman and pushed her towards the front door. He was then attacked by the man and stabbed repeatedly. The man was overpowered and arrested. P.C. Smith sustained a severed artery along with head and chest wounds. P.C. Fryers also received a shoulder wound. The wife of the attacker also sustained a punctured lung from a stab wound.

The attacker, Stephen Charlesworth, aged 34 years, appeared at Preston Crown Court in November 1986, where he pleaded guilty to wounding the two officers with intent to resist arrest and to unlawfully wounding his wife, Wendy. The court was told that Charlesworth had been receiving medication treatment for epilepsy, which carried a risk of making him aggressive and violent. Charlesworth was sentenced by Judge Sanderson Temple Q.C. to three years imprisonment.

Commending P.C. Smith, Judge Tempest said, *'In a desperately dangerous situation P.C. Neil Smith, heedless of his own safety, and with outstanding courage, physically placed himself between cold steel and a lady who was the intended victim.'*

Awarded 'William Garnett' Cup.

21ˢᵗ January 1988

Derek Peter MURPHY, Constable   **Merseyside Police**

Kenton Robert OWEN, Constable   **Merseyside Police**

Queen's Gallantry Medal

At 12.20a.m. on Thursday 21ˢᵗ January 1988, Constables Murphy and Owen were on mobile patrol in a police vehicle. They saw a van parked in a public car park with its headlights on, the engine running and the windscreen wipers operating, despite the weather being dry.

The officers decided to investigate. Constable Owen drove the police vehicle to within a few feet of the van stopping in front of it to prevent the van being driven off by the occupant. Both constables alighted from the police vehicle and approached the van to find a man in the driver's seat who appeared to be asleep. Constable Murphy roused the man and began to question him. As the man failed to give a satisfactory account of himself, Constable Owen decided to check the van's registration number through the Police National Computer. Information received revealed a discrepancy between the registration number and the type of vehicle.

When questioned further, the occupant reached into a holdall which was on the front passenger seat. Constable Owen saw him withdraw a sawn-off shotgun. The officer immediately shouted a warning to Constable Murphy. As the man alighted from the van he pointed the gun first at Constable Murphy's stomach, and secondly at Constable Owen's head, in both cases at close range. Constable Murphy, realizing that his colleague was in immediate danger, grappled with the gunman.

A violent struggle took place during which the gun was discharged twice by the gunman, on the first occasion at Constable Owen's head and then at Constable Murphy's stomach, missing both officers. The gunman broke free and ran towards his van. He appeared to be reloading the gun. Constable Owen ran to the police vehicle and drove it towards the gunman, trapping him in the doorway of the van.

When the police car reversed, the gunman attempted to run off, holding the gun. Constable Owen made a further attempt to stop the gunman by driving into him, knocking him to the ground. As the gunman attempted to run off again, Constable Murphy tackled the man, unaware that the gun was now lying on the ground. He was joined by Constable Owen. The man, who was in fact a wanted criminal, was eventually overcome, subdued and taken into police custody. The man was subsequently charged and convicted of a number of serious crimes.

Constables Murphy and Owen displayed gallantry of a high order, in overpowering an armed, violent and highly dangerous man, after he had discharged his weapon at them twice at close range.

L.G. 10/8/1989 Issue 51836 Page 9275

FURTHER INFORMATION:

Location of incident – Car park at Barlow Avenue, Bebington, Merseyside.

The gunman was Andrew Longmire, a serial rapist known as the 'Coronation Street rapist'. He had been the subject of 'Operation Osprey', a protracted investigation, and was later sentenced to life imprisonment for eleven rapes, three attempted rapes, aggravated burglary and firearms offences. Longmire had previously fled from Leeds Railway Station after threatening two British Transport Police officers with a sawn-off shotgun.

He received an additional life sentence in 2010 for a 12th rape, which he had been linked to following a cold case investigation. In 2017, he pleaded guilty to the rape of a 13th girl, who he raped in her own home in Great Lever in January 1982. Judge Timothy Clayson sentenced Longmire to an additional life sentence.

1st August 1988

Yvonne WILSON Mrs, Lately Constable   **Greater Manchester Police**

Queen's Commendation for Brave Conduct

For services in grappling with a robber known to be armed, holding on to him despite his gun being discharged, and assisting in his arrest.

FURTHER INFORMATION:

Her Majesty the Queen graciously awarded her Commendation for Brave Conduct to former Policewoman Yvonne Wilson in recognition of her brave actions on 1st August 1988, when an armed robbery occurred in Chadderton.

The incident involved two men who entered a post office with a double-barrelled sawn-off shotgun and a sledgehammer. Policewoman Constable Wilson, together with a colleague, arrived at the scene shortly after the commission of the offence, and due to good observations, effected the arrest of those responsible, recovering the money intact.

One of the offenders, in an attempt to evade capture, threatened Policewoman Wilson with the sawn-off shotgun which was pointed at her face. Despite this, she bravely grabbed hold of the barrel and managed to hang on to the prisoner until assistance arrived, During the struggle the gun was discharged, fortunately without consequence. A later examination of the weapon revealed that both barrels had been loaded with live cartridges.

(G.M.P. Annual Report 1990)

1989	
David John BRADFORD, Constable	**Greater Manchester Police**
Martin Edward HOULT, Constable	**Greater Manchester Police**
Queen's Commendation for Brave Conduct	

For services in pursuing an armed gunman while on mobile patrol, and in apprehending, disarming and arresting him.

L.G. 10/8/1989 Issue 51836 Page 9276

FURTHER INFORMATION:

Her Majesty the Queen graciously awarded her Commendation for Brave Conduct to Constables David John Bradford and Martin Edward Hoult, both of 'Q' Division (Oldham), for their pursuit of a gunman who had committed an offence of attempted robbery in Wakefield and had escaped in a stolen taxi.

Both officers had been on traffic duty during the early hours when they made contact with the stolen vehicle on the outskirts of Oldham.

A high-speed pursuit then took place during which the stolen vehicle was driven in a reckless and dangerous manner into West Yorkshire.

There, it collided with a wall and the man got out of the vehicle and pointed his pistol directly at Constable Bradford who was approaching to make the arrest. Constable Hoult managed to pull the man's arm away from the direction of his colleague and, following a violent struggle and with the assistance of other officers, the man was eventually arrested and disarmed.

(G.M.P. Annual Report 1989)

For services in seeking out an armed and dangerous man, who had made off after shooting Sergeant Bowden and a fellow officer while they were engaged on routine enquiries at a Motorway Service Station.

On locating the armed man, Sergeant Bowden was shot a second time, sustaining a serious injury. His colleague was found to be dead on arrival at hospital.

L.G. 1/7/1993 Issue 53360 Page 11214

FURTHER INFORMATION:

In the early hours of 14th September 1989, Inspector Raymond Codling, aged 49, in company with Sergeant James Bowden, 45, arrived at Birch Motorway Services between junctions 18 and 19, westbound, on the M62, looking for a white van, the details for which had been circulated by radio.

Insp. Raymond Codling

The officers saw a motorcyclist whom they approached, and he provided them with his details, which later proved to be false. A short time later they saw the man again, acting suspiciously, and the two officers approached him.

Bowden noticed that the man had a large knife in his belt and was holding his right hand inside his jacket. Bowden attempted to seize the knife, but the man pulled back and drew out a 9mm pistol. The man fired almost immediately at Bowden, but he escaped injury as the bullet was fired across his body and was deflected by the thick leather cover of his notebook in a breast pocket.

The man then shot Inspector Codling in the chest as he laid on the ground injured, a second shot was fired, killing him. Bowden attempted to give chase but was hit by a gunshot in the leg and was forced to take cover; he later recovered from emergency surgery. The suspect escaped.

After a manhunt, the gunman, later identified as Anthony Hughes from Baguley, was traced to a garage in Kendray, South Yorkshire. When officers entered they found Hughes' body; he had killed himself with the same gun used in the attack on Codling and Bowden. The gun had been stolen about two years previously from the car of a member of the Diggle Gun Club, near Oldham.

Hughes had previously carried out a series of armed robberies, and had served 15 years in prison for a string of violent offences including robbery, armed robbery, rape and impersonation of a police officer. At the time of the shooting he was wanted by Manchester Police in connection with a further three armed robberies. He had indicated his desire to kill a police officer following an earlier court appearance for a minor offence for which he was fined.

In 1991, a memorial to Raymond Codling was unveiled at Birch Services by Michael Winner, founder of the Police Memorial Trust, and the Home Secretary, Kenneth Baker.

Memorial to Inspector Raymond Codling – Birch Services, M62.
(Author's collection)

11th March 1991

Robert Ian MURRAY, Sergeant   **Greater Manchester Police**

Queen's Commendation for Brave Conduct

For services in disarming and arresting a man armed with a handgun, during an attempted robbery at a bank.

L.G. 15/5/1992 Issue 52922 Page 8408

On Monday 11th March 1991, Sergeant Murray, whilst off duty, was standing in a queue at the National Westminster Bank at Hollinwood Avenue, Chadderton. A man wearing a balaclava mask and carrying a handgun burst into the bank. He ordered the customers to get down on the floor. Sergeant Murray remained calm and told the staff to activate the attack alarm.

The gunman pointed the gun at him and shouted, *'Get down I mean it'*. The gunman turned away briefly, and Sergeant Murray ran across, grabbing the man's head and the gun barrel, forcing the man to the floor.

A violent struggle ensued, and Sergeant Murray got the gun off him without assistance and hit the man with the gun to subdue him. During the struggle, the Sergeant received injuries to his knee. The police arrived shortly afterwards, and the gun was found to be a replica. An 18-year-old youth later appeared before Oldham Magistrates Court in connection with attempted robbery.

Sergeant Murray joined Manchester and Salford Police in July 1972 and was promoted to Sergeant in 1981.

27th December 1992

Leslie Ann HARRISON, Constable   **Merseyside Police**

Terence MALONE, Taxi Driver

David MURRAY, Constable   **Merseyside Police**

Ruth Ann POLHILL, Constable   **Merseyside Police**

Harry James WAGNER, Constable   **Merseyside Police**

Queen's Commendation for Brave Conduct

For services in pursuing a man armed with a knife.

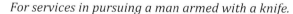

Following a reported burglary, Constable Polhill confronted the suspect and was threatened with a knife. She called for assistance and the suspect ran off pursued by the officer who was shortly joined by her colleagues, Constables Harrison, Murray and Wagner.

A violent struggle took place during which Constable Harrison was stabbed and badly injured. The suspect managed to free himself and ran off, pursued by Constables Murray and Wagner. The Constables found him and closed in and another violent struggle ensued.

At that point Mr Malone, a taxi driver, came upon the scene and stopped to give assistance. He was dragged from his cab by the suspect but managed to get into the rear of the vehicle as it was driven away by the suspect. The taxi was driven a short distance and the suspect then ran off. Mr Malone followed at a distance and was able to point out the suspect to further police officers who subsequently arrested him.

L.G. 30/6/1994 Issue 53720 Page 9471

FURTHER INFORMATION:

Location of incident – Wavertree, Liverpool.

Appearing at Preston Crown Court on 17th March 1994, heroin addict Stephen Doyle, aged 29 years, was convicted of the attempted murder of Constable Leslie Harrison and jailed for 15 years. Earlier he had been convicted of attempting to wound four police officers and a taxi driver as well as attempted burglary and aggravated vehicle taking.

Leslie Harrison required emergency surgery after being stabbed in the chest with a screwdriver, as well as twice in her arm. A surgeon had to cut open her rib cage and thrust a finger into a heart wound to stem the bleeding as she was given a blood transfusion during surgery.

It was revealed that she had previously been injured on two occasions, the first when, in 1990, she was hit over the head whilst patrolling in Toxteth and later sustained a dislocated shoulder after chasing a burglary suspect. (*The Guardian*, 18/3/1994)

The judge, Mrs Justice Smith, told Doyle: *'This was a very determined and very violent attack on a police officer in the execution of her duty. Were it not for a combination of great good luck and superb medical treatment, she would have lost her life.'*

Leslie was unable to return to work and was retired on medical grounds.

1993

Henry Donald MILNER, Q.P.M.
lately Detective Constable   **Greater Manchester Police**

Queen's Commendation for Brave Conduct

For services in attempting to prevent three youths from breaking into a vehicle.

The off-duty officer, whilst grappling with one of the youths, was beaten around the head by his two accomplices armed with staves.

On identifying himself as a Police Officer, one of the youths brandished a gun. Still holding on to one of the youths, the Constable was beaten across the wrist, and forced to loosen his grip.

His wrist was found to be broken. The youths fled but were subsequently captured and charged.

L.G. 2/7/1993 Issue 53360 Page 11215

FURTHER INFORMATION:

Previously awarded the Queen's Police Medal – L.G. 31/12/1990 Issue 52382 Page 26

<table>
<tr><td colspan="2">

26th February 1993

</td></tr>
<tr><td>**John Edward BARLOW, Constable**</td><td>**Greater Manchester Police**</td></tr>
<tr><td>**Paul LAWRENCE, Constable**</td><td>**Greater Manchester Police**</td></tr>
<tr><td>**Andrew Keith MACKAY, Constable**</td><td>**Greater Manchester Police**</td></tr>
<tr><td colspan="2">**Queen's Commendation for Brave Conduct**</td></tr>
</table>

For services in pursuing armed suspects following the wounding of a police constable.

The suspects were travelling at high speed in a car when spotted by Constable MacKay.

He gave chase and in the process two shots were fired by the fleeing suspects, hitting his vehicle. He persisted in his pursuit until his vehicle lost power as a result of damage caused by the two bullets.

Constables Barlow and Lawrence, who were following Constable MacKay, continued the chase and managed to apprehend one of the occupants of the car after it had stopped, and the suspects had attempted to escape on foot.

L.G. 1/7/1994 Issue - 53720 Page 9470

FURTHER INFORMATION:

Location of incident – Trafford Park Manchester and M62 Motorway.

On 25th February 1993, Denis Kinsella, Pairic MacFhloinn and Michael Timmins, three members of an I.R.A. active service unit, entered the gasworks at Winwick Road, Warrington, and planted bombs before leaving in a Mazda van. At 11.55pm that day, P.C. Mark Toker of Cheshire Constabulary saw the van in Sankey Street, Warrington. He stopped the vehicle after it failed to move off from traffic signals, which had changed to green. P.C. Toker breathalysed the driver, Denis Kinsella, with a negative result. When P.C. Toker asked to search the van, Pairic MacFhloinn pulled out a handgun and shot the officer three times.

The van drove off and was abandoned in Lymm where they hijacked a Ford Escort and bundled the driver, Lee Wright, into the boot. The Ford Escort was later sighted in the Trafford Park area and was pursued after it failed to stop for P.C. Mackay and went onto the M62 Motorway, heading towards Liverpool. P.C. Mackay's vehicle was hit twice by shots fired from within the Ford Escort and lost power due to damage to the cooling system. P.C.s Barlow and Lawrence continued the pursuit, which ended after the vehicle was abandoned on the M62 near Irlam after an eight-mile pursuit with speeds up to 90mph being reached. The occupants ran off and Kinsella and MacFhloinn were detained with Timmins escaping. Lee Wright was uninjured.

At approximately 4.10a.m., three bombs went off at the gas works and a gas holder was destroyed, sending a fireball into the sky. A fourth bomb failed to detonate.

Police later raided premises in Nottingham, arresting John Kinsella, the uncle of Denis Kinsella, and a cache of Semtex explosive was recovered. John Kinsella was later convicted of having explosive substances with intent to endanger life and sentenced to 20 years imprisonment. Denis Kinsella and Pairic MacFhloinn were convicted of causing an explosion, attempted murder, kidnapping and possession of firearms and were jailed for 25 and 35 years respectively. All were released early under the terms of the Good Friday Agreement. Michael Timmins was never found. (*Guardian*, 27/2/1993 & 11/2/1994)

Mark Toker was awarded the Queen's Police Medal in the Queen's Birthday honours list in June 1994. (L.G. 11/6/1994 Issue 53696 Page 28)

1995

Brian Rae DORAN, Temporary Inspector   **Greater Manchester Police**

Queen's Commendation for Bravery

For services in chasing a man armed with a knife and gun.

Following an affray during which two shots were discharged and knives produced, police were called. One of the armed men escaped by car, the other tried to run away.

Temporary Inspector Doran was in attendance and saw his officers chasing this second man. He then saw the man attempt to enter a vehicle to drive away. Knowing that the man was armed, he drove his police car in front of the escape vehicle, blocking its exit, the man then ran off. Although the suspect was armed with both a knife and a gun, Temporary Inspector Doran did not hesitate to follow the man on foot. He saw the man throw away the knife and then heard the sound of the gun being discharged.

He continued to pursue the man and at one point the man stopped and turned and at about 10 yards distance directly threatened him with the gun. The chase continued until they both entered a cul-de-sac and he saw the suspect drop the gun. He immediately moved to retrieve the weapon. However, the suspect having realised that there was no exit from the street also rushed to recover his weapon and succeeded in doing so.

Temporary Inspector Doran was again directly threatened but was saved from any further exposure to danger by the arrival of armed colleagues.

L.G. 30/6/1995 Issue 54088 Page 9054

FURTHER INFORMATION:

In court the judge commented, *'I should like to place on record my view that Sergeant Doran acted with courage, pertinacity and judgement, in seeking to arrest a man with what proved to be a loaded pistol.'*

Sergeant Doran was awarded the John Egerton Trophy.

1997

Malcolm James BECK, Constable   **Greater Manchester Police**

Queen's Commendation for Bravery

For services in the arrest of an armed suspect.

Constable Beck was on mobile patrol with a colleague when he saw two youths fighting and decided to investigate. He approached the youths to stop them fighting. On doing this one of the youths became extremely violent towards him.

As Constable Beck attempted to restrain him, the youth started to lash out and then pulled a knife and stabbed Constable Beck in the lower abdomen.

Initially Constable Beck thought that he had been punched but soon realised he had been stabbed. Despite this, he continued to hold onto his assailant, and radioed for assistance. Both men then fell to the floor and the struggle continued. The other youth then started to kick both Constable Beck and the assailant he was holding. Within minutes of Constable Beck's radio call for assistance other officers arrived and both youths were arrested.

L.G. 14/11/1997 Issue 54948 Page 12820

FURTHER INFORMATION:

Location of incident – Ashton-under-Lyne.

P.C. Beck received emergency surgery at Tameside Hospital and was off work for nine months.

The offender was jailed for four years and 6 months for wounding with intent and a three-year concurrent sentence for stabbing the man P.C. Beck tried to rescue. This man was also charged with attacking P.C. Beck but was cleared on a technicality.

Constable Beck was awarded the John Egerton Trophy.

1ˢᵗ January 1998	
Peter Chalkley SMITH, Inspector	**Greater Manchester Police**
Stephen John BENTLEY, Constable	**Greater Manchester Police**
Paul David HEAP, Constable	**Greater Manchester Police**
Queen's Commendation for Bravery	

For their actions in chasing and arresting a man armed with a sawn-off shotgun.

On 1ˢᵗ January 1998 at 12.30a.m. police officers attended a public house where a fight had broken out between a number of people.

Whilst they were trying to restore order at the scene they heard shouting that someone had a gun, followed by a gunshot from outside. Constable Heap looked out of the door and saw two men running towards the pub. One was chasing the other brandishing a sawn-off shotgun.

Constable Heap went back inside to inform his colleagues and warn the people in the building to take cover, and then looked back outside to see a number of people struggling with each other. There followed another gunshot and then the man being chased stumbled into the pub with a gunshot wound to his hand. At this Constable Heap, accompanied by Inspector Smith and Constable Bentley, left the premises and chased the gunman who had run off down the road with two other men.

On reaching a nearby junction, the men stopped and appeared to struggle with each other. The gunman then turned and levelled the shotgun at the pursuing officer, shouting for them to leave him alone. He then ran on with the other two men running off in other directions. All three police officers continued to chase the gunman and he again turned and pointed the shotgun at the officers shouting for them to leave him alone. He continued to run, and the officers followed at a close distance.

Soon afterwards the gunman entered an alleyway and stopped outside the entrance to a shop. He again turned and faced the police officers, shouting that if they did not leave him along he would shoot them. The officers continued to approach, and Constable Heap was able to strike him on the head with his baton, whilst Constable Bentley fired CS spray in his face.

Inspector Smith grabbed the gunman and managed to wrestle the gun from his grip. The three officers then successfully restrained and arrested him.

L.G. 23/3/2000 Issue 55799 Page 3342

FURTHER INFORMATION:

Location of incident – Toll Bar public house, Droylsden, Manchester.

The offender appeared at Manchester Crown Court charged with attempted murder, threats to kill and numerous firearms offences and was jailed for 12 years.

All three officers were awarded the John Egerton Trophy.

1998

Julia Vanessa BROWN, Constable   **Greater Manchester Police**

Queen's Commendation for Bravery

For services in confronting and disarming a woman with a knife.

Constable Brown and two other colleagues were called to an incident involving a woman who was drunk and in an agitated state, and who was threatening (with a petrol can and matches in her hand) to burn down her neighbour's house, Constable Brown and her colleagues restrained and managed to calm down the woman.

Constable Brown's colleagues were then called to another incident leaving her with the woman (then calm and lying on the ground). The woman became agitated again, got up and returned to her house where she picked up a knife and threatened to kill herself.

Constable Brown managed to grab the woman's wrist and force her to let go of the knife. The woman then ran into the kitchen and picked up another knife and walked into the rear garden.

As Constable Brown followed, trying to persuade the woman to drop the knife, the woman threatened the Constable, turned and stabbed her. Constable Brown's body armour took the force of the strike (though she suffered a fractured rib) and during the ensuing violent struggle Constable Brown managed to force the woman to release the knife.

The woman struggled free and ran back into her house followed closely by Constable Brown who wished to prevent another attack. At that stage Constable Brown was joined by further officers who assisted her in the arrest of the woman.

L.G. 3/4/1998 Issue 55087 Page 3858

7th November 1999

Paul ANDERSON, Police Constable   **Greater Manchester Police**

Queen's Commendation for Bravery

For his actions in chasing a man armed with a handgun.

Constable Anderson and a colleague attended an amusement arcade in response to a call that an armed robbery had just taken place. As the constables walked towards the entrance, they saw two men walking away who appeared to have just left the arcade.

P.C. Anderson approached them and asked them to stop. However, the two men broke into a run and as they did so, one of them removed a handgun from inside his jacket, pointed it at P.C. Anderson and told him to *'back off'*.

The two men then ran off with P.C. Anderson in pursuit. As the two suspects reached the junction with a side road the man with the gun raised his hand and fired two shots into the air about 12 paces from P.C. Anderson. The gun flash and the sounds of the shots were very clear. The men ran into a side road where P.C. Anderson momentarily lost sight of them but continued to give chase. As he turned the corner, he saw them enter a car park and run towards a parked car.

The armed man then turned towards P.C. Anderson and without warning fired at him, Anderson stopped, and the suspects got into the vehicle and drove off at speed. P.C. Anderson gave chase on foot until he lost sight of the vehicle. The men were later arrested and only then was the gun found to be loaded with blank cartridges.

L.G. 10/7/2000 issue 55909 Page 7551

FURTHER INFORMATION:

The amusement arcade was Nobles Amusements, Newport Street, Bolton. The getaway car was sighted by another officer who attempted to stop the vehicle on Bradshawgate. The vehicle was driven at up to 90mph on Manchester Road before being abandoned. At one stage one of the occupants pointed the gun out of the car window at the pursuing police vehicle. The robber was later identified from fingerprints left behind in the vehicle and on a car park ticket left inside.

In May 1999, Bryan Cooney (25) of Oatland Heights, Little London, Leeds, pleaded guilty to armed robbery and possession of an imitation firearm.

Judge Bruce Macmillan praised P.C. Anderson for his bravery and Iris Eden, one of the staff members, who secretly operated the alarm, delayed handing over money and manoeuvred the robber so his appearance could be recorded on CCTV.

Constable Anderson was awarded the John Egerton Trophy.

14th January 2003

Stephen Robin OAKE (deceased), Detective Constable   **Greater Manchester Police**

Queen's Gallantry Medal

Un-named Detective Sergeant   **Greater Manchester Police**

Queen's Commendation for Bravery

For their actions in tackling a man brandishing a knife in Manchester.

On 14th January 2003, a number of police and immigration officers attended a house, converted into flats, in Manchester to execute immigration warrants. They also possessed a search warrant under the Prevention of Terrorism Act.

Three men were found in the flat. Various checks were made, which took over an hour, and during this time the men were calm. After the verification process, the three men were arrested on suspicion of terrorism and preparations were made to secure any forensic evidence. Two suspects were in the bedroom with Detective Constable Oake when one of them made a determined attempt to escape.

4 Crumpsall Lane, Crumpsall, Manchester.
(Author's collection)

He punched the police officer standing in the doorway, ran past him into the kitchen where he acquired a knife, then he moved back towards the bedroom where he slashed out with the weapon.

Detective Constable Oake was repeatedly stabbed in the frenzied attack and was locked with the suspect for several minutes. He called out that the suspect had a knife and that he needed help. The Detective Sergeant attempted to assist Detective Constable Oake and was stabbed in the upper left arm.

He nevertheless decided to go forward a second time in an attempt to restrain the suspect. He managed to punch the man in the face but was stabbed once more. He was then pulled away from the suspect and other police officers eventually overpowered the man.

The suspect was found guilty of murder (22 years), two counts of attempted murder (15 years) and wounding with intent (8 years). All sentences to run concurrently.

L.G. 6/1/2009 Issue 58940 Page 115

FURTHER INFORMATION:

Location of incident – 4 Crumpsall Lane, Crumpsall, North Manchester.

Stephen Robin Oake was born at Poynton, Cheshire, on 21st April 1962 and joined Greater Manchester Police on 23rd July 1984. He served in the South Manchester Division until 1999, when he transferred to the Special Branch. In 2002, he was commended for his professional skills and expertise.

His father, Robin Oake, was a former Chief Constable of the Isle of Man Constabulary and holder of the Queen's Police Medal. A memorial is erected at Crumpsall Lane, Manchester, near to where he was killed and a street in Manchester was renamed 'Stephen Oake Close' in his memory.

Stephen Oake (aged 40) was a married man with three children.

His killer, Algerian illegal immigrant Kamel Bourgass, was later also convicted of conspiracy to commit a public nuisance by using poisons or explosives for which he was sentenced to an additional 17 years imprisonment.

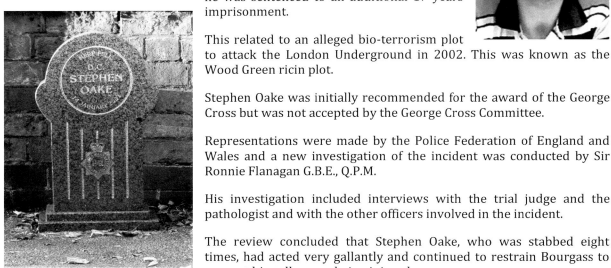

This related to an alleged bio-terrorism plot to attack the London Underground in 2002. This was known as the Wood Green ricin plot.

Stephen Oake was initially recommended for the award of the George Cross but was not accepted by the George Cross Committee.

Representations were made by the Police Federation of England and Wales and a new investigation of the incident was conducted by Sir Ronnie Flanagan G.B.E., Q.P.M.

His investigation included interviews with the trial judge and the pathologist and with the other officers involved in the incident.

The review concluded that Stephen Oake, who was stabbed eight times, had acted very gallantly and continued to restrain Bourgass to prevent his colleagues being injured.

Memorial to Stephen Oake, at 4 Crumpsall Lane, Crumpsall, Manchester. (Author's collection)

A revised submission resulted in the posthumous award of the Queen's Gallantry Medal.

22ⁿᵈ October 2004

Geoffrey Arnold HINCE, Constable   **Greater Manchester Police**

Queen's Commendation for Bravery

For his actions in tackling two robbers during a raid on a Post Office in Salford.

In October 2004 in the middle of the afternoon, Constable Hince was off duty and driving in Salford when he noticed two men wearing balaclavas, enter a Post Office.

One man was carrying a machete and the second man held a pick-axe. Constable Hince stopped his car and ran into the Post Office shouting *'Police'*. There were two members of staff in the shop at the time.

He ran towards one man and punched him in the face, knocking him down. The second man moved behind a screen, acting in a threatening manner and then attacked Constable Hince injuring him in several places on his arm and hand. The two employees joined in the fracas. A struggle ensued, and the man fell backwards onto the floor.

He was held down by Constable Hince, with the assistance of the employees. The other man joined in the affray. Constable Hince kicked out at him and he dropped the pickaxe and fled. The first robber was restrained for a few minutes until uniformed officers arrived at the scene.

The robber was sentenced to six and a half years and a further 12 months on recall of licence.

L.G. 7/2/2006 Issue 57894 Page 1745

FURTHER INFORMATION:

Location of incident – Adelphi Post Office, Oldfield Road, Salford.

One of the attackers was sentenced to six-and-a-half years in a young offenders' institution for robbery and wounding with intent to resist arrest.

Constable Hince was awarded the John Egerton Trophy and was awarded the annual National Police Federation Bravery Award, presented by Prince Charles. He was also commended by the Chief Constable.

4th July 2005

Paul LEIGH, Sergeant 582   **Lancashire Constabulary**

Lukmaan MULLA, Constable 3132   **Lancashire Constabulary**

Queen's Gallantry Medal

For their actions in dealing with a man wielding a firearm and other explosive devices.

During the early afternoon in July 2005, Constable Mulla and two colleagues attended an address in Rawtenstall, Lancashire to question a man following a complaint of harassment by a local woman.

The officers decided that a forced entry was necessary and an enforcer[52] was requested by radio. Sergeant Leigh arrived with the enforcer and Constable Mulla, with his colleague, forced open the door and entered the house. As the first officer approached the foot of the stairs he could see the suspect standing at the top holding a firearm. The man immediately raised the gun and shot the officer and discharged other shots out of the window which damaged vehicles.

Both officers retreated, and the injured officer collapsed at the side of the house. Sergeant Leigh realised that his colleague was badly injured, so he crossed the line of fire to give him support. The suspect then threw two lighted petrol bombs from a rear window which set a shed alight. Sergeant Leigh remained with his fallen colleague and a further two shots were fired.

Constable Mulla recognised the need for a first aid kit, which he obtained from a vehicle, and he too crossed through the line of fire to offer more help to the injured officer. After a while the Armed Response Unit arrived, rescued the injured officer and took control.

They were attempting a limited entry of the premises when they heard three more shots, so they kept the premises under observation. The man and his dog were found dead in the house the following morning.

L.G. 16/1/2007 Issue 58220 Page 533

L.G. 6/7/2007 Issue 58385 Page 9754 (Correction of first name for P.C. Mulla)

---

[52]   The enforcer is a hand-held steel battering ram used to break through doors.

Location of incident – Hardman Avenue, Rawtenstall, Lancashire.

The gunman was Stephen Hensby, aged 54 years, who had been involved in a long-standing dispute over eviction following the death of his mother. The wounded Constable was David Lomas.

Other officers involved in the incident were P.C. 989 Philip Bayliss, P.C. 1634 Peter Corser, P.S. 242 Wendy Jacobs and P.C. 421 Kevin Jones.

All officers involved in the incident were jointly awarded the 'William Garnett' Cup.

9th June 2012

Claire Louise MURPHY, Constable　　　　　　　　　　　**Greater Manchester Police**

Queen's Gallantry Medal

For saving the life of a woman who had fallen into a river.

On 9th June 2012, a 56-year-old woman was walking with two children aged 5 and 11 years respectively and their dog along the banks of the River Irwell in Salford. The river at the time was in full flow and the water level higher than normal due to heavy rainfall. One of the children threw the dog's ball into the river and the dog jumped into the river to retrieve it. However, due to the fast flow of the river and a steep vertical drop of some 2.5 metres from the river bank, the dog was unable to get out and became increasingly distressed in its failure to reach safety.

The woman leaned on a nearby branch and attempted to rescue her dog but the branch broke and she fell into the river. She too was unable to climb out and reach the safety of the riverbank. Fortunately, she managed to grasp some weeds and scrubs at the side of the bank and got a foothold keeping her head above water. The eldest child ran to get help. P.C. Murphy arrived at the scene and immediately summoned rescue services. She reassured the woman that help was on its way and encouraged her to hold on. She attempted to pass her utility belt as a safety line, but the woman was unable to reach it. With the river in full flow against her, the woman's grasp was weakening, her head going underwater several times.

She was struggling to retain her hold and there was a real risk of her being swept away. P.C. Murphy therefore took the decision to jump into the river to save her. She held the woman using her right arm, held onto a protruding rock with the other hand and wedged her foot against something in the river. To exacerbate the situation the foothold of the woman then gave way. She was pulled away leaving her with neither a foothold nor the clutch of weeds and just being held by the police officer. P.C. Murphy remained calm and continued to reassure the woman that help was on its way and she would be rescued.

P.C. Murphy knowingly put herself in an extremely dangerous, life threatening situation and displayed courage throughout the ordeal and her actions probably saved the woman's life. Due to the force and speed of the water, had either woman become detached from the river banking it is likely they would have been lost downstream. Throughout the incident she remained calm despite knowing that both her own and the woman's lives were at risk. She continually held on, despite the force of the river against her and showed great determination and resilience.

L.G. 11/12/2013 Issue 60713 Page 24589

FURTHER INFORMATION:

Location of incident – River Irwell, Agecroft, Salford.

The woman rescued was Mrs Lesley Coban (56), who had attempted to rescue her Staffordshire Bull Terrier 'Turk'. Turk also survived.

Appendix 1

The Tottenham Outrage

The Tottenham Outrage – Saturday, 23rd January 1909

At 10:30a.m. on Saturday 23rd January 1909, at the Schnurmann rubber factory at Chesnut Road, Tottenham, Albert Keyworth, a clerk, returned to the factory with the weekly payroll in gold, silver and copper coins. He returned there having been driven to the bank and back in the factory owner's car by the chauffeur, Joseph Wilson. On returning to the factory, Keyworth was grabbed from behind by Joseph Lepidus, a Latvian anarchist. Keyworth kept hold of the bag and both fell to the ground, with Lepidus attempting to throttle him in order that he would release his grip on the money bag. Joseph Wilson then came to assist and dragged Lepidus off Keyworth.

At this moment Paul Helfeld, the second Latvian robber, joined in running up to Wilson, firing several shots which all hit Wilson, but due to his heavy layers of clothing caused no injury and failed to penetrate. Upon Lepidus regaining his upright position, he fired once at Keyworth but the shot missed. Both men were armed with modern automatic pistols.

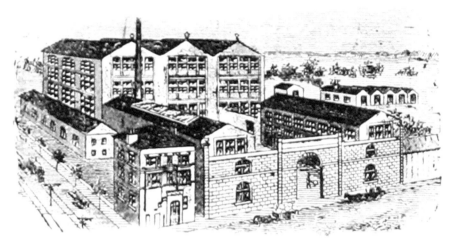

Schnurmann rubber factory, Chesnut Road, Tottenham.

Passing at the time was George Smith, a stoker at Hornsey Gasworks, who, hearing the commotion, tackled Lepidus as he left the factory area, bringing him to the ground. Whilst struggling on the ground, Smith was shot twice by Helfeld, in the head and in the collar bone, but survived. Tottenham Police Station was very near and, on hearing the shots, around 30 officers emerged in various stages of undress. Tottenham Police Station had a section house where single officers lived when not on duty. Two police officers, Constables Tyler and Newman, heard the shots and ran to the location of the noise.

The two gunmen ran from the scene, pursued by Tyler on foot and Newman with Wilson now back in his motor car, which also now contained the factory owner, Keyworth and another employee. By this time, two other constables, Bond and Fraser, had been alerted to the situation and joined the chase, along with further officers.

The car containing Wilson, Constable Newman and the others sped towards Helfeld and Lepidus. The driver, Wilson, had been encouraged by Newman to try to run them over. The car attracted a hail of bullets from the two men, wounding Wilson slightly. The car crashed, causing injury to those inside. Inadvertently caught up in the hail of bullets, a 10-year-old baker's delivery boy, Ralph John Joscelyne, was hit. He had been hiding behind a parked car after being frightened by the gunfire. He died in the arms of a bystander before he could be taken to hospital.

By this time, all those on foot had arrived at the scene where the motor car had crashed, and Constable Bond borrowed a small revolver from a member of the crowd and discharged four shots at the fleeing Lepidus and Helfeld, but all missed. (Firearms ownership was less strictly controlled than in modern times.)

Helfeld and Lepidus both headed towards a railway footbridge leading to Tottenham Marshes. In an attempt to cut them off, Constables Tyler and Newman ran across waste ground, out of sight of the armed offenders and protected by a high fence, and ended up with Tyler coming face-to-face with Helfeld and Lepidus as they ran out from the other side of the fence. Constable Tyler shouted, *'Come on, give in, the game's up.'* Helfeld took careful aim and shot Tyler through the head. Constable Newman stayed with Tyler and helped move him to a nearby private house, awaiting an ambulance. Five minutes after being admitted to hospital, Tyler was pronounced dead.

By this time, officers from all nearby stations were converging on Tottenham Marshes, some armed and others not. Lepidus and Helfeld had been forced to turn towards the River Lea. While they were searching for a crossing place, a number of civilian bystanders joined in the chase but were wounded.

The robbers crossed the river, and on arriving at a bridge, they rested and fired more shots at their civilian pursuers, injuring two more. Constable Nicod arrived on the scene, unobserved by the two fugitives. He crawled forward with a revolver, which failed to fire. He was noticed by Helfeld and Lepidus and was shot in the left thigh and leg. The two continued to be chased before being confronted by Sidney Slater, a horse keeper, who was fired at several times and disabled.

Constable Spedding also caught up and fired four shots from a borrowed revolver at the fleeing Lepidus and Helfeld, but all missed. Helfeld and Lepidus crossed a traveller encampment, firing at several people but caused no injuries. At Salisbury Farm the two rested, still pursued by civilians and police, and here William Roker was shot in the legs by Lepidus. The farmyard abutted Chingford Road, along which the Walthamstow Urban District Council trams ran. Lepidus then jumped onto a passing tram.

The driver was forced to stop the tram at gunpoint in order that Helfeld could catch up and board. The driver, Joseph Slow, managed to run off and hid on the upper deck. The conductor, Charles Wyatt, was forced to drive the tram with a gun pressed to his cheek with Helfeld exchanging fire with the pursuers.

The police commandeered another tram, and it was boarded by about 40 officers. Further along the road, the tram containing Helfeld and Lepidus was in danger of being overtaken by a horse-drawn carriage driven by Constables Williams and Hawkins, who attempted to shoot at the tram, but crashed after Helfeld shot the horse.

Edward Loveday (aged 63), a passenger on the tram, attempted to rescue Wyatt and was shot in the throat by Lepidus. Wyatt was told to stop and both robbers then jumped off the tram. They then stole a milk cart, shooting its driver, George Conyard, in the chest and arm as he attempted to stop them. They drove the cart along Farnham Road into Forest Road, where it crashed while negotiating a bend. Abandoning the milk cart, Helfeld and Lepidus hijacked another horse and cart, with Lepidus riding the animal and Helfeld firing into the large crowd of people in pursuit, made up of a number of police and civilians, some armed, and some on foot, with other riding bicycles and in cars.

The pursuing crowd was led by a motor car containing Constables Shakespeare and Gibbs, driven by Frederick Williams and also carrying Thomas Brown, armed with a double-barrel shotgun, who was exchanging fire with Helfeld and Lepidus. Sergeant Howitt and Constable Francis, hearing shots and police whistles, attempted to stop the horse and cart but retreated to cover after being fired upon several times. However, the officers caused the horse and cart to swerve and crash.

After abandoning the horse and cart, Helfeld and Lepidus fled. Lepidus climbed over a six-foot fence, leaving Helfeld behind. As the crowd neared Helfeld's position, he shot himself in the right eye, but survived the initial injury and was taken to the Prince of Wales Hospital. He died on 12th February.

Constable Ziething caught up with Lepidus, and was fired at several times by the fugitive, but the bullets passed through his clothing and into a civilian, Frederick Mortimer. Lepidus ran and was hidden from sight by a row of cottages. The end cottage was occupied by Charles Rolstone and his family; Mr Rolstone was out at work. Mrs Rolstone, attracted by the noise outside, came out, leaving her sons inside. A policeman ran past, ordering her inside and telling her to lock the doors. On returning she found the doors locked and through the window she saw a blood-stained man inside.

A crowd now assembled outside. Lepidus was seen at an upstairs window and a fusillade of shots followed. He was called upon to surrender but continued firing. Realising that Lepidus was upstairs, Constable Dewhurst and Charles Shaffer, who had been involved in the chase from the start, forced open a downstairs door and rescued the children inside. Sergeant Hart then searched the downstairs with the family dog which he sent upstairs.

Constable Eagles armed himself with a borrowed civilian pistol, climbed a ladder placed at the back of the cottage and opened a bedroom window. While looking through the window, Constable Eagles saw Lepidus point his firearm directly at him, but the officer could not operate his borrowed weapon due to the safety catch being faulty. Eagles rapidly climbed back down to the ground and was joined by Constables Dixon and Cater and Inspector Gould, who were all armed.

Four men then entered the house, namely P.C. Eagles, P.C. Dixon, P.C. Cater and Thomas Brown, a civilian. On opening the door to the stairs, P.C. Dixon called upon Lepidus to surrender but there was no reply. On ascending the stairs to a small landing, they saw feet under the closed bedroom door facing towards them. Eagles fired twice and Cater once through the door. This was followed by a shot inside the room.

Grave of P.C. Tyler, Abney Park Cemetery, Stoke Newington. (© Mike Higginbottom)

On entering the room, they found Lepidus bleeding from a wound to his right temple. Lepidus was carried out and was dead within minutes. Autopsy results would reveal that the calibre of bullet which killed the anarchist did not match either Cater's or Eagles's firearms, and that Lepidus had killed himself with his own weapon.

Grave of P.C. Tyler, Abney Park Cemetery, Stoke Newington. (© Mike Higginbottom)

The three officers risked their lives in an attempt to arrest this man, knowing that he had already killed two persons, including a police officer.

The official report lists 7 wounded police officers and 17 wounded civilians.

The chase took place over two and a half hours, covering a distance of around six and a half miles. It is estimated that around 1,000 members of the public were involved and 100 police officers. The robbers had fired around 400 shots.

P.C. William Frederick Tyler was aged 31 years at the time of his death and was stationed at Tottenham Police Station. He lived with his wife, Emily, at Arnold Road in Tottenham. They married in 1903 but had no children.

At the funeral of P.C. Tyler, no fewer than 3,000 policemen were in the procession and there were 500,000 people on the two and half mile route between P.C. Tyler's home in Arnold Road, Tottenham, and Abney Park Cemetery. The other victim, Ralph Joscelyne, was buried at the same time in a grave near that of P.C. Tyler.

Never before had there been such a widespread demonstration of deep public sorrow at a police funeral. The blinds of all the houses on route had been closely drawn and shops were closed for the day with black shutters put up as a sign of mourning. Flags were lowered to half-mast, and mourning cards were being sold to members of the public.

The country was shocked at this incident, and the Commissioner of Police, Sir Edward Henry, pressed the Home Secretary, Mr H.J. Gladstone, to reward the officers involved. In due course, a recommendation was placed before His Majesty, King Edward VII for an award to be created.

Grave of P.C. Tyler, Abney Park Cemetery, Stoke Newington.
(© Mike Higginbottom)

This award was to become the King's Police Medal. The first officers awarded the medal were those singled out for their actions during the Tottenham Anarchist Outrage, namely Constables John William Cater, Charles Dixon and Charles Eagles.

All three officers were promoted to the rank of Sergeant and awarded ten pounds from the Bow Street Reward Fund and were presented with a medal from the Carnegie Hero Trust.

There was no recognition of the gallantry of P.C. Tyler. His widow, Emily, was granted a pension of £15 per year. A public appeal raised £1,055 but the money was invested, and she was only permitted to receive the interest from it.

The robbers, Jacob Lepidus and Paul Helfeld, were born in Riga, Latvia, which was then in Russian control. It is generally believed the names are false identities. It is recorded that both were living in Paris in 1907, when the brother of Jacob Lepidus was killed when attempting to assassinate the French President. This occurred when the bomb he was carrying exploded prematurely.

Anticipating police attention, Lepidus and Helfeld fled to Scotland, where they lived until their money ran out, when they headed for London. Both were members of an anarchist organisation originating in Russia and other revolutionary organisations. It is believed both had criminal records in Latvia.

Appendix 2

Liverpool City Police Gallantry award winners

1940 - 1941

LIVERPOOL CITY POLICE

Members of the Force Decorated for Gallantry during Enemy Action over Liverpool,
1940-1941

Con. 272E Young (Commendation)	Con. 215H Tarbuck (B.E.M.)	Con. 413R Gardier (P.W.R., E Div.) (B.E.M.)	Sgt. 17E Blackburn (Commendation)	Con. 294K Cameron (Commendation)	Con. 529R Lewis (P.W.R., B Div.) (Commendation)	Con. 327H Hunter (B.E.M.)	Con. 289E Roughley (Commendation)	Sgt. 36A Claydon (G.M.)
	Con. 100B Morrisey (Commendation).	Con. 139A Crann (G.M.)	Con. 52E Murphy (B.E.M.)	Con. 347A Gren (G.M.)	Con. 17E Spicer (G.M.)	Con. 656R Davies (P.W.R., B Div.) (G.M.)	Con. 164E Metcalfe (Commendation)	
Sgt. 28B Carson (Commendation).		Con. 243A Baker (G.M.)	Chief Supt. Nichols. formerly (Supt. E Div.) (G.M.)	Insp. Black (B.E.M.)	Sgt. 11E Smith (G.M.)	Sgt. 26E Watson (Commendation)	Con. 258A Symington (B.E.M.)	
Con. 264B Green (G.M.)	Sgt. 7E Collins (G.M.)	Sgt. 19A Garland (G.M.)	Mr. T. M. Skelton (C.C. of Hyde), formerly (Insp. E Div.), (B.E.M. and Bar)	Con. 66E Gannaway (B.E.M.)	Con. 413R Gardier			

SEPTEMBER, 1944

361

Appendix 3

The William Garnett Cup winners

Year	The William Garnett Cup Award Winner(s)	National award					
		GC	GM	KC QC	BEM	KPM QPM	QGM
1930	P.S. 656 John Henry BARBER P.C. 563 Thomas Edward BRADBURN						
1931	P.S. 1697 COLLINS P.C. 1489 WELCH						
1932	P.C. 180 Herbert HAYES					★	
1933	No award made						
1934	P.C. 382 Edward HALLIDAY P.C. 1950 Richard ROBINSON					★	
1935	P.C. 33 William BENSON						
1936	P.C. 1975 James Trott BELL					★	
1937	P.C. 1996 Stanley DOBSON					★	
1938	Inspector Harry WILD					★	
1939	P.C. 2190 Jack JEAVONS					★	
1940 – 1948	No awards made						
1949	P.C. 1365 COOPER						
1950	P.S. 863 John Robert LEACH					★	
1951 – 1953	No awards made						
1954	P.C. 2301 Andrew WHIGHAM			★			
1955	P.C. 811 WESTHEAD						
1956	P.C. 259 HORNBY P.C. 839 SMITH						
1957	P.S. 2362 KENYON						
1958	P.C. 365 CLARK						
1959	D.C. 1670 David MANDER						
1960	No award made						
1961	P.S. 2394 HARRISON				★		
1962	P.S. 2388 WALLWORK P.C. 225 FLEMING			★			
1963	P.C. 2107 LEWIS P.C. 769 HUGHES				★		
1964	P.C. 1206 ROGERSON						
1965	P.C. 10 BUCK				★		
1966	D.S. 916 MOORES P.C. 2939 HUGHES				★		
1967	P.C. 2482 FORREST			★			

Year	Name						
1968	P.C. 1172 ASHWORTH						
1969	PC 1375 WESTHEAD						
1970	D.S. 4711 MATHEWS						
1971	Superintendent RICHARDSON	★					
1972	P.S. 1930 STILL P.C. 5727 DEAN			★			
1973	P.C. 2363 RAINFORD						
1974	P.C. 1826 ATKINSON						
1975	Inspector William DUNCAN						
1976	P.S. 3086 GREEN P.C. 3545 PEERS						
1977	P.C. 324 HELM P.C. 5865 John WILSON						★ ★
1978	D.C. 25 LEVER W.P.C. 6110 BARTRAM			★ ★			
1979	P.C. 5865 John WILSON.						
1980	P.C. 1167 HARRISON W.P.C 6196 WRIGHT			★ ★			
1981	W.P.C. 6189 EDDOWES						
1982	P.S. 627 SUMNER P.C. 2966 SMITH						
1983	W.P.C. 6133 BRADLEY P.C. 562 CONNOLLY P.C. 1956 MORRISON P.C. 253 ABRAM			★			
1984	No award made						
1985	P.C. 457 ECKERSLEY						
1986	P.C. 318 SMITH			★			
1987	P.C. 985 LOWE						
1988	P.C. 2022 SWINDELLS P.C. 1489 MEADOWS P.C. 1720 COTTAM						
1989	D.S. 1870 FISH P.S. 1808 RAE P.C. 1144 CHAMBERS						
1990	P.C. 552 BARBER						
1991	P.C. 301 WHITEHEAD						
1992	P.C. 6043 McKEAN						
1993	P.S. 541 BLEZARD						
1994	P.C. 1678 ROBERTS						
1995	D.C. 6126 PEEL D.C. 2506 NISBET						
1996	P.C. 2392 KHAN						
1997	No award made						

Year		GC	GM	KC/QC	KPM/QPM	QGM	
1998	Inspector ARMITAGE P.C. 2006 YOUNG						
1999	D.C. 1251 LALONDE P.C. 1766 MILNES P.C. 2079 BENTLEY						
2000	P.C. 165 Paul HARRISON P.C. 470 Steve MILLER						
2001	P.C. 1161 David BOWER P.C. 811 Julian BRASSINGTON P.C. 2540 Matthew LEIGH						
2002	No award made						
2003	D.C. 2174 Ian LAWRENCE						
2004	P.C. 2565 Neil COOKSON						
2005	P.S. 582 Paul LEIGH P.C. 3132 Lukmaan MULLA P.C. 3856 David LOMAS P.C. 989 Philip BAYLISS P.C. 1634 Peter CORSER P.S. 242 Wendy JACOBS P.C. 421 Kevin JONES						★ ★
2006	P.C. 3862 James SADDOO P.C. 3584 Victoria WILSON						
2007	P.S. 2035 Mark PASS P.C. 2762 Nathan JONES P.C. 2562 Frank SMITH						
2008	No award made						
2009	P.C. 4004 Katie JOHNSON P.C. 1494 Ian TINSLEY						
2010	No award made						
2011	P.C. 479 Marc RIGBY P.C. 2629 Ian McGINTY						
2012	D.C. 2455 Kim CARBUTT P.S. 2353 Rick FRITH						
2013	P.C. 3729 Dave PINNINGTON						
2014	D.C. 1373 Karen KENWORTHY D.S. 145 Damian McALISTER						
2015	P.C. 3253 Martin COX P.C. 2988 Darren EDWARDS P.C. 1450 Lee BROWN P.C. 2411 Louise POINTER P.C. 4232 Helen BLACKBURN						
2016	P.C. 4452 Ben BARNES						
2017	P.C. 2621 Peter LUCAS P.C. 3656 Gary HOLLIDAY P.C. 2076 Peter BLACK						

GC   = George Cross
GM   = George Medal
KC/QC = King's/Queen's Commendation for Brave Conduct
KPM/QPM = King's Police Medal / Queen's Police medal (for Gallantry)
QGM   = Queen's Gallantry Medal

Appendix 4

The John Egerton Trophy winners

The John Egerton Trophy winners

Year	The John Egerton Trophy winners	Further information
1983	P.C. Alan SHAW	
1984	P.C. Bob SALMON	
1985	No award made	
1986	P.C. Neil MURRAY	
1987	P.C. John O'ROURKE	Awarded Queen's Commendation for Brave Conduct
1988	P.C. Graham HOLLINGSWORTH	
1989	A/D.S. Joe HENNIGAN	
1990	P.C. LE CHEMINANT	
1991	No award made	
1992	P.C. Chris GAINES	
1993	P.C. Peter MORRIS	
1994	P.S. Brian DORAN	Awarded Queen's Commendation for Brave Conduct
1995	P.W. Angela DAWSON	
1996	No award made	
1997	P.C. Malcolm BECK	Awarded Queen's Commendation for Brave Conduct
1998	P.C. David SMITH	
1999	Inspector Peter SMITH P.C. Paul HEAP P.C. Stephen BENTLEY	Awarded Queen's Commendation for Brave Conduct
2000	P.C. Paul ANDERSON	Awarded Queen's Commendation for Brave Conduct
2001	P.C. Michael DAVIES P.C. Steve LAMBERT P.C. Steve JONES	
2002	D.C. Andrew EVANS	
2003	P.C. Stephen CHARVILL P.C. Martin WARD	
2004	P.C. Andrew HALLSWORTH	
2005	P.C. Jason WILLIAMS	
2006	P.C. Geoff HINCE	Awarded Queen's Commendation for Brave Conduct
2007	P.W. Claire TITTERINGTON P.C. Stephen WORRALL	
2008	No award made	

2009	S.C. Paul CHALLIS P.S. Stuart CHARLESWORTH S/Insp Simon JONES P.C. Alastair JONES	
2010	P.C. Paul CHALLIS P.C. Alastair JONES P.S. Stuart CHARLESWORTH S.I. Simon JONES	
2011	P.C. Philip BAINBRIDGE P.S. Christopher FLINT	
2012	P.C. Gary MARSHALL	
2013	P.C. David URIE	
2014	P.C. David FRAME	
2015	P.C. Graeme BLACK P.S. Paul HAMER	
2016	P.C. Edmund BARKER	
2017	P.C. Rob SHAKESPEARE	
2018	P.C. Mohammed NADEEM	

Bibliography and further reading

Abbott P.E. & Tamplin J.M.A, *British Gallantry Awards* (Nimrod Dix & Co., 1981)

Ashcroft, Michael, *George Cross Heroes* (Headline Review, 2010)

Aurora Publishing, *Our Blitz, Red Skies over Manchester* (Aurora Publishing 1994 – Facsimile, first published 1945)

Barton, Geoffrey, *The Tottenham Outrage and Walthamstow Tram Chase* (Waterside Press, 2017)

Bassie, Gavin F., *Liverpool's Finest, The History of the City's Fire Brigade* (Trinity Mirror North West & North Wales, 2008)

Blundell R. H. and Wilson G. H., *The Trial of Buck Ruxton* (William Hodge & Company, 1937)

Brown, Mike, *Put that Light Out!, Britain's Civil Defence Services at War 1939-1945* (Sutton Publishing, 1999)

Cowley, Richard, *Policing EOKA: The United Kingdom Police Unit to Cyprus 1955 – 1960* (Peg and Whistle Books, 2008)

Critchley, T. A., *A History of Police in England and Wales* (Constable and Company Ltd, 1978)

Ellis, John, *Blackpool at War. A History of the Fylde Coast during the Second World War* (The History Press, 2013)

Fairhurst James, *Policing Wigan, The Wigan Borough Police Force 1836-1969* (Landy Publishing, 1996)

Goslin, R. J., *A History of the Bolton Borough Police Force 1939-1969* (1970)

Green, Andrea, *MG's on Patrol* (Magna Press, 1999)

Farmery J. Peter, *Police Gallantry, The King's Police Medal, the King's Police and Fire Services Medal and the Queen's Police Medal for Gallantry 1909-1978* (Periter and Associates Pty Ltd, 1995)

Hardy, Clive, *Manchester at War* (First Edition Ltd, 2005)

Hebblethwaite, Marion, *One Step Further, Those whose gallantry was rewarded with the George Cross*, Supplements 1- 4 (Marion Hebblethwaite, 2017)

Ingleton, Roy, *The Gentlemen at War, Policing Britain 1939-45* (Cranborne Publications, 1994)

Laybourn, Keith, *The General Strike of 1926* (Manchester University Press, 1993)

Laybourn, Keith, *The Battle for the Roads of Britain* (Palgrave McMillan, 2015)

Liverpool Daily Post and Echo, *Bombers over Merseyside: This was Merseyside's Finest Hour: The Authoritative Record of the Blitz 1940-1941* (Liverpool Daily Post & Echo, 1943 & reprinted 1983)

McKenna, Joseph. *The I.R.A. Bombing Campaign Against Britain, 1939–1940* (McFarland & Co., 2016)

Metcalfe, Nick MBE, Q.G.M., *For Exemplary Bravery, The Queen's Gallantry Medal* (Writersworld, 2014)

McDermott, Phillip, *Acts of Courage, Register of the George Medal, 1940-2015* (Writersworld, 2016)

McGreal, Stephen, *Wigan in the Great War* (Pen and Sword Books, 2016)

Noonan, Gerard, *The I.R.A. in Britain, 1919-1923, 'In the Heart of Enemy Lines'* (Liverpool University Press, 2014)

Perkins, Anne, *A Very British Strike* (Pan Books, 2007)

Pythian, Graham, *Blitz Britain, Manchester and Salford* (The History Press, 2015)

Stallion, Martin & Wall, David S., *The British Police* (2nd Edition) (Police History Society, 2011)

Symons, Julian, *The General Strike* (House of Stratus, 2001)

Taylor, Denis, *999 And All That* (Oldham Corporation, 1968)

Willoughby, Roger, *FOR GOD AND THE EMPIRE, The Medal of the Order of the British Empire 1917-1922* (Savannah Publications, 2012)

Index

Awards

Merit Badges and Commendations..................28
The Gerald Richardson Memorial Trophy.308
The John Egerton Trophy 339
The Kay Taylor Trophy.........................28
The O'Donnell Trophy....................28, 255
The Rhodes Marshall Trophy 28
The Smith Cup 27
The William Garnett Cup 24

Civilians

ALEXANDER, George Stanley..................207
BAGGOTT, Kathleen Winifred 85
BARTNIK. Francis Anthony 290
BATES, Henry Abel............................203
BONAR, Eric Watt "Jock" 106
BOWYER, Frederick Albert...................137
BRADLEY, William James......................237
BRYCE, John..................................192
CATON, John...................................54
CHALLIS, Stanley 207
CHAMBERLAIN, Alexander.......................54
CODLING, Inspector Raymond 343
COLLINGS, Maurice............................185
COOGAN, Thomas...............................275
COPE, Lily....................................54
COPPARD, Thomas...............................54
COUSINS, Henry James.........................185
DAVIES, Christopher Matthew.................292
DEMAIN, David Jack 268
DICK, Robert.................................278
DISBERRY, William.............................54
EVANS, Walter................................141
FISHER, Thomas...............................245
FLEMING, Norman Robert 242
FRIEL, John..................................277
GARTH, Richard................................54
GRAHAM, Abraham Clark.........................54
GRANT, Thomas Joseph.........................189
GRAY, Patrick Joseph 242
GROGAN, Edward...............................292
HANDLEY, William Derek.......................290
HEALD, William................................54
HEXTER, Basil................................168
HIGHTON Charles..............................239
HOOTON, Eileen, Mrs..........................240
HUGHES, Roland Hugh..........................248
HUNT, Philip.................................239
HUTCHINSON, George............................54
JOHNSON, Eric................................275
JOHNSON, Jilbert..............................54
KAVANAGH, Bertie.............................189
KEW, Thomas...................................54
LEATHAM, Ernest Sydney 193
MALIK, Javed Mahmood.........................317
MARTIN, Harry................................151

MATHEWS, Francis.............................274
MEEHAN, John Joseph..........................137
NUTT, George..................................54
O'GARA, John Joseph..........................185
PICKERING, James Clark.......................149
PRITCHARD, Robert............................146
ROUTLEDGE, William...........................207
SEDDON, Peter................................239
SEERY, William................................54
SHEPHERD, Maisey J............................54
STANDRING, Thomas............................274
SWEENEY, Annie, Mrs..........................237
SYKES, Thomas................................258
TATTERSALL, Thomas............................54
TAYLOR, Charles...............................54
TAYLOR, James................................210
TAYLOR, Richard...............................54
TILL, Edward.................................259
TOLEN, Thomas................................187
WHEELER, George Ernest.......................194
WILKINSON, Mary Agnes.........................54
WILLIAMS, Miss, Muriel Ruth 201
WILSON, Roy Anthony..........................259

Commendations

King's Commendation for Brave Conduct....16
Queen's Commendation for Brave Conduct 16
Queen's Commendation for Bravery 16

Garnett Cup Winners

ABRAM, Patrick Richard 333
BARBER, John Henry 25
BELL, James Trott 115
BRADBURN, Thomas Edward 25
BRADLEY, Angela 333
BUCK, Raymond George.........................280
CONNOLLY, Gordon 333
DEAN, Christopher 312
DOBSON, Stanley 117
FLEMING, John Jack...........................265
FORREST, James Gerald 293
FRYERS, William Armistead 340
HALLIDAY Edward..............................110
HAYES Herbert................................106
HELM, Robert.................................325
HUGHES, Roger................................286
JEAVONS, Jack................................122
LEIGH, Paul..................................353
MOORES, Robert...............................286
MORRISON, Colin..............................333
MULLA, Lukmaan...............................353
RICHARDSON, Gerald Irving....................302
ROBINSON Richard.............................110
SMITH, Neil Howard...........................340
STILL, Charles Ian...........................312
WALLWORK, John...............................265
WILD, Harry..................................120

WILSON, John Stuart..322

King's Commendation for Brave Conduct

ALEXANDER, George Stanley.........................207
ATKINSON, John James.....................................144
BAILEY, Richard..168
BATES, Henry Abel...203
BATTERSBY, Peter..235
BEAVERSTOCK, John Charles 235
BECKETT, William..172
BEESTON, Thomas William 212
BESFORD, James..183
BIRCHENOUGH, James.......................................220
BLACKBURN, Charles Frederick....................197
CAMERON, James..178
CARSON, John...190
CHALLIS, Stanley 207
CLARKSON, Herbert Emsley............................139
COLLINGS, Maurice..185
COOK, Albert..209
DALGARNO, George Henry 199
DAVENPORT, Arthur, M.M 166
DICKINSON, Vernon Francis 173
ERICSON, William R.E..199
EVANS, Robert John...199
FISHER, Thomas Harold Ruben.....................140
FISK, Harry Charles 144
FRASER, Charles...185
GILLBANKS, Isaac Joseph..................................235
GLAISTER, Joseph..236
GREGORY, William...166
HAGGART, Alexander Francis Livingstone201
HAYES, Thomas...199
HEXTER, Basil...168
JONES, Stanley Percival 183
LEECH, Frank..165
LEWIS, David Charles...190
LISTON, Henry Thomas.......................................139
LOMAS, William Reginald 173
MAULT Leslie..231
McCARTHY, Thomas Joseph..............................183
McCLINTOCK, William James..........................172
METCALFE, Robert Henry...................................197
MORRISEY, Norman..190
MORRISON, Joseph Dickinson.........................139
NICHOLAS, Vere Rogers......................................220
O'GARA, John Joseph 185
PENNINGTON Edward..149
POTTER, Charles Lathom...................................230
PRENDERGAST, Frank 168
PROCTOR, Robert..164
PROCTOR, Samuel...167
REDFERN, Ernest Alfred 175
REES, Leonard...199
ROBINSON, William Edward.............................171
ROUGHLEY, Thomas 197
ROUTLEDGE, William...207
SLIDDERS, John Finlayson.................................234
SMITH, Fred Hall..208
STEEN, Ian Douglas 158

SUMMERS, John Edwin..159
WAPPETT, Joseph Stanley 228
WARDROP, Alexander Duncan 169
WATSON, Alfred..197
WILLIAMS, Muriel Ruth 201
WRIGHT, George Swan..230
YOUNG, William Arthur.......................................197

Medal Recipients

Member of the Civil Division of the Most Excellent Order of the British Empire

LAWRENCE, Sydney..161
WHITE, Frank...274

The British Empire Medal

ADAMS, James Munro 274
ALKER, Thomas..165
ANKERS, Elymer 201
BARTON, Joseph 218
BIGLAND, Charles 150
BLACK, James 192
BOWYER, Frederick Albert...............................137
BOYD, Arthur Diamond 181
BREWER, John Thomas 155
BRITCH, John..94
BRYCE, John 192
CAIRNS, Charles Leslie.......................................207
CALLAGHAN, Thomas..203
CATTERALL, Paul..205
COOPER, William...85
COTTIER, William Henry 183
CROSBY, Fred 203
DENNEY, John Vincent James.........................155
DIXON, Philip...210
DOBSON, William Alban....................................199
DOWNWARD, Henry Harper 162
EGERTON, Thomas..87
EVANS, Walter 141
FALLON, Albert Edward 206
FISHER, Thomas 245
FOX, Albert Edward...101
GANNAWAY, Harry 194
GARDLER, Sidney John.......................................194
GEE, Norman Blundell.......................................157
GEORGE, William..166
GRANT, Thomas Joseph 189
HANLON, William...175
HUMBLE, Alfred William....................................138
HUNTER, William..193
IRWIN, Edward..208
JONES, Archibald Idwal......................................160
KAVANAGH, Bertie 189
KYTE, Bernard..210
LEACH, John Robert..155
LEATHAM, Ernest Sidney..................................193
LONGSTAFFE, John Jackson.............................223
MARKIN, Francis George 162
MARTIN, Harry...151
McCLORRY, Edward Gerard..............................155
MOIR, Albert...148
MORRIS, Thomas Edward..................................173

MORRIS, William............................173
MORRISON, Cuthbert Dickenson...............155
ROXBURGH, Richard.........................141
RUSS, Edward..............................170
SCOTT, Henry Donald.......................182
SKELTON, Thomas Morton....................141
SMITH, William............................161
SMITHWICK, William Burnett.................89
SUMNER, Thomas.............................94
SYMINGTON, George Robert..................189
TARBUCK, James............................205
TAYLOR, Francis John......................163
TAYLOR, James.............................210
WHYMAN, Leslie Gordon.....................136
WHYTE, Andrew.............................161
WILES, James Buxton.......................170
WILLIAMSON, Tom...........................218
WILSON, Thomas Ellis......................136
WOODWORTH, George..........................86

The British Empire Medal (Bar to)
SKELTON, Thomas Morton............... 194, 197

The British Empire Medal for Gallantry
ASHWORTH, Alan............................267
BEATTIE, Eric William.....................246
BENNETT, John Francis Ivor................263
BONNER, Walter Alan.......................268
BROWN, John Dugdale.......................290
BUCK, Raymond George......................280
BULLOCK, Henry Martindale.................279
CLARKSON, William James...................278
COLLINS, James Patrick....................312
DENT, Arthur..............................313
DICK, Robert..............................278
EDWARDS, Geoffrey Seymour.................263
EDWARDS, Leslie Wyn.......................278
FELTON, Brian.............................278
GARDNER, Joseph...........................270
GRAY, Edward......................... 302, 310
HANCOX, Joseph............................296
HANLEY, Edward....................... 302, 311
HARRISON, William.........................261
HUGHES, Arwyn.............................270
HUGHES, Roger.............................286
HUGHES, Roland Hugh.......................248
LEE, Joseph James.........................269
LEWIS, Harold William.....................278
LEWIS, Thomas Raymond.....................270
LUCAS, Thomas Henry.......................281
MATHEWS, Francis..........................274
McDONALD, James Brian.....................312
METCALFE, Ian Charles.....................314
MOORE, George Donald......................288
MOORES, Robert............................286
MURPHY, Edward............................270
MURPHY, Walter Brian......................259
PRIEST, Graham David......................273
SASS, William John........................273
SMITH, Edward Gordon......................300

TAYLOR, Derek Peter.......................290
TORKINGTON, Michael John..................295
VERTH, Archibald..........................248

The Colonial Police Medal for Gallantry
SEWART, Alan..............................243

The Edward Medal
COPPARD, Thomas............................54
GRAHAM, Abraham Clark......................54
KEW, Thomas...............................54
TATTERSALL, Thomas........................54

The George Cross
NEWGASS, Harold Reginald..................144
RICHARDSON Gerald Irving..................302
WALKER, Carl..............................302

The George Medal
BAKER, Herbert Frederick Collier..........187
CARSWELL, Robert..........................263
CLAYDON, Harold Frederick.................177
CLEGG, James..............................151
COLLINS, Daniel John......................189
COUSINS, Henry James......................185
CRANN, Edward.............................176
DAVIES, Thomas Arthur.....................143
DAVIES, Thomas Owen.......................263
EBEL, Mark Vincent R.N.V.R................194
FORSHAW, David Charles....................146
GARTLAND, Christopher John................187
GREEN, Percy Albert.......................197
HAMPSON, Ian..............................302
HILLIS, Andrew............................302
HOLLIDAY, Thomas Edward...................154
IRVINE, Kenneth...........................283
JACKSON, Patrick..........................302
LOCKETT, Thomas Arthur....................245
MACKAY, Kenneth...........................302
McCARTHY, Thomas Joseph...................146
MEEHAN, John Joseph.......................137
NICHOLS, Edward...........................137
PICKERING, James Clark....................149
PRITCHARD, Robert.........................146
ROBERTS, Robert William...................263
ROSE, Frank...............................233
ROSS, Alexander...........................149
ROWLANDS, Arthur Rees.....................263
SCOTT, Victor James.......................146
SCULLY, Thomas............................180
SMITH, Thomas.............................180
SPICER, Frederick Albert..................197
TOLEN, Thomas.............................187
UREN, John Edward Willington..............187
WATKINS, Emlyn Arthur.....................318
WHEELER, George Ernest....................194
WRIGHT, Harold Alexander..................134

The King's Police and Fire Services Medal
ATKINSON, Ernest..........................229
BENN, Thomas Arthur.......................179
DAVIS, Robert William.....................211
JONES, Francis Henry......................227

LACEY, Leslie Walter......179
LEACH, John Robert......232
McNAUGHTON, Donald Neil......217
MOORE, Charles......219
RATCLIFFE, James......227
ROTHERHAM, Arnold......224
SIMMONS, Harry......224
THORLEY, William Binch......225
WINDLE, Raymond......224

The King's Police Medal
ADAMSON, Christopher......33
ASHMAN, Edwin William Alfred......119
BAILEY, Richard......68
BEESLEY, George......36
BELL James Trott......115
BENSTEAD, James......74
BOLAS, Michael......68
BOUCHER, William Edwin......68
BOWDEN, Henry......66
BRADBURY, Herbert......45
BRAITHWAITE, Thomas......102
BROCKLEHURST, Fred......54
BROTHWOOD, George......95
BROWN, Thomas......62
BROWN, Thomas James......62
CLARKE, John Harold......89
CLYNES, John......40
CORK, Nicholas......60
CORLETT Robert Alfred......75
CROMPTON, William Anderson......114
DOBSON Stanley......117
DODD, Francis Edward......123
DODD, George......127
ENTWISLE, Joseph......98
FOX James......62
GIBBONS, Thomas Parnell......38
GITTINGS, Walter......113
GREEN, William......39
HALLIDAY, Edward......110
HANDLEY, William......72
HARDACRE, James......45
HARRISON, Thomas Smith......123
HAYES, Herbert......106
HESKETH, Walter......108
HODGSON, William Bramwell......54
HUDSON, Stephen......76
JAMES, William......79
JEAVONS Jack......122
JOHNSON, Thomas......95
JOLLEYS, Ambrose......52
JONES, John......63
JONES, Thomas......71
KENT, John Nelson......44
LEECH, Frank......90
LEWIS, Richard......67
LINAKER, Henry......33
MACLACHLAN, Cyril......78
MARR, William Alexander......104
MATTINSON, William Guthrie......97

McGUIRE, James......32
McMAHON, James......121
MOFFATT, D'Arcy Benson......54
MONKS, Jack......37
NEWSHAM, Richard......54
OAKES, George Albert......54
PETER, William Parker......77
RICHARDS, Edward......98
ROBINSON, Richard......110
ROTHERY, Thomas......35
RYLANCE, Willie......88
SAVAGE, Alonzo......54
SEBBORN, Robert Arthur......118
SKELLERN, Arthur James......110
SLOAN, Daniel Devine......54
SMITH, William Henry......91
SOUTHERN, George Rigby......78
TATE, Thomas......73
TAYLOR, Hariph Richard......59
THOMAS, Albert......77
TIERNAN, John......113
TONGUE, Samuel......68
WARDLE, Thomas Herbert......79
WEARING, William Andrew......54
WILD Harry......120
WOOFF, William James......100
YATES, Arnold......109

The King's Police Medal(Bar to)
JONES, John......88

The Medal of the Order of the British Empire
AINSCOUGH, Ralph......41
BARNES, Frank......45
BOOTH, John......45
COOKSEY, Thomas Brett......41
DUCKWORTH, John William......45
JONES, John......41
PERCIVAL, John S.......41
RILEY, Eli Hudson......45
ROBERTS, John......45
RYLANCE, Willie......41
SCHOFIELD, Walter Riley......45
SMALLEY, Edward......45
WALKER, Richard Thomas......45
WARE, Edward Samuel......45

The Queen's Gallantry Medal
DAVIES, Thomas William......320
HELM, Robert......325
HENAGHAN, Denis......324
LEA, John Frederick......320
LEIGH, Paul......353
MULLA, Luckmaan......353
MURPHY, Claire Louise......354
MURPHY, Derk Peter......340
OAKE, Stephen......351
OWEN, Kenton Robert......340
POWER, George Kenneth......323
WILSON John Stuart......322

The Queen's Police Medal for Gallantry

O'DONNELL, James 249

Medals

The Albert Medal 12

The British Empire Medal 19

The Colonial Police Medal 23

The Edward Medal 12

The George Medal 22

The King's Police Medal 14

The Medal of the Order of the British Empire
....19

The Queen's Gallantry Medal 22

The Queen's Police Medal 15

Police Forces

Accrington Fire 45

Barrow-in-Furness 282, 288

Blackburn 249, 279

Blackpool 37, 44, 212, 230, 290

Bolton 276, 294

Bolton Fire 205

Bootle 136, 146, 148, 149, 185, 199, 207

Church Fire 45

Colne Fire Brigade 36, 59

Farnworth Fire 98

Greater Manchester ...316, 317, 318, 319, 321,
330, 338, 339, 341, 342, 343, 344, 345,
346, 347, 348, 349, 350, 351, 352, 354

Lancashire 33, 35, 38, 39, 45, 52, 60, 62, 67,
71, 73, 76, 77, 79, 85, 86, 87, 94, 95, 98,
100, 101, 102, 106, 110, 115, 117, 120,
121, 122, 136, 151, 154, 155, 157, 158,
159, 203, 206, 211, 217, 219, 224, 225,
229, 232, 239, 243, 261, 265, 270, 280,
286, 293, 297, 302, 312, 313, 322, 325,
326, 329, 330, 332, 333, 340, 353

Liverpool and Bootle .292, 296, 298, 299, 300,
301, 312

Liverpool City 62, 72, 74, 89, 91, 97, 110, 113,
118, 123, 127, 137, 141, 143, 176, 177,
178, 179, 180, 187, 189, 190, 192, 193,
194, 197, 205, 218, 223, 227, 228, 231,
233, 234, 235, 236, 237, 238, 242, 246,
247, 263, 268, 269, 270, 273, 275, 277,
284, 285, 286

Liverpool Fire 134, 138, 144, 181, 201

Liverpool Market Police 89

Manchester and Salford 295, 314, 315

Manchester City .40, 68, 75, 78, 108, 109, 162,
165, 166, 167, 168, 169, 172, 173, 175,
209, 210, 245, 248, 262, 274, 275, 283,
288, 289

Manchester Fire 161

Mersey Tunnel 327

Merseyside 315, 316, 320, 323, 324, 328, 331,
332, 340, 344

Oldham 104

Oswaldtwistle Fire 45

Preston 32, 259

Rochdale 237, 267

Salford 66, 77, 90, 114, 119, 140, 160, 161,
162, 163, 164, 165, 170, 171, 172, 258

Salford Fire 139, 150, 208

Southport 220

Warrington 260, 272, 281

Wigan 297

Wigan Fire 41, 63, 88, 203

Queen's Commendation for Brave Conduct

ABRAM, Patrick Richard 333

ADAMSON, Douglas 276

ALLOTT, George 315

ANDREWS, Robert Edward 260

BAILEY, Oliver Charles 330

BARLOW, John Edward 346

BARTRAM, Elizabeth Dianne 326

BENTLEY, Stephen John 348

BOOTH, Stanley 299

BOWDEN, James Geoffrey 343

BOWERS, Percy 262

BRADFORD, David John 342

BRADLEY, William James 237

BRADSHAW, Bryan Peter 316

BRADSHAW, Trevor 321

BROWN, Donald James 319

BUTLER, Jack Picton 315

BYRON, Geoffrey 320

CARO, Maurice Murray 260

CHALKLEY, Donald 285

CLARKE, Lawrence Stanley 289

COLLINS, Arthur Graham Ferguson 247

COOGAN, Thomas 275

COTTON, Kenneth Paul 272

COTTON, Percy Allan Shelton 274

COVILL John 249, 255

DAVENPORT, Raymond 332

DAVIES, Christopher Matthew 292

DAVIES, Thomas Edward, ...320

DEAN, Christopher 312

DEMAIN, David Jack 268

DORAN, Joseph 275

DORAN, Nicholas 320

DUNNE, Joseph 274

EDWARDS, Brian 316

EGERTON, John 338

ELLERSHAW, Derrington Stephen 317

ELSBURY, Fred 237

FAWCETT, Andrew 328

FELTON, Brian 268

FLEMING John Jack 265

FLEMING, Norman Robert 242

FORREST, James Gerald 293

FRIEL, John 277

FRYERS William Armistead 340

GIBSON, George Harold 317

GRAY, Patrick Joseph 242

GREENER, Samuel Joseph 301

GREENWAY, William Walter 237

GREENWELL, Edward McDonald 298
GRISDALE, Anthony George 288
GROGAN, Edward 292
HALLIWELL, Peter 249
HANDLEY, William Derek.............290
HANNIGAN, Michael Joseph 289
HARRIS, Richard Thomas 319
HARRISON, John...............249
HARRISON, Leslie Ann 344
HARRISON, Philip Quintin............330
HEAP, Paul David...............348
HIGHTON Charles...............239
HOOTON, Eillen, Mrs...............240
HOULT, Martin Edward...............342
HUGHES, John Desmond 238
HUGHES, Owen Stanley 274
HUNT, Philip. 239
JOBSON, Alan 283
JOHNSON, Colin Edward 277
JOHNSON, Eric...............275
JOLLY, Barry...............315
JONES, Christopher Anthony 275
JONES, Harold Powell...............299
KEIR, Alastair Andrew...............319
LAMBERT, Lieut Charles Graham...........324
LAWRENCE, Paul...............346
LEACH, Eric...............285
LEVER, Geoffrey Gerald...............326
LEWIS, Harold William...............268
MACKAY, Andrew Keith 346
MALE, John...............272
MALIK, Javed Mahmood...............317
MALONE, Terence...............344
MARSDEN, Alan Geoffrey...............301
MARSHALL, William...............292
MAWDSLEY, Thomas...............327
McCARTHY, John...............261
McFALL, Reginald...............284
McLOUGHLIN, William...............258
McMillan, Pauline...............323
MILNER, Henry Donald, QPM 345
MOSS, Arthur Reginald 315
MURRAY, David...............344
MURRAY, Robert Ian...............344
O'ROURKE, John Paul...............339
OWEN, Jeffrey Richard...............299
PARK, Keith 294

PEACH, Frank Theodore...............297
PITCHER, Hubert Noel...............272
POLHILL, Ruth Ann...............344
POLLITT, Barry Joseph...............330
QUINE, Doris Elizabeth...............242
REDPATH, Stephen Drummond...........302
RIDYARD, Harry...............276
RILEY, David Walter 332
RILEY, Jack...............249
ROOKE, John William 284
ROSKELL, George Frederick 242
SEDDON, Peter...............239
SINCLAIR, Thomas Paul William 328
SMITH Neil Howard 340
SMITH, David James...............298
SMITH, Graham...............258
SMITH, Peter Chalkley 348
SMITH, Sheila Ann 323
STANDRING, Thomas...............274
STEPHENSON, Anthony...............283
STILL, Charles Ian 312
STOREY, Harry...............274
SWEENEY, Annie, Mrs...............237
SYKES, Thomas...............258
TAYLOR, Donald Thomas...............294
TAYLOR, Nora Mary...............300
THOMPSON, Ian Charles...............331
TILL, Edward...............259
TOWNSEND, Joseph Gerard...............285
TWYFORD, Raymond...............288
VALLELY, John...............282
WAGNER, Harry James 344
WALLWORK, John...............265
WAUGH, Brian David...............284
WHIGHAM, Andrew...............239
WIGGINS, John Graham...............286
WILSON QGM, John Stuart...............329
WILSON, Roy Anthony...............259
WILSON, Yvonne Mrs...............341
WOOD, Alan William...............299
WRIGHT, Kim Patricia...............330
Queen's Commendation for Bravery
ANDERSON, Paul 350
BECK, Malcolm James...............347
BROWN, Julia Vanessa 349
DORAN, Brian Rae...............347
HINCE, Geoffrey Arnold 352

PRINTED AND BOUND BY:
Copytech (UK) Limited trading as Printondemand-worldwide,
9 Culley Court, Bakewell Road, Orton Southgate.
Peterborough, PE2 6XD, United Kingdom.